Fallacy 24+
Appeal to tradition/
Historian fallacy.
2nd book the signal and the
noise.

# Winning
# Decisions

# Winning Decisions

## GETTING IT RIGHT THE FIRST TIME

J. Edward Russo and Paul J. H. Schoemaker

With Margo Hittleman

CURRENCY
DOUBLEDAY
New York
London
Toronto
Sydney
Auckland

A Currency Book
PUBLISHED BY DOUBLEDAY
a division of Random House, Inc.
1540 Broadway, New York, New York 10036

Currency and Doubleday are trademarks of Doubleday,
a division of Random House, Inc.

Book design by Chris Welch

Library of Congress Cataloging-in-Publication Data

Russo, J. Edward.
Winning decisions : getting it right the first time / J. Edward Russo and Paul J. H.
Schoemaker ; with Margo Hittleman.— 1st ed.
p. cm.
Includes index.
1. Decision making. I. Schoemaker, Paul J. H. II. Title.
HD30.23 .R876 2002
658.4'03—dc21
2001032293

ISBN 0-385-50225-7

First Edition: January 2002

Currency Books are available at special discounts for bulk purchases for sales
promotions or premiums. Special editions, including personalized covers, excerpts of
existing books, and corporate imprints, can be created in large quantities for special
needs. For more information, write to Special Markets, Currency Books, 280 Park
Avenue, 11th Floor, New York, NY 10017, or e-mail *specialmarkets@randomhouse.com*

3   5   7   9   10   8   6   4

To Daniel Kahneman for his lifelong exploration of the mind of the decision-maker, continually taking us in new directions and revealing hidden patterns of preference, belief, and value;

To his equally remarkable collaborator, the late Amos Tversky, for his pioneering insights and rigorous formulations of the most fundamental problems and principles of the field; and

To the late Herbert A. Simon, a founder and intellectual leader of cognitive science over the last half century, for the model of his life.

# Acknowledgments

Our book draws on multiple intellectual disciplines—from behavioral decision theory and decision analysis through artificial intelligence and problem-solving to group dynamics and creativity. In each discipline are dedicated researchers whose collective efforts have formed the intellectual basis for all that you will read below. We acknowledged some of these scholars by name in our early book *Decision Traps* (Doubleday, 1989) and our gratitude to them continues in this work.

In addition, we have benefited from the stimulating intellectual climates where we worked as academics, especially the University of Chicago (where we first met in the early 1980s), Cornell University, and the Wharton School of the University of Pennsylvania. Our colleagues there have provided much-appreciated support and challenge to our thinking over the years. Paul especially acknowledges John C. Hershey for our continuing dialogue in the context of our joint executive education at Wharton, as well as Howard C. Kunreuther and Paul Kleindorfer for numerous stimulating discussions while writing our joint book *Decision Sciences: An Integrative Perspective* (Cambridge Press, 1993). Thanks go as well to George Day, Roch Parayre, Howard Perlmutter, and Harbir Singh for our wide-ranging discussions about decision-making in organizations.

We are also grateful to the thousands of managers who have heard us speak about decision-making over the years. Their valuable feedback—whether as questions, survey responses, or follow-up conversations and consulting—compelled us to respect more fully the complex challenge of real-world, real-time decisions. These numerous seminars and workshops were conducted at various universities, in public forums, and at the invitation of companies. There are too many for all to be listed, but we acknowledge in particular the following organizations:

University of California at Berkeley, University of Chicago, Cornell University, CEDEP at INSEAD, Duke University, University of North Carolina, MIT, and the Wharton School for their support of our executive education workshops; and

Abbott Laboratories, Arthur Andersen, Cargill, Coopers & Lybrand, CUES, Eli Lilly, General Motors, Harris Bank, IBM, Johnson & Johnson, Knight-Ridder, Lever Brothers, Lucent, National WestMinister Bank, New York Life, Royal Dutch/Shell, State Farm, and the U.S. Forest Service for their repeated in-house offerings of our executive decision programs.

Several individuals played essential roles in the making of this book.

John Oakes teamed up with us in the mid-1990s to design a management training program based on our book *Decision Traps*. We have benefited not only from his great interest in this subject and his vast experience in training and human resource management, but as much from his patient insistence on practical and user-friendly expositions of our more obtuse concepts and techniques. He helped sharpen our exercises while adding many tools and tips where they were needed. Our intellectual journey with him changed our own thinking, as reflected in the present writing, and we acknowledge his substantial contribution with gratitude.

Richard Roll, CEO of RealHome.com, Inc., volunteered his time and risked the exposure of his decision processes to all who read chapter 10. It is one thing to make a decision; it is another to observe and describe it; and it is still more to reveal it with candor to two critical scholars for commented publication. For all of the above, Richard has our gratitude and respect.

In addition, we are indebted to our writer, Margo Hittleman, who undertook the challenging task of getting two strong-minded decision researchers—living in two different cities—to see eye to eye on numerous theoretical issues and applied questions. Her patience, discipline, insight, and professionalism brought much-needed structure and coherence to our original thinking. Whatever merit the writing style itself possesses goes to Margo. She performed admirably under deadline, and without her this book would not have been published in its present form and at this time.

We thank Barb Drake for her remarkable clerical and administrative support as well as Angela Horne for her contribution as a reference librarian. In addition, we thank Roger Scholl and Stephanie Land at Doubleday for their editing.

# Contents

# Contents

# Decision-Making in the Real World

*In the affair of so much importance to you, wherein you ask my advice, I cannot for want of sufficient premises advise you what to determine, but if you please I will tell you how.* —*Benjamin Franklin*

THE AMERICAN BOTANIST and explorer David Fairchild recounts the following tale. "I had been dining with our old friends, the Arthur Bullards, and late in the evening Herbert Hoover came in. He dropped wearily into an easy chair, as if he had just come from his office. Mr. Bullard said something to him about my going on a long plant hunting expedition. He looked up in a tired way and asked, 'Does he have to make decisions on such a trip? If not, I'd like to go along. I'm tired of making decisions—one after another all day long. My view of Heaven is of a place where no one ever has to make a decision.' "[1]

If you are like many professionals we know, you can echo President Hoover's sentiments. But you are unlikely to find his Heaven manifest on earth. If anything, more people are making more decisions—and are being forced to make them faster—in an increasingly unpredictable and less forgiving environment, where more is at stake than ever before.

Whether you work in business, government, professional services, education, or the not-for-profit sector, the same scenario probably reigns. High speed rules decision-making as well as everything else. "In a world that moves at Web speed, time cannot be sacrificed for better quality, lower cost, or even better decisions," recently observed John Roth, president and CEO of Canada's Nortel Networks.[2]

Whatever their role and organization, most professionals have to make a decision "now"—followed by another decision "now," followed by yet another. If that weren't challenging enough, more is at stake than ever before. The terrain for today's decision-maker is a minefield in which any misstep can provoke a devastating explosion. In this sped-up world, you are likely to have exactly one shot to get a decision right, not three. And if you get it wrong, you have less time to correct mistakes and reestablish credibility. It's enough to make anyone tired. But those very challenges can provide unprecedented opportunity and strategic advantage—*if* you can embrace the responsibility for making good, fast, frequent decisions, and *if* you can do so better than those against whom you compete.

Simple enough to say, we concede. But how can a decision-maker rapidly assess the situation, gather needed information, consider it thoroughly, and reach an intelligent conclusion? How can one make good, fast, frequent, *winning* decisions? Bookstores are filled with volumes describing the challenges facing organizations today and offering platitudes instead of solutions. Remember "work smarter, not harder"? Unfortunately, no one told you *how* to work smarter. Too often the mantra became just one more way to get you to work harder.

In this book we truly will teach you how to work smarter. We believe that decision-making prowess is a skill that *can* be learned—and that *should* be learned. Why do well-intentioned, smart, experienced professionals make poor decisions far too often? We believe it is because they haven't been taught a disciplined process for making winning decisions. Left to fend for themselves, they've relied on intuition, brains, luck, common sense, and training within the narrow bounds of their professional expertise. We're not denigrating those attributes. Unfortunately, in today's professional environment they are seldom sufficient to maintain your edge—and they surely won't be enough in the future.

## Why Decision-Making Is Increasingly Challenging

How many of the following characteristics describe your decision-making environment?

- ❑ **Information overload.** You have an avalanche of information literally at your fingertips, but much is conflicting and of uncertain reliability.
- ❑ **A galloping rate of change.** You must make intelligent decisions about moving targets. What's fact today may be fiction tomorrow.
- ❑ **Rising uncertainty.** The days of predict-plan-execute are gone. Discontinuities are the norm.
- ❑ **Few historical precedents.** You must decide correctly within new organizational models (such as virtual organizations) and about new technologies or electronic commerce with little historical experience to guide you.
- ❑ **More frequent decisions.** Standard operating procedures have been replaced by decisions tailored for individual customers, suppliers, partners, products, and cases.

❑ **More important decisions.** In today's flatter organizations, many are making decisions that have the potential to affect the well-being of the entire firm. These decisions were once made only by those at the top.

❑ **Conflicting goals.** You must deliver short-term, but also experiment and "learn" to prepare for long-term, which is, of course, just the many short-terms yet to come.

❑ **More opportunities for miscommunication.** Cross-functional and multinational teams are becoming the norm, where function-bound and ethnocentric views of the right answer can quickly derail a decent solution.

❑ **Fewer opportunities to correct mistakes.** In a fast-paced world, you have less time to correct mistakes and reestablish credibility.

❑ **Higher stakes.** In our Winner-Take-All society, fewer people will be big winners. And if you're not one of them, you may well find yourself pushed to the sidelines.[3]

## BECOMING AN EXPERT DECISION-MAKER

Year by year in almost every sport, the best coaches learn more about the processes involved in great athletic achievement as well as better ways to teach those processes. It's because of these coaches' systematic attention to the process of reaching peak performance that athletes are able to set new records nearly every year.[4]

Even those of us with no hope of setting a new record for athletic prowess recognize the value of good coaching. Few golfers who want to improve their game simply get out the clubs, take to the links, follow their intuition, and hope for the best. If you want to shine in front of your colleagues on the golf course, you arrange for lessons from a professional coach, the best one you can find. So, too, if you want to improve your tennis game, speech delivery, or most any other skill.

Yet those same people who would not hesitate to schedule a series of private lessons with the local golf pro are largely self-trained in decision-making. In this arena, and perhaps this arena alone, they assume that intuition, repeated experience, and their general intelligence will see them through. Unfortunately, intuition and repetition are unreliable teachers at best. Amateur swimmers' intuition tells them to take their head out of the water to keep breathing. Their instinctive goal: to stay alive. Then they repeat that head-lifting move over and over until it becomes habit. Competitive swimmers, however, have learned to overcome this compelling instinct and keep their face as close to the water as possible. Their goal, as their coach will continuously remind them, is not just to stay alive, but to win the race.

Even more unfortunate for untutored decision-makers, research shows that the less competent people are, the less likely they are to know it. Over-confidence is a deep-seated human characteristic, one we discuss more in chapter 4 as a pervasive trap for untrained decision-makers. New research suggests that the dangers of overconfidence are even greater than one might think. Not only do most people tend to hold overly favorable views of their intellectual and interpersonal abilities, but those who are least accomplished most *over*estimate their performance and ability.[5] In other words, those who most need training to improve their decision-making abilities are the least likely to recognize it. Instead, like drunken drivers who are certain that their reflexes are unimpaired, they proceed with the mistaken impression that they are doing just fine.

We will tell you in chapter 4 how to recognize the ways in which you may unwittingly overestimate what you know. (Those exceedingly confident about their decision-making prowess may want to peek at that chapter first.) Fortunately, however, becoming a skilled decision-maker is no more complex than becoming a skilled athlete. The process can be taught—and it can be learned. Researchers in decision-making have discovered that, like untrained swimmers who lift their head too far out of the water, untrained decision-makers also make characteristic errors. They frequently define their problems in ways that cause them to overlook their best options, for instance. Or they fail to collect key factual information because they have too much confidence in their own judgments. There are predictable pitfalls that trap unwary decision-makers as well as field-tested strategies to help keep you on solid ground. In this book we will show you those pitfalls and coach you through strategies that work in the real world.

Through this coaching you will examine the process of decision-making systematically and learn how each part of the process contributes to an excellent decision. You will learn to recognize the subtle ways in which even the best decision-makers err, and apply effective techniques for resolving even the most difficult and complex decisions. To bring it all together, you must then practice this approach consistently, like a disciplined athlete in training, to avoid errors and improve personal performance. And as in athletics, no matter how good you already are, you can always become better.

## BUT WHO HAS THE TIME?!

By this point you may be thinking: "Nice idea, but who has the time to go through a detailed process and intricate techniques? I need to make that decision *now*!"

In fact, just as a good golf swing does not take longer than a bad one, asking the right questions when facing a complex decision does not take longer than asking the wrong ones. In fact, it saves time. Granted, our step-by-step process may at first slow down your decision-making while you are learning new skills and superior techniques. Just like that good golf swing, it requires slow motion and practice while you are learning. But once grooved, the result is superior. Over time it becomes second nature.

In our experience, much time is wasted in meetings and deliberations because people focus on the wrong issues, don't ask the right questions, fail to examine the data critically, or don't really know what they want. All this adds up to muddling your way through the decision, with wrong turns and backtracking, rather than utilizing a bold and confident process that leads to timely, successful results. As one manager we know recounted in exasperation, "Why do we never have enough time to do it right the first time, but we somehow can find the time to *redo* it three or four times?"

Indeed, we believe that a good decision-making process will save time in the long run since you will make the right decision the first time. When you consider the waste in time and effort your wrong decision produces, not to mention the blot on your reputation and personal friction it may cause, a "quick" decision may not be that quick after all.

## THE BASIS FOR DECISION COACHING

The insights and strategies in this book are built on thirty years of pathbreaking academic research in a field known as "behavioral decision research"—research that looks at how real people make real decisions. Traditionally, researchers who studied decision-making asked themselves how decisions *should* be made. Then they created mathematical models for people to follow. Unfortunately, those who tried to apply their elegant theories found the real world so complex that the models rarely helped much.

Along came scholars such as Daniel Kahneman at Princeton and the late Amos Tversky at Stanford—widely acknowledged as pioneers in behavioral decision research—who recognized the necessity of examining decisions made by real people.[6] They looked at the mental approaches we all use as we make decisions—both those that help us reach our goal and the flawed mental shortcuts and biases that sidetrack us. Their research incorporated earlier work by the late Herbert Simon, the 1978 Nobel Prize laureate in economics,[7] on how people process information, and it has been added to by their students and other researchers who have followed. Taken together, this research maps the process by which ordinary people can become excellent decision-makers. However, this important information, published mostly in academic journals and textbooks, has remained largely inaccessible to the lay reader.

In *Winning Decisions*, we have built on key lessons and insights to make these ideas readily available to those who want to become better decision-makers.[8] We have also built on our previous book, *Decision Traps* (Doubleday, 1989), but now focus much more on applications, solutions, and tools than on the traps themselves. In addition to our own research in the field, we draw on more than twenty-five years of working with executives, managers, MBA students, and other professionals. We began our decision coaching when we were both professors and researchers at the University of Chicago's Center for Decision Research in the late 1970s. We have continued our research and teaching about managerial decision-making—Jay as a professor of marketing and behavioral science at Cornell University's Johnson Graduate School of Management; Paul as research director of the Emerging Technologies Management Research Program at the University of Pennsylvania's Wharton School and through his company, Decision Strategies International, Inc.

Combining our experience with both research and teaching, we have built a simple four-stage process that provides a broad, conceptual framework for approaching virtually any decision. We have added a series of strategies and techniques that can be honed over time to equip you with reliable yet versatile tools for making winning decisions. Our goal is to provide you with a system that you can competently apply to the decisions you must make today. For those interested in the underlying research itself, you'll find it cited in numerous endnotes that elaborate upon the text.

Top corporate managers, lawyers, financial analysts, advertising executives, public officials, leaders of not-for-profit organizations, and physicians—people who share little more than the burden of making decisions—report that decision coaching, based on this process, has dramatically improved their results and forever changed the way they work.


**THE PLAN FOR THIS BOOK**


The structure of this book parallels our four-stage process. In each chapter you will find general principles, major lessons, and easily identifiable tools. Our goal is to enhance your critical thinking and decision-making skills, show you how to identify and avoid common decision-making traps, build a toolbox of useful skills, and have a greater impact on your organization's decisions. To do so, we address topics such as:

- Reframing issues so you don't solve the wrong problem
- Improving the quantity and quality of your options
- Making intelligent decisions in the face of uncertainty
- Converting expert yet conflicting opinions into useful insights
- Making group decisions work to your advantage
- Creating environments that enhance feedback and learning

At the end of each section you'll find a box labeled "Decision-Making Under Fire." In it, we offer tips about how to adapt these tools and processes when time is exceedingly tight. In addition, we engaged in some real-time decision coaching through a live case that illustrates the entire decision-making process. The story of RealHome.com, an Internet business launched in March 2000, is told in chapter 10. Internet start-ups are known for requiring frequent, fast decisions in an extremely competitive and unforgiving environment. We took a decision that RealHome founder and CEO, Richard Roll, was facing during the summer of 2000 (when this book was being written) and followed it through its conclusion in early 2001. The case appears as chapter 10, a capstone illustration of the struggle and skills of a good decision process. As the case unfolds over time, we apply a selection of the principles and tools we have discussed in the preceding chapters to the RealHome.com decision and share with you the insights Roll and his colleagues gained through this exercise.

Before we move on to the decision-making process itself, a few "disclosures." First, you should know up front that we bring a "cognitive" slant to our approach. Decision-making is a complex process involving cognitive (thinking), social, and emotional components. Our work with managers and other professionals has led us to believe that the key challenge in making powerful decisions is a cognitive one: decisions should be made with the head, not the gut. We have found that this is the arena professionals least understand, and in which they most often misstep. Thus, we emphasize the cognitive aspects of the game, and show you how to apply cognitive skills to deal with the interpersonal dynamics that can often derail a decision-making effort. While understanding social components such as organizational politics or emotional intelligence can be helpful, we are not going to coach you on those; there are superb books on those subjects (see the endnotes for a list of our favorites).[9] Nor will we tell you how to resolve emotional blocks rooted in past experience that may complicate your decision-making process (although we will coach you on how to reduce the biases they may introduce).

Second, we can't eliminate the complexity inherent in most important decisions. This book is not about simple solutions, but rather about a sound process for framing problems correctly and making the right decision. Like any coach, we will give you the tools, skills, and basic principles to help you prepare; but when the clock is running, you have to play the game.

Third, the field of "behavioral decision research" is still developing. As researchers ourselves, we are pained by how many important research questions cannot yet be definitely answered.[10] Much, however, is known. The factors that distinguish good decision-making from mediocre efforts are increasingly clear. And decision-makers need that knowledge now, not when the last scientific "t" has been crossed and final scholarly "i" dotted. Thus, while the principles and tools we present are firmly grounded in scientific research, we have extended, interpreted, and generalized from that base.

Finally, like any skill, a good decision-making process will only become truly yours with practice. We encourage you to use this book as a training manual. Try the exercises in each chapter. Select several tools to apply the next time you are in the office. Take careful note of what you find helpful. Add it to your decision-making repertoire.

There's an old joke about a man who is asked if he can play the piano. "I don't know," he replies. "Give me a piano and let's find out." To most of us, his hubris is funny. Yet many professionals take the same approach to decision-making. And that's not so funny. We believe that one can only get so far on optimism and guts alone. In the end you need practiced skills and a sound process. Today's world is no place for amateur—or arrogant—decision-makers, for in our Information Age the race will go not to the strong but to the cognitively swift.

# Winning Decisions

## CHAPTER 1

# Setting the Course

Nothing is as frightening as ignorance in action.   —*Goethe*

L ET'S BEGIN WITH a quick experiment. You'll soon find that we, as educators and researchers, have a fondness for experiments. We encourage you to try these simple exercises whenever they appear. You'll learn more quickly the general principles we're trying to convey. More important, you'll learn about yourself and how you make decisions. Armed with that knowledge, you can better choose whether to replace your habitual approach to decision-making with some of the ones we suggest. And whatever the outcome of the "tests," we promise: no grades.

Imagine you have in front of you two coins. Both are biased: coin #1 has a 55 percent probability of turning up heads; coin #2, a 45 percent probability of yielding heads. The coin you select will be flipped only once. If the head appears, you get $10,000 tax-free. If the tail turns up, you get nothing.

**Coin #1: 55% chance of heads**   **Coin #2: 45% chance of heads**

Playing the odds, you choose coin #1. It's flipped . . . and lands tails up. You get no money. Curious to see what would have happened with the second coin, you flip it. It lands heads up.

Using a scale of 1 to 7 (where 1 is "clearly made a wrong decision" and 7 is "clearly made a right decision"), how good was your decision to choose coin #1? Answer:

Consider a second situation. You are the CEO and sole proprietor of a small company faced with the choice of promoting only one of two new products. Product 1 has a 55 percent chance of success, and a corresponding 45 percent chance of failure. Product 2 has a 45 percent chance of success, with a 55 percent chance of failure. If the product succeeds, you will personally receive an after-tax net profit of $10,000. If it fails, you receive nothing. Note that these probability estimates capture all the information that can be reasonably known at this time. They are based on market research, past experience with similar products, specific marketing plans for each product, a realistic estimate of the quality of the execution of those marketing plans, and a thorough consideration of such external factors as competitors' responses, the chance of an unexpected competitive entry, and so on.

You choose Product #1. It fails. However, Product #2, unexpectedly launched by your closest competitor, succeeds.

Using a scale of 1 to 7 (where 1 is "clearly made a wrong decision" and 7 is "clearly made a right decision"), how good was your decision to choose product #1? Answer:

Did you give your decisions a score of 7, indicating that you made the best possible decision given the information you had? (You should have.) Or did the unsatisfactory outcomes sour your assessment? How you answered the questions above tells you an important characteristic of your decision-making. It reveals whether you evaluate the quality of your decisions primarily in terms of the *process* you used to weigh the alternatives and come to a conclusion or on the basis of the *result* you obtained.

When we ask this question in our executive education seminars, most people will agree that choosing coin #1 was the right decision, based on mathematical probabilities. But a considerable number refuse to rate the decision as 7 (excellent) or even 6, and some insist it was the totally wrong decision. They can't bring themselves to recognize a good decision *process* (choosing the coin that puts the odds in their favor) when faced with a poor *outcome*. When we put the question into a business context like the product launch, people are even more reluctant to rate the decision a 7 (only about half as many do as in the coin toss). The poor outcome weighs even more heavily on their minds.

## PROCESS VS. OUTCOME

This outcome-focus among most decision-makers is not surprising. After all, most organizations reward—or penalize—people based on the *outcomes* of their decisions. Results are what matter. You are given a raise or bonus for being highly productive. You are offered a promotion when the projects you manage consistently turn out well, and passed over for plum assignments when they fail. This organizational preference for outcomes is understandable. It exists in part because outcomes are usually easier to assess and are often more objective than assessments of process. The new service you decided to offer, or the new product you decided to launch, proves profitable or not. The team you lead performs well, completing its task on time and within budget, or it doesn't.

The focus on outcomes goes beyond ease of observation, however. Many people believe that good outcomes *necessarily* imply that a good process was used. And they assume the converse to be true as well: that a poor outcome necessarily signals a poor or incompetent process. One division president we know captured this view starkly when he rhetorically posed the following question. "I can promote one of three people," he said. "One has a track record of 50 percent mistakes. The second, 25 percent mistakes. And the third, no mistakes. Who do you think I will promote?" He expected us to answer: the person with no mistakes.

Instead we responded with a question of our own: "How does an experienced manager boast of a track record with no mistakes? The only way we know to have a track record of no mistakes is to do nothing." In an organization where one mistake can derail a career and mistakes are judged only on outcomes, people become afraid to make decisions. They become afraid to do anything. Furthermore, if the track record is based on just a few "big" decisions instead of numerous smaller ones, a focus on outcomes carries the risk of rewarding good luck—or penalizing bad luck. A focus on process would, instead, allow him to truly find the most worthy candidate for promotion. Unfortunately, this executive was not convinced. We hope you, however, will be.

As consultants, researchers, and teachers, we are as pragmatic and results-oriented as anyone. We aim for good outcomes and are pleased when they occur. Throughout this book, however, we will argue that your best hope for a good decision *outcome* is a good decision *process*. That is because we believe that decision-makers must focus on what is actually under their control.

To better understand the process vs. outcome dilemma, consider with us where good results come from. Three things influence outcomes, or results:

(1) Deciding (the thinking and decision process),
(2) Doing (implementation and other factors under your control),
(3) Chance (uncontrollable factors, luck).

By definition, you can't control those factors in the chance category (although you can seek to move more factors under your control and leave as little as possible to chance). And in contrast to the coin toss, the outcome in most real-world decisions depends not only on the quality of the decision process, but also on a mixture of implementation and chance that is difficult to disentangle. A good process, even when tied to excellent implementation, won't guarantee a good outcome 100 percent of the time. Bad luck happens to us all. But clearly, the closest to a guarantee of a good *outcome* is a good thinking/decision *process* followed by good implementation.

## The Three Factors That Determine Outcomes

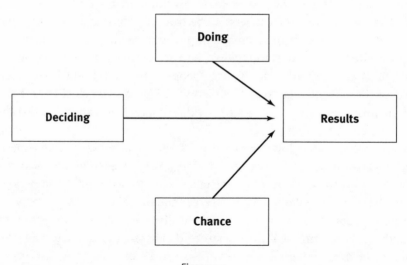

*Figure 1-1*

Fortunately, the organizational bias toward assessing only outcomes is beginning to wane. Robert Rubin, former treasury secretary of the United States, recently noted that "decisions tend to be judged solely on the results they produce." But he continued, "I believe the right test should focus heavily on the quality of the decision-making itself. . . . It's not that results don't matter. They do. But judging solely on results is a serious deterrent to taking the risks that may be necessary to making the right decisions. Simply put, the way decisions are evaluated affects the way decisions are made. I believe the public would be better served, and their elected officials and others in Washington would be able to do a more effective job, if judgments were based on the quality of decision-making instead of focusing solely on outcomes. Time and again during my tenure as Treasury Secretary and when I was on Wall Street, I have faced difficult decisions. But the lesson is always the same: good decision-making is the key to good outcomes. Reject absolute answers and recognize uncertainty. Weigh the probabilities. Don't let uncertainty paralyze you. And evaluate decisions not just on the results, but on how they are made."[1]

The person who uses a good decision process and is rewarded with a good outcome deserves the ensuing accolades. But someone who uses a good process and is met by failure deserves praise as well, for this person may simply have fallen prey to a bad break. Likewise, someone who employs a poor decision process but is met with world-class success deserves neither praise nor promotion for this fortunate individual is simply the recipient of dumb luck. Such luck happens, but you certainly wouldn't want to bet your career on it. You just can't count on luck alone. And so, we invite you to take a moment to reconsider your assessment of the two decisions at the beginning of this chapter. If you weren't able to assign yourself a 7 for clearly making the right decision, see whether you might be able to now. And then read on, as we show you what we have found to be the key elements of a good decision-making process. As Dwight D. Eisenhower said, "Plans are nothing. Planning is everything."

---

Lesson: Your best hope for a good *outcome* is a good decision *process* followed by good implementation.

---

|  |  | Outcome | |
|---|---|---|---|
|  |  | *Good* | *Bad* |
| **Process Used to** | Good | Deserved Success | Bad Break |
| **Make the Decision** | Bad | Dumb Luck | Poetic Justice |

## A GOOD DECISION-MAKING PROCESS

Would you tell me, please, which way I ought to go from here? asked Alice.
That depends a good deal on where you want to get to, said the Cat. I don't
much care, said Alice. Then it doesn't matter which way you go, said the Cat.[2]
—*Lewis Carroll, from* Alice's Adventures in Wonderland

Unlike Alice, most of us do care where we get to, so it does matter which way we go. We need a coherent road map, designed to save us from ending up in the kind of topsy-turvy worlds that Lewis Carroll delighted in creating.

Dividing the decision-making process into four stages can provide just that needed guide.[3] These four stages provide the backbone of almost any decision process, and consciously or not, every decision-maker goes through them. They are:

1. **Framing:** Framing determines the viewpoint from which decision-makers look at the issue and sets parameters for which aspects of the situation they consider important and which they do not. It determines in a preliminary way what criteria would cause them to prefer one option over the other.

2. **Gathering Intelligence:** Intelligence-gatherers must seek the knowable facts and options and produce reasonable evaluations of "unknowables" to enable decision-making in the face of uncertainty. It's important that they avoid such pitfalls as overconfidence in what they currently believe and the tendency to seek only information that confirms their beliefs.

3. **Coming to Conclusions:** Sound framing and good intelligence don't guarantee a wise decision. People cannot consistently make good decisions using seat-of-the-pants judgment alone, even with excellent data in front of them. A systematic approach will lead to more accurate choices—and it usually does so far more efficiently than hours spent in unorganized thinking. This is particularly true in group settings.

4. **Learning from Experience:** Only by systematically learning from the results of past decisions can decision-makers continually improve their skills. Further, if learning begins when a decision is first implemented, early refinements to the decision or implementation plan can be made that could mean the difference between success or failure.

In real life, of course, the process is not quite as linear—or as distinct—as our four stages suggest. Indeed, information discovered in the "intelligence-gathering" stage may inspire you to go back and reframe your decision. Moreover, a complex problem (the relocation of your business, for instance) may entail a series of smaller decisions, each of which may involve several framing decisions, several intelligence-gathering efforts, and several coming-to-conclusions steps.

In spite of this inherent complexity, it helps to think about each of these activities of your decision separately. You can't guard against the characteristic errors of each stage unless you learn to recognize which part of the decision you are working on at any given moment. Fortunately, avoiding these errors is easy once you have learned to recognize the stages and their common traps.

Our four-stage process is a framework, not a series of rigid rules. Follow the paths we suggest only as far as you feel is required for the decision at hand. Use them flexibly. Be aware, however, that every good decision-maker must go through the first three stages. They will happen with you, or without you, poorly or wisely, controlled or ad hoc. If you skimp on the stage crucial to the issue you face, you will pay the price. You can manage these stages now, or they can run over you later.

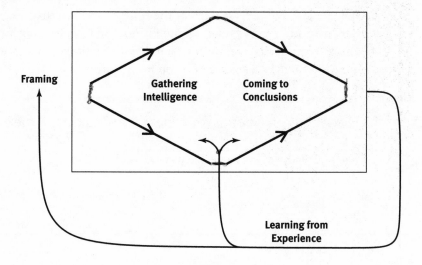

*Figure 1-2*

## Four Stages of the Decision Process

*Note that the first two stages are primarily expansive. In them, you will be trying to expand your options, challenge your assumptions, add to your knowledge, and diversify your interpretations. In contrast, the second two stages are primarily convergent. You will be trying to narrow in on the preferred option and summarize your learning into a few pithy lessons for the future.[4]*

## WHERE DO YOU SPEND YOUR TIME?

One key to managing these four decision-making stages is deciding how much time to devote to each. Most untrained decision-makers allocate their time by happenstance, often overlooking framing entirely, plunging directly into gathering intelligence, and rushing on to the next decision before they've taken time to learn from their experience.

Here's another exercise. Think about an important decision you made recently. This could be a decision about which candidate to recommend for a job that must be filled, which consultant or contractor to hire, whether the proposed budget and timeline for your project will be sufficient, whether a pilot venture ought to be expanded (or be canned), whether your organization should offer new products or services, or any of the myriad other decisions you face in a typical workweek. How did you divide your time among the four decision stages? What percentage of the time devoted to that decision was allocated to framing? To gathering intelligence? To reaching conclusions? To learning from experience? In hindsight, how would you allocate your time if you were to make a similar decision in the future?

## Exercise: How Do You Spend Your Decision-Making Time?

How did you divide your time in an important decision you recently made?

| Stages | Time Allocation |
| --- | --- |
| Framing | —% |
| Gathering Intelligence | —% |
| Coming to Conclusions | —% |
| Learning from Experience | —% |
|  | 100% |

When we asked participants in our executive education seminars how they allocate their decision-making time, they reported the figures in the box below. The bulk of their time is usually devoted to gathering intelligence and coming to conclusions; the least time is spent on framing. Only about 13 percent of their time, on average, is devoted to "lessons learned" analyses and other ways of learning from experience. Almost all experience anxiety, frustration, and conflict with others before a decision is reached.

At the end of our seminars these same people tell us they are going to focus more on framing and learning from experience. They now understand that with a good frame, they'll be able to delegate much of the information-gathering because they will be able to tell people what to seek and how to find it, and they'll also be able to spend less time agonizing about the choice itself. Subsequent follow-up discussions with some of these managers have shown that this is what actually happens; they experience less aggravation and conflict, and find group meetings more productive and enjoyable.

## Where Do Managers Spend Their Decision-Making Time?

The second column shows how managers say they have typically allocated their decision-making time. The last column shows how they intend to allocate their time after learning this decision-making process.[5]

| Stages | Actual Time Allocation | Intended Time Allocation |
| --- | --- | --- |
| Framing | 12% | 22% |
| Gathering Intelligence | 40% | 33% |
| Coming to Conclusions | 35% | 22% |
| Learning from Experience | 13% | 23% |

## DECIDING HOW TO DECIDE

The four major decision stages we just described consume almost all of a good decision process. Chapters 2 through 9 elaborate upon them and provide practical tools to deal with their challenges. Expert decision-makers, however, know they must devote a portion of their time to making choices about the decision process itself—choices that are likely to determine the character of the entire effort—*before* plunging into Stage 1. In this preliminary stage, you will need to evaluate the nature of the decision, decide *what* it is that you need to decide, identify which stages of the decision process will be most critical, evaluate how much time to devote to each stage, and devise a plan for managing the decision, getting help, and so on. In academic jargon, we call this preliminary assessment the "metadecision."[6] The American educator John Dewey said it well when he noted that "A problem well stated is a problem half solved."[7] Too often, pressed for time and an immediate answer, amateur decision-makers plunge into a decision-making process without stopping to ask questions such as:

- What is the crux of the issue that I am facing?
- How do I believe decisions like this one *should* be made?
- How much time should I spend on each stage—as a first guess?

- Can I draw on feedback from related decisions and experiences that I have faced in the past to make this decision better?
- What are my own relevant strengths and weaknesses?

By skipping this initial assessment and plunging into the decision process, managers involved in a complex negotiation for example may fail to ask themselves how they should formulate the right response to their adversary's proposal. Money-losing companies may not ask themselves what is the crux of the challenge in reviving their business. Executives discussing new products may not think through how new product development decisions should be managed. The symptoms of personal conflicts may simply be managed at the surface rather than addressing the rifts' deeper causes. People often find themselves wasting time that could be focused more efficiently. Worse yet, they try to solve the wrong problem.

A carefully constructed metadecision can actually save time and money. Some choices that you make now (either consciously or by default) will affect what happens in later stages. For example, a key meta-question considers whether the decision should be made alone or in a group. Japanese managers encourage open communication from the beginning of a decision-making process to the end: they will seek input from the employees crucial to a product's success, for example, to get commitment and to anticipate potential problems. Although this consensus-oriented style of making decisions slows down the up-front deliberations, it greatly speeds up the decision's subsequent implementation.

## CHANGING THE QUESTION AT PEPSI

Consider this classic example of how a good metadecision powerfully transformed Pepsi-Cola's previously unsuccessfully attempts to challenge Coke's dominance of the soft drink market in the 1970s. The result: Pepsi catapulted from a distant second to Coca-Cola to a fierce competitor in the marketplace.

John Sculley, better known as the former chairman of Apple Computer, was Pepsi's vice president of marketing at that time. As he recalls in his autobiography, *Odyssey*, Pepsi executives were certain that Coca-Cola's distinctive, hourglass-shaped bottle was Coke's most important competitive advantage.

"The bottle design nearly became the product itself," Sculley recalls. "It made Coke easier to stack, more comfortable to grip, and more sturdy to withstand a vending machine's drop. As much a part of this country as Mom and apple pie, it was the only company logo a person could pick up in his hand."[8]

Trying to compete with Coke's bottle, Pepsi spent millions of dollars and many years studying new bottle designs. But although the Pepsi "swirl" bottle, introduced in 1958, served as the company's standard packaging for nearly two decades, it never achieved the recognition of the Coke bottle.

In tackling the problem of how to compete with the Coke bottle, Sculley made an excellent metadecision. In other words, he asked and answered the crucial questions, "What is the crux of this issue? How should problems like this be approached?" He realized that the heart of the problem was not to try to compete directly with Coke's bottle (Pepsi's focus in the past) but to "nullify" its strengths. He decided to approach the problem by shifting the ground rules to alter the whole playing field, "pulling back and asking what the customer really wanted."

Sculley also realized that the company simply did not know enough about consumers to identify what they really wanted, and therefore it could not conduct its marketing decision process in the right way. So before he even tried to assign the bottle question to a new task force, Sculley created an opportunity to learn from a kind of feedback the company had never used before: he launched a careful test to study how families actually consumed Pepsi and other soft drinks *in their homes*.

The company allowed 350 families to order soft drinks weekly in whatever quantity they wanted at discount prices. "To our astonishment," he recalls, "we discovered that no matter how much Pepsi they ordered, they would always consume it." Sculley had discovered what all marketers now recognize as a key fact about snack foods—however much you can persuade people to buy, that's how much they'll consume.

"It dawned on me that what we needed to do was design packages that made it easier for people to get more soft drinks into the home."

Now Sculley could move on to the first of the four decision-making stages: properly framing the issue of competing against the Coca-Cola bottle. "It became obvious that we should change the rules of the competition entirely. We should launch new, larger and more varied packages."

Pepsi began a new intelligence-gathering stage, decided to launch a new group of larger packages, and established new systems to learn from feedback in the stores to refine the packaging strategy still further.

The results were dramatic. Coca-Cola couldn't convert its famed hourglass silhouette bottle into a larger container. Pepsi's market share not only expanded dramatically, it drove the long unassailable Coke bottle into extinction in the U.S. market and beyond.

Lesson: Before plunging in, take time for an initial assessment in which you ask yourself how this kind of decision should be made.

  **Take time to decide how to decide.**

When you start work on any major issue, spend a few minutes—and occasionally a few hours—thinking about the larger issues you are facing. You'll save time and aggravation in the long run. Before any major decision process is launched, review the questions in the accompanying box. The first two questions are the most crucial. The others serve to illuminate them. At the end of this preliminary exercise, you should have a good sense of which stages are most important to the decision at hand, and how much time and resources each deserves.

## Worksheet: Deciding How to Decide

### *Crucial questions*

1. What's the crux or primary difficulty in this issue? Which of the four stages in the decision process will be most important?
2. In general, how should decisions like this one be made (e.g., alone or in groups, intuitively or analytically, etc.)? Where do my own strengths and weaknesses lie? Where do I need help? (Be honest.)

### *Other questions*

3. Must this decision be made at all? Does it need to be made now? Should it be made by me? What parts can I delegate or do jointly?
4. How much time have decisions like this one taken in the past? How long should this decision take? When should it be made? Are the deadlines real or arbitrary? If they are arbitrary, can I negotiate to extend them?
5. Can I proceed sequentially from framing to gathering intelligence to coming to conclusions, or must I move back and forth among the parts of the decision process on this issue?
6. Where should I concentrate my time and resources? How much time should I expect to spend on each stage of the decision process? Do I face a difficult job framing this choice? Will intelligence-gathering be the biggest challenge? Will I have difficulty making the decision systematically even after I have completed the framing and intelligence-gathering?

7. Can I draw on feedback from related decisions and experiences I have faced in the past to make this decision better?
8. What are my own skills, biases, and limitations in dealing with an issue like this? Do I need to bring in other points of view? Which other points of view would be helpful?
9. How would a more experienced decision-maker, whom I admire, handle this issue?
10. Does this decision greatly affect other decisions? If so, what are the cross-impacts?

Intelligently deciding how to decide is probably even more important in group settings than in individual decision-making. While an individual who has started in the wrong direction can turn around and start over fairly easily, changing the direction of a group can be like turning a battleship: slow and awkward.

Thus, in addition to the questions above, two other questions should be asked before beginning any major group decision process.

11. What should I use this group for?
12. In which of the four key elements of the decision process (framing, intelligence-gathering, coming to conclusions, and learning from experience) should the group participate? What is the role of the group as a whole in each one of these stages?

As the Pepsi example demonstrates, a good initial assessment is crucial. Often excellence or sloppiness in decision-making is established in the metadecision that is made, sometimes without the decision-maker even knowing it. Yet nothing else can yield more improvement in less time than making more thoughtful decisions about *how* to decide rather than *what* to decide. By taking the time to contemplate how strategic decisions should ideally be made, Sculley's good metadecision at the start of the decision-making process led him and his Pepsi colleagues to a brilliant solution. Lewis Carroll's Cheshire Cat is correct: knowing where you want to get to is crucial to determining which way you ought to go. If you set out for the wrong destination, it will not be of much use in the end, even if you manage to arrive there intact and on time.

## Metadecisions Under Fire

When time gets short, amateur decision-makers plunge right into gathering information, believing that they lack the time to engage in the more thought-intensive initial stages.

The clock is ticking—and they want action fast. Beware! No matter how little time you have, you cannot afford to skip making a good metadecision. Particularly when your time is limited, you must plan how to best allocate it among the four decision-making stages, *based on an understanding of where the decision-making difficulties lie.* If you don't do this well, you may waste more time than you "save" because you risk solving the wrong problem.

At a minimum, ask yourself two questions:

1. Which stage is the crux of the difficulty? That is, at its core, is this decision a framing problem, will it be solved by gathering enough of the right intelligence, or will reaching a group consensus be the greatest obstacle?
2. Are there past cases from which we could learn? Will a few phone calls (made privately, to some trusted colleagues) reveal the key knowledge needed to make this decision well?

To illustrate, consider the following scenario. You and your colleague have prepared a joint sales presentation to a new client. You both travel to their location and present your talk, which is well received. In fact, the client likes it so much that they request a thirty-minute break and then wish to resume to discuss price and time schedules. You are not prepared for this. Normally, you have at least a week between delivering a sales pitch and preparing a budget. What should you do when suddenly under the gun, considering that this is an important potential project for you and your firm?

The metadecision here is not what price to quote but how best to use the limited time you have (thirty minutes) to properly resolve this issue. Whereas normally the crux of this problem would center on information gathering—about the client's budget, past experiences, competitive bids, etc.—this time, framing is key and also learning from experience. So you and your colleague might spend fifteen minutes discussing how to view this urgent price quote request (from its being a negotiation ploy aimed at getting you to commit under pressure to a genuine desire to conclude a deal because of the client's internal needs and deadlines). Can you somehow postpone the quote but agree on principles? Should the quote be based on "cost plus" pricing to assure a reasonable profit margin or reflect "value pricing" so as to extract the most the client is willing to pay? Should this case be viewed on a pure transaction basis or more from a long-term relationship perspective? A few quick phone calls back to the office by you or your colleague may help settle these issues. And then, in the meta-phase, consider lessons learned from past cases where you had to decide under pressure. Did you ever commit prematurely to a low bid? Has the desire to close the deal, or the limited time available, ever prevented you from considering important contingencies? Lastly, ask how someone you admire (e.g., your boss, Winston Churchill, Bill Gates) would approach this problem. That's what the meta-phase is all about: deciding how to decide.

Finally, be careful not to create false time pressure. Many decision-makers, when they reflect honestly, acknowledge that most time-pressured decisions initially had adequate deadlines, but the lack of an appropriate framework to guide the stages of the decision-making process (i.e., the absence of a good metadecision) consumed what would have been enough time to make the decision well. Also, many managers will admit that the deadline was artificial or even arbitrary. Always ask whether a delay in the deadline (of a week, a day, or even an hour) would appreciably improve the decision-making approach. Of course, such extra time must then be put to good use.

The bottom line: there is rarely a good excuse for not taking some time—even if it is just a few minutes—to think about how you will decide.

# Decision-Framing

## CHAPTER 2

# The Power of Frames

Seek simplicity, then distrust it.   —*Alfred North Whitehead*

I N 1 9 8 9, ENCYCLOPAEDIA Britannica sold over one hundred thousand copies of its multivolume encyclopedia and set a sales record of $627 million. Only five years later, sales had plummeted 53 percent. The reason for the stark drop? CD-ROM, with its advantages of exciting graphics and color, lower manufacturing costs, and high consumer appeal, had entered the market. But while Microsoft offered cut-rate deals on its Encarta CD-ROM or gave it away free with computer purchases, Britannica continued to market its sets of encyclopedias for almost as much as it cost to buy a computer. In fact, in spite of the new technology's growing appeal, Britannica's management chose to offer only a very limited electronic license of the series' content. Their enormous sales staff remained dedicated to selling books.

By the time the company's leaders realized the full impact of CD-ROM on their business, they had insufficient money and time to develop new technology or license partners. In 1995, CEO Peter Norton resigned. And while the Britannica brand is still recognized as the quality leader for authoritative information, it is doubtful whether the company will ever be able to regain its erstwhile market dominance.[1]

Shortsightedness? Flawed strategy? Poor planning? Yes, at least in part. The causes of executive mishap can be numerous, and it is difficult in hindsight to unravel the myriad strands that weave a particular pattern of failure. Nonetheless, we believe that in the case above (and numerous others), previously successful corporate leaders made losing decisions because they used a sensible-sounding—but fundamentally limited—view of the world to structure their decision-making process. They framed their problem poorly. Britannica executives apparently framed their issues narrowly from a print book publisher's perspective—maybe without even realizing they were doing so. In the changed business environment of the 1990s, their once winning "book publisher" frame became a losing one. As a result, each subsequent step in their decision-making was thrown off track. They missed key information that might have led them to an entirely different conclusion. Worse yet, they seemed not to have appreciated what they had missed. When it came time to reach a conclusion, they overlooked the best options. Sometimes these options weren't even on the decision-making table.

Had the Britannica executives known how to consciously evaluate their frame and how to reframe themselves from "book publishers" to one among many companies helping children and adults gain a knowledge advantage in a highly competitive world, they probably would have responded differently. They might have recognized, for example, that families' limited discretionary spending on knowledge resources was increasingly being allocated to computers and electronic products. With such new information, Britannica executives might have made some very different, potentially winning, decisions.

Before we talk more specifically about what frames are and how decision-makers can use them to ensure winning decisions, consider one more framing story, this time with a happier ending. Faced with a stalemate that almost destroyed their joint venture, two telecommunications equipment manufacturers who dominated their respective and complementary niches, learned to use framing skills to ensure their joint success.

In the early 1990s, a $2 billion high-technology manufacturing company and its partner had independently developed a sealed station protector, part of the equipment needed to connect telephone lines to each other. Recognizing the opportunity to build on each other's reputation, they decided to form a joint venture to develop, manufacture, and market this product together. But as so often happens in joint ventures, conflict in the meeting room shredded a plan that looked great on paper. Engineers from both companies wanted to preserve as much of their respective existing designs as they could. Afraid of giving away design secrets, neither group would tell their counterpart about significant shortcomings in its own products.

After eighteen months of stalemate, the consortium decided to produce both designs, thereby doubling the development, tooling, and manufacturing investment required. At last, with the relationship in jeopardy, there was a breakthrough. By finally agreeing to an open discussion of the advantages and disadvantages of both designs, the teams uncovered a key difference in perspective. The first manufacturer had long focused its expertise on exceptional sealing technology, exceeding the industry standards in that area. That expertise defined its perspective during design discussions. Its partner, while meeting industry standards for sealing capabilities, had developed its expertise on grounding. That expertise was framing its perspective.

Once the engineers had refocused the discussion from the differences in design to the differences in expectations (i.e., the misalignment of their frames), the two teams were able to appreciate the value of their particular perspectives. They then built a far better "shared" frame by combining the critical highlights of each. Applying this new frame to the two designs, they found that neither would have passed muster in the market. By focusing so intently on what had made them successful in the past, engineers for both companies were unable to see how the same formula might lead to failure in the future. The final result: they created an entirely new design, ending the impasse, saving about $250,000 in tooling and two person-years in design costs while protecting their market position. And maybe just as important, they had developed a new frame that could be applied to get the same benefits from future joint venture projects.

---

Lesson: The perspectives through which we view the world limit the decision-making options we can see and influence how effectively we can communicate and "sell" those options to others.

---

## ADOPTING A FRAMING PERSPECTIVE

Most people intuitively know something about frames. They allude to them when they talk about "thinking outside the box," "not being on the same page," or "it's all in how you look at it." We experience frames when we meet people who just seem to immediately understand us, with whom we "click," as well as in the frustrating alternative of trying to talk with others who just don't seem to "get it" no matter how much we try to explain.

These different ways of looking at the world can be explained by what cognitive scientists call "frames." Frames are mental structures that simplify and guide our understanding of a complex reality. Everyone must inevitably adopt some kind of simplifying perspective. We are bombarded daily with far more information than we could ever hope to process or use. Even prior to the glutted Information Age, our environment was far too complex for the human brain to process every piece of information available. If we didn't focus our attention on some things and ignore others, we would quickly be consumed solely with trying to make sense of the world around us.

Most people rarely pay any more attention to this automatic mental process than they do to walking. However, as the Britannica story so starkly shows, we can pay a high price for this much-needed simplicity, for our frames limit our perspective and distort what we see. The analogy of a window frame illustrates the difficulties. Architects designing a new house choose where to place windows to give a desired view. But no single window can reveal the entire panorama. When you choose which window to look through—or even if you decide to keep track of what's happening through three different windows—you will never see everything. In fact, you may miss an important event occurring just outside the limits of your frame.

---

Lesson: "Frames"—mental structures that simplify and guide our understanding of a complex reality—force us to view the world from a particular, and limited, perspective.

---

But frames do more than limit our view; they can themselves be hard to see and change. Continuing with the window analogy, you can see the broadest panorama by standing close to the window, with your nose pressed against the glass. But to see the window itself and, more important, to notice that the room may have other windows offering different views, you must step back. So too with frames. People often find it hard to see their frames unless they have been trained to do so or warned that they are there. Yet if you don't recognize that you are looking at the world through only the eastern window, you'll never know when you need to check the view from the south. And when decision-makers confuse the view they see from one—or even two—windows with the entire panorama, they can get caught off guard, thinking their decision-making perspective is more complete than it really is. That leads to the kind of off-the-mark decisions that the Britannica executives made and the kind of conflicts the technology engineers encountered. Often, a frame difference is the major cause of policy disagreements or the key barrier to the implementation of a chosen policy. One person may insist she sees a forest outside the window; a second may insist it's an ocean view. If they do not realize they are looking out of different windows—or through different frames—they may argue endlessly about who is right rather than stepping back to explore the alternative view. (For other ways that frames distort what we see, see the accompanying box.)

Lesson: When we forget that our frame does not capture all of reality, we can be lulled into thinking that our decision-making perspective is more complete than it really is.

## How Frames Distort What We See

Frames guide our thinking in an overly complex and otherwise chaotic world, helping our mind make useful connections and not be distracted by irrelevant ones. However, frames can play tricks on our minds. Here are some of the built-in dangers of frames:

- **Frames filter what we see.** They control what information is attended to and, just as important, what is obscured. Remember: no single window can reveal the entire panorama.
- **Frames themselves are often hard to see.** Just as we have to step back from a window to see that it's there, so too do we have to "step back" from our frame to see that we are viewing the world through a particular perspective.
- **Frames appear complete.** Frames simplify the world. They do not capture all of reality, leaving gaps. But since our mind tends to fill in such gaps, we usually don't even notice that anything is missing.
- **Frames are exclusive.** We typically see one frame at a time. It's hard, after all, to simultaneously look out the windows on both the north and west sides of a room.
- **Frames can be "sticky" and hard to change.** Once we are locked into a frame, it can be difficult to switch, especially without conscious effort. When people have emotional attachments to their frames, changing frames can seem threatening.

To see how different frames can provide different perspectives on the same situation, consider the following two ways to frame the routine act of buying or selling a car. Think first of that buyer-seller exchange as an economic transaction. What things come naturally to mind? Most people find that they focus on issues of price, value, reliability, seamless service, credit ratings, negotiating the best deal, warranties, and so on. We can call this perspective on buying and selling a "transactional" frame.

Now think of this same act in terms of a relationship between buyer and seller (a "relational" frame). What aspects of the exchange now come naturally to mind? Probably you thought about things like trust, honesty, consistency, communication, rapport, building mutual confidence, alliances and partnerships, creating a win-win outcome, cooperation, follow-up, and so on.

Neither frame is right, and neither is wrong; both provide important information about the buying-selling activity. But notice how each frame drew your attention toward certain aspects of the buyer-seller exchange and away from others. And as you can easily imagine, if a buyer has adopted a relational frame while the seller operates from a transactional one, each is likely to wonder why the other person is "behaving poorly" or "just doesn't get it."

Similarly, consider two ways to frame the employer-employee relationship, frames that are increasingly coming into conflict in today's rapidly changing economy. Traditionally, many employment relationships have been framed as a "family," highlighting lifelong relationships, loyalty, interdependence, mutual responsibilities, security arising from continuity, sticking it out through the hard times, a "we're all in this together" mentality, collective identity, and so on. That frame still rings true for many companies, such as S. C. Johnson and others, who pride themselves on the "family" underpinnings of their corporate culture.

Recently, however, many workers (particularly young educated workers in the U.S.) are framing themselves as "free agents." This frame—popularized by the downsizing of the 1990s and new opportunities in a virtual economy—highlights mobility, independence, security arising from one's skills rather than one's loyalty, selling those skills to the highest bidder, continually seeking the next opportunity, one's identity as a professional (e.g., a market researcher, software designer, or intellectual property lawyer) rather than as a part of a specific company, and so on. They are the CEOs of Me Inc.

Again, neither frame alone captures everything of value in an employee-employer relationship. But when it comes to making decisions, the way people frame a problem—i.e., the particular perspective they (often unconsciously) adopt—exerts enormous power over the options they will recognize and the solutions they will favor. An organization that frames itself as a family, for example, will approach the problem of what to do about an employee whose job performance is suffering from alcohol abuse very differently from an organization that subscribes to the "free agent" frame. Remedies such as paid leave, company-sponsored counseling, and an in-house support group fit naturally within the family frame. That same employee, viewed within the free agent frame, is likely to be seen as "responsible for himself." An ultimatum to quit drinking, unpaid leave, and even firing are logical consequences within this frame.

---

Lesson: The way we frame a problem exerts enormous control over the options we recognize and the solutions we choose.

---

## Some Competing Thinking Frames

|  | One Frame | Another Frame |
| --- | --- | --- |
| Buyer-seller exchange | A transaction | Part of a relationship |
| Customer with a complaint | Potential litigant | Free informant |
| Negotiation | Competition, win-lose | Joint problem-solving, win-win |
| Competitors | A person or organization trying to take our customers | A person or organization trying to take our profits |
| Time | A limited, finite resource; an input to productivity | Unlimited; goes on forever; a background to work and relationships |
| Training | Cost | Investment |
| Work group | Sports team | Parts of a smooth-running machine |
| Organization | Collection of contracts | Community of people[2] |

## WHAT'S OUTSIDE YOUR VIEW?

Remember the well-known parable of the six blind men and the elephant? The first man, feeling the massive side of the elephant's body, was sure the animal in front of him was just like a wall. Another, with his hands wrapped around the elephant's leg, insisted it was like a tree. The third, grabbing the elephant's tail, argued that it was really most like a rope. And so on. Each had important information about this new reality, but none had the complete picture. Each was partially right, and all were wrong.[3]

So too with frames. As we saw with the examples of the buyer-seller exchange and the employer-employee relationship, frames tend to draw our attention to certain aspects of a situation, highlighting them, while leaving other equally important aspects in the shadows, obscured from view. The "transactional" frame highlights price, delivery, product specifications, and so on, while leaving the relational aspects of the exchange in the shadows. Conversely, the "relational" frame highlights longer-term issues such as trust, cooperation, and a mutually satisfying outcome while shadowing shorter-term economic considerations.

Unfortunately for decision-making, elements lurking just outside our view (that is, in the shadows of our frame) can come back to haunt us later. Consider this real-life example from a major pharmaceutical company. In order to reduce cost, the manufacturing group had increased the carton size about 15 percent on all dimensions for the same quantity of medication. They thought they would save their company much money. The marketing team, however, was soon in an uproar. Why? The product had to be kept refrigerated, and the customers that distributed it to patients had only limited refrigerator space. Because the repackaged product took up more space per unit of drug, the clients had to order less product. Rather than saving money, the larger carton was costing the company plenty—in lost income and customer dissatisfaction.

This is a classic example of how shadows trip up decision-makers. The traditional manufacturing frame emphasizes such things as product quality, efficiency, cost reduction, innovation, product availability, and enhancing profits. From these perspectives, the cost-lowering larger carton looked like a no-brainer. Issues related to how customers use and store the product, typically in the shadows of the manufacturing frame, did not even show up on their decision-making radar screen.

---

Lesson: Frames draw our attention to certain aspects of a problem while leaving others in the shadows, hidden from our view.

---

If we look carefully, we can often see objects obscured in the shadows. But just as a flashlight illuminates certain objects and leaves others in the shadows, it also excludes some objects from view entirely, leaving them completely in darkness. Likewise, frames impose boundaries, leaving some options, consequences, or considerations so far into the shadows that they are banished from view altogether. These mental boundaries may take the form of geographic regions, time frames, functions, budgets, and the like. A common framing boundary is captured by the expression "yes, we should do it, but it is not in our budget for this year."

Can you see the frame and its boundary?

Those who use the "not in this year's budget" argument adopt an accounting frame; the boundary is the fiscal year. Of course, shareholders don't really care about such internal artifacts as budgets and fiscal years. They want managers to do what is right for the business. Decision-makers who think only in domestic terms (thereby excluding international implications), or ignore anything beyond, say, three years (bounding out the more distant future), or measure only with economic yardsticks (disregarding either humanistic or more strategic considerations) may all "bound out" options they ought to consider.

In a classic example of frame boundaries, leaders of the U.S. auto industry in the early 1970s framed their environment primarily in terms of the United States. Japan and the Middle East were "bounded out" of their strategic analyses. As a result, industry executives discounted the market penetration of the Japanese auto industry, deriding their products as "econoboxes." They did not foresee the rise in demand for more energy efficient cars precipitated by the 1973 and 1979 oil crises. By the time they did include those elements in their frames, it was too late. The U.S. auto industry went from an export surplus to a $60 billion import deficit in two decades. Imports rose from 1 percent in 1965 to over 30 percent in 1987.

Lesson: A frame's boundaries may leave the best options (or some options' consequences) so far in the shadows that we miss them altogether.

## WHAT DO YOU MEASURE AGAINST?

Frames also influence our thinking through the yardsticks and reference points they lead us to adopt. How you measure success or progress, for example, depends on your frame. In years past, General Motors' Central Foundry Division, which makes engine blocks and crankshafts, measured its success by the tons of metal it poured each quarter (i.e., framing in terms of "raw materials input"). Today, it emphasizes yardsticks such as "net good pieces delivered," framing its measurements in terms of "output" instead. GM found that although the input yardstick is easier to compute, such a frame obscures important issues such as quality, safety, and even efficiency.

Similarly, many companies used to measure success only through the traditional "bottom line" financial frame. The rising popularity of the "balanced scorecard" expands that old frame to include other yardsticks such as customer satisfaction, comparisons to competitors, operational efficiency, employee morale, and innovation. When this new frame with its new yardsticks is applied, the resulting conclusions about whether the organization has been successful may change dramatically.

Whatever yardsticks we use to measure performance, most contain a reference point or marker that distinguishes good from poor performance. Although reference points are often numerical, like a sales target or rate of return, they need not be. After all, not everything that is important can be measured (nor is everything that we can measure important). Consider how we might assess society's progress on equal job opportunity, and then ask what frame or reference point is being used. In evaluating the status of career opportunities for women or minorities, for example, some tend to measure progress against a historical reference point, emphasizing how far these groups have come. Others tend to measure job opportunities against the ideal standard of complete equality, and contrast that with the current status of white males. Depending on which reference point we use, we can either focus on how much progress has already been made or emphasize how far we still have to go. As in the classic question about whether the glass is half empty or half full, neither frame is perfect; each offers only a partial view.

---

Lesson: The frame—and the yardsticks—you use may dramatically bias how you interpret information and what conclusions you reach.

---

## OUR FRAMES ARE ROOTED IN OUR EXPERIENCE

Years, even decades, of functional training and experience can powerfully frame people's views of their entire company or business generally. They learn to "think like a marketer"—or an accountant, engineer, psychologist, scientist, and so on—without realizing that applying a narrow frame to every decision they face will lead them to poor (or at least limited) conclusions. Here's a typical example from an automotive products company that was losing money. A parent-company task force asked key managers to investigate the decline. They found that the marketing group blamed the lack of advertising and promotional support. The sales group blamed the lack of promotion and dealer-support programs. The manufacturing and distribution group insisted the problem was inaccurate forecasting by the marketing and sales groups, which caused poor production planning and high costs. The finance department pointed to budget overruns by all departments and unreliable forecasts from the marketing group. The legal department blamed a lack of new franchising and licensing agreements, which meant that the company lacked distribution outlets.[4]

As with the blind men and the elephant, no one analysis was completely right, and no one completely wrong. Left to their own functional frames, no one group could develop a sufficiently broad analysis of the problem—or its solution. Consequently, the best managers reach across the narrow frames of different departments, bringing them together in a more robust whole. In this case the corporate task force concluded that the division president had discouraged interdepartmental cooperation. In failing to do that, the president of this division had failed in his job.

Cultural backgrounds are also powerful sources of frames. Consider the framing disparities experienced by two U.S. MBA students who took a one-year internship in Japan. After extensive interviews in the U.S., both had reached verbal agreements concerning salary and benefits with their future employer, a large Japanese government organization. When they arrived in Tokyo, they were invited to sign employment contracts. In the interim, however, the organization had experienced financial difficulties, and the contracts contained a base salary lower than the figure discussed in the interviews and had no provisions for vacation, sick leave, or bonuses. One of the students saw the new contract as a breach of agreement. Operating from his U.S. "legal" frame, with its emphasis on binding written agreements, he believed that the organization had broken its promises and tried to exploit him. Further, he feared that by signing the new contract, he would be agreeing to abide by its terms for the entire year. Before signing he insisted that the salary figure be raised to the original level and that two weeks vacation and a week's paid sick leave be added to the contract.

His Japanese employers, operating from their "social cooperation" frame, viewed the contract as more of an "agreement to agree" than a legally binding document. (Within this frame, written contracts may be left deliberately incomplete, recognizing that circumstances may change. All employees are members of the "family" and as such, expected to share both the pain and the gain.) To the Japanese managers, the American student's behavior conveyed a lack of trust and an unwillingness to cooperate. The situation deteriorated rapidly, with the student returning home early, breaking the contract he had tried so hard to formalize.

The second student signed the contract immediately, deciding that regardless of the contractual terms she would still learn a great deal about how Japanese companies operate. As the weeks passed, she found that vacation time could be had by asking for it. She was given several bonuses that brought her salary level up to more than the figure quoted to her originally. And when an accident left her unable to work for close to a month, she was not only given paid leave but found that her coworkers visited her in the hospital, ran errands for her, and offered emotional support. All in all, she enjoyed a remarkable experience.

## KNOW YOUR OWN FRAMES AND THOSE OF OTHERS

How can decision-makers avoid the built-in biases and blind spots that frames impose? The first step is awareness, identifying the frames used by you and those you work with. (In the next chapter we will show you how to evaluate and, when necessary, change your frames.) Although discovering frames can be time-consuming at first, it need not be repeated for every decision you make. Once you know your dominant frames—and those of the people with whom you interact most regularly—you will find that those frames resurface in most situations. (In fact, this step is a particularly effective way to prepare for a group meeting.) With practice you will find that, after a few targeted questions, you can quickly catalog the dominant frames operating in any new situation. The following tools and exercises will help you begin to identify the frames you and others use.

 **Conduct a frame audit.**

The easiest way to analyze a frame is to take a "divide and conquer" approach. Rather than trying to see the entire frame, begin by looking at the individual components. Ask what assumptions you are implicitly making about your industry, business, or profession. Try to define the boundaries, and explore the highlights and shadows. What's emphasized? Minimized? Included? Excluded? What are the yardsticks and reference points used?

Consider the origin of the frame: why do you think about the problem in the way that you do? Common reasons might be cultural or educational training, professional experience, organizational norms, and so on.

To discover other people's frames, try asking yourself: "What matters most to them? What do they talk about most often?" Ask also, "What do I naturally consider that they rarely mention? What messages do they seem to filter out?" The first questions reveal their highlights; the second, their shadows. To do this well will require that you temporarily drop any attachment to your own frame. As we tell our students, to walk a mile in someone else's shoes, you must first remove your own.

Finally, bring your organization's frames to the surface to understand what type of thinking dominates the environment in which you work.

**Compare your frames to others.**

To help you notice your own frame (i.e., to stand back from the window), ask yourself, how might others in the same (or a different) industry think about this? A different functional area or profession? Another culture? What are the alternatives that you automatically exclude but a colleague or competitor would not? You may be completely right to exclude them, but you are drawing boundaries differently from your colleague or competitor. Noticing the differences can help you see the characteristics of your own frame.

American and Northern European managers, for example, tend to adopt a functional frame for their organizations. This leads them to highlight questions such as "Who does what?" "Which functions are most essential?" and "How do the functions interrelate?" Southern European managers, on the other hand, have traditionally tended toward a social frame. This frame highlights questions such as social status ("Who is above whom?") and the structure of authority ("Who reports to whom?").[5] What matters is the social network and where you (or others) fit in.

---

## Frame Analysis Audit

*Use questions like the following to analyze a current frame, a frame you are considering adopting, or the frame of someone you must communicate with.*

❏ What issue(s) does the frame address most?
❏ What boundaries do I (we, they) put on the question? In particular, what aspects of the situation do I (we, they) leave out of consideration?
❏ What yardsticks and reference points do I (we, they) use to measure success?
❏ What metaphors—if any—do I (we, they) use in thinking about this issue?
❏ Why do I (we, they) think about this question this way? What training or experience frames the way I (we, they) view the world?
❏ What does the frame emphasize? Minimize?
❏ Do other people in my (our, their) profession or industry think about this question differently? How? Why? Are their frames successful?

---

 **Learn about your organization from other perspectives.**

Medical residents are increasingly required to spend a week as a patient to help them look at their profession through this very different frame. The Korean company Samsung sends its executives to U.S. business schools with two purposes. The first is to learn about American business principles and practices. The second is to learn about America. When their formal training ends, the Samsung executives are required to spend one month traveling in the U.S. by any means of transportation they choose *except* by airplane. The result: they come face-to-face with many aspects of American life that they wouldn't see if they flew business class from New York City to San Francisco.

In the past, some companies used eighteen-month job rotations to help employees develop an appreciation for other frames. However, as costs have increased, this practice is declining. One low-cost way to learn about your own and others' frames is to take a short (one to two-week) course in a functional area other than your own. If you work in marketing, for example, try taking a short course in finance— and vice versa. One of the biggest benefits of earning an MBA is learning the full portfolio of functional frames, from accounting and operations to strategy and organizational behavior.

 **Appreciate newly emerging frames.**

Track frame shifts occurring in your industry, profession, nation, or worldwide. How are people currently changing the way they frame important questions? What do these frames highlight or leave in the shadow?

Kinko's, originally established as a low-price copy shop for college students, was one of the first companies to recognize the emerging "free agent" frame of self-employed professionals and start-up entrepreneurs. Better and sooner than their rivals, founder Paul Orfalea and his colleagues figured out how to apply this new frame to their own business. By the early 1990s, Kinko's had repositioned itself as a state-of-the-art service center for self-employed professionals, with a marketing campaign touting each of their shops as "Your Branch Office." Open twenty-four hours a day, seven days a week, they provided round-the-clock administrative support and access to the high-end technology typically available only at large corporations: high-quality printers, scanners, digital cameras, specialized design software, and real-time videoconferencing along with workstations, telephones, FedEx service, and even scissors, staplers, and paste.[6]

Likewise, the emergence of the Internet has forced many people to rethink long-standing business models, and indeed, the deeper-thinking frames that underlie them. In an Internet frame the emerging highlights are speed, convenience, global availability, and price competition. We can sit in our pajamas at 10 P.M. on a Sunday evening and order a new sweater (or automobile, or watch) from a seller located anywhere on the planet. And pity those who have "distributor" in their title, for "middlemen" are bounded out of the frame entirely. Contrast this with the old business frame's highlights of loyalty, service, business as part of a community's social network, and keeping money in the local community. Once again, neither frame is "right" (or "wrong"). People must decide for themselves whether investing their money in the local economy is more important than obtaining the lowest price. But as a decision-maker, it's imperative that you understand how people are framing important questions and what those frames highlight and shadow.

Here are some other frames we see emerging in a wide range of industries and professions. Can you identify their highlights and shadows, boundaries, yardsticks, and reference points? We've listed the older, competing frames in parentheses to help you notice the different perspectives.

- Real-time, 24/7 (vs. 9 to 5)
- Balanced scorecard (vs. economic bottom line)
- Knowledge management (vs. swapping stories at the water-cooler)
- Learning culture (vs. performance culture)
- "Coopetition" (vs. competition alone)
- Virtual organizations (vs. face-to-face, bricks and mortar)[7]

## WHAT METAPHORS DO YOU USE?

Metaphors can play a profound role in many people's frames.[8] Think of the human brain as a muscle. What actions for improving brainpower come to mind? Many people say things like stretch it, exercise it, ensure that it receives sufficient rest and nutrition. Now think of the human brain as a computer. How might you improve brainpower? Using this frame, people often answer: increase memory, input better data, develop the ability for parallel processing, create better software (e.g., new ways to handle information).

Experienced decision-makers choose metaphors carefully to highlight important facets of the situation at hand, helping them think about the current situation in terms of another one that they understand better. Amateur decision-makers, on the other hand, automatically use one or two metaphors to frame almost everything. (Consider the colleague who talks about every situation as a football game, a family, or a military engagement.) In doing so, they limit the options they can see, sometimes excluding the best ones from consideration.

The next time you read a book by one of the latest business gurus (some of the most avid users of metaphors), ask yourself, how does this metaphor function as a frame? What does it highlight, and what does it shadow? Peters and Waterman, in their best-selling book *In Search of Excellence*, chose the following metaphor to frame new product development: "Experimentation . . . resembles nothing so much as a game of stud poker. With each card, the stakes get higher and with each card, you know more, but you never really know enough until the last card has been played. The most important ability in the game is knowing when to fold."[9]

When we share this analogy with managers, they agree that it is a good metaphor. After all, with most development projects, you never know for sure until after the fact whether it has been worthwhile. And, as the project gets rolling, each major step becomes much more expensive than the last— and it's harder to quit. The crucial management decision is whether—and when—to fold (i.e., to cut your losses). Knowing how to revise the odds in light of new information is crucial. Just as in poker, players possess both private and public information, with the latter increasing over time (like new cards being turned). Finally, you need the poker player's mental toughness to fold quickly and start over again whenever the current hand stops looking promising.

People have a much harder time, however, identifying what is not captured by the metaphor (i.e., what's in the shadows). This is one of the problems with frames; people rarely notice in what ways they are incomplete. As our executive education students ponder what aspects of new product development are concealed by the stud poker metaphor, they propose the following: New product development is not necessarily a zero-sum game. Many players might win or lose due to regulatory action (as in biotechnology) or market acceptance (as with personal computers). Second, players do not receive a new hand each round, nor ones that are entirely dictated by chance. Finally, some collaboration is permitted in new product development (through strategic alliances), but usually taboo in poker. And, above all, the rules of the game are not fixed.

Finally, we ask them, "What other metaphors could illuminate the problems of new product development?" Answers include gardening, oil drilling, and biological evolution. With these alternatives in mind, they can consider which specific development decisions might be better made within the stud poker frame, and which might benefit from the perspective offered by a different metaphor.

---

Lesson: Metaphors, when chosen carefully, can highlight important facets of a situation. But when one metaphor is used indiscriminately to frame all decisions, it limits the options that can be seen, possibly excluding the best ones from consideration.

---

 **Explore the metaphors used.**

What are your favorite metaphors? What images do you regularly use to describe situations or explain behavior? What metaphors do your boss, team members, partners, and competitors use most often? Use the elements of those metaphors to help expand your view of highlights and shadows. Try to become more sensitive to the imagery in people's speech and view it as a window into their hearts and minds.

## IT'S ALL IN HOW YOU FRAME IT

Different frames are what make it so difficult for people from different functional or cultural backgrounds to communicate with each other. Without a conscious understanding of framing that helps people recognize the value of another person's view, there may not be, literally, a meeting of the minds. It is not unusual to encounter deep frame conflicts in decision-making situations, especially when people don't appreciate that we all operate from incomplete frames. Every decision-maker has stories of stalemate and conflict, sometimes attributed to individuals' "personalities." These conflicts can generate outright hostility, accusations of private agendas, or questions about competence or ethics. In fact, often they just stem from unidentified frame differences.

Opportunities for frame conflict have increased as many organizations turn to cross-functional teams to help address the problem of myopic thinking and frame blindness. Assembling people with different backgrounds (and presumably, different frames) can bring forth a broader range of ideas, help them see into the shadows of their individual frames, develop alternative frames, or at least, stretch their existing frames to include new highlights. But as we all know, such cross-functional teams are not without their own problems, particularly when team members are oblivious to the issues of framing, frame blindness, and the lack of completeness inherent in their personal views.

The well-publicized conflicts between physicians and hospital executives as today's U.S. healthcare system undergoes fundamental changes is a good example of a conflict arising from frame differences. In a typical physician's frame, doctors are independent service providers who use the resources of hospitals, laboratories, specialists, and so on to help patients. Hospitals are simply one location offering specialized resources where they can treat their patients. In the business frame held by a growing number of management-trained hospital executives, doctors are an asset of a well-managed hospital, and a hospital is a business that offers its customers many services, one of which is access to physicians. What gets lost in the highly-charged interpretations of morality and competence that often accompany such discussions is that each of these frames offers highlights *essential* to the provision of high-quality, cost-effective medical care. These highlights include the value of a single decision-maker with the medical expertise to coordinate all facets of a patient's care, as well as the need for efficient use of resources, and sensible tradeoffs between costs and benefits. Ultimately physicians and healthcare executives will have to understand—and appreciate—elements of the others' frame and, together, develop a new, more robust frame that incorporates elements of both.

Lesson: Interpersonal conflicts are often rooted in unidentified frame differences.

## Frames, Mental Models, and Paradigms

The terms "frame" and "framing" have their origin in the academic fields of cognitive science and artificial intelligence. For those interested in a bit more theory on how frames operate—and their relation to other mental constructs such as *mental models* and *paradigms*—we offer this overview. Additional readings are suggested in the endnotes.

Cognitive scientists have devoted a great deal of time to studying complex mental processes like perception, memory, and reasoning. How these processes relate to each other—and to the underlying physiology of our brains—is only partly understood. However, we do know enough about framing in action to coach decision-makers on how to avoid framing blunders and use framing tools to improve their decisions.

Cognitive scientists believe that we organize our understanding of the world into "mental models"—a rich network of concepts and relationships that capture the essence of both concrete objects, such as a car or a computer, and abstract constructs such as democracy, family, competitor, and leadership. A simplified mental model of a car, for example, would contain the features most people consider central in their definition of a car (see figure 2-1). At the core of the model we would probably find a chassis, engine, brakes, wheels, steering mechanism, and fuel tank. As the model becomes a bit more intricate, we'd include additional features such as a windshield, exhaust pipe, cooling system, and lights. These features are important, but they are not the *core*—the first things people think of when they think of what makes an object a car.[10]

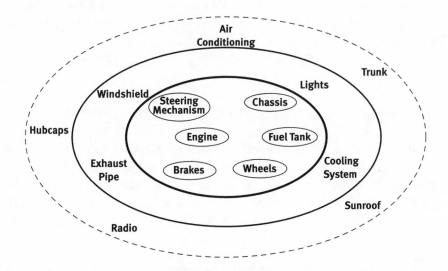

*Figure 2-1* **Mental Model of a Car (Simplified)**

An adult brain contains thousands of mental models, which have developed over decades of education and experience. Much of decision-makers' special knowledge about their professional activities may be represented as a collection of mental models.

Frames are at the tightly woven structural core of these mental models, what we might call the mental model's "essence." They often reside in our memories and are usually evoked or triggered automatically. Whereas trying to change any substantial portion of a mental model can take weeks, months, even years, because of the vastness and strength of its interconnected network, frames can be exposed, understood, and realigned in less time. Thus, mastering frames is particularly useful to decision-makers.

The frames we use can be either borrowed or constructed.[11] Every culture teaches powerful thinking frames (such as democracy) to its young. We unconsciously borrow these frames and apply them to diverse situations. A person's occupation and education, capturing years of training and experience (e.g., learning how to think like a lawyer, engineer, or accountant), similarly produce powerful thinking frames. They become a permanent part of our mental repertoire, and we use them broadly. In fact, many thinking frames become so deeply ingrained in groups or organizations that people cannot change them when the circumstances call for it. When large groups use these widely shared mental models to define their reality, we call them paradigms.

In contrast to the broad thinking frames that we internalize through years of socialization and then borrow to apply to a wide range of situations, we sometimes construct frames to organize our thinking about a specific topic, situation, or decision. For example, when we develop criteria to evaluate possible vacation options, whom to hire for a job opening, or where to open a new retail outlet, we may construct a frame tailored to the problem and decision at hand. Although thinking frames and constructed frames differ in their origin and depth, their impacts on our decision-making processes bear enough similarities that we can talk about them together.

## "AS SIMPLE AS POSSIBLE, BUT NO SIMPLER"

In our experience, decision-makers' most demanding job is to manage the process by which they—and their organizations—select winning frames. As important as broad visions are, frames are typically where the thinking rubber meets the action road. The way we frame a problem will circumscribe the options we recognize. When a single mental framework is repeatedly and indiscriminately applied to different situations, we are likely to use it to misframe decisions. In fact, the more frequently a frame is used, the more likely it is to be used indiscriminately. Remember the Britannica story with which we began this chapter. Even a historically successful frame can lead to a poor decision when it is inappropriately used. Frames also influence how effectively we can communicate and "sell" our perspectives to others. For these reasons, framing forms the foundation of a good decision-making process—and poor framing is one of its most lethal flaws.

Albert Einstein admonished his colleagues: "Make it as simple as possible, but no simpler." That's good advice for decision-makers as well. Frames enable us to simplify the world. However, we must ensure that in doing so, we don't *over*simplify it, obscuring or bounding out the best options. In this chapter we gave you some ways to recognize the frames you and others use. In the next chapter we'll show you how to evaluate your frames, create more robust frames, and turn frame conflict into a competitive advantage. By understanding how to identify, evaluate, and when needed, change frames, you can make a profound difference in your organization's problem-solving and decision-making prowess.

CHAPTER 3

# Creating Winning Frames

The test of a first-rate intelligence is the ability to hold two opposite
ideas in mind at the same time and still retain the ability to function.
                                                    —*F. Scott Fitzgerald*

A N   O L D   S T O R Y about a Franciscan priest and a Jesuit illustrates well
the gentle art of frame control. Both were heavy smokers and somewhat troubled about this human frailty, especially when praying to the
Lord. The Franciscan decided to see his prefect and asked: "Father, would it
be permitted to smoke while I am praying to the Lord?" The answer was a
resounding no. The Jesuit also sought counsel, but framed his question
somewhat differently: "Father, when in moments of weakness I smoke,
would it be permitted to say a prayer to the Lord?" The answer: "Yes, of
course my son."

We leave it for others to judge if the Jesuit really found a superior frame
long-term. After all, smoking harms your health. However, he does demonstrate the nuanced skills of frame control.

Decision-makers have a special responsibility to consciously control their
frames, rather than be controlled by them, and to overcome, as far as possible, the inherent limitations of any single frame. This doesn't mean you must
continually reframe every aspect of life. For most decisions you or your organization already have an adequate frame. It does mean, however, that you
must *notice* and *evaluate* your frames. For if you frequently use an inappropriate frame—that is, if you continue to simplify in ways that blind you to what
is most significant about the situation—your decisions will inevitably cause
difficulties for you and your organization. And without a conscious understanding of framing, people may not recognize the value of another person's
view, be it in interpersonal interactions or in group decision-making.

Unfortunately, most people don't select frames, they often adopt them unconsciously. In the last chapter we showed you how to identify what frames

you and others are using. This step—Awareness—is the first step in good framing. In this chapter we will show you how to take strategic control of your frames (and, to the extent possible, influence the frames of others) to create the kind of broad, novel, *winning* perspectives that can form a sturdy foundation for successful decision-making.

To do this well entails two more steps: evaluating whether your existing frames fit the problem at hand, and, if necessary, finding or building a better frame.

---

## Three Steps to a Winning Frame

1. **Awareness:** Notice what frames you and others are using.
2. **Evaluate fit:** Evaluate whether your frames fit the problem at hand. If they match, you're on track. If not, proceed to step 3.
3. **Find or build a better frame.** For yourself, find a better frame, or build one if necessary. When working with others, help them change their frames.

---

### STEP TWO: EVALUATE FIT

Unlike developing awareness of existing frames, which you need to do only periodically, you must evaluate the appropriateness of your frame for every situation. This needn't be a lengthy process. Sometimes a two-minute check will be just fine. For example, if you are a lawyer facing a purely legal problem, you can use your legal frame to structure your decision.

However, framers beware! As we saw in the last chapter, decision-makers often confidently use frames that are outdated or just plain wrong to "solve" their problems—with disastrous consequences. And too often, a single view or thinking frame dominates our approach to everything. In complex situations it is rare that any single frame will be adequate. Remember, different frames highlight and obscure different aspects of any situation. Frames should be fitted to the problem rather than used out of habit, dictated by convention or, worst of all, blindly imposed by others.

You're not alone, however, if you find it easier to notice the blind spots in other people's frames than in your own. How can we identify a poor frame, given that our frames filter what we see and then trick our minds into believing that they are more complete and appropriate than they are? The answer: we must consistently challenge our own frames, honestly examining their fit. This is easier said than done—but if you are willing to be truly honest with yourself, it is possible. Here are some strategies that can help. As with frame awareness, don't try to evaluate the entire frame at once. Rather, "divide and conquer," matching each part of your frame to the problem to ascertain fit.

 **Observe the symptoms of frame misfit.**

Poor results, unexpected outcomes, inconsistencies, and difficulty communicating with others are all symptoms of a potential framing problem. Start by considering the possibility that your frame may be wrong or, at least, not perfect. Try to falsify it. For example, if your frame says customers care mostly about price and only secondarily about service, try approaching your customers from the opposite direction.

A major investment firm, trying to increase the number of female MBAs it was hiring from business schools, reasoned that they should be able to hire more women if they screened more women, so they increased the number of women interviewed during their recruiting visits to business school campuses. Unfortunately, their strategy failed. The number of women accepting jobs at their firm remained abysmally small. The company's executives could have assumed poor performance by the interviewers or concluded that female MBAs simply didn't want to work at investment firms. Instead they began to investigate their entire recruiting practice, examining the questions they asked candidates, their interview procedures, and even the places in which they were recruiting. Their conclusion? Their traditional investment banking frame, which defined what constituted a "good investment banker," led partners to question candidates primarily about their previous "deal experience." In such an interview, only those who had worked on Wall Street before business school (primarily men) could shine.

Noticing the misfit between their frame and their goals, they developed a new frame that highlighted the ways in which people could add value to the firm in the future. Instead of focusing on previous deals, interviewers began asking job candidates to talk about how they would contribute to the firm's mission. The interviews shifted radically in tone and substance. Boasts from former Wall Street stars were replaced by nontraditional candidates—men as well as women—describing a range of managerial skills, creative experiences, and diverse work styles. The executives also lengthened the interviews from thirty to forty-five minutes, which enabled them to focus more on the candidates' skills, ideas, and experience rather than on first impressions and whether the candidate fit their traditional frame of an investment banker (e.g., how "comfortable" they were with a particular candidate). Not only did their hiring of women increase, the firm returned to one prominent business school the following year to find that it was earning a reputation as a great place to work.[1]

 **Evaluate the quality of assumptions.**

Challenge all the assumptions in your frame. Are they appropriate and realistic? Are other assumptions possible? Recognize how your assumptions direct your attention and lead you to filter information. It is likely that some of these assumptions are explicit, while others will lurk below the surface. Ask yourself whether changing an assumption would change the preferred course of action.

For example, GM's assumptions about itself and the world in the early 1970s presumed an isolated U.S. market, an abundance of cheap gas, dominance of styling over technology, alienated workers, and limited social unrest. These assumptions, which worked when technology was simple and gas was cheap, kept executives from noticing the many signals that the world was profoundly changing.[2]

Similarly, in the mid-1990s, many American credit unions assumed that they would undoubtedly continue to enjoy tax-exempt status, could count on the long-term loyalty of their members as a competitive advantage, and would continue to attract top employees at low market wages because of a shared belief in the credit union philosophy. Only a few years later they saw bank-supported bills introduced in Congress that threatened their tax-exempt status, began to lose their most profitable members to banks and other financial service providers, and found increased competition for good employees.

**Question your boundaries, yardsticks, and reference points.**

Identify the origins of your measuring points, or those used in your company. Decades ago, Ford, GM, and Chrysler used each other as their reference points. Sears compared itself primarily against Montgomery Ward and J. C. Penney, whose stock prices were prominently displayed next to Sears' in the lobby of its former Chicago headquarters. One benefit of globalization and the benchmarking movement (where you compare yourself against "best current practice") is a healthy broadening of reference points, and of frames of mind in general. Since the early 1980s, Ford, for one, has been adamant about *not* comparing its quality to that of its two domestic rivals, but instead focusing on the best in its industry, which includes the Japanese and German car companies, among others.

Often the simplest and most appealing yardstick is not the right one to use. For example, a U.S. corporation might measure the bottom line of its Dutch and Italian subsidiaries in dollars, or in guilders and lira. On the one hand, using U.S. currency makes it easy to compare the performance of all operations, domestic and foreign, on a single yardstick. On the other hand, the managers of a foreign subsidiary need to compete with domestic firms whose strategic decisions are based on local currency. When the home office uses a dollar yardstick to evaluate a potential project, decision-makers must factor in the uncertain fluctuations of the foreign exchange rate. This may make a project look riskier than if it were judged by a local currency yardstick; the company may pass up a project as too risky that domestic competitors rightly see as attractive.

Using the wrong reference point can turn a good decision into a mediocre one. On the other hand, a shift of reference point can reinvigorate an organization. General Electric CEO Jack Welch regularly insists that his managers reframe their boundaries to stimulate higher performance. If managers report that GE holds a 60 percent market share for a particular product, Welch will insist they redefine the market more broadly, such that GE holds only 10 percent of the newly defined market. By redrawing the boundaries, Welch reframes his managers' view of their divisions as less dominant, undercutting tendencies toward complacency and unleashing latent creativity and initiative.

 **Seek other opinions.**

Seeing your frame is akin to seeing your nose—others do it better than you do. Seek a devil's advocate to challenge the assumptions of your frame and point out shadows. Often the best devil's advocates are those people you continually disagree with. Though most of us feel more comfortable with people who share our views, they are the least likely to see the frames they share with us. Try getting opinions from people whose background or training differs from yours. Sacrifice some congeniality for learning.

 **Role-play your adversaries and stakeholders.**

Temporarily adopt your competitors' viewpoint as well as that of your shareholders, employees, regulators, suppliers, auditors, and whoever else matters most to the decisions you make. We recommended this kind of approach in chapter 2 to help you identify your frames; you can also use it to evaluate their fit. What is their frame? What do they include that you don't? Do any of their highlights, boundaries, yardsticks, or reference points fit your situation better than your own? Remember, they may not be right, but at least it will give you another perspective to consider.

 **Compare old frames to new realities.**

How do present conditions compare to previous circumstances? What elements are the same, and which are different? Do adjustments in the frame need to be made to match the new realities? Consider the emerging frames discussed in chapter 2. What do they include that you might have overlooked?

Federal Express, whose name has become synonymous with the U.S. overnight delivery system, was spectacularly unsuccessful when it exported its U.S. model to Europe in the late 1980s. Its winning U.S. approach called for a dedicated fleet of planes, one central hub, and standardized procedures for processing packages. But a single hub in Brussels added costly customs delays, and differences in national cultures frustrated FedEx's attempt to standardize its procedures. The bottom line: annual losses as high as $200 million. In 1992 the company scrapped its intra-European express delivery, laid off 6,600 employees, and closed more than 100 European facilities.[3] Had executives compared their old U.S. frame to the new European realities, they might have avoided making such a costly mistake.

 **Challenge yourself.**

Look not only through the window of your frame, but in the mirror. Ask yourself whether the problem is really one of execution, or the result of an outdated (or inappropriate) frame. Remember, this can be a private analysis. You owe it to yourself to be totally honest.

## How Effective Are Your Frames?

To assess whether your frames serve you well, professionally or personally, answer the following questions as honestly as you can. Ask the opinions of others you trust as well.

1. Do your frames prompt you to ask the right questions most of the time?
2. Have you tested or challenged your frames, or have others tried to do so?
3. Are your frames decisive in the sense of helping you resolve tough issues?
4. Are your frames easily communicated to and understood by others?
5. Do key stakeholders accept your frames as a guide to joint action?
6. Do your frames achieve sufficient simplicity (without being too simple)?
7. Are your frames adaptive and up-to-date with respect to the changing times?
8. Do your frames generate solutions that achieve the desired results?
9. What are some notable failures of your frames? Where have they led you astray?
10. In which cases did your frames allow you to see the forest for the trees?
11. What are some of the deeper assumptions that underlie your frames?
12. What are some of the origins of these assumptions in your past experience?
13. How do the frames of those you admire differ from your own?
14. What frames are used by those more successful than you?
15. Have you improved your framing skills over time? In which ways?

## STEP THREE: FIND OR BUILD THE MOST APPROPRIATE FRAME

By now you've thoroughly analyzed and evaluated your current frames. Suppose you have concluded that your frames do not adequately fit the realities of the current situation. Can you change your way of thinking? We believe that you can. There are several elements to this skill, but much of its success relies on having a repertoire of frames to work with. Using multiple frames offers the best way to notice how you have simplified your perspective and recognize when you need to broaden it. Some of the tools, below, can help you and others expand your perspective, "think outside the box," and generate alternative frames.

Changing other people's frames (or those of your organization as a whole) is more challenging. Most of us are all too familiar with the kinds of stalemates that can arise when a diverse team must make a complex decision or when we must convince someone higher up in the organization to choose a particular course of action. Can you lead other people to change their frames? Not always. But it can be done sometimes. The skills to do so (some of which are described below) are one hallmark of an excellent leader.

In addition to the tools we offer, reframing also requires a willingness to live with discomfort for a while. That can be challenging for most organizations, but it is a small sacrifice when compared to the costs of mental inertia.

### Finding alternative frames

No thinking frame is complete. To discover or create the best frame, it can help to have multiple frames to work with. Here are a variety of ways to generate alternative frames.

 **Tailor to fit.**

Borrow a broadly applicable frame, but customize it to your specific situation. Ask yourself: what other decisions are similar to this one? What frames were used in those cases? What elements are different in this case?

This is exactly what small companies that adopted "guerrilla marketing" did. Faced with the need to fight a much larger competitor, some borrowed the frame used by guerrilla fighters battling much larger, well-equipped armies. They kept a low profile; capitalized upon flexibility and being fast on their feet; chose low-cost, high-impact attacks on market awareness (e.g., word-of-mouth and postering) rather than the brute force of big bucks (e.g., sixty-second TV spots); exploited every weapon in their arsenal; and targeted their efforts to gain product acceptance to precise, valued market segments.

 **Use outsiders to get different viewpoints.**

How would your competitor define the problem? A marketing manager? An engineer? An entrepreneur? A regulator? Someone from a different industry? Someone from a different culture? Even someone from a different generation? Ask people who usually disagree with you: "How do you see it?" "What am I overlooking?"

Explore the views of professionals experienced in these types of problems or decisions. Ask who within your company might have this kind of expertise. Are there any articles or seminars that might provide helpful insight? Can you hire the expertise you need on a permanent or consulting basis? A major pharmaceutical company, considering the possibility of marketing a new drug over-the-counter as well as through the more traditional prescription route, hired two marketing managers from Procter & Gamble to complete its eight-person team. The company wanted a P&G-type perspective on direct marketing to consumers to stretch the boundaries of its frame.

Similarly, after British Petroleum (BP) had repeatedly failed to find a profitable way to produce its Andrew field in the North Sea, it shifted its approach. In a major departure from established practice, the development team invited seven key contractors—who would normally bid on the project only after it had been fully developed by BP's staff—into the problem-solving effort. Working on their own, BP managers could not reduce projected costs to develop this geologically complex field below $676 million. Once the contractors got involved, every problem, component, and assumption was examined. Breakthrough solutions were found, from employing horizontal wells to cost sharing to offshore construction of an integrated deck. The end result was a new budget of $560 million for the project, with penalties for overruns and bonuses for savings. The project came in just below $444 million and was completed six months ahead of schedule. The seven contractors shared a bonus of $69 million, a worthwhile frame-busting exercise indeed.[4]

 **Use subgroups.**

Whenever two groups are given the same task (as in the "Seeing into the Shadows" exercise below), each group is likely to notice different highlights. When constructing a list of criteria for a decision frame, for example, try having two groups generate their lists independently; then combine the lists and select the most relevant factors. This is an excellent way to reveal shadows that might otherwise be overlooked.

 **Adopt multiple frames to guide decision-making.**

When we set out to write this book, we adopted two different author frames. The first was a "professor/scholar" frame, which focused on the needs of our students and peers for a book they could study. Such a frame highlights respected academic research that would substantiate the claims we were making, appropriate citations for those who want to read the original research themselves, depth and completeness of material, and so on. At the same time we also adopted an "author/consultant" frame which focused on the needs of our professional readers for a book that would easily translate into on-the-job action. This second frame highlights anecdotes to which readers can easily relate, practical tools that can be readily applied, an accessible text that can be understood without in-depth study, etc. Since we (Jay and Paul) have been trained to operate from the scholarly frame, we followed our own advice to "use outsiders to get different views" by inviting a professional writer (Margo) to collaborate with us; part of her job was to ensure that the highlights of the "author/consultant" frame remained in view. Throughout the writing process, the three of us continually shifted from one frame to another when making decisions about what material to include and how to present it, while also trying to shed as much light as possible on our potential shadows and blind spots.

 **Shift metaphors.**

Whenever you (or someone else) uses a strong analogy or imagery, be on guard: you are about to be framed. The connections that automatically fire in our brain are dictated by that metaphor. To avoid these limitations, use several alternative metaphors to illuminate the issue in a new way. To succeed in your profession, should you act more like a general, a religious leader, a mountain climber, or a competitive swimmer? To succeed in the industry you're thinking of entering, should your company behave more like a football team, an orchestra, or the parts of a Japanese garden? (Use of the garden metaphor has been credited with helping the Japanese focus on the long-term, like growing a tree, and acting cooperatively, like symbiosis.) Often, a combination of elements from several different frames offers the best picture of a problem.

A creative example of shifting metaphors took place during World War II when U.S. government agents questioning the loyalty of Japanese-Americans would ask, "Who do you want to win this war: America or Japan?" Recognizing that the framing of this question was not appropriate to their situation (they loved both countries), some Japanese-Americans tried to shift the discussion from a military frame to a family frame. Thus, they responded, "Who do you want to win when you see your mother and father fighting? You just want them to stop fighting."

 **Think via analogy.**

When engineers first tried to build airplanes or strong, tall structures, they derived inspiration from biological analogies such as birds flying (or gliding) and bees building sturdy hives. The essence of synectics (a Greek word referring to combining components) is to join seemingly unrelated elements—such as beehives and huge iron-and-concrete structural designs. By moving away from the problem to a distantly related phenomenon and then trying to analogize, powerful ideas may result. Try it for yourself: what can a Swiss army knife teach you about how to organize your division? (Think of interchangeable parts, complementary tools, multipurpose pieces, compactness, the links between form and function, etc.)

## MODIFYING OTHER PEOPLE'S FRAMES

Modifying others' frames is challenging. It cannot always be done. But that doesn't mean you shouldn't try. Particularly in group decision-making, the ability to help group members modify frames as needed can determine whether you wind up with a stalled team or a successful conclusion.

 **Stretch an existing frame.**

It is often easier to get others to stretch their frame by including additional highlights or criteria than to change it totally. The accompanying exercise, "Seeing in the Shadows," offers one way to help people stretch their frame. Here are some examples of companies that have stretched their frames.

At a major pharmaceutical company, the R&D and manufacturing divisions had traditionally focused on quality. By beginning to talk about "speed to market" as an attribute of quality (and in the process, generating the notion of "quality-speed"), corporate leaders were able to stretch their employees' functional frames to include an additional highlight. They then stretched the frame even further, introducing "economic value added" as another key attribute. Whatever their functional frame, employees throughout this company now approach any major decision by asking how it will affect "quality-speed-value."

Consultant and author Gary Hamel has suggested that traditional organizations would do well to stretch how they frame decisions to allocate resources. In a provocative article entitled "Bringing Silicon Valley Inside," he contrasts the traditional corporate "stewardship" frame, where access to capital is tightly controlled at the top and the status quo reigns, with Silicon Valley's "entrepreneurship" frame, where unconventional ideas attract funding on their own merit, no matter what title the innovator holds. His advice: stretch the traditional central planning, *resource allocation* frame to incorporate the *resource attraction* highlights of Silicon Valley operations. Ninety-two-year-old, 102,000-employee Royal Dutch/Shell did just that when a manager in one of its largest divisions created the GameChanger process, giving a small group of employees $20 million to allocate to their peers who had innovative, promising entrepreneurial ideas. It took some coaching before employees used to conventionally defined work projects began to think like entrepreneurs, but of the company's five largest growth initiatives in early 1999, four began with GameChanger funding.[5]

**Challenge the yardsticks and reference points.**

Shifting yardsticks can help reframe the thinking of others. For example, if a project budgeted at $100,000 is completed for only $90,000, a sharp employee will express this accomplishment as an impressive absolute: "I saved the company $10,000." If, however, the same $100,000 project costs $110,000, that savvy employee will minimize the overrun by claiming: "I stayed within 10 percent of the budget."

A small consulting firm hired by a Caribbean resort to cut costs changed reference points to help a resistant manager shift his frame. The consultants found an efficiently run resort that was ignoring important ways to make more money. By focusing its marketing exclusively on a small, traditional clientele, it was neglecting convention business and joint reservation and marketing opportunities with other resorts. The consultants saw the missed chances as "opportunity costs"—costs of forgone opportunities. Opportunity costs can rarely be directly measured, but the consultants' frame wisely treated them as equal in importance to outright waste. Thus the consultants told the resort's management that these opportunity costs should be attacked as aggressively as out-of-pocket costs, and urged a new approach to marketing. The manager, a "self-made" man, couldn't see their point. He was determined to eliminate current waste, not embark on new opportunities envisaged by the consultants. Finally the consultants thought of a way to switch the manager's reference point from current revenues to what revenue *would be* if the right opportunities were seized. "By not taking these actions," they said, "you are losing $72 million a year." Now they had his attention. Later, the consultants confided to us that the $72 million estimate was rather "speculative." But making up a number was the only way they could find to present the situation within the manager's frame.

## Exercise: Seeing Into the Shadows

Try the following exercise to learn two ways to overcome the limitations of shadows and boundaries—and to help people stretch their frames.

To begin, spend a few minutes developing a set of criteria that you could use to select your company's top managers five to ten years from now. What skills, attributes, or experiences will these people need to have? These criteria should be able to help you pinpoint the kinds of people you should be hiring, promoting, and investing in to ensure that your company will have the leadership it needs in the future.

Ask a colleague to develop a similar list, without revealing your list. It would be particularly instructive to choose a colleague from a different department or background, or one who's older or younger than you.

Compare the two lists. In all likelihood you will find that you have written down somewhat different criteria, and that your combined list is more complete than either of your individual lists. Each of you will have included important criteria that the other person overlooked.

---

Lesson: It is useful to have more than one person, or one group, independently develop criteria to solve a problem.

---

Now, compare your list of criteria with the following lists developed in one of our executive education seminars. We asked one group of managers engaged in this exercise to imagine that they were venture capitalists developing a list of criteria they could use to evaluate entrepreneurs in whom they might invest. We asked a second group to imagine that they were athletic directors developing a list of criteria for selecting a new basketball coach.

They came back with the following lists:

| **Entrepreneur** | **Basketball Coach** |
| --- | --- |
| Risk-taker | Ability to recruit |
| Visionary (creative) | Win/loss record |
| Able to sell/persuade | Developer of talent |
| Adaptive | Ethical |
| Decisive | Develops strong game plans |
| Self-disciplined | Positive external image |
| Resistant to failure | Players' graduation rate high |
| Customer-focused | Good town-college relationships |

Are there additional criteria, drawn from these lists, that would strengthen the list you developed? In our seminars, many managers report that they would add persuasion skills, drawn from the entrepreneur criteria, and recruiting skills from the basketball coach criteria—skills that were usually overlooked in the construction of their original lists.

---

Lesson: New highlights can be drawn from the shadows by taking an "outside" perspective.

## CONSTRUCTING A NEW FRAME FOR A NEW SITUATION

In evaluating fit, you will sometimes find that your old frame is outdated. For example, those trying to apply the old "distribution channel" frame to the Internet (e.g., viewing the Internet as a new mechanism through which existing products and services can be sold) will miss the most profound aspects of the e-commerce revolution. The old frame obscures new products and services that might be created, new competitors poised to enter established markets, new ways of structuring organizational and work relationships, and changes in consumer expectations and buying criteria. Simply "stretching" the old frame or changing reference points will not provide the perspective you need for competitive decision-making. At other times, conflicts among competing frames within a decision-making group seem to prevent resolution. In both these cases, and others like them, you need the ability to create a new frame appropriate to the situation at hand.

 **Create a shared frame.**

Often, when a group is faced with a seemingly insurmountable stalemate, the culprit is unrecognized frame differences. You can break the stalemate by helping the group to build a new, *shared* frame. As the engineers learned (in the story that we told at the beginning of chapter 2), no one frame is complete; thus, a new frame that blends elements from several different frames is likely to result in stronger decisions.

Begin by asking people questions such as "What should our goals be?" or "What criteria should we consider?" In a group that has been experiencing conflict, it can help to ask people to send their individual lists to one person, who will then combine the responses and send them to the entire group. By removing names from each response before distributing, you can often defuse the problem of having people respond to individual personalities rather than to the merit of their ideas.

When the Johnson Graduate School of Management at Cornell University was first developing its elite Park Leadership Fellows Program several years ago, the faculty and administrators assigned to build the program found themselves in such a stalemate. Some of those on the committee, framing their charge as "building an elite program," wanted to offer the Park Fellows a variety of special educational and professional opportunities that would communicate their special status. Others, for whom the school's traditional frame as an "egalitarian, friendly learning environment" was most important, resisted any solutions that might divide the student body. After months of impasse—and with the arrival date for the first group of students rapidly approaching, one of us (Jay) was appointed to chair the committee. He asked committee members four questions: (1) What are the various goals of the program? (2) How can the program be used to help the Johnson School achieve its mission and specific goals? (3) On what criteria will we judge the success of the program; how will we know that it was successful? (4) What are the three most important things you want to say to our various stakeholders about the value of the program a year from now?

Each individual e-mailed their responses to Jay, who then compiled and circulated them (without names) to the entire group. Working with the joint list, the group was quickly able to agree on three goals for the program: (a) elevating the quality of all the school's MBA students, (b) improving the educational value added to all MBA students, and (c) enhancing the reputation of the school. Decisions were then weighed against these criteria, and the extent to which they added to or detracted from each goal evaluated. While it would be disingenuous to say that conflict disappeared completely, for the first time program planning proceeded rapidly and without the argumentative quality that had characterized earlier meetings.

---

Lesson: Since no one frame is complete, a new frame that blends elements from several different frames is likely to result in stronger decisions.

---

## Constructing a New Frame for a New Situation:
### *Balancing the Past and the Future in South Africa*

As South African apartheid crumbled, the country's new leaders faced a harrowing decision. How were they to come to terms with the gross violations of human rights throughout the apartheid era while moving forward to create a new, well-functioning, multiracial society?

Archbishop Desmond Tutu, winner of the 1984 Nobel Peace Prize, talks about the two historical frames proposed for dealing with such situations (a Nuremberg-style trial or general amnesty), and why they were unviable alternatives. A Nuremberg-style trial (a frame he refers to as "retributive, or victor's justice") highlights accountability, the punishment of aggressors for crimes committed, the satisfaction for victims at seeing justice done, and the importance of remembering the past. In its shadows, however, lay the probability of a bloody coup by the police or military, who still retained their weapons; the huge financial burden of defending state employees in a trial; the impossibility of meeting the legal standard to prove beyond reasonable doubt that the crimes occurred when often the only witnesses still alive were the perpetrators; simmering resentments of those forced to submit to retributive justice; and the perpetuation of the cycle of violence and retribution. As Tutu writes, "While the Allies could pack up and go home after Nuremberg, we in South Africa had to live with one another."

The second historical frame—general amnesty, as used in Chile—suggests letting bygones be bygones. Highlighting forgiveness and the future, this frame would have avoided provoking a military coup. In its shadows, however: national amnesia, simmering resentments by the victims of apartheid as their experiences were denied once again, and the oft-learned lesson that the past continues to haunt unless it has been dealt with adequately.

Writes Tutu: "[We] had to balance the requirements of justice, accountability, stability, peace and reconciliation. We could very well have had justice, retributive justice, and had a South Africa lying in ashes—a truly Pyrrhic victory if ever there was one. Our country had to decide very carefully where it would spend its limited resources to the best possible advantage."

In response, the South African leadership developed an entirely new frame, one Tutu calls "restorative justice." Through the Truth and Reconciliation Commission, which he chaired, perpetrators of racial crimes were granted amnesty in exchange for publicly and fully disclosing their crimes. This new frame drew elements from each of the two historical frames, emphasizing forgiveness and healing (from the general amnesty frame) and accountability, the validation of the past, and punishment (from the retributive justice frame). By providing details of their crimes, aggressors not only validated victims' experiences but revealed details that are now part of the national historic record. Perpetrators were punished through public humiliation and the psychological costs of facing the victims and their own families (the divorce rate, for example, jumped as family members learned for the first time of their actions).

Finally, this newly constructed frame added an additional highlight not present in either of the two historical frames: a concept known in some South African languages as *ubuntu*, which can be loosely translated as an awareness of shared humanity, or the essence of being human. This concept captures traditional African values of social harmony and community as the greatest goods and recognizes that since every individual is part of a greater whole, each is diminished when others are diminished.

Tutu credits the creation of this new frame (and the insistence by the nation's leadership that it be adopted) as the primary reason for South Africa's relatively peaceful transition to representative democracy rather than the bloodbath that had been predicted. He now travels throughout the world suggesting that a similar frame (and frame flexibility) might help resolve long-standing conflicts in Northern Ireland, the Balkans, the Middle East, Southeast Asia, the Sudan, and elsewhere.[6]

## APPLY THE ROBUSTNESS TEST

If you can find one frame that captures an entire situation better than any other, run with it. In many cases, however, you won't find one frame clearly superior to the others. Even a new, blended frame may not be sufficient. In these cases you must search for a solution that points toward success under several different approaches. Try making the decision in several frames, one after another. If the same option appears to be the best solution in multiple frames, you are fortunate enough to have found a "robust" solution.

The wonderful "Parable of the Kitchen Spindle" (first published in the *Harvard Business Review* in 1962) illustrates the power of robust solutions.[7] In this story, a restaurant owner found his cooks and waitresses bickering about orders, especially during peak hours. He consulted four specialists, representing four different academic disciplines.

A *sociologist* framed the problem in terms of status and hierarchy: the cooks resented receiving orders from the lower-status waitresses. He recommended sensitivity training for both the cooks and the waitresses. An *anthropologist* stressed cultural norms, especially concerning sex roles. The male cooks disliked having their actions initiated by women. He recommended that a senior cook be given authority to manage the system—he could tell the waitresses where to leave their orders and parcel them out among the cooks.

A *clinical psychologist* diagnosed the problem in terms of sibling rivalry: the cooks and the waitresses were like brothers and sisters competing for the approval of the boss, who had become a parent figure to them. He recommended weekly counseling sessions for both groups to improve communication. Finally, an *information theorist* blamed "cognitive overload." At peak times, too many orders had to be memorized, resulting in tension and friction around the kitchen. He recommended that waitresses punch the orders into a new computer system, which would display the right order at the right time for each cook.

The manager was thoroughly confused. He feared he could not afford any of these solutions. What if he invested in one of them and it did not work? In desperation, he mentioned the problem to a junior cook. "You know, in the restaurant where I used to work they had a rotating thing in the kitchen and we clipped our orders to it," he replied. "The cooks could just turn it around and pull off an order each time they were ready to start cooking something new. It made everything a lot easier. Do you think that would work here?"

The boss said he didn't know. So he took the idea back to the four experts. Each continued to recommend the course of action first proposed, but each also said the kitchen spindle might help alleviate the problem. The sociologist said the spindle would align statuses, since the orders would have to wait until the cook got them. The anthropologist said the spindle would impersonalize the initiation of action, thereby freeing the cook from the despised reversal of sex roles. The psychologist said the spindle would reduce the friction-causing interaction between cooks and waitresses, minimizing sibling rivalry. The information theorist said the spindle would give the system external memory, comparable to a computer, by recording the orders on paper.

The boss installed the kitchen spindle and it was a smashing success. He never had to consider any of the experts' other advice. The moral, of course, is that when a decision makes sense through several different frames, it is probably a good decision.


## THINK LIKE THE RABBIT: THE SKILLS OF FRAME ALIGNMENT

Framing skills can also help sell others on your point of view. Often, such attempts fail because your frame differs from theirs. Learning how to align your message with your listeners' frames often can move them from opposition to "buy-in."[8] In other words, sell your message in words that they want, or need, to hear. This is what the consultants to the Caribbean resort did when they shifted their reference points from "opportunity costs" to "lost revenue."

Marketers and salespeople know this point well. Frank "Buck" Rogers, in *The IBM Way*, notes: "When I'm asked, 'What products does IBM sell?,' I answer, 'IBM doesn't sell products. It sells solutions' . . . An IBM marketing rep's success depends totally on his ability to understand the prospect's business so well that he can identify and analyze its problems and then come up with a solution that makes sense to the customer."[9]

A hospital management firm used frame alignment to turn around declining business in eighteen newly purchased hospitals. With limited capital for physical improvements, the management firm decided to offer a kind of joint venture (a percentage of ownership at 15 percent below market value) to the leading physicians in the cities of its eighteen new hospitals. Framing the offer in terms of financial gain drew acceptance from local physicians in seventeen of their eighteen hospitals. At the final site, however, the physicians viewed the firm's offer as too oriented to the "bottom line"—and they refused it. After some thought, the management firm came back with a reframed offer, highlighting quality of care. Through partial ownership, physicians could gain more influence over the quality of care provided to patients. The physicians accepted.

Here's another, well-focused use of frame alignment. After searching for months, the manager of a market research department at a major U.S. corporation had finally identified an outstanding candidate, whom we shall call John Smith. Smith, however, was not interested. The job description, drafted six months earlier by a previous manager, consisted of five single-spaced pages detailing "duties" and "responsibilities"—and did not appear to offer Smith the opportunity he was looking for. In fact, the word "opportunity" was mentioned only twice in the eighteen-hundred-word write-up. After reviewing her interview notes, studying Smith's personnel file, and calling two previous supervisors and a former coworker to understand what motivated Smith, the manager rewrote the job description. She reduced the five-page document to a one-page memo highlighting four bullet points. Then she added several new points that she knew especially mattered to Smith: "Commitment from Management" and "Opportunities for Personal Growth." Although the job duties had not been substantively altered, when she showed the reframed description to Smith and again expressed her enthusiasm, he accepted on the spot, saying: "This is exactly what I was looking for."

In fact, the skills of frame alignment are often the best ways to persuade *up* the organizational ladder. Presenting your solution within someone else's frame is far easier than trying to change their frame.

## Framing Under Fire

Every decision is embedded within a frame. The question is whether you control the frame—or the frame controls you. While it's often useful to uncover or construct frames systematically and organization-wide, when in a time crunch you can perform your own analysis, or perhaps involve a small working group. This needn't take a long time. Most of the exercises in the preceding chapters (e.g., conducting a frame audit; exploring the metaphors used; evaluating the quality of your frame's assumptions, boundaries, and reference points; comparing old frames to new realities; or adapting alternative frames) can be completed in an hour—and often less.

However, if even an hour is more time than you have, you can build a frame for any decision in less than five minutes. Ask yourself:

- What are the three (five, etc.) most important objectives to aim for in this decision?
- What are the yardsticks, reference points, and boundaries inherent in my frame? How might someone in another organization approach these measures?

You can usefully invest an additional five minutes by consciously noting the higher-level thinking frames you typically adopt, and the biases they may entail. If you are a lawyer, for example, who mostly deals with adversarial problems, consider how that frame may limit your options. Ask yourself:

- Is my perspective on this problem balanced and sound? What biases might my frame entail, and how can I broaden or refocus the frame to bring in other perspectives?

The danger of the five- or ten-minute frame, of course, is that one or more essential criteria remain hidden, outside your view. Therefore, if you have five more minutes, contact someone you respect who thinks about things differently from you, such as a colleague in a different profession, a golf buddy, or your spouse. (You've probably noticed by now the frequency with which we recommend asking others for their point of view— it's quick, easy, cheap, and often the single most useful thing you can do.) Ask them the same questions you just asked yourself. Consider any new criteria that arise as possible additions to your frame.

## CULTIVATE FRAME COMPASSION

A final word on managing frames. Be aware that people's attachment to their frames is emotional as well as cognitive. Physicians and nurses who joined the healing profession are understandably upset about changes that frame health care primarily as a business. Former Soviet citizens accustomed to communism may prefer "the devil they know" (e.g., scarcity, long lines, and limited opportunities to accumulate wealth, but guarantees that their basic needs would be met) over the devil they don't know (e.g., capitalism's competitive arena with winners and losers). Churchgoers accustomed to male clergy may just feel very uncomfortable with female priests or ministers.

Try to appreciate people's emotional commitment to their frames. Especially if core values are involved, people usually need considerable time to adapt. Some never will. Don't assume that what is clear to you will also be clear to others. Cognitive filters and emotional ties to old frames will frustrate many a change effort.

On the other hand, to the extent that you can develop your frame management skills, you will ensure more successful decisions and also win the hearts and minds of those around you. The following story captures it well. There were once three hod carriers. (A hod is a handheld trough for carrying objects like bricks.) A traveler to a European city many centuries ago passed the first hod carrier and asked him what he was doing. "Carrying bricks," he replied curtly, in a disdainful tone that made it clear the answer was obvious. A few minutes later the traveler came upon a second hod carrier and asked him the same question. "Doing my job, feeding my family," he said. Not long after, the traveler passed a third hod carrier. His response to same question? He smiled and proudly asserted: "I'm helping to build a cathedral."

Good framing is as much an art as a science, but it is an art that can be learned. If you can use these framing tools better than your competitors, you will have a distinct advantage. If you can't, you may wake up one morning to find *yourself* framed.

# Improving Your Options

The real voyage of discovery consists not in seeking new landscapes but in having new eyes.   —*Marcel Proust*


ENGINEERS AT A petrochemical complex in Venezuela were in a quandary: a large storage tank had been built directly in the path of a major new pipeline. After a series of meetings, three options were proposed: (1) move the storage tank with a crane, (2) strip the tank down and rebuild it in the correct place, or (3) change the new pipeline route. None of these options were particularly attractive. The first was risky (the tank might break in transport), the second and third were expensive and time-consuming. Finally, after many fruitless meetings, a brainstorming session was held and someone spoke up: "Let's build a pool around the empty storage tank, fill the pool with water, and move the storage tank to its correct place." That one additional option turned what could have been a costly decision into a successful maneuver.[1]

Options are the lifeblood of decisions. Without good alternatives to choose from, it is impossible to make a good decision. For this reason, skilled decision-makers rarely restrict themselves to the alternatives presented, preferring instead to expand the choices available. Whether your decision merits spending one day—or only one minute—on this step, you should try to discover at least one new alternative to add to those already on the table.

In this interlude we examine *how* to improve the options at your disposal. We treat it as an "interlude" because the process of generating options falls between "framing" and "intelligence gathering" in our four-part framework. It fits in neither phase alone and is vital to both. Some options will follow naturally from the frame you choose, whereas others will be discovered or refined through excellent intelligence-gathering. Still other options can be generated through creativity techniques designed to help you find new insights and connections. First, we will look at some ways to generate better options by generating *more* options. Then we will explore two tools that can help create better alternatives by generating *more flexible* options.

## INCREASING YOUR OPTIONS

Just as a good frame focuses your attention on certain issues and hides others, it also suggests particular options to be considered, relegating others to the shadows. In the petrochemical company case above, reframing the heavy storage tank as a floating object suggested a completely different way to solve the problem. Likewise, a CEO concerned about lagging sales will naturally consider one set of options when viewing the problem through a production frame, and a rather different set of options when viewing the problem through a marketing frame. In the production frame, solutions such as improving production efficiency (so as to lower manufacturing costs) and improving product quality (so the product compares more favorably to its competitors') immediately come to mind. In the marketing frame, other options naturally arise, such as adding features to better differentiate the product and meet customer desires, or providing better incentives to the sales force.

Thus, even if concerns about lagging sales have been properly framed as a manufacturing problem, marketing options should not be ignored as possible solutions. This is especially true if the options suggested by the manufacturing frame don't seem to offer a rich or satisfying array of possibilities. Of course, if your frame suggests only a paucity of options, you should question whether you have the right frame (or whether a single frame can, in fact, do justice to the issues you face).

The task of generating better options calls upon skills and tools from the fields of creativity and innovation. Several key principles set the stage.

◆ **The more options you generate, the greater your chance of finding an excellent one.** Although this point may seem trivial, many decision-makers do not generate enough options because they fail to appreciate the out-of-sight, out-of-mind rule. The options you see are but a small sample of all the options that exist. It usually makes good sense to cast a wider net. The more options you consider, the greater your chance of finding a truly excellent one. You should only stop generating more options when the cost and delay of further search are likely to exceed their benefit.

✧ **Don't prejudge or filter ideas prematurely.** To unleash your full creative power, generate additional options first, then evaluate them. A judgmental attitude—in which you try to evaluate ideas or options as they come up—is the kiss of death to creativity. In large hierarchical organizations, many good ideas never make it to the top because people self-censor, failing even to offer their ideas for consideration. Other times managers filter out what they deem to be foolish or otherwise undesirable alternatives. Premature screening criteria can throw the baby out with the bathwater. Sometimes it takes a while for people to realize an idea's potential. Art Fry, the 3M corporate scientist who came up with the idea for the enormously profitable Post-It Notes, recounts that at first his colleagues couldn't conceive of "repositionable notes" and thus couldn't believe there was a market for them. Only after he began giving away sample notes to key people in the organization did they begin to appreciate their versatility.

✧ **Shift your perspective to see things in a new light.** No matter how good your frame, it will prevent you from seeing all the options. That's the nature of frames. Too often we search only in the neighborhood of the existing problem for solutions and come up with the usual list of stale ideas. We try what marginally worked before without being truly creative. Temporarily shift your perspective—and you may discover an excellent alternative hiding in the shadows of your previous frame. Vinton Cerf, one of the creators of the TCP/IP protocols that help form the common language of the Internet, notes: "Creative people let their minds wander, and they mix ideas freely. Innovation often comes from unexpected juxtapositions, from connecting subjects that aren't necessarily related."[2] Breakthrough thinking requires an attitude and resolve to be bold and break the mold.[3]

We introduced a number of creativity techniques in the previous chapter to help you generate better frames. They are equally useful in helping generate more and better options. After all, reframing serves to provide a different, hopefully more robust perspective—thus enabling you to see different alternatives. In particular, we recommend previously mentioned techniques such as **shifting your metaphors, thinking via analogy,** and **random association techniques.**

In addition, here are some other techniques that can help you double or triple the number of ideas put on the table. Although many of those additional ideas may be impractical or foolish, it only takes one good new option to make the exercise worthwhile.

**Challenge your assumptions; ask others.**

One of the simplest and least costly approaches is to ask: "What options have I overlooked?" Robert Dennard, the IBM researcher who invented DRAM (more commonly called RAM), which made the desktop computer possible, says: "Good ideas come from asking questions. I'm constantly asking questions: Why are things the way they are? How can we do that better? Innovation comes from believing that everything has the potential to be improved."

One company we know periodically brings together their corporate account managers to share each person's most novel approach to handling customers' problems and opportunities. The resulting list is then circulated, and managers are encouraged to contact each other for further information.

As in the framing phase, you are most likely to get new information by asking those whose frame is different from yours—those outside your organization or industry, from a different functional area, or with whom you often disagree. In the accompanying "brainstorming" tool, we describe how some organizations have begun using their customers to help them think of new options. At Xerox's famed Palo Alto Research Center (PARC), director John Seely Brown recruited a group of young people to brainstorm with the staff scientists about what the workplace would be like in the year 2010. The BrainStore, an "idea-factory" in Biel, Switzerland, also turns to young consultants when they need new kinds of solutions to their clients' problems. Their "BrainNet" is a fifteen-hundred-person global network comprised mainly of young people age thirteen to twenty; the BrainStore often mixes those young people with members of its client teams during creative workshops.[4]

 **Temporarily change your frame.**

Having the right frame prevents you from drowning in a sea of possibilities and helps you focus on the right issues. However, your frame may also cause you to place in the shadows some good options you should in fact consider. Hence, once you get to generating options, it may actually be beneficial to shift your frame—temporarily—to shake the tree of options again and make sure you've got most of its fruits. Xerox's PARC and the BrainStore described above value young people's thinking precisely because they haven't yet absorbed corporate frames and thus are more likely to think outside them.

Frederick Smith, CEO of FedEx Corporation, describes such a frame shift in his organization: "I don't think that we understood our real goal when we first started Federal Express. We thought that we were selling the transportation of goods; in fact, we were selling peace of mind." With that frame shift, new options immediately became obvious. FedEx offered customers a website and automated phone access to track their packages right from their desktops. In the process they saved $500 million a year.

Sometimes this shift in perspective requires a particularly creative frame shift. This is how the Venezuelan petrochemical company solved its storage tank problem. Viewing the problem as originally framed, people could see the storage tank only as "big, heavy equipment," and this defined the solutions they could envision. By looking at the tank from a new perspective—as "a floating body"—a new option became apparent.

Union Oil Company employed this kind of creative thinking process to deal with hundreds of miles of gas pipelines springing leaks across the desert. How to efficiently pinpoint the leaks? Think stink. Rather than methodically examining the pipelines inch by inch, the company injected ethyl mercaptan into the lines. This odorous substance is only mildly noticed by humans, but to turkey vultures it smells like rotting flesh. Wherever the olfactory-keen birds alighted to lick a leak, a fix-it squad quickly followed.[5]

 **Use brainstorming to enable creativity to flower.**

Brainstorming is an effective way to quickly generate new options. However people will only be creative if they know their ideas will not be ridiculed or scorned. To make brainstorming work, insist that participants withhold judgment or comment on the ideas presented until the session is over. You want to create a climate in which creativity is valued and rewarded, and where people feel comfortable sharing their thoughts.

Don't let "the way it has always been done" keep you from recognizing these new opportunities. To illustrate, we asked a group of credit union executives to brainstorm ways to get their members (who are both the owners and customers) to help create, produce, and deliver credit union products and services. In just a few minutes they came up with a multitude of new ideas, including:

- Let customers use the Internet to order checks, enter address changes, and download copies of financial statements.

- Allow customers to create their own loan terms (amount, duration, payment schedules, prepayment options, etc.) and then have the credit union quote a competitive interest rate.
- Pay existing members to bring in new members, new product ideas, customer complaints, etc.
- Bring key users of new services into the organization as part of the new product development team.
- Involve especially loyal or discriminating members in honing some core competencies such as customer service, credit collection, or financial advice.

 **Foster a culture of curiosity.**

The next time a colleague insists: "We can do either 'x' or 'y,' " you might respond: "And what are some other options?" Encourage people to think creatively about all decisions. It is hard to mandate or script creativity at the moment it is needed. Instead, to the extent you can, foster a culture that rewards innovation in matters large and small, whether in your own group or the organization as a whole.

British Airways' "First & Fast" procedure—in which first-class luggage is loose-loaded last into the aircraft's hold and off-loaded first, arriving quickly at the luggage claim carousel—began with the curiosity of Ian Hart, a baggage handler working at London's Heathrow Airport. Hart found himself frequently asked the same question. Passengers noticed that bags with yellow and black tags always seemed to arrive first at the carousel and wanted to know how they could get those tags for their bags. Hart realized that the customers asking him this question were always the first people off each airplane, that is, British Airways' first-class passengers. After some detective work he discovered that the current system unintentionally gave priority handling to standby passengers' luggage (the ones with the yellow and black tags) and left first-class passengers' luggage to be unloaded last. Hart proposed a change in the system, and eventually his idea was used on all of British Airways' inbound wide-body flights. Within a year the average time for first-class luggage to arrive at the carousel dropped from twenty minutes to less than ten.[6]

If the lack of innovative options is a recurring problem in your organization, we recommend that you consult one of the many excellent books on creativity (listed in the endnotes); they offer many more tools than we can provide here.[7]

## FINDING MORE FLEXIBLE OPTIONS

Generating more options will generally give you more *better* options. However, in a truly volatile environment, even a multitude of options may not
solve your problem. When the future cannot be anticipated with any degree
of certainty, the degree of *flexibility* afforded by an option becomes an important part of its overall value. Increasingly, the best decision-makers are
adding what has come to be called "real-options thinking" to their tool kit.[8]
Real-options thinking is not just a new management technique, but rather a
new management *frame* that recognizes the dynamic nature of the highly uncertain, rapidly changing environments many decision-makers face—and
builds flexibility into the options they choose right from the start.

In the old management frame, decision-makers created The Plan. Given
the top-down, command-and-control structure of most organizations, this
plan was more or less carved in stone. You committed to a course of action,
and you followed through. After all, your boss, who had more than enough
to do, would have had to approve any changes. And he (and in the old management frame, it was usually a "he") would have been as likely as not to ask
why you didn't plan it right the first time. After the arduous task of pushing
the plan up through the management structure for approval the first time
around, the last thing anyone wanted to do was go back to the boss and tell
him the plan needed to be revised. In this old frame, the plan was a roadmap
with the route carefully but indelibly marked. A manager's job was to follow it.

The new real-options frame stretches the traditional frame to include one
more key highlight: it recognizes that no matter how well one plans, some
uncertainty will always remain. And in some arenas—such as those related
to investments in emerging technologies, early-stage R&D, entering new foreign markets, and so on—that uncertainty will be sizable. Decision-makers
must still commit to a plan. But instead of the indelibly marked route, the
stretched frame takes into account many possible routes to the same destination. It recognizes that unanticipated road construction might make the
old highway more attractive than the Interstate, or that snow in the Rockies
might close the mountain pass you were expecting to use. When the future
is uncertain, it pays to leave your options open. In a fast-changing and unpredictable environment, organizations need not only speed, but agility.

The real-options frame allows decision-makers to see that alternative
routes to the same destination are real options. Better yet, it invites decision-
makers to actively create even more options by systematically restructuring
decisions so as to increase future flexibility. In doing so, they build in opportunities to defer, expand or contract, terminate, or otherwise modify projects

as the future unfolds, opting to take full advantage of potential favorable developments while limiting the negative effects of adverse ones.

Enron Corporation built in such real options when they opened three gas-fired power plants in northern Mississippi and western Tennessee in mid-1999. Extremely inefficient, the plants generate electricity at an incremental cost 50 to 70 percent higher than the industry's best, making them far too costly to run most of the time. But these less efficient plants also cost significantly less to build. So Enron can let the plants sit idle, then fire them up when electricity prices rise (as they did briefly soon after the plants opened—jumping from $40 per megawatt-hour to an unprecedented $7,000). With such unpredictable volatility in price, Enron executives are betting that they can make money from these new plants, even if they operate only a week or so per year. In fact, in an interview with *Business Week*, Enron president and CEO Jeffrey Skilling credited real-options thinking with helping Enron transform itself from a U.S. natural-gas pipeline company into a global player that trades commodities including gas, electricity, water, and telcom bandwidth.

Hewlett-Packard has also successfully employed real-options thinking. Following the most cost-effective manufacturing approach, HP inkjet printers for overseas markets were customized at the factory, then shipped to warehouses in finished form. The problem: it was hard to predict demand, so HP would wind up with too many printers configured for, say, the Italian market, and too few for the French. Using the real-options approach, HP executives took a counterintuitive step: they increased the production cost of the inkjet printers by delaying customization until the machines arrived at the warehouses. But they also saved $3 million a month by more effectively matching supply to demand.[9]

Our colleague William Hamilton at the Wharton School suggests viewing the options approach as a cycle, as summarized below.[10] The basic steps are:

1. **Adopt an options perspective.** To develop and manage options you must first see them. Most decisions present options, but these are frequently ignored or undervalued. Without a fundamental frame shift, future opportunities may not even be recognized as real options.
2. **Create and structure options.** Some real options are inherent in the alternatives as presented. Others can be created by building additional flexibility into the decision process. By structuring decisions to increase future discretion, decision-makers can generate new options and increased value.
3. **Value your options.** How much are your real options worth? What price should you pay for creating flexibility? Decision-makers who view their alternatives through the lens of traditional financial analysis may

be blinded to real options. Further, unlike traditional valuation formulas, real option valuation is an ongoing process, not a one-shot deal. As each decision is made and intermediate outcomes are known, the value of the remaining options will change.[11]

4. **Implement the real options approach.** The value of real options is realized only through careful management over time. You will need to know *when* to exercise your option, and when to simply let it expire. We return to this subject in Interlude C.

To illustrate, consider this decision: should we build a new manufacturing plant? The choice would be easy if only we knew the future demand for the plant's output. In the traditional static view, the top half of Figure A-1, we are forced to live with a best-guess prediction about that uncertain future demand. Then we work back to compute the expected value of building the plant (−$50,000) versus not building it ($0). In the real options view, the plant is designed in such a way that its output can be easily increased or decreased as, over time, the actual demand becomes known. As the bottom half of figure A-1 shows, the resulting expected value is much greater when the plant is designed in advance to provide flexible capacity.

 **Look for or create "future" options.**

The greater the uncertainty inherent in your decision, the greater the value of managerial flexibility and, thus, of real options. Ask yourself: at what points in time (or in the evolution of the project) might we be able to alter the timing of revenues, costs, and other outcomes? Can we defer or accelerate portions of the project? What actions could we take to capitalize on better-than-expected outcomes? How might we mitigate the effects of worse-than-expected outcomes? In other words, have back-up plans in place before running into trouble.

 **Use "portfolio" thinking.**

Smart investors know that having a well-diversified portfolio is the greatest protection against the risks of any single investment. The risks inherent in any one holding are at least partially offset by the (different) risks of another holding. By creating a "portfolio" of options, you can afford yourself the same protection. The risk in any one option may be partly hedged by the risks of another option, making the portfolio as a whole less risky than the sum of its parts.

Too often, people look at options in isolation. But seasoned decision-makers will naturally see connections between two projects that others

## (a) Static View of Plant Investment

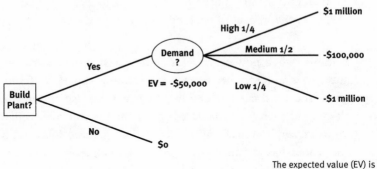

**High 1/4** — $1 million

**Medium 1/2** — -$100,000

**Low 1/4** — -$1 million

Demand ?

EV = -$50,000

Yes

No — $0

Build Plant?

The expected value (EV) is negative, so don't build the plant.

## (b) Flexible View of Plant Investment

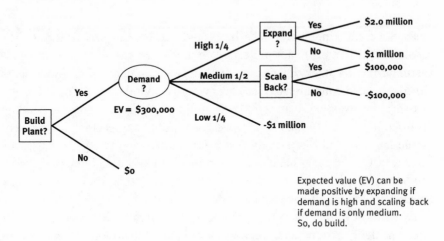

Expand ?
Yes — $2.0 million
No — $1 million

High 1/4

Medium 1/2

Scale Back?
Yes — $100,000
No — -$100,000

Demand ?

EV = $300,000

Yes

Low 1/4 — -$1 million

No — $0

Build Plant?

Expected value (EV) can be made positive by expanding if demand is high and scaling back if demand is only medium. So, do build.

*Figure A-1* **Options Thinking**

regard as separate. Ask yourself whether you can find pairs of alternatives such that when conditions hinder the success of one, they promote the success of another. The portfolio perspective asks:

1. Which options are mutually exclusive and which are not?
2. What is the impact of each option on the others?

For example, when new cars aren't selling well, the used car market
and auto parts industry are usually performing superbly. If you own
both new and used car dealerships, you may find some alternatives
less risky (and therefore, viable options) than if you owned just one
or the other. Or, suppose you are considering three job candidates,
each of whom has distinct strengths and weaknesses. Usually, you
would consider these options to be mutually exclusive. But are they?
Ideally, you would like to blend them into an optimal portfolio of
traits crucial to the position to be filled. Although you can't fuse
people, you could try to hire two of them in a job-sharing arrange-
ment and thus get much closer to the ideal skill set for the job. This
is the spirit of portfolio thinking. Of course, part-time work may
not be a feasible option—either for the company or the prospective
employees—but it should at least be considered.

Portfolio thinking should also be brought to bear on the financial risks
associated with many major projects. Looking at the risk of an individual investment (be it a stock or a new project) in isolation of all other investments
already made or contemplated may lead you to a poor decision. The U.S. bank
Natwest, for example, lost over $200 million in its middle market lending
portfolio in the early 1990s in part because it didn't appreciate fully that economic factors would impact its real estate, cable, and energy loans in the
same way. On the other hand, if a new project is likely to fail under the same
conditions in which other projects would succeed, then its risk is actually
lower than you might have thought.

In addition to finding options that are not mutually exclusive, you must
also consider question #2 above: how would pursuing option A (e.g., launching a new advertising campaign) impact—for better or for worse—option B
(e.g., co-branding with a strategic partner), and vice versa? Once you better
understand how options might affect each other, you can then examine the
options in terms of their combined effect on the bottom line.[12]

Understanding the full range of your options early in the decision-making process puts you on stronger footing in later stages. By considering up-front how you might deal with choices you may face in the future, you will more fully understand the dynamic natures of your options, and you can begin to gather the appropriate intelligence about their inherent risks and opportunities as well as the probabilities that any given future will occur.

PHASE II

# Gathering Intelligence

CHAPTER 4

# Avoiding Distortion and Bias

The empiricist thinks he believes only what he sees, but he is much
better at believing than at seeing.  —*George Santayana*

I N  T H E  E A R LY 1990s a greeting card company, wanting to attract more
of its core customers (women age thirty to fifty) into its stores, decided
to expand its product line by selling fresh flowers. Conservative by culture, the company rarely committed itself to a new idea without undertaking
a significant amount of market research, planning, and preparation. So the
company began collecting information. Focus groups were held, with the response from participants extremely positive. Facilities were investigated. Personnel needs were identified. Costs were estimated. Everything indicated
that the venture would be a winner. The project was given the green light. A
fresh flower facility opened in the Midwest. The company's major stores
were outfitted with refrigeration units to keep the flowers cool and fresh. Bo-
tanical experts were hired to ensure that quality and care were taken in the
acquisition and distribution process. Stores began receiving shipments of
flowers.

In spite of all this careful planning, the venture flopped. Flowers literally
withered and died on the shelves. The flower division was quickly closed
down and the equipment sold. Fortunately, the company took the time to figure out where it had gone wrong. The biggest mistake they found: distortions
and biases in the information they gathered and in its interpretation.

We'll come back to the details a bit later in the chapter. But here's the
problem in brief: confident that fresh flowers would be a great complement
to the company's current projects, the company tended to interpret the available information favorably. They did not ask enough questions that would
have proved their theory wrong. Apparently they did not fully appreciate that
the information they had gathered was incomplete.

Two decades ago, a chapter on gathering intelligence might have focused primarily on how to gather *information*. Today, the real question for decision-makers is how to create *intelligence*. Whatever their field, decision-makers face a barrage of information, available at their fingertips, often at virtually no expense. A few clicks of the mouse alone can provide an avalanche of data and information on any subject imaginable.

The real challenge then is to turn *information* into *insight*. To do so, we must understand how even smart, experienced professionals introduce distortions and biases in synthesizing and evaluating information. While figuring out what information you need and how best to gather it depends on the specific decision you face, the distortions and biases we discuss are universal.

On paper, the process for gathering intelligence appears trivial:

1. Ask the most appropriate questions.
2. Interpret the answers properly.
3. Decide when to quit searching further.

If only it were that simple. In practice, there lurks a series of all-too-human traps in each step, traps that stem from common biases in the way people—in the absence of training—process information. In this chapter we shall focus on those biases and offer some simple tools that can help raise your awareness of those biases to mitigate their pull. In particular, we focus on the hidden costs of undue optimism and false efficiency. Don't get us wrong: we're not advocating pessimism or inefficiency. But *undue* optimism and *false* efficiency regularly trip up decision-makers, leading to major miscalculations and faulty choices. These phenomena can cause problems throughout the entire decision-making process, but they particularly affect the gathering of intelligence. As the greeting card company executives so painfully learned, they make us think we know more than we do—which often means we examine too little information, formulate too few hypotheses, select and interpret information to make it better fit our prior beliefs, and fail to think critically in making judgments. They lead us to rely on the most available information rather than the most valuable; to anchor our estimates unduly on convenient starting points; and to finish our search too soon.

## THE HIDDEN COSTS OF UNDUE OPTIMISM

Most successful professionals like to believe that they are hardheaded realists. They take pride in making decisions that are data-driven and in consistently separating opinion from fact. And often, they do just that. But an unrealistic view of our knowledge and ability can lead to undue optimism about what we do and don't know. Just consider the following quotes, selected from hundreds that we could have used in their place.

That idea is so damned nonsensical and impossible that I'm willing to stand on the bridge of a battleship while that nitwit tries to hit it from the air. —*Newton Baker, U.S. secretary of war in 1921, reacting to the claim of Billy Mitchell (later Brigadier General Mitchell) that airplanes could sink battleships by dropping bombs on them.*

Heavier-than-air flying machines are impossible. —*Lord Kelvin, British mathematician, physicist, and president of the British Royal Society, spoken in 1895.*

A severe depression like that of 1920–21 is outside the range of probability. —*Harvard Economic Society, Weekly Letter, November 16, 1929.*

I think there is a world market for about five computers. —*Thomas J. Watson, chairman of IBM, 1943.*

They couldn't hit an elephant at this dist____ —*General John B. Sedgwick, Union Army Civil War officer's last words, uttered during the Battle of Spotsylvania, 1864.*[1]

Successful. Expert. Respected for their knowledge and rigorous thinking skills. And adamantly certain they were correct.

How could people of such high caliber be so wrong?

The most obvious answer is that they made an error in judgment, a mistake that could befall even the best decision-makers. But we believe their main error was one much more nefarious to a decision-maker than an occasional mistaken belief. Their major mistake was holding their beliefs with utter conviction without considering whether the available information justified the depth of that conviction. We categorize such overconfidence, along with other biases stemming from an inflated sense of knowledge and ability, under the broad rubric "undue optimism." (Narrowly defined, optimism refers to a positive view about the chance of success. Our broader definition extends it to overly favorable views about not just Lady Fortune, but about the skills, knowledge, and abilities that let us navigate the unruly waters of life.)

A systematic intelligence-gathering process might have shown each decision-maker that he had no grounds to be so certain. When John Wingate Weeks succeeded Newton Baker as U.S. secretary of war, Mitchell's squadron of tiny planes got a chance to demonstrate its power. They promptly turned a supposedly unsinkable dreadnought into a permanent part of the ocean floor. Baker, who had returned to Cleveland and resumed a successful law practice, was fortunately spared having to stand on the bridge during the assault. But nothing could spare him from the devastating distinction of having been so publicly proven wrong.

---

Lesson: Good decision-making requires not only knowing the facts, but understanding the limits of our knowledge.

---

What leads so many hardheaded realists to undue optimism about their knowledge? The same kind of cognitive processes (and their inherent distortions) that we discussed in the chapters on framing. And like our tendency to see the highlights of our frame and ignore the shadows, we barely notice that these biases are there:

## SIZING UP WHAT YOU KNOW

Confucius stated it simply: "To know that we know what we know and that we do not know what we do not know, that is true knowledge." Unfortunately, few untrained decision-makers have a good grasp of the limits of their knowledge. Like the successful (and wrong) leaders quoted a few pages back, they are unjustifiably confident about the extent of their knowledge. They are *overconfident*.

Psychologists have dubbed this human tendency to overestimate our own knowledge and abilities the "Lake Wobegon effect," after Garrison Keillor's fictional town in which "all the children are above average." Adam Smith commented on the pervasiveness of overconfidence in young people when he noted their "overweening conceit in their own good fortune" as they sailed off into the sunset or took up arms in battle.[2] Although many never returned alive, the death statistics hardly made a dent in these young heroes' belief in their own invincibility.

Here's one example of how this sort of overconfidence—an exaggerated belief in what one knows—distorts decision-making. A loan offer at a major commercial bank felt that his colleagues did not understand their changing competition as well as they thought they did and were refusing to notice signs of coming trouble. He approached his boss with this concern and proposed measuring the degree of confidence his colleagues had in their knowledge about the bank's competitors. His boss insisted there was nothing to worry about. After all, he argued, "No one is more realistic than a banker." Despite this overconfident answer, the boss agreed to the test—but only he would take it. The loan officer's test first asked for best estimates for questions like: "What was the total dollar value of new commercial loans made by Competitor X last year?" and then for *ranges of confidence* around those estimates (that is, the boss was asked to state how confident he was that his answer to the question was accurate by specifying a ballpark range).

To his surprise, he failed miserably. To his credit, he then asked all eleven other loan officers to take the same test. Every one of them flunked. One problem was that they did not know the answers to specific questions about their competitors. But the deeper problem was that they did not know that they did not know. Had they been in the midst of an important business decision, that unfounded certainty would have kept them from checking their facts.

A similar quiz, this time focusing on general rather than industry-specific knowledge, appears below. The quiz contains ten trivia questions, and you can do well on the test without knowing the actual answers for any of them. It measures not how much you know about the subjects asked, but rather how well you know what you *don't know*. As with frames, it is usually easier to see other people's overconfidence than our own. We believe that like the loan officer's reluctant boss, you may be surprised at how poorly you do. Try it before reading further, particularly if you are apt to be confident.

---

## Exercise: How Confident Are You?

For each of the following questions, provide a low and high guess such that you are 90 percent sure the correct answer falls between the two. Your challenge is to select a range that is neither too narrow (overconfident) nor too wide (underconfident). If you succeed, you should have nine hits and only one miss—that is, your answers should be correct 90 percent of the time.

1. What is the weight of an empty Airbus A340-600 (in kilograms or tons)?
2. In what year did John Steinbeck win the Nobel Prize for Literature?
3. What is the distance (in kilometers or miles) from the Earth to the Moon?
4. What is the air distance (in kilometers or miles) from Madrid to Baghdad?
5. In what year was the construction of the Roman Colosseum completed?
6. What is the height (in meters or feet) of the Aswan High Dam?
7. In what year did Magellan's crew complete the first naval circumnavigation of the globe?
8. In what year was Mohandas K. Gandhi born?
9. What is the surface area (in square kilometers or miles) of the Mediterranean Sea?
10. What is the gestation period of the great blue whale (in days)?

Answers: (1) 218,000 kilograms or 240 tons; (2) 1962; (3) 384,400 kilometers or 238,850 miles; (4) 4,308 kilometers or 2,677 miles; (5) A.D. 80; (6) 114 meters or 375 feet; (7) 1522; (8) 1869; (9) 2,510,000 square kilometers or 970,000 square miles; (10) 335 days.

Did you get more than one question wrong? If so, you are not alone. Of the more than two thousand American, Asian, and European managers to whom we have given a ten-question quiz like this one, less than 1 percent met the challenge. Most miss four to seven questions out of ten.

"But," you may be thinking, "whether I know the distance from the earth to the moon or the year in which Mohandas K. Ghandi was born is irrelevant to the decisions I need to make; if it were relevant, I could easily find the correct answer." In other words, you might ask, if a question falls outside my area of expertise, shouldn't I be excused if my confidence interval misses it?

We think not. How much you know about history or geography may or may not matter in your life, but how much you know about yourself—about your own knowledge—matters a great deal. Cognitive researchers call this kind of knowledge *"metaknowledge"*—knowing what it is we do, and do not, know. Whether you know a lot or a little about a subject, you are still responsible for knowing the limits of your knowledge. The data, facts, expertise, and subject knowledge we carry around is called *primary knowledge*. If you had a lot of primary knowledge about the subject of one of our questions, your 90 percent confidence interval should have been narrow; if you knew less, it should have been wider. In either case, your 90 percent confidence intervals should, by definition, capture the true answers 90 percent of the time.

Good decision-making depends on having both good *primary knowledge* and good *metaknowledge*. Indeed, in one way a poor sense of what we do and don't know (poor metaknowledge) poses a far greater danger to a decision-maker than limits on our subject-specific (primary) knowledge. When our subject knowledge is lacking, we realize that we must do additional research or hire a consultant (whether a business consultant, physician, or tax attorney). But when metaknowledge is lacking, we blithely proceed to reach a conclusion without even noticing that we don't have all the primary knowledge we need to make a sound decision.

As the American humorist Will Rogers said: "It's not what we don't know that gives us trouble, it's what we know that ain't so." His warning is more relevant than ever as knowledge becomes rapidly outdated by an ever more quickly changing reality. One can usually find the primary knowledge needed—as long as we realize that we need to look for it in the first place.

---

Lesson: A poor sense of what one does—and does not—know poses as much danger to decision-makers as does limited knowledge of a subject.

---

## OVERCONFIDENCE ON THE JOB

Might you be overconfident on our trivia test, but estimate accurately in your regular work? Perhaps. We and other researchers have found that the job relevance of the questions does indeed affect results, possibly because experience reduces overconfidence. Managers in a computer firm did better on firm-specific questions (58 percent misses) than on those covering their entire industry (80 percent misses). Data processing managers, too, showed less overconfidence on industry-specific items (42 percent misses) than on general business facts (62 percent misses).[3]

However, even with the most job-relevant questions, overconfidence does not vanish. Every group we have ever tested believed it knew more than it did about its industry or company, still missing three to four times as many questions as they should. Our own research with managers is confirmed by a large body of similar results from different professions, levels of expertise, ages, and nationalities involving varying degrees of probability. When chemical industry managers, given company- and industry-specific questions, were asked for 50 percent confidence ranges (meaning they could miss half the time), the correct answer lay outside their ranges 68 percent of the time. Physicians diagnosing for pneumonia erred as badly as the managers. Even scientists, using quantitative models and statistical error theory, have historically been overconfident in their estimates of physical constants like the speed of sound. A cross-cultural study, conducted with Asian managers of several nationalities, further confirms the ubiquity of overconfidence.[4]

The problem persists in the heart of business. One manager at a Fortune 500 company studied company files for information on the completion times of more than eighty projects. He obtained the original estimates of completion times (in person-days) and compared them with the times actually taken. Sometimes the estimates were correct: For projects where the firm had directly comparable experience, actual completion times averaged 3 percent less than estimates. But when the firm tried to do something new, it almost always suffered from overconfidence about how quickly it could do the work. Completion times averaged 18 percent above the original estimate, and too often fell outside the high end of people's confidence ranges.

Thus even experts, who by definition know a lot about a specialized topic, are rarely able to express precisely how much they do not know. Technically speaking, we find that few people are "well calibrated"; that is, few people can accurately assess their uncertainty. In decision-making, this translates into underestimating risk, missing deadlines, overrunning budgets, or massively off-track decisions.

Overconfidence can strike whole organizations.[5] Think of Ford's Edsel: the company halted market research two years before the product's introduction because it was afraid that researchers working with the public would let information about Ford's "great idea" leak out.[6] Recall Chicago's Continental Bank in the late 1970s: it apparently felt sure that energy loans were secure because the price of oil could do nothing but rise. Unfortunately for them, oil prices collapsed in the mid-1980s, causing the bank to become insolvent and be taken over.[7]

## OVERCONFIDENCE IN INVESTING

There is growing evidence that overconfidence is a major cause of investment losses by personal investors. Simply put, if you feel confident that you can pick stocks, you'll trade more as new information provides the basis for new purchases. Several large studies found that investors, on average, seldom recover their investment costs, including brokerage commissions and the so-called bid-ask spread (the difference between a stock's sale price and purchase price).[8] Ignoring these costs creates a more positive picture than is warranted, and that is for those investors who try to keep track. Many simply rely on their impressions about their past trades, remembering the winners better than the losers. All of this fuels overconfidence. As the expression goes, "don't mistake a bull market for brains."

## IS OVERCONFIDENCE EVER USEFUL?

Participants in our executive education seminars often resist the idea that they should fight overconfidence. They tell us: "I need to feel confident to work well." We agree with them that confidence in one's knowledge and abilities is often a good thing. All of us need self-confidence to function. Moreover, to succeed in many endeavors, you have to project confidence even when it cannot be justified. Because people often equate confidence with competence, you had better sound confident if you want your opinions to be treated as credible. It is seldom easy to stand up at an important meeting and say, "I'm not sure." Instead, people go out on a limb.

When it comes time to *implement*, overconfidence can be an asset. Risky but worthwhile projects might never be undertaken if a few key people did not have an unrealistic belief in their chances of success. When "positive thinking" is used deliberately and strategically, it can yield excellent results. As Goethe wrote, "For a man to achieve all that is demanded of him, he must regard himself as greater than he is."

However, if the motivational value of overconfidence is clear, its downside—especially in decision-making—is too often overlooked. *Undue* confidence can backfire—causing us to bet on plans, people, or projects that a more realistic appraisal would have rejected.

How do you motivate others by convincing them that something is achievable—without falling victim to an unrealistic belief yourself? Look at how great generals have led their troops. They try to avoid all distortions in their planning. They ask tough questions. They face the hard realities. Yet once they decide on a battle plan and head out to the campground to rally the troops, they exude confidence.

Managing overconfidence means that when you gather intelligence or make a decision, you should be careful to think in a realistic mode. But when the time comes to implement the decision, go all out for success. Persuade others to get on board, and to work enthusiastically. The ideal professional thinks like a *realist* when making a decision, but works like an *optimist* when implementing it.

---

Lesson: Separate "deciding" from "doing." Be a *realist* when deciding; confine optimism to implementation.

## SEEING WHAT YOU BELIEVE

Not knowing the limits of our knowledge will invariably trip us up. But other dangers, in a menagerie of mental biases, lurk in the thicket of information that we must forge through on our way to a winning decision. Each of these biases reinforces our undue optimism and inflated self-image.

First, most of us possess a built-in tendency to favor evidence that supports our current beliefs and to dismiss evidence that challenges them. (Psychologists call this tendency "confirmation bias.") It's existence is not surprising. Confirming evidence gives a mental reward. Every shred says: "You're on the right track. You're doing a good job." Disconfirming evidence, on the other hand, says: "Your idea wasn't as good as you thought."

But while the tendency to seek confirmation is seductive, it is acutely dangerous to decision-makers, causing them to neglect evidence that might undermine their ideas. In our Information Age, a biased search can quickly turn up hundreds of pieces of evidence that seem to confirm a hypothesis—even if the hypothesis isn't true. This confirmation bias can lead a decision-making process far off course.

Successful scientists know this tendency well. The nineteenth-century British evolutionist Herbert Spencer, a contemporary of Charles Darwin, held a mechanistic view of the natural world, believing that the cosmos evolved from less to more complex. But as historians of science have noted:

> "Spencer began, like a scientist, with observation; he proceeded like a scientist, to make hypotheses; but then, unlike a scientist, he resorted not to experiment, nor to impartial observation, but to selective accumulation of favorable data. He had no nose at all for 'negative instances.' Contrast the procedure of Darwin, who, when he came upon data unfavorable to his theory, hastily made a note of them, knowing that they had a way of slipping out of memory a little more readily than the welcome facts!"[9]

Unfortunately, when it comes to our intelligence-gathering efforts, many of us are closer to Spencer than to Darwin. James R. Emshoff and Ian I. Mitroff, two professors working at the Wharton Applied Research Center in the mid-1970s, studied strategy formulation in America's largest companies. In dozens of companies, they found well-paid executives simply using the latest sophisticated computer information systems to produce data supporting the strategies they had already decided to adopt. Many of the strategies failed miserably for reasons that should have been predictable—with or without the computers. "The key issue isn't getting the right facts but challenging the right assumptions," they noted. In fact, they found that the greater the access to more information, the more people used it selectively to support preconceived positions, erroneously assuming that the quality of their decisions had improved.[10]

Based on an inside account that we received, we believe that confirmation bias lay at the root of the greeting card company's failed flower strategy cited at the beginning of this chapter. According to our source, the company felt confident that the flower business would be successful, and sure enough, all the information they gathered supported their belief. In the focus groups, for example, people were asked if they would buy flowers from the company's stores. To the delight of the company, they said "yes." Customers weren't asked, however, *when* and *how* they usually bought flowers. Only too late did the company learn that people typically buy flowers at the end of their normal shopping routine; the company's stores, however, were usually the first or second stop on their list. Further, customers did not like to go to malls (where most of the company's stores were located) if they had to make a special trip solely to buy flowers. In those instances they found the corner florist much more convenient.

Wishful thinking also distorts how we interpret information, and it does so far more often than diligent professionals would like to believe. Consider this study of financial analysts. They were presented with fourteen hypothetical events that could affect stock prices and asked how likely it was that each event would occur. They were also asked to determine whether each event would be good for their investments, or not. The result: the more positive they thought an event was for their investments, the more likely they thought it was to occur.[11]

---

## Distortion of Information

Wishful thinking causes us to view our preferred outcome as more likely to come to pass. Yet even when there is little to wish for, when our preferences are just forming and can change momentarily, we may interpret new objective data to align with those preferences. One of us (Jay) has observed people in many different professions make choices. In one study he provided six sworn statements to prospective jurors. The case involved a boy's mother who was suing a small construction company. The child had been injured when a porch railing, built by the company, collapsed. The sworn statements came from the carpenter who built the railing and from witnesses to the accident. Each juror in the study was presented with the same sworn statements, but in a different order. The findings: jurors were likely to interpret each new piece of evidence so that it supported whatever conclusion they were already leaning toward. That is, those who perceived the initial testimony as faulting the carpenter were more likely to conclude that later testimony supported their initial perspective. Those who viewed the first testimony as suggesting the construction company and carpenter were *not* to blame interpreted later testimony in a way that supported that initial view. Regardless of which of the two verdicts people favored, each individual tended to believe that newly provided information favored the alternative they were leaning toward at that time. Imagine what happens when managers committed to a new project—having invested substantial amounts of time and perhaps money—are faced with additional information. Will they hear what it truly says, or will they hear what they want it to say?[12] As we like to remind our Ph.D. students who are eagerly researching their thesis, "if you torture the data long enough, it will confess."

Given our tendency to see what we believe and to hear what we want, a penchant for disconfirming thinking can be a decision-maker's best friend. When making predictions or forecasts, we often lean toward one perspective. The natural tendency is to seek support for our initial view rather than look for evidence that will prove us wrong. Unfortunately, the more complex and uncertain a decision is, the easier it is to find one-sided support. Realistic confidence requires seeking *disconfirming*, as well as confirming, evidence. Like Darwin, we must make a habit of recognizing and remembering evidence unfavorable to our preferred views.[13] Such a critical attitude is common to most of those we remember as the "great" thinkers of their day. It has been said of Leonardo da Vinci that "He wouldn't take yes for an answer."[14] Whatever the evidence at hand, he always wanted to probe more deeply.

Lesson: Don't be too quick to take "yes" for an answer. Make it a habit to seek evidence that disproves your favorite theory or desired outcome. Always consider and test multiple hypotheses.

 **Ask disconfirming questions.**

In any intelligence-gathering process, deliberately ask an appropriate number of potentially disconfirming questions. Especially when numerous possibilities exist, it is a crucial skill to eliminate efficiently the many blind alleys one might get stuck in. Consider disconfirming not only your ideas, but also your data sources. Often, estimates and forecasts are biased because a source of data is consistently providing wrong information.

A former MBA student, Jay Freedman, began his career as an analyst at the investment firm Kidder, Peabody and Company. Within six years of leaving school, he was ranked the number two household products analyst in America by *Institutional Investor* magazine. When gathering intelligence on a company, Freedman deliberately asks questions designed to "disconfirm" what he believes is true. If he thinks the disposable diaper business is becoming less price competitive, for example, he will ask executives a question that implies the opposite, such as "Is it true that price competition is getting tougher in disposable diapers?" This kind of question makes him more likely than competing analysts to get the real story.

This approach can also save time, effort, and money wasted implementing a "solution" to the wrong problem. As a chemical engineer fresh out of college, Robert Ruebusch went to work for a multinational oil company at their chemical plant in Houston, Texas. The company believed it was losing a large amount of gas through a five-inch flow vent on top of a large raw material feed tank. As the junior members of the team, Ruebusch and another young colleague were sent to spend a hot night on top of this tank measuring the amount of gas escaping through the flow vent. The tank was capped by a rounded dome, with a protective side railing only near the access ladder. "With the light of a very large waste gas flare nearby and ropes tied around our waists, anchoring us to the partial side rails near the tank ladder, we dutifully proceeded to periodically sample and measure vapor flow rates from the tank's vent stack in search of the alleged material escaping from this vent," Ruebusch recalls.

Trying to stay awake so they wouldn't fall off, the young engineers had a lot of time to think. "As the night proceeded," he continues, "we began to doubt the logic of the 'theory' that this vent stack was the culprit responsible for the large loss of material. And then we asked ourselves, 'If the alleged amount of material was escaping from this little vent stack across the time period in question, how fast would the vapors have to be escaping?' Out came the slide rules. . . . We realized that if the amount lost was escaping through the flow vent in the time allowed, it would have blown us to the moon. If only we had asked that question a day earlier in the air-conditioned confines of our office."

 **Entertain and test multiple hypotheses.**
Many explanations exist for every observation. Make it a habit to explore a variety of possible explanations before predicting an outcome or reaching a conclusion so that you don't miss the hypothesis that

will bring you closest to the right answer. During World War II, the famous British mathematician Alan Turing deciphered Germany's renowned Enigma machine for encoding military messages. Because the Germans thought their code unbreakable, they decided the British must have developed a superb spy network. Focusing on confirming evidence, they devoted all their energy to finding the spies and, indeed, found an alarming number of them. They never attempted a simple test of the possibility that their codes had been broken. They could have easily sent fake messages and observed British naval responses. But they were so sure they were right, they failed to pursue and test alternative hypotheses.

 **Engage in contrary analysis.**

In addition to testing alternative hypotheses, think of reasons why your favored hypothesis, data, or beliefs might be wrong and try to prove them so. Ask others to offer counterarguments as well.

Several studies have demonstrated the power of generating counterarguments. In one, a major company tested its managers by asking questions such as whether the company's liabilities at the end of the next quarter would be greater or less than its current liabilities. One group of participants was asked just to circle the "greater than" or "less than" answer and then state how confident they were about their prediction. On average, this group guessed that they would be correct 72 percent of the time. However, they actually picked the correct answer only 54 percent of the time. They were overconfident by 18 percent.

A second group was asked to think of "the major reason why the alternative circled might be wrong" *before* assessing the probability that they were correct. Then they were allowed to change their answer if they wished. This group estimated, on average, a 73 percent probability that they would be correct, essentially the same rate as the first group. However, they picked the correct answer 62 percent of the time. Their level of overconfidence was only 11 percent, a reduction of nearly two-fifths, thanks to a single counterargument.[15] Clearly, thinking first and then guessing is better than blind guessing. And the effect is twofold. Those providing counterarguments circle a different answer and/or express lower confidence in that pick.

However, is this practical? It depends. We think it would be an excellent idea for major capital budgeting requests to have a counterargument section in which managers are asked to identify the major reasons not to go ahead. And if the project does fail later, managers should be rewarded if the actual causes of failure were clearly identified in this contrarian section of the report.

A warning, however. To be useful, this process must be taken seriously, with serious consequences (both good and bad) for the managers involved. Otherwise it may degenerate into a useless formality or, worse, corporate "gaming" (i.e., managers withholding their genuine concerns in favor of saying whatever gets the budget approved).[16]

  **Assess other people's metaknowledge.**
Too often in group decision-making, the person expressing the most confidence drives the process. Over time you can usually determine someone's credibility, that is, the degree to which they have good metaknowledge, based on experience and feedback. But you can also seek to reveal undue confidence by asking probing questions, such as asking people to explain *how* they know what they assert to know, the *process* they used to arrive at their conclusions, the evidence they can muster pro and con, and so on. And be skeptical if they don't seem to have answers to any of those questions. Unless they have a stellar track record, don't accept their estimates with blind faith.

## THE HIDDEN COSTS OF FALSE EFFICIENCY

Just like optimism, efficiency can be valuable. We recommend that all good decision-makers begin by asking: What information would make this decision easy? What is the quickest, easiest, and least expensive way to gather that information? In some cases, that may be all that is needed. Bertrand Russell made this point well when he noted: "Aristotle could have avoided the mistake of thinking that women have fewer teeth than men by the simple device of asking Mrs. Aristotle to open her mouth."[17] Wherever possible, one should favor *simple* intelligence-gathering approaches. However, there are well-documented traps inherent in the quest for efficiency that can leave decision-makers with a false sense of security—and poor intelligence. Two of the most dangerous shortcuts in the intelligence-gathering phase are:

(1) the tendency to pay too much attention to the most readily available information, *and*

(2)  the tendency to excessively anchor opinions in a single statistic or fact that from then on dominates the thinking process.

As we have seen, overconfidence and a preference for confirming evidence can bias what information we *seek*. The common shortcuts we discuss in the section that follows distort how we *filter* or *interpret* the information we have.

## BELIEVING WHAT YOU SEE

Before continuing, please answer the following questions:

- Have violent crimes by U.S. youth increased or decreased during the 1990s?
- Have violent crimes committed on school grounds in the U.S. increased or decreased in that decade?
- Has the number of very young offenders (under age thirteen) arrested for murder in the U.S. increased or decreased between 1970 and 2000?

Before reading further, consider how you arrived at your judgments. Did you ask yourself questions like, "How often have I heard about American young people being involved in violent crime? How often have I heard about school shootings? How often have I heard shocking stories about young children who kill? How many news reports have I heard about the widespread problem of youth violence?" Perhaps not consciously. But if you are like most people, your impressions probably developed from the instances of youth violence you have heard or read about.

In fact, violent crimes committed on school grounds, and by youth in general, have been on the decline in the United States. Youth homicide arrests dropped 56 percent from 1993 to 1998, according to the FBI; the number of youth under age thirteen arrested for murder is at its lowest point since 1964 (the first year the statistic was kept). Likewise, the number of school-related student homicides remained relatively stable through the 1990s at 30 to 35 per year, including 1998–99 (the year of the Columbine shootings).[18]

But if you thought youth violence was on the increase, you are not alone. Sixty-two percent of people polled by the *Washington Post* in 1999 said they believed children were getting more violent. Seven in ten Americans think a school shooting was "likely" to happen in their communities. (In fact, a child had just a one in two-million chance of being killed in a U.S. school in 1998–99.) And during the same one-year period that school-associated violent deaths *dropped* 40 percent, the number of people who feared a school shooting in their community *increased* 49 percent. These distorted views impact decisions. Schools, for example, are installing more metal detectors, conducting more locker searches, and imposing more suspensions and expulsions for threats.[19]

Some people instinctively realize that they can fall victim to "availability bias." They know that they base some judgments on evidence that comes most easily to mind. They also know that television, newspapers, and other readily available information sources can skew their views of reality. And they know that the information that is most "available" is not always the most representative or relevant. However, few put these realizations together when making important judgments.[20]

Availability bias takes several forms. Our perceptions are distorted not only by the most available and the most vivid information, but also by the most *recent*. For example, imagine yourself at a cocktail party, discussing whether to buy a new Volvo or Saab. Suppose that a consumer survey leads you to favor the Saab. A stranger overhearing your decision chimes in with a disaster story about his Saab: the brakes failed twice in the first year. Will you buy your Saab?

Statistically, your sample of car owners' opinions has increased from 1,000 to 1,001. Thus, the painful tale of one Saab's flaws should carry no more than a one-thousandth weight. Not only do the story's concrete, vivid details overwhelm such reasoned consideration, but we tend to overemphasize the most recent information we receive. That's why the last person to get the boss's ear often has the advantage and why the closing arguments of a trial can sway the jurors (if they still have an open mind).

The "recency effect" can mislead troubleshooters. In one case, whenever a large chemical company received a customer complaint about its industrial solvents, a technical specialist (typically a chemical engineer) analyzed the problem and rendered a diagnosis. Often the expert diagnosed incorrectly. A new diagnosis had to be made. This continued until an adequate solution was found.

The company's quality control manager suspected that an availability bias was causing inaccurate diagnoses. He devised a test. He presented each of these experienced engineers with five solvent complaints, along with a list of plausible causes. He asked the engineers to assign a probability to each of the possible causes for each of the five cases. He reviewed the answers along with the recent cases handled by each engineer. Those who had recently experienced a particular cause deemed it much more likely—by a factor of anywhere from 15 to 50 percent across the five test cases. In other words, the typical engineer tended to believe that a new problem's most likely cause was the one that had been the true cause of the most recent, similar problem encountered by that engineer.

The manager estimated that the company and its customers were losing about $2.6 million a year because recency effects were biasing problem diagnoses. To correct for this, he and his engineers analyzed past experience and prepared a guide with the actual probabilities that any particular cause would produce particular symptoms. "My people are superbly trained chemical engineers," he admitted later, "but they've never been trained in making critical judgments."

Lesson: Our perceptions of the "facts" are often distorted by the most available, most recent, or most vivid information.

## AVOIDING AVAILABILITY BIAS

Without conscious attempts to compensate for these biases, it is quite natural to assume that the "most available" information is the "most relevant"—and to underestimate the relevance of information that is not readily available. This is even more so when that information is highly memorable, vivid, and, as in the case of school shootings, shocking. Many decision-makers get caught by this trap, even when they *think* they are being careful.

The "vividness" bias is particularly hard to overcome. That is why people tend to be more afraid of highly reported, horrific accidents such as airplane crashes, earthquakes, and nuclear meltdowns than the more common but underreported (and less dramatic) at-home accidents, drowning or electrocution. The vividness bias, however, needn't relate to a horrifying situation. The pleasure of being wined and dined by a possible new supplier is more vivid than dry reliability statistics. We may know it exerts undue influence upon our perceptions. Yet we often cannot overcome or suppress it fully.[21]

In spite of their hold on our attention, you can often improve decision-making dramatically by simply understanding—and compensating for—these biases.

 **Use representative data.**
Make sure to base your decision on truly representative data. Make it a habit to check whether your data set might in some way be

unrepresentative. Consider whether you are being unduly influenced by information that is simply the most available, recent, or vivid.

 **Modify procedures to compensate for information biases.**
One bank found that its sales force constantly favored selling whatever services were most recently described in training sessions. A division of the bank marketed about thirty information services and reporting systems. But rather than choosing from the entire portfolio of services and recommending those truly appropriate to customers' needs, salespeople too often suggested those they had most recently learned about. Sales calls were wasted and fewer products were sold.

When one of the bank's managers discovered this "recency bias" after hearing us lecture, the bank modified its sales training to ensure that each seminar concluded with a description of how the product under discussion fit into the bank's overall product line. And it produced a pamphlet that could be used to consistently remind the sales force about all the available products and the types of customers that each could best serve.

## The Boston Murder Hoax

On October 23, 1989, Boston was rocked by a horrifying murder case. Carol Stuart, a white pregnant woman, was killed in her car; the baby, born prematurely, died. Her husband Charles Stuart, who was driving, blamed the killing on a black assailant. Public attention was riveted on the investigation, with the entire city pressing for progress. It was not long before the police found and charged William Bennett, a thirty-nine-year-old unemployed black man with a prison record. The problem: Bennett was innocent. Stuart's brother eventually came forward to reveal that Charles had killed his wife and unborn child himself.

The Boston Police Department's failed intelligence-gathering process had severe consequences. An innocent man was charged. Resources were squandered. And the Boston police lost much of what little goodwill they had in the black community, and valuable credibility elsewhere in the city.

In making a decision about whom to charge, the police officers fell victim not only to pervasive racial biases, but to cognitive ones as well. These cognitive biases—a search for confirming evidence, the tendency to believe that what comes to mind most easily or quickly is the most likely, and undue attention to the most vivid information—sent the investigation careening off track.

In any complex case, confirming evidence usually can be found if you look hard enough—or believe hard enough. In the Stuart case, looking hard meant a police drag-net for young black men in the Mission Hill area where police found the couple after they were shot. Hundreds of innocent African-American men were stopped by police—and sure enough, incriminating evidence was soon found. Bennett was identified by Charles Stuart from his hospital bed and later in a police lineup.

How could Stuart have identified the accused twice if he had never seen the man before? Coaching by the police, claimed some. In fact, if you believe hard enough in your current theory, coaching a witness may not even be deliberate. A facial expression or catching your breath as the "right" mug shot is shown can do the job—especially if the witness is as eager as you to confirm your solution to the crime.

The media's overreporting of black-on-white crime laid the foundation for the avail-ability bias. As we saw with the school shootings earlier in the chapter, we tend to be-lieve what is most often cited. Similarly, people paid too much attention to concrete, vivid information (Charles Stuart's frantic calls for help, a pregnant woman killed, her premature baby's seventeen-day fight for life, and the tragedy of a seemingly perfect couple) relative to tedious (but damn useful) statistics. In fact, roughly one-third of women who are murdered are killed by their husbands or boyfriends. Given such data, the husband should automatically have been a prime suspect, even more so because he was present when the crime occurred and there were no other witnesses. But statistics are dull; and a pregnant mother's fatal wounds, gripping.

The lessons in the Boston murder hoax are not only about the sociopathic mind of Charles Stuart, but about the minds of all of us. If racial bias runs deep, our cognitive bi-ases run deeper—and even experienced professionals, who might be expected to know better, too easily succumb.[22]

## DOES YOUR "ANCHOR" WEIGH YOU DOWN?

Suppose you are trying to decide whether to enter the widget business. You need to estimate the size of the market for widgets five years from now as well as the appropriate salary for a plant manager. Most people, consciously or unconsciously, start with a number that easily comes to mind—say, the number of widgets sold last year and the salary of the current manufacturing supervisor. Then they adjust up or down to reflect other issues that matter.

Although this procedure seems sensible, it suffers from a major defect: *people usually adjust insufficiently.* The initial number affects the analyst's mind and keeps the final judgment from moving as far as it should. Researchers call this phenomenon "the anchoring bias"—the tendency to focus on one value or idea (the "anchor") and not adjust away from it sufficiently. Anchoring is a common shortcut when people need to make an estimate, and it creates many problems in intelligence-gathering and decision-making.

It is typical to provide a best guess before we give a ballpark range or confidence interval. For example, we usually estimate next quarter's unit sales before we come up with a confidence range (if at all). The sales estimate becomes an anchor point and drags the high and low brackets, preventing them from moving far enough from the best estimates. The result: the high and low guesses aren't far enough apart, so what we think is a 90 percent confidence range may only be 60 percent.

How strong is the best estimate's pull? To answer this question, we went back to our trivia questions (like those we used earlier to demonstrate overconfidence) and presented them to two groups of managers. One group was asked to start by giving us a best estimate to answer the question. Only after that were they asked to provide their 90 percent confidence interval. The second group was asked only to supply a confidence range without ever committing to (and possibly anchoring on) a best guess.

How did they compare? The first group scored 61 percent misses (compared to the ideal of 10 percent). The second group, in contrast, performed better. Because their confidence intervals were wider, they scored only 47 percent misses. Thus, having people provide a range in which they thought the correct answer would fall, *without* first anchoring on a specific number, reduced error substantially.

Again, what if we move from trivia to information that is professionally relevant. We asked nearly one hundred managers: "What is your best estimate of the prime interest rate six months from now?" This was in 1983, when the real prime was around 11 percent.

Their average guess was on target: 10.9 percent. This unanchored question serves as a control group benchmark.

Then we surveyed a second group with these two questions:

1. Do you believe that six months from now the prime rate will be above or below 8 percent?
2. What is your best estimate of the prime rate six months from now?

We wanted to see if the first question, designed to anchor subjects on 8 percent, would "drag" estimates below those of the unanchored group. It did. The average guess was now 10.5 percent, or 40 basis points below the unanchored group. When we anchored a third group at 14 percent ("Do you believe that six months from now the prime rate will be above or below 14 percent?"), their average estimate was 11.2 percent.

Note how subtle anchoring can be. We didn't even tell participants we thought 8 percent and 14 percent were reasonable guesses. Many information sources with an interest in the outcome of your decision will use this kind of strategic anchoring—mention of a statistic to encourage the listener to anchor on it—to influence decision-makers' perception of the issues.

This common reframing tactic works well in negotiations when the initial anchor appears reasonable. Different starting points yield different answers and they are always biased toward the starting point, or anchor. So in many negotiations, the crucial issue is whose anchor will be accepted as the appropriate reference point. In one study with real estate agents, it was found that using different anchors (in the form of high versus low listing prices) caused differences in the "independent" appraisals on the order of 9 percent of the home's value.[23]

Do interest rate anchors work just because listeners assume that the person offering the anchor knows something they don't? In other words, does the anchor drag the estimate because the listener has good reasons to believe it is genuinely informative (in which case the "drag" might suggest the listener is behaving sensibly)? Unfortunately for our pride in our own rationality, the answer is no. Several studies have deliberately used random anchors that could not possibly have been perceived to contain useful information. The results? Random anchors can affect people's opinions just as much as credible anchors.

You can try the following experiment at your next party. We conducted it with our MBA students. Ask people: "What are the last three digits of your home phone number?" Suppose the last three digits are 781, then say, "Do you think Attila the Hun was defeated in Europe before or after A.D. 781?" (i.e., use that random telephone number as an anchor).[24]

After they answer (and without telling them whether they were right), ask: "In what year would you guess Attila the Hun was actually defeated?"

The correct answer is A.D. 451. Not surprisingly, few of our MBA students knew that. Surprisingly, however, the telephone-number anchor dramatically affected the years they gave. The lower the value of the anchor, the lower the average estimate of the year of Attila's defeat. Since the students knew that their own telephone number was used as the starting point, they had no logical reason to pay attention to the anchor. Yet it clearly did influence their judgments.

---

Lesson: Readily available (but not necessarily relevant) numbers or ideas distort our final judgments because people fail to adjust away from them sufficiently.

**Be aware of the anchoring effect.**
You can guard against the dangers of anchoring in several ways. Most fundamentally, you can make people aware of the dangers. That can be especially helpful if you see a consistent bias in the estimates your organization produces, and you can warn your colleagues to watch out for it in the future. If, for example, company forecasts are always too close to the previous year's numbers, tell the people who make them—and their bosses—that they need to guard against this bias.

 **Provide a range first, not a single-point value.**
One of the most effective de-anchoring techniques we know is to move directly to providing a confidence range without first providing a "best guess" answer. Although this de-anchoring technique has yet to be verified outside the controlled laboratory, we see no reason why it should not work as well in real environments. How effective it is will depend on your ability to focus on the confidence interval and block out of your thinking any earlier estimate that might serve as an anchor. And later you can just use the midpoint of the range as your point estimate if you need one.

 **Work with multiple anchors.**
Approach *key* estimates from several starting points. Think of a few plausible numbers you could anchor your estimate on: for example, last year's sales, a continuation of the five-year moving average for sales, a consensus of independent analysts' expectations of sales, an optimistic forecast, a pessimistic forecast, etc. "Best-case" and "worst-case" scenario pricing will also provide multiple anchors.

When Boeing launched its 747 airplane, no competition existed for an airplane that could hold more than two hundred people. It should have been a hands-down profit-generator right from the start. Unfortunately, it took the company fifteen years to break even. Why? Boeing, which was great at building airplanes, didn't do as well at prophesying costs. Airplanes must be priced long before they are built. Following standard practice for a new product or service, Boeing priced the 747 by estimating its cost and adding a profit margin. However, they anchored the cost too low.

Unexpected labor strikes and technical problems caused the plane to cost far more than they had expected. Had they used *multiple* anchors (e.g., "value pricing" based on what customers were willing to pay, the closest competitive substitute in the marketplace, or the best—and worst case scenarios—in addition to their estimated cost), they might have set a higher price from the start.[25]

 **Avoid considering only incremental solutions.**
Anchoring can affect complex qualitative judgments as well as numerical estimates. Indeed, few organizations ever formulate policies by comprehensively analyzing their situation. Most limit themselves to a choice among alternatives that differ only slightly (i.e., incrementally) from existing policies. A company experiencing turnover of employees, for instance, will try minor rules changes to deal with employee dissatisfaction rather than attempt to determine and fix the root cause.[26]

Because no decision-maker can thoroughly analyze every problem, the incremental approach may be a sound way to make many decisions. But incrementalist anchors can destroy good ideas. When a competitor surprises your firm by introducing a new product, don't anchor your thoughts exclusively on the exact product your competitor has introduced. By the time your "me-too" product comes out, its design may already be outdated. Instead, focus your thoughts on the customer's real needs—find out what the customer wants done and find a better way to do it.

 **Remain open to new information.**
Remember, it's not over until it's over. Before ending the information-gathering phase, ask yourself: what have I overlooked? Get answers from others as well. Until the decision is made, remain open to new information, new options, new criteria, and even new frames.

## Intelligence-Gathering Under Fire

Often the greatest danger to good intelligence-gathering is not insufficient time, but your own mental biases and distortions. Thus, any investments you make in training yourself and your colleagues to realistically assess what you do and don't know will pay off when intelligence must be gathered quickly. The key to intelligence-gathering under fire is to (a) identify the basic intelligence you need, (b) get it as quickly as possible, and (c) not distort it once it's in your hands. Also, be aware of information you wish you could have (but can't due to time pressure), and the ways in which what you don't know may hurt you.

Your investment in developing a good frame also will pay off in this stage, as you should now know what criteria are most crucial to your decision and what's lurking in the shadows. Ask yourself two kinds of questions (the first will help you identify and get the minimum intelligence you need; the second will help ensure that you don't get fooled by wishful thinking or confirmation bias):

☐ What's the single most important piece of information that will enable me to assess the decision options? How can I get it most easily? Does the information I need already exist in someone's files (or in their head)?
☐ What's the biggest disconfirming question I can think of, the one that would completely change my decision? How can I most easily get that question answered?

Here's a hypothetical example. Imagine that a company planning a two-month market research test on two versions of a new product learns that its key competitor has just introduced a similar product regionally, without any apparent testing. Product managers must now decide quickly whether their competition chose the right version; if so, they will have to roll out their own version quickly to capture market share. Clearly, the long-planned two-month research study placing different versions of the product in five hundred homes to gather intelligence on consumer preferences will take far too long.

But consider instead a one-week product placement with two hundred consumers, using increased incentives to complete an online survey every two days. In addition to asking consumers what they like and don't like about the product (pro/con reasoning), market researchers could employ the prospective hindsight tool (see the next chapter) with a question like: Assume you're unhappy with this product three months from now. Why might that be?

This "under fire" approach provides the key decision information needed (i.e., which product stacks up more strongly with consumers), while seeking solid disconfirming evidence (if either product is going to fail, why will it?) Finding ways to obtain the answers to the two sets of questions we posed above may take some creativity, but they will provide you with key intelligence quickly. Sometimes time pressure is good. People often delay a decision while waiting for information that is not really important or could not change the decision. Time pressure focuses the mind on what is truly important.

## FOREWARNED IS FOREARMED

Overconfidence, wishful thinking, and a preference for confirming evidence can foster undue optimism or bias the information we *seek*. Shortcuts such as relying critically on the most available, recent, or vivid information, or anchoring estimates on inappropriate figures, reflect false efficiency, distorting how we *filter* or *interpret* the information we have.

In many situations, awareness may be all a decision-maker needs to accurately assess how much is known, limit availability biases by gathering information systematically, minimize the drag of anchoring, and so on. In fact, armed with heightened awareness, good decision-makers often devise their own solutions to the problems of undue optimism and false efficiency. Recall the head loan officer who was certain that he and his staff knew their competitors quite well. After failing the overconfidence quiz, he took immediate action. Each officer was required to contribute information to a "competitor alert" file. And each was required to check the file weekly to gain a more realistic appraisal of their competition. Within three weeks a loan officer found information in the file signaling that a major client was contemplating a shift to another bank. The competitor was not one of the city's major commercial banks, and the size of the loan exceeded the competitor's legal lending limit. However, by joining with another institution, it was able to offer a loan large enough to meet the client's needs. Thus alerted, the loan officer in charge of the account convinced the client not to switch banks, saving $160,000 in annual revenue.

However, in other situations, particularly those involving complex decisions with a high degree of uncertainty, more sophisticated intelligence-gathering tools are needed. We turn to these in the next chapter.

## CHAPTER 5

# Intelligence in the Face of Uncertainty

*Never test the depth of a river with both feet.* —*African proverb*

**M**OST PROFESSIONAL RACE car drivers wish for good weather on the day of the big race. Rain is troublesome. At fast speeds, even excellent drivers can lose control and wipe out. Some race car drivers, however, pray for rain. Why? Because they know that they can manage adverse conditions better than their competitors. Wet roads and poor visibility may hinder every driver, but it hinders the most skilled drivers less than their slightly-less-accomplished peers. It gives them a competitive edge. Likewise, you benefit from sharper intelligence-gathering when facing high uncertainty.

It is in the intelligence-gathering stage that most decision-makers seek to overcome uncertainty. They hope that more information will at least reduce, if not eliminate, the discomforting doubt. The intent seems logical. And in part, it is. Many of us were trained to manage just that way. We learned that distilling past performance and future prospects to a set of numbers was crucial. Vague projections and expressions of doubt were signs of analytic weakness. So, faced with uncertainty, many decision-makers ask for more facts, believing (with some justification) that more information will let them pinpoint which of the various options will succeed. They may demand precise forecasts—and ignore all the uncertainty embedded in them. They feel justifiably annoyed at colleagues who offer only loose estimates and wishy-washy "on the one hand, . . . but on the other hand" analyses.

Unfortunately, in a world characterized by rapid change and discontinuities, decision-makers are dealing not so much with trends as with surprises. Numerical precision may offer only a false sense of certainty. And even if real certainty were possible (and increasingly, it's not), the cost of obtaining it

has become unacceptably high. Delay long enough and you'll be left cough-
ing in the exhaust of the car that just sped past. So what's a decision-maker
to do?

We believe that decision-makers must reduce uncertainty as far as they
can, then they must *manage* it. Managing uncertainty doesn't mean accepting
vague projections, making wishy-washy recommendations, or abandoning
planning. It does, however, mean redefining rigor. In an uncertain environment, rigor is not found in precise single-point predictions, but rather in precisely defined uncertainty estimates. It is not obtained by selecting the *one*
right vision for the future, but through a rigorous *process* that will enable you
to anticipate and prepare for *multiple* futures.

Murphy was right: If anything can go wrong, it will—and decision-makers
would do well to incorporate his wisdom into the decision-making process.
The challenge for decision-makers is not to eliminate all surprises, but to
anticipate—and prepare for—them. To do that, you must *acknowledge* uncertainty: uncover it, recognize it, understand it, and deal with it in an unbiased
way. Most decision-makers know that as they gather information on the
likelihood of a project's success, they must also assess the risks of failure. Yet
few spend much time trying to *systematically* identify all the things that could
cause a decision to fail or *quantifying* the chances that those events will occur.
And even fewer consider the numerous ways they might capitalize upon uncertainty, turning it into a competitive advantage.

The tools in this chapter will help you do just that. The best tool for your
task will depend largely on what type of uncertainty you face. Select the simplest tool possible, without underestimating the complexity of the decision
you face. The accompanying diagram, developed by several management consultants at McKinsey & Co., nicely illustrates the spectrum of possibilities.[1]
At Level 1, on the far left, the future is relatively clear. While some uncertainty exists, it is well within the range of what can be predicted by a single
forecast. If you are facing a Level 1–type problem, the first two tools in this
chapter—confidence-range estimates and training people to become better
calibrated—should be sufficient. They will help you better define the limits
of what's known and quantify the uncertainty that remains.

At Level 2, your decision-making must incorporate several possible futures, but the alternatives are few, discrete, and relatively easily defined. The
next set of tools—pro/con reasoning, prospective hindsight, and fault trees—
should do a nice job of helping you expose hidden sources of future problems
and opportunities. As uncertainty increases to a range of *interrelated* variables
(Level 3), more sophisticated tools are required. Scenario planning and
options thinking can help here. Decision-makers who can expand their imag-
inations to see a wider range of possible futures will be much better posi-

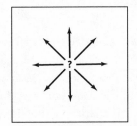

**True Ambiguity**
*No basis to forecast the future

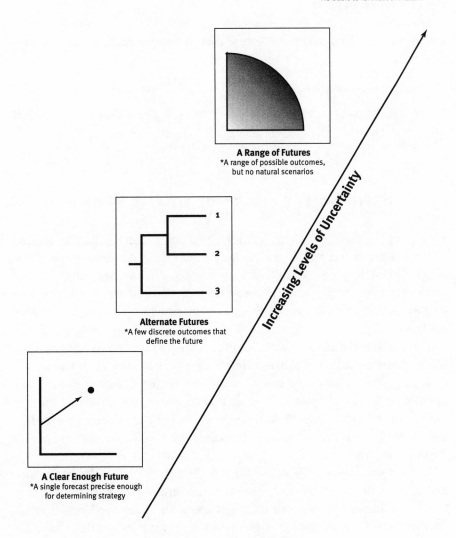

**A Range of Futures**
*A range of possible outcomes,
but no natural scenarios

**Alternate Futures**
*A few discrete outcomes that
define the future

**A Clear Enough Future**
*A single forecast precise enough
for determining strategy

Increasing Levels of Uncertainty

*Figure 5-1* **Levels of Uncertainty**

Source: McKinsey & Co.

tioned to take advantage of the unexpected opportunities that will inevitably come along.

Finally, at Level 4, a truly ambiguous environment requires learning and agility, as decision-makers can never anticipate enough of the future in advance. Level 4 problems arise when entering new markets, exploring embryonic technologies (such as the Internet), or beginning operations in foreign countries and cultures. In such cases you will need to supplement the tools in this chapter with a framework and additional tools that enable you to learn quickly from experience. We turn to learning from experience in Interlude C and chapters 8 and 9.

If you can use these tools effectively, you will find that uncertainty is no longer the enemy but rather can give you a competitive edge. In fact, you may start to welcome it as your friend.

---

Lesson: Never pretend uncertainty is smaller than it is. Reduce uncertainty as far as you can, then *manage* it.

---

## DEFINING THE LIMITS OF WHAT'S KNOWN

Except for the most mundane decisions, you will face a significant element of uncertainty in every decision. The last chapter strikingly demonstrated the dangers of misjudging the limits of what you know. How, then, do you assess accurately how much you really know in situations where so much is unknown? And how do you quantify how big the risks imposed by uncertainty really are?

Our answer: abandon the false comfort of single-point predictions in favor of **confidence-range estimates**. Here's an example that shows what we mean. Suppose you tell your boss that you are "reasonably sure" you can sell 200,000 widgets each year for the next three years. You know that doesn't mean you will sell *exactly* 200,000 a year. But what then does your estimate say? Indeed, do you, yourself, know exactly what you mean? How sure is "reasonably sure"?

What if, in retrospect, sales are 175,000 the first year, 140,000 the second, and 230,000 the third. You and your boss could argue endlessly over whether the discrepancies between your estimates and actual sales were "reasonable." Further, you would be hard-pressed to decide for yourself whether your self-confidence was well deserved or needs refinement.

Now suppose instead you say: "I estimate that we will sell between

180,000 and 220,000 units next year. I am 80 percent sure." This kind of estimate can be far more useful than a numerically exact (but not exactly correct) prediction. It allows your organization to plan the future with as much knowledge as currently exists or to invest in getting better information if the uncertainty is too great. Further, once a confidence-range estimate has been made (e.g., "I am 80 percent sure"), you can ask, "What additional information would allow us to narrow the range with an even higher level of confidence?" Narrower ranges and higher levels of confidence mean less uncertainty in the decision-making process. Providing levels of confidence will help you consciously assess whether your knowledge is sufficient or whether you need to seek *additional* information before making a decision on a complex issue. In this way you can better assess whether the additional information is worth the added costs (and the related delays).

Finally, this kind of estimate enables you to learn much more easily from experience. Now you can assess your accuracy and decide whether your confidence was justified.

In the example above, in at least two of the three years (or more accurately, in four out of five years), actual sales ought to fall within your range. Since you said you were 80 percent sure, you should be right 80 percent of the time.

---

Lesson: Confidence-range estimates can be more useful to decision-makers than a numerically exact (but not exactly correct) single-point prediction.

---

## BECOMING WELL-CALIBRATED

Setting confidence ranges (or asking your colleagues for their confidence ranges) is not much help, however, unless people have a fairly accurate assessment of just how much they really know. Unfortunately, as we saw in the last chapter, this is rarely the case. The hypothetical example above illustrates the problem: sales failed to fall within the range forecasted three years in a row. If you had bet your reputation on your forecast, it would have been not just embarrassing for you, but problematic for your company as a whole. Such outcomes also signal that a dangerous gap exists between what you actually know and what you *think* you know. In this case, you would have fallen prey to that dangerous predator: overconfidence.

Fortunately, becoming "well-calibrated"—that is, learning to forecast confidence ranges more accurately—is a teachable, learnable skill. Feedback and accountability can help. Feedback that is accurate, timely, and precise tells us by how much our estimates missed the mark. Accountability forces us to confront that feedback, recalibrate our perceptions about primary knowledge, and temper our opinions accordingly.

U.S. Weather Service forecasters are one of the few professional groups who have been found to be well calibrated (another is experienced public accountants). When U.S. Weather Service forecasters predicted a 30 percent chance of rain, as they did 15,536 times in one statistical study, it rained almost exactly 30 percent of the time. This superb calibration holds along the entire range of probability, except at the highest levels. When a 100 percent chance of rain is predicted, it actually rains only 90 percent of the time. This prediction error reflects deliberate caution on the part of the forecasters.[2]

Royal Dutch/Shell, the Anglo-Dutch oil and gas giant, has used feedback with great success to help its geologists become better calibrated. The company's executives noticed that newly hired geologists were wrong much more often than their levels of confidence implied. For instance, the junior geologists would estimate a 30 percent chance of finding oil, but when ten such wells were actually drilled, only one or two would produce. This type of overconfidence cost Shell millions of dry-well dollars.

These judgment flaws puzzled Shell's senior management, as the geologists possessed impeccable credentials. How could well-trained individuals be overconfident so much of the time? Put simply, their primary knowledge was much more advanced than their metaknowledge. To develop a better sense of the *limits* of their knowledge required repeated feedback, which was coming too slowly and costing too much money.

In response, Shell designed a training program to help geologists develop calibration power. As part of this training, the geologists received numerous past cases of drilled wells that incorporated the many factors affecting oil deposits. For each case they had to provide best guesses for the probability of striking oil as well as ranges as to how much a successful well might produce. Then they were given feedback as to what had actually happened. The training worked wonderfully: now, when Shell geologists predict a 30 percent chance of producing oil, three out of ten times the company averages a hit.[3]

---

Lesson: Feedback and accountability can teach people to develop a sharper sense of how much they do—and do not—know.

---

In both cases, the U.S. Weather Service forecasters and the Royal Dutch/Shell geologists were given precise, timely feedback about repeated judgments in a field whose knowledge base is relatively stable. Both groups were also held accountable by their supervisors or professional colleagues for the accuracy of their confidence judgments. Within a day, weather forecasters receive feedback about whether or not it rained, and their predictive performance is factored into their salary increases and promotions.

In most professions, however, you won't get good feedback automatically. Thus, you won't learn to calibrate unless you or your organization works to *create* systematic feedback. We'll discuss ways to make sure you learn from the results of your decisions in chapters 8 and 9. But you needn't wait until the outcomes of your predictions are clear to become smarter about just how much you know for sure; the following two tools can help you learn to do so now.[4]

 **Provide ranges and confidence levels for estimates.**

Erroneous forecasts not only hurt the forecaster's reputation, they may hurt the company as a whole. To preserve an accurate sense of uncertainty in the decision-making process, reorient your estimating processes to provide accurate **ranges** and **confidence levels** rather than dangerous single-point predictions. Insist that your staff do the same. Consider whether additional information would allow you to narrow the range with an even higher level of confidence—and determine if the decision warrants the extra time and cost.

Choose the confidence level appropriate to the issues and risks at hand. It may not be worthwhile to narrow the confidence range in every case. For example, when building a complex new oil refinery, where the downside risks are high, you may want to incorporate even extreme swings in oil prices. In that case, perhaps a 95 percent confidence range on future crude oil price levels should be assessed. However, for estimating regional sales levels, you may want a 50 percent range, if you can cope more easily with surprises outside that range.

Sometimes, you may want to provide both a 90 **and** a 50 percent confidence range. For example, if you are shipping a package from the U.S. to Europe, you may be able to predict a two- to five-day delivery with a 50 percent confidence level, and a one- to six-day delivery with a 90 percent confidence level. Articulating the two alternatives can help you decide whether just one level of confidence is sufficient—or what's needed is more information, or even another alternative (such as mapping the full probability distribution).

**Provide accelerated feedback and training to help people calibrate.**

Simple experiments with trivia questions, such as the "test" we provided in chapter 4, have demonstrated the efficacy of accelerated feedback. Just the exercise of taking this quiz improves people's sense of how much they do and don't know. This kind of training can be especially effective for new employees—and is far less expensive than waiting for employees to learn from costly experience.

You can obtain important feedback on your calibration in your own professional field without waiting for the outcome of the decisions you're making today. Here's how: Create a test that asks for range estimates and levels of confidence in response to questions relevant to your profession. If you're in a position to do so, give this test to all professionals in your department and to all new employees. In any event, take it yourself.

A test for personnel managers might include such questions as:

1. Among professionals hired in the last five years, how many have failed to be promoted on schedule?
2. How many applicants for systems analyst positions did advertisements in major out-of-town newspapers generate?
3. What percentage of our job applicants are minorities or women?

And so on. In response to each question, give your best range estimate for a given level of confidence (say 80 percent). Then secure the exact answers from appropriate sources. Does the frequency with which real answers fall within the ranges you provided match the levels of confidence you gave? If you have ten questions with an 80 percent confidence level, then the correct answer should fall within your range for 8 out of those 10 questions. If the real answers fall within your ranges significantly **less** often than you anticipated, then you'll know that in providing estimates for real decisions, you must expand your ranges. Keep practicing with this kind of constructed test until you can consistently succeed. Over time you will surely get better.

Remember that learning to recognize how much you know and don't know is the key issue, not actually coming close to the right answers. If personnel managers recognize that they don't know what share of professionals progress on schedule, they can do research to find out. But if these managers believe they know and they're wrong, they are likely to adopt incorrect policies without any research at all. In most business decisions, ignorance is *not* bliss. Rather, it spells big-time trouble.

## FIND THE HIDDEN FUTURE PROBLEMS

The estimation techniques presented above will help when you have a fairly good sense about where you stand. But what about when ambiguity increases? In such situations, selecting *one* version of the future can be a dangerous bet, as a major pharmaceutical firm found out. In 1993, the Clinton administration was aggressively pressing its proposal to change the healthcare system in the United States. The company's leaders, with change so clearly on its way, decided to move ahead of the curve. Assuming that some version of the Clinton healthcare proposals would become America's new public policy, they took proactive steps, such as substantially reducing their workforce. But just eighteen months later the landscape shifted. The Clinton plan had derailed. And the company, which had hitched its future to the reform, was caught running in the wrong direction. They had to hire back some of the staff they had just fired. They lost tens of millions of dollars in training and relocation costs. And they missed their sales forecast by more than at any other time in the company's history.

Trying to nail down the *one* right path, closing other doors so as to move decisively ahead with the "winning" alternative, may have been possible when the future was more predictable—and the environment more forgiving of mistakes. In today's world it's not only foolhardy, but idiotic. Rather than trying to pick the "most-certain" future, decision-makers must learn to capitalize upon the doubt, generating multiple views of the future as a way to preserve the inherent uncertainty.

Thus, while you can't foretell the future, you can be ready for whatever it brings by trying to expect the unexpected. By definition, the unexpected is difficult to anticipate—even though we know it is inevitable. Overconfidence and availability bias cause people to underestimate the difficulties they will face: too few unexpected events that *might* delay a project come easily to mind when people are planning it. As a result, many organizations fail to complete projects within the time they originally forecast or don't deliver products or services at the costs they originally hoped.

When you must deal with several possible but still easily defined futures, techniques such as pro/con reasoning, prospective hindsight, and fault trees can help you identify the potential causes of future problems and opportunities more clearly, avoid the tendency to see your preferred outcome as more likely, and incorporate uncertainty into the decision-making process. The first two are "back of the envelope" techniques, often taking less than ten minutes to complete. Fault trees take a bit more time to construct but can be extremely useful, especially for repetitive decisions.

As uncertainty increases, with several interrelated possible futures, you will need to turn to the more sophisticated scenario planning techniques. People operating under severe time pressures may be tempted to reject building fault trees or creating scenarios so as to "save time." But doing so often causes surprise and losses. In recent years, companies such as Hewlett-Packard and Xerox have launched efforts to anticipate problems in the early stages of their design processes, because they recognize that the alternative includes frustration, delay, reputational damage, and high costs. And even these more comprehensive techniques can be used in a simple, scaled-down version, depending on the magnitude and complexity of your decision.

---

Lesson: Rather than trying to pick the one "most-certain" future, preserve inherent uncertainty by generating multiple views of the future and trying to expect the unexpected.

---

## PRO/CON REASONING: A BALANCED VIEW

Answer this question: who will be the next elected leader of your country's government? Now assign a probability that your answer is correct. If you're like most people, when we asked you for the probability that you will be right, you begin to think of reasons why your chosen candidate is likely to win the next election. Now consider the reasons you might be wrong, or the reasons why some other candidate might win the election. To do that, you probably will have to think of reasons that weren't initially on your mind.

Here's our point: few decision-makers evaluate decision alternatives impartially. Rather, most of us naturally prefer one alternative over the others. There's nothing wrong with this per se. But when it's time to quantify the risks and opportunities inherent in each alternative, we must impose discipline to overcome the pull of wishful thinking and confirmation biases. Research shows that forcing people to look at arguments both for ("pro") and against ("con") their expected outcome is a good way to ensure intellectual honesty and a balanced view. When people generate arguments both for and against their favored view, they pick the right answer more often and have more accurate calibration in assigning confidence levels.[5]

**Use pro/con reasoning to ensure a balanced view.**
This technique is quick and highly effective. List the reasons why your favored alternative is likely to succeed and why the other options are likely not to. Now list the reasons why it is likely to fail (or why another alternative has a better chance of success). If after five or ten minutes you're not satisfied that you're getting to the right issues, try the next technique.

## PROSPECTIVE HINDSIGHT: "BACK TO THE FUTURE"

Monday morning, after the football team has lost, every fan can see why the quarterback's pass to the tight end was a bad idea. The same is true after a political election, or when a competitor succeeds in acquiring a takeover target, or when you lose a key client. Hundreds of "Monday-morning quarterbacks" declare that the quarterback (or whoever was calling the plays in the losing organization) should have anticipated the problem. After all, it's so easy to see it now.

Similarly, in hindsight, it is easy to laugh at Newton Baker's inability to imagine an airplane sinking a battleship, or to shake our heads at Thomas Watson's inability to envision a digital future. In hindsight, our vision is often 20/20. Too bad it isn't so in *foresight*.

But perhaps it can be. A number of experiments suggest that you can harness your ability to explain events in hindsight to better anticipate *possibilities* that still lie ahead.[6] Such "prospective hindsight" can be a valuable supplement to fault trees and scenarios when you need to contemplate an uncertain future. To see how this might be so, try the experiment below for yourself.

## Exercise: Mental Time Travel as an Aid to Imagination

To test the effect of prospective hindsight on yourself and others, create two groups. Give question A to one group and question B to the other.

A. How likely is it that a woman will be elected the leader of your country in the first election after the next one? Think about all the reasons why this might happen. For specificity, provide a numerical probability.

B. Imagine that the first election after the next one has just occurred and a woman has been elected the leader of your country. Think about all the reasons why this might have happened. Then provide a numerical probability of this actually occurring.

Most people find that version B, in which the respondent pretends to be using hindsight, generates a greater number of paths to the event and a higher numerical probability.

---

We tested this technique with several groups of managers and MBA students. We gave each a brief description of a new employee including the person's job, company, industry, and personal ambitions. Using such vignettes, we asked half to generate plausible reasons why the new employee *might quit* six months from now. They generated an average of 3.5 reasons per person. The other half were told that the new employee *had quit* and were asked to generate plausible reasons why this had happened. The hindsight group generated an average of 4.4. reasons (25 percent more). Furthermore, the reasons were different in tone: more specific and more closely linked to the episode at hand.

We believe that the impact of prospective hindsight will be even greater with real decisions involving large stakes. So if you doubt whether you or your colleagues have sufficient insight into the myriad of causes that could produce success or failure for your project, engage in some mental time travel.[7]

 **Use prospective hindsight to stimulate insight.**
To use prospective hindsight in decision-making, simply pretend that whatever project or situation you are evaluating has already occurred. Then postulate the possible outcomes in hindsight. For example, assume that a year from now your project turned out to be a fiasco, then list reasons why it failed. You'll probably see more reasons for an event when you pretend it has already happened than when you simply ask yourself why it might occur.

## FAULT TREES: PATHS TO TROUBLE

If your list of pros and cons is getting long, or you need to present them clearly to others, or you want to preserve them for a future decision, you may need a more systematic approach. One of the simplest is to construct a fault tree, a hierarchical diagram designed to help identify all the paths to some specific "fault" or problem. Fault trees detail the many ways in which a complex system might fail. By doing so, they help people visualize more clearly

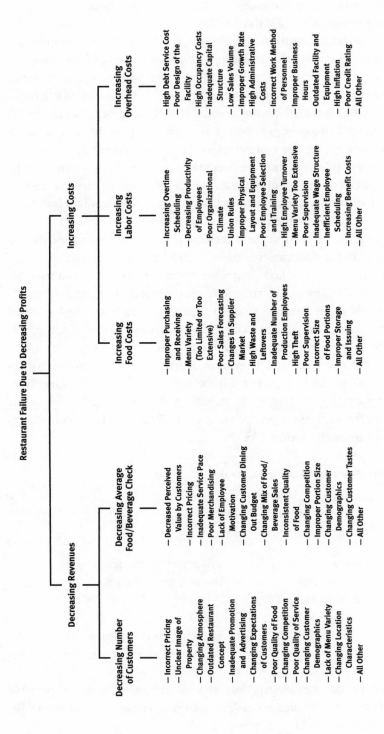

# Restaurant Failure Due to Decreasing Profits

## Decreasing Revenues

### Decreasing Number of Customers
- Incorrect Pricing
- Unclear Image of Property
- Changing Atmosphere
- Outdated Restaurant Concept
- Inadequate Promotion and Advertising
- Changing Expectations of Customers
- Poor Quality of Food
- Changing Competition
- Poor Quality of Service
- Changing Customer Demographics
- Lack of Menu Variety
- Changing Location Characteristics
- All Other

### Decreasing Average Food/Beverage Check
- Decreased Perceived Value by Customers
- Incorrect Pricing
- Inadequate Service Pace
- Poor Merchandising
- Lack of Employee Motivation
- Changing Customer Dining Out Budget
- Changing Mix of Food/Beverage Sales
- Inconsistent Quality of Food
- Changing Competition
- Improper Portion Size
- Changing Customer Demographics
- Changing Customer Tastes
- All Other

## Increasing Costs

### Increasing Food Costs
- Improper Purchasing and Receiving
- Menu Variety (Too Limited or Too Extensive)
- Poor Sales Forecasting
- Changes in Supplier Market
- High Waste and Leftovers
- Inadequate Number of Production Employees
- High Theft
- Poor Supervision
- Incorrect Size of Food Portions
- Improper Storage and Issuing
- All Other

### Increasing Labor Costs
- Increasing Overtime Scheduling
- Decreasing Productivity of Employees
- Poor Organizational Climate
- Union Rules
- Improper Physical Layout and Equipment
- Poor Employee Selection and Training
- High Employee Turnover
- Menu Variety Too Extensive
- Poor Supervision
- Inadequate Wage Structure
- Inefficient Employee Scheduling
- Increasing Benefit Costs
- All Other

### Increasing Overhead Costs
- High Debt Service Cost
- Poor Design of the Facility
- High Occupancy Costs
- Inadequate Capital Structure
- Low Sales Volume
- Improper Growth Rate
- High Administrative Costs
- Incorrect Work Method of Personnel
- Improper Business Hours
- Outdated Facility and Equipment
- High Inflation
- Poor Credit Rating
- All Other

*Figure 5-2*

the possible causes of future problems and therefore help them to realistically assess the likelihood of difficulties.

For example, if you wanted to examine the reasons why a restaurant might
fail (so you could realistically assess and minimize the risk of investing in a
new restaurant), you might construct a fault tree with the primary set of
branches representing the major kinds of failures. Then you would list subgroups of causes within each major branch. In each subgroup, include an "all
other" category to cover those causes you haven't thought to specifically
mention. Here's a fault tree that corresponds to this example.

To be useful, fault trees must be reasonably complete, at least in identifying the major categories of potential trouble. If they are not, chances are that
even specialists will fail to realize what is missing. "Availability bias" takes
over: people assume that the causes they have listed will account for almost
everything that could go wrong, and they dramatically underestimate the impact of events in the final category of "all other" causes.

A study that one of us (Jay) conducted demonstrates this caveat well. He
asked a group of eighty restaurant and hotel managers studying at Cornell's
School of Hotel Administration to use a fault tree to estimate the likelihood
of causes for restaurant failures.[8] One group was shown a list of six specific
reasons why fewer customers might dine at a restaurant, along with a final
category for "all other" causes. They were instructed to estimate the chances
that each cause would be the culprit if the restaurant failed. And they were
specifically warned to remember to include in the "all other" category any
other reason for failure beyond the six specifically listed. The combined results of their estimates looked like this:

**The Hospitality Managers' Response (Group 1)**

*Reasons for Decreasing Numbers of Customers*

Incorrect Pricing
Unclear Image
Changing Atmosphere           93% probability that failure would
Outdated Restaurant Concept   be due to one of these six causes
Inadequate Promotion and Advertising
Changing Customer Expectations

All Other ⟶ 7% probability that failure would
be due to some other unlisted cause.

A second group of managers was shown an expanded list of possible
causes—the original six causes plus six additional causes, as well as the "all
other" category. Here's how they responded:

**The Hospitality Managers' Response (Group 2)**

*Reasons for Decreasing Numbers of Customers*

Incorrect Pricing
Unclear Image of Property
Changing Atmosphere ⎱
Outdated Restaurant Concept ⎰ 46% probability that failure would
be due to one of these six causes
Inadequate Promotion and Advertising
Changing Customer Expectations

Poor Quality of Food
Changing Competition
Poor Quality of Service ⎱
Changing Customer Demographics ⎰ 50% probability that failure would
be due to one of these six new causes
Lack of Menu Variety
Changing Location Characteristics

All Other ⟶ 4% probability that failure would be due
to some other unlisted cause.

Notice the discrepancy. If there had been a 50 percent probability that one of the six *new* causes shown to Group 2 could be responsible for the restaurant's failure, then those causes should have been accounted for by Group 1 in the "all other" category. If the members of Group 1 *had* accounted for them, their estimate for the "all other" category should have been close to 54 percent. Instead, it was only 7 percent.

Why? What's out of sight is out of mind. Because such causes of customer decline as poor food and poor service had not been listed on the original chart, even these experienced executives vastly underestimated their possible impact. The longer list of causes shown to Group 2 made the additional six causes more obvious, and thus more available for their consideration.

We don't know for sure whether the probabilities produced by any of the managers were accurate. But we do know that thinking about a list of twelve possible causes of failure, rather than six, would greatly benefit a decision-maker trying realistically to avoid future problems. The more causes listed on the fault tree, the less likely people are to overlook them.

 **Use a fault tree to systematically organize possible paths to trouble.**

Fault trees are relatively simple to construct. On the primary "branches," list the major categories of potential problems that might befall your chosen alternative. Then list subgroups of causes within each major branch, including an "all other" category. To be useful, however, fault trees must be reasonably complete, and the major categories of potential trouble should not overlap. Remember: even directly warning people that other causes may exist and should be listed in the "all other" category doesn't overcome the blindness imposed by availability biases. Instead, make sure you have listed as many causes as possible. Then ask people to extend the fault tree even further by providing space for them to list additional possible causes.

Fault trees produce especially useful estimates if you break a large project into parts and try to estimate the time required for each component. You'll usually find that you can estimate some parts of the project accurately because you have done similar work before. You won't need a fault tree for those components. But after you have estimated the components based on your past experience, you can then create fault trees to gauge the problems you'll face in the parts of the project you know less well.

## SCENARIO PLANNING: PATHS TO THE FUTURE

Among the many tools available to decision-makers, scenario planning—a disciplined method for imagining possible futures—stands out for its ability to capture a whole range of possibilities in rich detail and organize them into scriptlike narratives that paint in vivid specifics how the future might unfold in one direction or another.[9] Whereas fault trees highlight individual causes, scenarios focus on the *joint* effect of many overlapping causes.

By expanding the range of possibilities without drifting into unbridled science fiction, scenario planning can help us understand how the various strands of a complex tapestry move when one thread is pulled. When you just *list* possible problems (as with a fault tree), you and your colleagues may tend to disbelieve them in isolation. But when you explore the possible problems together, you may realize that certain combinations could magnify each other. For instance, an increased trade deficit may trigger an economic recession, which in turn creates unemployment and reduces domestic production.

Scenarios work by dividing our knowledge into two areas: (1) things we believe we know something about and (2) elements we consider uncertain or unknowable. The first component—trends—casts the past forward, recognizing that our world possesses considerable momentum and continuity. For example, we can safely make assumptions about demographic shifts and substitution effects of new technologies. Of course, nothing is ever absolutely certain—not even death and taxes—but to leave everything uncertain will cause paralysis in most organizations. The second component—true uncertainties—are things such as future interest rates, results of political elections, rates of innovation, the worldviews that will dominate, and so on.

Scenario planning is especially useful when:

- Uncertainty is high relative to decision-makers' ability to predict or adjust.
- Too many costly surprises have occurred in the past.
- The company does not perceive or generate new opportunities.
- The quality of strategic thinking is too routine or bureaucratic.
- The industry or field has experienced significant change or is about to.
- The organization wants a common language and framework, without stifling diversity.
- There are strong differences of opinion, with multiple opinions having merit.
- Your competitors are using scenario planning.

Numerous organizations have applied scenario planning to a great range of issues, from relatively simple, tactical decisions to the complex process of strategic planning and vision building. We became convinced about the power of scenario planning through our work with Royal Dutch/Shell where one of us (Paul) worked for two years. Shell has used scenarios since the early 1970s as part of a company-wide process for generating and evaluating its strategic options.[10] Shell has been consistently better in its oil forecasts than other major oil companies, and saw the overcapacity in the tanker business and Europe's petrochemicals earlier than its competitors. In the early 1980s, Anglo-American Corporation of South Africa convened an international group of experts to explore South Africa's future through scenarios. The resulting scenarios posited two dramatically different political and economic futures. Subsequent scenario planning helped further shape that country's policy debate and influence the agenda for profound political reform. One of us (Paul) has helped organizations employ this tool to estimate future environmental liability, anticipate healthcare cost containment and regulatory control, assess the consequences of deregulation in electric utilities, determine the shifting dimensions in financial services, and develop a strategic vision for an R&D division. In short, the technique is applicable to virtually any situation in which a decision-maker would like to imagine how the future might unfold.

Harrah's Casino in Atlantic City used scenario planning to solve a tactical problem: how to deal with the high costs incurred when inclement winter weather forced them to cancel previously booked entertainment. Casinos traditionally have used high-profile entertainment acts to draw patrons. Harrah's Atlantic City has a $5 million budget to operate its theater, with a typical gig costing around $150,000. Unfortunately, in the northeast United States, winter snowstorms are a key uncertainty. Predictions of bad weather can cause many customers to stay home, and the storms themselves can force last-minute cancellations. The entertainer fees, however, are already committed. The cost to the casino of cancelled shows is high.

The solution, however, wasn't obvious. They couldn't afford to close the casino entirely for the winter months. Booking less expensive entertainers was risky. If competitors offered a higher-quality act and the weather was good, Harrah's wouldn't fill their hall.

So Harrah's manager Dave Jonas, who had taken one of our executive education seminars, convened his staff for some scenario planning. For several days the group brainstormed other ways to market the casino. Then they plotted the attractiveness of each option against diverse scenarios: from good weather to bad. One unorthodox option stood out as a winner across all the scenarios. Although it flouted standard operating procedure in the industry, they had found a robust solution.

Their plan? They would close the showroom for the winter, booking no acts. But on weekends where they would normally have booked an entertainer, they would mail an offer for "supplemental cash" (coupons that could be used like cash in the casino's games) to their customers. The size of the offer was relative to how much that customer typically spent. They rolled out the new plan in January. The first two weekends were snowy. Customers stayed home, but the casino had no entertainment contracts to honor. Also, they cut back on labor and other costs, missing their operating revenue target by only 10 to 15 percent. Then, the third weekend arrived and it was sunny and dry. Customers came out in droves to cash in their coupons; revenues were at a record high, exceeding the anticipated bottom line. The supplemental cash solution proved so successful that Harrah's Atlantic City now uses it to market the casino during other traditionally slow times: midweek, early in the month, and during holiday weekends.[11]

 **Construct scenarios to envision multiple futures.**
Here's a brief description of how one of us (Paul) constructs scenarios. (Readers should note that scenario planning can take many forms, and many variations are possible. While a detailed analysis of this tool is beyond the scope of this book, we have listed a variety of sources in the notes to this chapter. In addition to describing the process in more detail, they also offer case studies of scenario planning in action.)

1. **Define the scope.** Set the time frame and scope of analysis (e.g., products, markets, geographic areas, technologies).

2. **Identify the major stakeholders.** Who will have an interest in these issues? Who will be affected by them? Who could influence them? Think about each player's role, interests, and power position, and ask how and why they have changed over time.

3. **Identify basic trends.** What political, economic, societal, technological, legal, and industry trends are sure to affect the issues you identified in step 1? Briefly explain each trend, including how and why it exerts its influence on your project. Everyone participating in the process must agree that these trends will continue; any trend on which there is disagreement belongs in the next step.

4. **Identify key uncertainties.** What events whose outcomes are uncertain will significantly affect the issues you are concerned with? As above, consider factors that are political, economic, societal, etc. For each uncertainty, determine possible outcomes. It is not important to account for all the possible outcomes of each uncertainty; simplifying the possible outcomes is sufficient. For instance, you may want to think in terms of three possible interest rates (high, medium, and low) rather than hundreds of them. The purpose is not to cover all possibilities, but to span the great majority of them.

5. **Construct initial scenario themes.** Once you have identified trends and uncertainties, you have the main ingredients for scenario construction. One recommended approach, useful if some uncertainties are clearly more important than others, is to select the two biggest uncertainties and two widely different outcomes of each uncertainty. Then crossing them in a matrix generates four possible scenario[12] themes or "seeds." These are illustrated in the accompanying figure, drawn from an actual scenario project for credit unions.

6. **Check for consistency and plausibility.** Ask yourself whether any of the initial scenarios generated above are implausible, internally inconsistent, or irrelevant. For example, an initial scenario may assume both full employment and zero inflation. That's an unlikely combination. To test internal consistency, ask: Are the trends compatible within the chosen time frame? (If not, remove the trends that don't fit.) Do the scenarios combine outcomes of uncertainties that go together? (If not, eliminate that possible pairing from the scenario.) Are major stakeholders placed in positions they do not like and can change? (If so, your scenario will evolve; try to describe the new scenario, which is more stable.)

**Changes in Playing Field?**

|  | Minor | Profound |
|---|---|---|
| **Gradual** | **Scenario A:** Status Quo | **Scenario B:** Wallet Wars |
| **Radical** | **Scenario C:** Technocracy | **Scenario D:** New World |

**Impact of Technology?**

*Figure 5-3* Scenario Design: 2x2 Matrix

7. ***Develop scenarios.*** By now, some general themes should be emerging that are strategically relevant to your project. Flesh out these themes by incorporating additional possible outcomes and trends from your lists that are compatible. Rearrange the scenario elements to create two to four relatively consistent, plausible scenarios. These scenarios should describe generically different futures rather than variations on one theme. They should cover a wide range of possibilities and highlight competing perspectives. Although uncertainties, by definition, appear in all the scenarios, they can be given more or less weight in different scenarios.

8. ***Identify research needs.*** At this point you may need to do further research to flesh out your understanding of uncertainties and trends. For example, do you really understand how a key stakeholder will behave in a given scenario or how closely market share correlates with price? Do you need to study new technologies not yet in the mainstream of your industry, but which may be someday?

9. ***Develop quantitative models.*** You can take any scenario to the next step of specificity by quantifying it, that is, by numerically estimating the impact of the trends and uncertainties. For example, models can help quantify the consequences of various scenarios in

terms of price behavior, growth rates, market share, and so on. Royal Dutch/Shell has developed a model that keeps oil prices, inflation, GNP growth, taxes, oil inventories, interest rates, and so forth in plausible balances. As decision-makers imagine different outcomes of key uncertainties, they can use formal models to keep from straying into implausible scenarios.

10. *Evolve toward decision scenarios.* Finally, in an iterative process, you must converge toward two to four distinctly different scenarios that you will eventually use to test your strategies and generate new ideas. (While a broad range of variables may emerge, it is important to keep the focus narrow.) Retrace steps 1 through 8 to see if the scenarios (and any quantitative models from step 9) address the real issues facing your project. Are they relevant? Internally consistent? Do they describe generically different futures rather than variations on one theme? Do they describe an equilibrium or state in which the system might exist for some length of time? (It does little good to prepare for a possible future that will be short-lived.) If you answered "yes" to each of the questions above, you are done. If not, repeat the steps and refocus your scenarios the way an artist judges the balance and focal point in a painting. Half of this judgment is art, half is science.

## SCENARIOS IN THE ORGANIZATIONAL CONTEXT

A few additional tips about scenario planning: Balancing a scenario planning team to include many viewpoints—including contrarians—is essential. (Chapter 7 explains further why teams with diverse and moderately conflicting views tend to make higher-quality decisions.) It also can be extremely useful to include smart frontline workers in this planning process rather than just those at the "top." When the people who deal with the everyday details of your organization get involved, they often see implications that are not obvious to others.

When creating global scenarios, it's not always necessary to start from scratch. Rather, you might start with existing scenarios produced by research centers and think tanks, and then build on them. In the early 1990s, for example, the Dutch Central Planning Bureau, a leading government agency, issued wide-ranging twenty-five-year global scenarios.[13] For more complex or important decisions, the scenario exercise may benefit from engaging experienced facilitators, as there are many things that can be done to make the process go more smoothly.

Finally, depending on your organization, scenario planning can be challenging at the start. Keith Kendrick, vice president for AT&T's Universal Credit Card Service, offers the following thoughts about integrating scenario planning into an organization that hasn't used it before. His group used scenario planning in the mid-1990s to look at alternative futures for how consumers might pay for their purchases. Cybermalls, intelligent agents, and other technology developments were changing their business—and the technology or direction that will dominate was not at all certain. As a result of the scenario planning process, AT&T began operating in "a cybermall environment," replacing some toll-free services with e-mail services, developing new payment techniques, and forging alliances with firms experimenting with new "smart card" applications.

Here is what Kendrick observed about the process itself.

Scenario planning is challenging because it involves asking people to think about things that are extremely uncomfortable. . . . Participants may feel that the process is addressing things that won't happen, or that it's the annual strategic planning function in disguise. . . . But scenario planning is not about preparing a plan. It's more about going forward. Our scenario planning experience began when a small group of us became convinced that despite our success as a company, emerging industry trends presented high risks and uncertainties. . . .

Inviting a cross-section of people in positions of control to participate in this type of meeting introduces a variety of biases that can impact the scenario planning process. For example, some managers like control and feel threatened by a process that may diminish or change their area of responsibility, or introduce changes. . . . [O]thers draw comfort from the process because it helps them understand what was previously unknown or ambiguous.

There are several things you can do to facilitate the scenario planning process. Talk about what other companies are doing. Take the focus off the idea that "this is our strategic business plan." Focus on strategy, not budgets. Help the group get comfortable with the notion about thinking five years out. Put them in a very comfortable hotel. Identify "committed" individuals who feel strongly about the scenarios being developed, and get them and others from their group(s) involved. It may be appropriate to separate the forward thinkers from those who are locked in the status quo. Also, identify technology partners who have resources needed to participate.

We learned some good lessons as a result of our scenario planning exercise. . . . Everything we wrote about the "cybermall" 20 months ago has happened or is happening.[14]

## KNOWING WHEN ENOUGH IS ENOUGH

If a little information is good, a little more will be better. Right? Not necessarily. In their desire to reduce uncertainty, many decision-makers ask for too much information. They believe—mistakenly—that more information will give them a clearer picture of the future. However, more information helps only to the extent that you can use it intelligently. In fact, vast amounts of data may only confuse matters. Here's a simple study that demonstrates this point well.

Horse race handicappers typically use "past performance charts," which give nearly a hundred pieces of information on each horse and its history, to determine the likelihood that any given horse will win a race.[15] In this study, researchers watched eight handicappers make predictions for numerous races. However, they limited the handicappers to using only five pieces of information per horse from the charts. The handicappers could use any five nuggets of data they wanted, and different handicappers often selected different pieces of information. The researchers then asked the handicappers to make the same predictions using ten pieces of information per horse, then with twenty pieces, and one last time using forty pieces of information for each horse in the race. In addition, they asked the handicappers, in each case, to estimate the likelihood that they had correctly picked the winning horse. The results are shown in figure 5-4.

The research question of interest was whether the handicappers became more accurate in picking winners as they were given more information. They themselves felt that they would be. Their confidence in their predictive ability increased as the amount of information they were allowed to use increased. In reality, however, they were as accurate in their predictions using five pieces of information as they were using twenty or forty. More information helped little to improve the quality of their decisions. However, their secondary knowledge—their ability to correctly predict how much they knew—declined dramatically. The more information they had, the more overconfident they became (without becoming more accurate).[16]

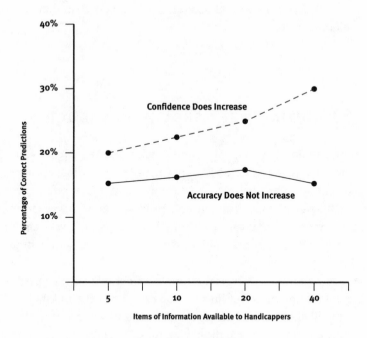

*Figure 5-4* **Horse Race Handicapping**

Lesson: Ask yourself whether you may be collecting too much information. More information increases decision-makers' confidence, but not necessarily their accuracy.

Herein lies the danger for decision-makers. Past a certain point, more information will make you increasingly confident about your knowledge but may do little to improve the accuracy of your predictions. And so we return to the main theme of this chapter: don't pretend you can reduce uncertainty any more than you really can. In "The Power of Frames" (chapter 2) we quoted Einstein's admonition to "Make things as simple as possible, and no simpler." Here we warn you: Make things as certain as possible . . . but no more certain. Instead, incorporate uncertainty into your decision-making process, and you will be prepared for whatever lies ahead. Learn to manage it well, and like the top race car drivers in inclement weather, you will find yourself cruising ahead of your less savvy competitors.

INTERLUDE B

# Technologies for Aiding Decisions

What do machines mean for us then? . . .
They offer the possibility of achieving ever
higher and more nuanced goals. —*Romano Guardini*[1]

A HOST OF emerging innovations will soon change the way decisions are made, supplementing human intelligence with sophisticated "artificial intelligence" (AI) technologies. Unfortunately, most of these technologies have not yet penetrated the managerial decision-making arena. It may not be long, however, before they do. For that reason, we want to pause for a moment from our discussion of the stages in a good decision-making process and give you a preview of the technological future. We have placed this interlude[2] between the chapters on "gathering intelligence" and "coming to conclusions" because these emerging technologies will impact both stages of the decision-making process. More important, they will serve as a bridge between them.

Consider WiseUncle, a young company to which one of us (Jay) serves as chief scientific advisor. The company has been developing a product called Advisor, intelligent software to aid consumer decision-making. Although version 1.0 was still being developed as this book went to press, we expect one or more computer manufacturers to have installed the software on their websites by the time you are holding this book in your hands. By mimicking the informed dialogue that would occur between a decision-maker and a trusted, expert advisor (hence the name "wise uncle"), the software creates an interactive environment to help decision-makers bridge the gap between their needs, wants, and preferences (an intelligence-gathering activity) and a decision about the best option to choose (in the drawing conclusions phase).

The capabilities of this kind of software are not limited to decisions about which computer to buy, but because that will be WiseUncle's first application, it's the example we will use to illustrate technology-aided decision-making. If you were using Advisor to help you decide which new personal computer to buy, the first few screens might ask you whether you currently own a PC and, if yes, why you believe you need a new one. Your answers to the initial questions determine the subsequent questions posed. If you need a new computer, for example, because your current one is too slow, Advisor asks you why. Is it due to new applications? Large databases? Heavy downloads over telephone lines? The dialogue would continue until the system has an adequate picture of your needs.

Once those needs are identified, however, they have to be matched to the available options (viz., processor, memory, speakers, sound and video cards, etc.). It's not difficult to imagine how combining the different available components quickly explodes into billions of final options to choose among. Advanced AI technology solves this enormous optimal selection problem. To be useful to decision-makers, such solutions not only have to be feasible and accurate, they must also be fast. Most people don't enjoy answering a string of questions without getting any clear benefit, or even any comments, until a recommendation finally appears on the screen. So the Advisor system enables you to request a preliminary recommendation after only a few questions have been answered. You can then watch the recommendation become increasingly customized as you provide more information about your intended uses, expected needs, and personal preferences.[3]

## THE UNDERLYING TECHNOLOGIES

The new decision-aiding systems use two different kinds of AI technologies, rule-based systems and network structures. The most powerful decision-aiding systems, such as Advisor, are typically hybrids that combine these technologies.

***Rule-based systems*** are built on a series of "if, . . . then. . . ." building blocks. For example: "If the consumer says that playing music is an intended use for the new computer, then (a) a high-end sound card is a likely need and (b) ask about adding high-quality speakers." Such systems are very flexible and can evolve over time to become highly sophisticated. That is, designers can keep adding rules to make them function increasingly better. (They can eventually encompass tens of thousands of rules.) Such rule-based systems have already proved effective in well-delineated decision-making domains like diagnosing thyroid disorders and playing the game of backgammon.[4] They are particularly adept at the "intelligence-gathering" aspects of the decision-making process.

The most sophisticated of these rule-based systems can be made even more flexible through what is called **"fuzzy logic."** Unlike the precision of traditional computer programs, fuzzy systems improve performance by thinking more like humans, who use not only black-and-white categories but are especially good at thinking in "gray" terms as well. They use categories with fuzzy boundaries to make inferences about whether, for example, an elevator is fast or slow, just as human experts use fuzzy definitions in defining such concepts as tall, cheap, efficient, etc.[5] Is there always a black-or-white answer to whether a consumer needs the fastest (and most expensive) processor, or whether a standard and cheaper one is adequate? Fuzzy logic enables a more flexible answer.

*Network structures,* on the other hand, serve as a computational bridge, matching huge amounts of extracted information to the best available option, a "coming to conclusions" function. Three kinds of network structures are common. **Bayesian networks** use conditional probabilities to link the strength of the connection between "input" (e.g., the decision-maker's needs, wants, and preferences) and "output" (decision options such as the several billion possible computers). The option with the highest probability is the one that is recommended. The complexity of the network and the accuracy of the linkage probabilities are the main determinants of its success. (Experts provide these essential probabilities that, for example, an expressed need to play video games requires a particular video card.)

*Neural nets* mimic the network of neurons in the human brain such that the activation of "input" nodes (which, again, might reflect the intensity of the decision-maker's needs, wants, and preferences) "propagates" throughout the network to result in the activation of the "output" nodes. If the output nodes represent the computer components, the most activated processor, memory, etc. are the ones that are recommended. Neural nets are more flexible than Bayesian networks and can more easily adapt to experience over time. If certain links in the network are frequently "activated," those connections grow stronger. Conversely, if certain pathways are rarely traversed, that part of the neural net may atrophy. Neural nets are built by "training" them on actual decision-making cases, such as the needs of a consumer (the input) and the best product as chosen by an expert (the output).

*Genetic algorithms* mimic features of evolutionary biology in that they use a trial and error process to see which adaptations survive best in certain environments. The key is to set up mutable programs that compete and undergo some form of "natural selection" in a simulated environment. To offer a different (and real) example, competing sets of rules may be created to determine credit approval. As feedback becomes available (either simulated or real) about the performance of the initial selections, adjustments are made in the rules to improve performance over time. Some of these strategies for improvement are already programmed in (hence the label "algorithm"), whereas other improvements are akin to random mutations, some of which work and some of which don't.[6]


## OUR PREDICTIONS

We have used an example of consumer decision-making (purchasing a personal computer) in this discussion because all of us are consumers and can relate to the complex barrage of decisions involved in trying to determine whether the processor should be 1.4 or 1.5 gigaHertz, or whether the 32MB NVIDIA GeForce 2 MX 4X AGP graphics card is really better than some other equally obscure alternative.[7] Such decision dilemmas are compounded when shopping online, although they certainly aren't limited to the virtual realm. Most people can recall a time that they set out to buy a complex product, but quit before making a purchase decision because they weren't sure which option was best.

The technologies we've just described, however, will be used increasingly to aid managerial decisions. And these will include the "fuzzier" decisions with their greater uncertainty, not merely the more technical ones like optimizing airline routes or schedules.[8] In the spirit of the trends that are a crucial input to scenarios (see chapter 5), we offer some of the driving forces that will make these kinds of decision aids more common in the not-too-distant future. We see the following trends and possible developments over the next five years.

The underlying technologies—rule-based systems, Bayesian networks, neural nets, genetic algorithms, and fuzzy systems—will grow in sophistication and scope. Indeed, in some decision domains they will become as good as (or better than) all but the best human advisors. These systems will become increasingly adept at building the bridge between decision-makers' goals and preferences, and determining the best option for them. Returning to purchase decisions for a moment, making the right choice among relatively complex products with many diverse options (e.g., automobiles, computers, insurance policies) is like hitting a moving target because the options themselves are constantly upgraded by new technology. By the time you buy your next car or computer, new features and capabilities must be considered in your decision-making. These AI-based technologies cannot only provide the advice linking people's needs to available products, but they can be updated with the latest products (and information on them).

At the same time, bandwidth into the home and office will continue to expand, such that multimedia and virtual modeling will increasingly be used to let managerial decision-makers see and interact with the available options (e.g., views of alternative locations for a new retail outlet or recorded video interviews of job candidates). In a consumer's decision about which personal computer to buy, 3-D images of the machines being considered will be rotated and fitted virtually to see how each matches available desk space, the office décor, and so on.

Of course, this optimistic scenario may be undermined by security and privacy concerns, the difficulties of protecting intellectual property, and, of course, user acceptance. The latter, in turn, hinges on how good the artificial systems really are and their ease of use. However, given our Information Age's imbalance between available information (about an ever-increasingly multitude of options, we might add) and the necessary advice to choose wisely among those options, it's safe to assume that decision-aiding technologies will continue to be improved over time and their range of application expanded.

# Coming to Conclusions

CHAPTER 6

# Choosing: A Pyramid
# of Approaches

*Life is the art of drawing sufficient conclusions from insufficient premises.* —*Samuel Butler*[1]

YOU'VE CREATED A frame that captures the essence of your problem. You've generated good options. You've collected excellent intelligence, incorporating uncertainty into the mix. You're ready to decide. Will you make the best choice?

Not always. Many people pose their questions carefully, collect their intelligence brilliantly, but then "wing it" when it comes to actually deciding. They would do better to have a proven set of "choosing techniques," consciously selecting the right one for the job.[2]

Benjamin Franklin gave one such technique, now familiar to most decision-makers, but at that time one of the first documented attempts to systematically compare the subjective trade-offs between alternatives. Writing in 1772 to the famed British scientist Joseph Priestley, Franklin reflected:

[M]y way is to divide half a sheet of paper by a line into two columns; writing over the one Pro, and over the other Con. Then, during the three or four days consideration, I put down under the different heads short hints of the different motives, that at different times occur to me, for or against the measure. When I have thus got them all together in one view, I endeavor to estimate their respective weights; and where I find two, one on each side, that seem equal, I strike them both out. If I find a reason pro equal to some two reasons con, I strike out the three. If I judge some two reasons con, equal to some three reasons pro, I strike out the five; and thus proceeding I find at length where the balance lies; and if, after a day or two of further consideration, nothing new that is of importance occurs on either side, I come to a determination accordingly.

And, although the weight of reasons cannot be taken with the precision of algebraic quantities, yet when each is thus considered, separately and comparatively, and the whole lies before me, I think I can judge better, and am less liable to make a rash step, and in fact I have found great advantage from this kind of equation, in what may be called moral or prudential algebra.[3]

It was clear to Franklin that a systematic approach would allow him to "judge better," but that conclusion is not yet as widely accepted as one might expect. In fact, the number of people advocating that professionals "get in touch with their intuition" is on the rise. Given the frenetic pace at which we all now operate and the unceasing demands for fast, frequent decision-making, that's not surprising. But how accurate is intuition? Conversely, are analytical approaches really worth the time they require? We believe, as we have advocated throughout this book, that decision-makers ought to use the simplest technique *sufficient* for the task at hand. But that requires a conscious, evaluated choice. In reality, too many decision-makers decide by default, allowing inexperience, convenience, or haste to make the choice for them. In this chapter we present four types of choosing techniques (intuition, rules of thumb, decision weighting, and value analysis) and describe the promises and pitfalls of each. In doing so, we hope to provide you with a sound basis for selecting the most appropriate approach.

We have also placed these choices in a "pyramid" to indicate that higher approaches are used less frequently than lower ones and for more important decisions. The techniques at the lower levels of the pyramid are rapid and often executed automatically with little attempt to follow a deliberate process. The higher ones are more time-consuming and costly, but yield greater accuracy and reliability in complex environments. Some near the top will likely require technical assistance to use. We conclude the chapter by suggesting how to determine which method is most appropriate, and with some guidelines for spreading these techniques throughout your organization.

Note: The higher the method is in the pyramid, the more accurate, complex, and transparent it is. We use a pyramid shape to show that higher approaches are used less frequently and for more important decisions than are lower ones.

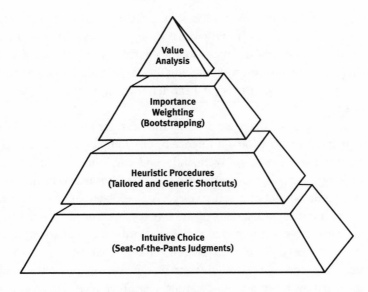

*Figure 6-1* **A Pyramid of Choice Approaches**

## LEVEL 1: WHEN YOU JUST KNOW

Intuition has understandable appeal. It's quick, easy, and requires no tedious analyses. And it can sometimes be brilliant. When based on extensive learning from past experience, it may truly reflect "automated expertise."[4] You have likely experienced automated expertise in situations so familiar that you grasp the key issues instantly, without any conscious analytical thought.

Researchers who have studied "intuition" find that these "gut" or "sixth sense" decisions actually follow a coherent path, but one that takes place so rapidly that people can't notice themselves doing it. When applying automated expertise, highly seasoned professionals reach into their mental storehouse of past experience and rapidly match patterns of the current decision and context with those of an old situation. Then the matched pattern "fires off" the old action in the new situation.

In a fast-paced world, this kind of intuition has an understandable appeal. If you're a firefighter or emergency medical technician, it may be the only option. And when the situation truly matches ones you have faced numerous times in the past, more systematic approaches may be unnecessary and a waste of time.

Unfortunately, as a decision-making tool, intuition also has significant drawbacks. It's hard to dispute choices based on intuition because the decision-makers can't articulate their own underlying reasoning. People "just know" they're right, or they have "a strong sense of it," or they're relying on "gut feel." You can't tell if the *process* is good or bad, because there's no process to examine. It's so quick, so automatic, there is no way to evaluate its quality. So how are you to know whether a decision based only on intuition is one worthy of your trust or a capricious mistake that will be wildly off the mark?

To those who study decision-making, the most striking feature of intuitive judgment is not its occasional brilliance but its rampant mediocrity. Consider this study. Nine radiologists were independently shown information from ninety-six cases of suspected stomach ulcers and asked to evaluate each in terms of the likelihood of a malignancy.[5] A week later, after these x-ray specialists had forgotten the details of the ninety-six cases, they were presented with the same ones again, but in a different order. A comparison of the two sets of diagnoses showed a 23 percent chance that an opinion would be changed.[6] Not one of the radiologists was perfectly consistent, and some were inconsistent to an alarming extent. Certainly such results support the standard advice to seek a second opinion in important medical decisions. What is especially unsettling is that you may be able to get that second opinion from the same doctor a week later!

The radiologists are not alone in their inconsistency. Consider the CEO who angrily demands, "What idiot made this decision last year?" and must be politely told, "You did, sir." Few of us realize how much our memory failings, mental limits, momentary distractions, and fatigue can influence our judgments from one day to the next. (In fact, we remember much more easily those flashes of intuitive brilliance, causing us to overvalue our intuition because we over-remember its successes.) Like overconfidence, this illusion of consistency—and our real-world inconsistency—is a widespread and hidden threat to good decision-making. It's seldom documented, however, because we rarely make the same decision twice and step back to compare our results.

To capture the ubiquity of this phenomenon, we once ran a simple experiment with our MBA students. We asked 128 students to intuitively predict the grade point average (GPA) of 50 past applicants. All had since been admitted and graduated, so we (but not our students) knew the true GPAs. The applicants were listed in random order (without names) and described only by the standard information listed in their completed applications, such as test scores, college grades, etc. Three weeks later we asked the 128 students to repeat this task and challenged them to be as consistent with their initial predictions as they could.[7] They performed slightly worse than the radiologists, *even though they knew they were being tested on consistency in a class on decision-making.*[8] Imagine the level of error that creeps in when people are not on guard.[9]

Lesson: The successes of intuitive choice are exaggerated and its risks greatly underappreciated.

## LEVEL 2: SHORTCUTS WITH "RULES OF THUMB"

*Put your home on the market in the spring: seven of ten home sales occur between April and July.*

*When pricing seasonal clothing, mark up the wholesale price by 60 percent and discount the retail price every two weeks by 20 percent until the entire inventory is gone.*

*When setting production costs, estimate the weight of the plastic part, calculate the cost of the material, and then multiply this dollar figure by two for processing, assembly, shipping, etc.*

Much of our decision-making is rule-based. And like intuition, decision-making rules have their place.[10] A good rule provides a clever shortcut through a dizzying maze of possibilities. They enable us to arrive at the right answer, or a close approximation, most of the time—without expending a lot of effort in the process. In fact, without decision-making rules we could never complete all the estimates and choices we must make in daily life. You may have a rule, for example, that says you will delegate attendance at weekly interdepartmental budget meetings to your subordinate unless you hear that a crucial item is on the agenda. That's far more efficient than repeatedly studying the question of whether you will attend interdepartmental budget meetings, collecting information about the agenda of each one, and then making a well-reasoned decision each time.

Unfortunately, people don't always use rules judiciously, and they often don't realize their inherent distortions. They may continue to use a good rule of thumb that's become outdated or inappropriate to the decision at hand. And in that blindness lurks the danger. Trammel Crow made a fortune in commercial real estate in Texas by breaking the sacred rule that warehouse and office space should be built only after tenants have signed up. Building on speculation positioned him well for the boom years. But when the local economy went bust, rigid abidance by his new rule nearly ruined his successors. Knowing how to recognize decision-making rules—and understanding their inherent biases—can keep an inappropriate rule from distorting your final decision. In the sections that follow, we explore several of the most common types of rules.

## Sample Rules Used in Business

When writing an ad, use sentences of no more than twelve words.

—David Ogilvy, founder, Ogilvy & Mather International

The individual with responsibility for implementing a decision should be part of the decision-making process.

—Eugene Webb, former associate dean, Stanford Business School

Never make a personnel judgment the first time it comes up. Never fire someone without sleeping on it.

—Alfred P. Sloan, Jr., former chairman of the board, General Motors

Set a maximum of three to five corporate goals in a year.

—John Hanley, former president, Monsanto

Round numbers beg to be negotiated, usually by counteroffer round numbers. Odd numbers sound harder, firmer, less negotiable.

—Mark McCormack, business author

Build a 20 percent pessimism quotient into all expectations. Overestimate by 20 percent the amount of time it will take to accomplish a plan. Underestimate by 20 percent the expected results.

—Robert Townsend, former president, Avis Rent-a-Car; author, *Up the Organization*[11]

**Generic Rules**—Many decision-making rules exist to help us screen and sort information. Each has its own characteristic biases. Here are two examples.

The "dictionary rule" is commonly used to rank options starting with the most important factor, and then moving down the list one attribute at a time. (It's so-named because this process is similar to how words are alphabetized in a dictionary.) For example, suppose you want to select one of several law firms or advertising agencies. Many people consider word-of-mouth recommendation the most important criterion. Using the dictionary rule, you would start by grouping those firms that have all received strong recommendations (the first attribute) and then interview this top tier. Next you would rank those firms based on how well they did in the interview (the second attribute). If ties still remain after this second screen, you might create a third cut by ranking the firms on their fees or bids. In a similar vein, a company might first rank its projects on the basis of expected returns, and only in cases of ties or near ties, consider other attributes such as timeline or strategic fit.

Because this dictionary rule gives enormous power to the first attribute, it works best when one attribute is much more important than the others. However, it can exclude from consideration good options that are very strong on attributes 2, 3, 4, and 5, but not as strong as others on attribute 1. In this way, it can cause you to miss what could be your most attractive option when the attributes are closer in importance. It can also lead to false comparisons—and poor decisions, as one well-known food products company discovered when its market share continually eroded (see "How A Smart Cookie Crumbled" below).

The "threshold rule," used to screen options against preset criteria, is also common. Most companies require that investment projects have projected financial returns that pass a preset "hurdle" rate. That's a threshold rule. The threshold rule is often used to decide what sort of house to purchase, what car to buy, or what person to hire. Banks employ a threshold rule when they use preset lending criteria to screen each applicant, approving the loan only if *all* criteria are met. Although useful, such a rule can be too unforgiving. Someone who passes all the bank's criteria with flying colors except for one payment default will not get a loan, which may well be the lender's loss.

## How a Smart Cookie Crumbled

The consequences of rules can at times be subtle. A U.S. food company was mysteriously losing market share in five product categories.[12] The culprit: a dictionary rule. The rule, commonly used in the industry to make decisions about new product formulations, such as cookies, goes like this:

Replace the current product with a cost-reduced version if:

1. Consumers do not rate it lower in overall satisfaction, and
2. The new product formulation is cheaper per unit sold.

The company used sophisticated consumer acceptance tests, focusing on overall taste, texture, visual appeal, and so forth to compare the current and new versions. It also used appropriate statistical tests and introduced the new version only if the rating differences were not statistically significantly worse. Nonetheless, after lower-cost versions had been introduced over several years, market share declined in five distinct product categories (such as cookies, cake mixes, etc.). The declines were not due to industry trends, competitor action, or shifts in consumer preferences. What happened?

The answer lies in the danger inherent in the dictionary rule. Consumers didn't notice the loss of quality from one change to the next, but the cumulative effect of *several* changes made a noticeable difference. The company had tested each new version only against the current one and not against any of the previous formulations. Consequently, it failed to detect the gradual decline in quality.

The scientific techniques this company was using, such as the statistical tests, are embedded in a decision system that was itself flawed. We'd like to report a happy ending, but cannot. Managers received credit for cost savings with each reformulation. The assistant brand manager who discovered and persistently complained about the rule was ignored and resigned in frustration. Senior management eventually noticed the decline in sales and ordered a "from scratch" reformulation. This process produced competitive products again, but at a high cost. And because the firm continued to use the faulty decision rule for deciding whether to substitute cheaper versions, it remained exposed to another gradual and "mysterious" decline in market share.

**Industry- and Occupation-Specific Rules**—In addition to generic rules, thousands of industry- and occupation-specific rules determine when we change price, replace parts, launch a new product, sell a property, and even hire people. Sometimes the rule is exceedingly simple, such as "change the oil in your car every three thousand miles." (Of course, this rule is hardly optimal since it ignores road conditions encountered, loads carried, driving habits, maintenance of the car, its age, and other factors. But, in general, it works much of the time.) Other times the rule is more complex. Fund-raisers in one presidential campaign followed these three rules: (1) the candidate will only show up at an event that will raise at least $10,000 dollars; (2) whenever you get more than five people in a room, ask them for money; (3) all fund-raising events must have a second purpose, such as a media event or selecting volunteers.

In a box above, we listed a number of rules commonly used in business. Often these guidelines are "golden rules," honed and tested through time to balance effort and accuracy. Much of the time they work just fine. But when the environment has changed due to deregulation, new technologies, shifts in consumer preferences, or whatever, it is likely that some of the old rules have become outdated. The evaluation tool that follows (see box) will help you test whether your rule is still golden or ready for an overhaul.

**Users Beware**—Decision-makers who don't recognize the nature of their rules and the hidden dangers they pose will sooner or later pay the price of ignorance. Rules are often worthy attempts to gain speed and accuracy. They eliminate the random inconsistency of intuition and greatly simplify complex tasks. And unlike intuition, they are transparent; the underlying process used by the rule is clear. Rules, however, don't take into account all of the relevant information, and they may not allow superior performance on some attributes to make up for poor performance on others. Even a seemingly scientific rule has built-in dangers, and they can be subtle, as the cookie company found out. So scrutinize the rules you use for the information they leave out and the attributes they emphasize at the expense of others. In sum: make sure your simplifying rule fits the situation, or your "clever" shortcut may send you careening over the cliff.[13]

---

Lesson: Those who don't recognize the nature of their rules—and the biases inherent in them—will sooner or later pay the price of ignorance.

---

## A Systematic Approach to Evaluating Your Rules

Here are six steps to help you decide if your favorite rule is ready for an overhaul. Two cases illustrate each step.

| Step | Case A. Auditing Interest Income | Case B. Pricing a Walkie-Talkie in New Midwest Markets |
|---|---|---|
| 1. Identify an important rule of-thumb or shortcut calculation in your firm. | Interest applied to end-of-month asset levels should add up to yearly total. | Price by finding closest match of this product in comparable known markets. |
| 2. Give an example of where this rule comes close to the correct answer. | End-of month balances fairly reflect average monthly balances over the year. | Criteria used to establish matches reflect key demand factors in the new area. |
| 3. Give an actual example of where it failed badly because of the external environment being atypical. | Deposits are mostly received early in the month or withdrawals occur unevenly. | Indianapolis seems like St. Paul but is not growing as fast, which matters here. |
| 4. Construct cases where the rule would produce | Clerk intends to defraud and thus makes sure | Competitor knows this pricing rule and focuses |

| Step | Case A.<br>Auditing Interest<br>Income | Case B.<br>Pricing a Walkie-Talkie in<br>New Midwest Markets |
|------|------|------|
| disastrous results (to understand its limits). | month-end figures match year total. | on markets where it yields too high a price. |
| 5. Generate possible improvements on the rule (from in-house, competitors, con-sultants, etc.). | Take several random dates within each month and use those as averages. | Study markets where pricing was clearly off and then develop better criteria. |
| 6. Test the new rules, either in real world pilot settings or via simulation. | Compare old and new rules on past fraudulent cases. | Try both pricing schemes in new test markets or in ones with strong competitors. |

## LEVEL 3: WEIGHING IT OUT

As decisions increase in complexity and importance, the dangers of intuition and simple rules rise accordingly. Automated expertise is reliable only for de-cisions you have made dozens—or better yet, hundreds—of times. Simple rules are just that: simple. They are not designed to cope with situations characterized by great complexity or uncertainty. When you are facing an im-portant decision that is complex, uncertain, or unique, you must find a sys-tematic way to rigorously evaluate the strength of the evidence and then pick the choice that the weight of the evidence favors. This is where decision or importance weighting techniques come in.

Benjamin Franklin outlined one such weighting technique. His approach (cited at the beginning of this chapter) works well when only two alterna-tives exist. However, when you must rank numerous options without losing valuable information, it's time for a weighted decision model. These models work much like Franklin's simple list of pros and cons, only more precisely. They enable decision-makers to list all important variables, give some factors more weight than others, apply those weights, and add up the results to get an overall score for each alternative.[14] (A more detailed description of how to build such a model appears below.)

Given the inherent limitations of intuition and rules of thumb, one might expect decision-makers to be delighted with the more consistent approach provided by modeling techniques. Weighted decision models can help process large amounts of information without losing valuable pieces. They never suffer from distraction, fatigue, boredom, or random error. They are consistent, week after week. And once the model is built, the rating scheme and weights can be used again for future decisions.

Yet in spite of these obvious advantages, most people treat these kinds of analytical models the same way many young children treat a plateful of creamed spinach or canned broccoli: with a nearly instinctive distaste. They are particularly resistant to the idea that simple techniques can validly make such subjective evaluations as hiring a senior associate or launching a new product. For some, that resistance may stem simply from unfamiliarity with the statistical techniques involved. Many more, however, subscribe to the widespread assumption that human judgment is more discerning than a model. They are reluctant to believe that simple mathematical calculations can match the complexity of the human mind.

The evidence, however, proves otherwise. When computer models were first introduced by banks many decades ago to assist in loan decisions, few loan officers believed that a simplified model of their own seasoned judgments could come close to their professional performance. Even the researchers who conducted those early studies expected such simple models to be no more than a floor that might support the intuitive expertise of new, not-yet-skilled loan officers. Imagine everyone's surprise, however, when that supposed floor turned out to be a ceiling! Few loan officers could outperform the models.[15]

Still inclined to favor "expert" judgment over a more systematic technique? Consider the Colorado highway safety study. Colorado state officials had to decide how to allocate scarce funds to improve highway safety. Traditionally, decisions as to which road segments would be upgraded were made by "expert intuition," as well as in response to political pressure from people who recently had relatives killed in an auto accident.

In the study, twenty-one experienced Colorado highway engineers were presented with information such as lane width, curves/mile, grade, traffic volume, intersections, and so on for thirty-nine segments of a two-lane rural highway and were asked to predict which segments were the most dangerous. A weighted decision model was built based on the same criteria. Finally, the seven-year accident rate was calculated for each highway segment to provide an objective assessment of highway safety.

How did the experts do? On a scale where 1.00 represents a perfect match with the actual accident rate, their predictions achieved only .50. Even the most accurate engineer's predictions achieved only a .64 match. And the model? When compared against the true accident rate, its predictions achieved a .80 match.[16] No one with the skills of an experienced highway engineer enjoys being replaced by a model, especially a simple one that just multiplies and adds. But if you were driving on Colorado's rural roads, would you rather that safety improvement decisions be made by engineers or by the weighted decision model?

Study after study—in a wide range of fields—has come to the same conclusion: the benefits of *consistency* provided by a decision-making model usually exceed any losses of human *complexity*[17] (applied unreliably).

---

Lesson: Substituting a simple, but systematic, model for a human expert's intuition is usually better than intuition alone.

---

 **Build a decision-weighting model.**

Here's how to build a weighting model, along with an example to demonstrate each step.

1. Say it in numbers. Make the criteria or attributes in your model numerical.
2. Assign importance weights to each factor, based on their relative importance.
3. Compute the final measures. (This step naturally lends itself to a spreadsheet analysis. But when assessing just a few alternatives, it is also easily performed with a hand calculator or even by ranking options on the back of a paper napkin.)

Suppose you are judging applicants to an MBA program (or to any position in your organization). You could simply read the application folders and decide to accept or reject each applicant. That's intuition. And if you're experienced at recruiting, you may possess enough "automated expertise" derived from years of practice to do it reasonably well. But, like our MBA students or the radiologists, you would probably give different answers from one week to the next. You could also rank the applicants based on a dictionary or threshold rule, but that might cause you to neglect important information. Decision weighting will allow for a more systematic, consistent approach.

To begin, you must first identify and quantify the factors you will use to make your decision. In this case, the relevant factors would likely be quality of the personal essay, selectivity of the applicant's undergraduate institution, undergraduate major, college GPA, work experience, and scores on the

Graduate Management Admission Test (GMAT). Some of these factors are already quantified, such as the GPA and GMAT scores. To quantify the other factors, rate them on some numerical scale (or have an independent expert rate them for you). In Figure 6-2, we list all of these factors as they naturally occur. Note that all factors, including those that are verbal, must be rated numerically before proceeding to the next step. For instance, the verbal readings of the Personal Essay might be transformed as follows: Excellent = 5, Strong = 4, . . . Poor = 5.

| Applic. # | Personal Essay | College Major | College GPA | Work Exper. | Gender | GMAT Verbal | GMAT Quant. |
|---|---|---|---|---|---|---|---|
| 1 | Poor | Science | 2.50 | 10 | Male | 99% | 60% |
| 2 | Excellent | Business | 3.82 | 0 | Male | 70% | 80% |
| 3 | Average | Other | 2.96 | 15 | Female | 90% | 80% |
| 117 | Weak | Business | 3.10 | 100 | Male | 98% | 99% |
| 118 | Strong | Other | 3.44 | 60 | Female | 68% | 67% |
| 119 | Excellent | Science | 2.16 | 5 | Male | 85% | 25% |
| 120 | Strong | Business | 3.96 | 12 | Male | 30% | 58% |
| Ranges: | 5 Levels | 3 Levels | 2.0–4.0 | 0–100 | 2 Levels | 0–100 | 0–100 |

*Figure 6–2* **Setup for a Linear Model**

Second, weigh the importance of each factor relative to the others. This is the heart of the decision weighting technique. There are several ways to do this. The easiest is to allocate a hundred points across all the factors. For instance, you might decide that the personal essay should count for 5 percent of the decision, the undergraduate major should count for 10 percent, and so on, until you have reached 100 percent (see the accompanying table, third column).[18]

Finally, multiply each factor's score by the appropriate weight and add all the weighted scores to come up with an overall score for the applicant. For instance, an excellent personal essay would translate into five points (a score of 100 for "excellent" multiplied by 5 percent. Using spreadsheet software, a computer can crunch the numbers, freeing your attention for the critical judgments in steps 1 and 2: picking the factors you consider significant enough to include in the model and deciding what weights to assign them. As long as you make sure to include all the important factors, this kind of "subjective" model (so-called because you *subjectively* assign weights to each factor) will work well.

## BOOTSTRAPPING: BUILDING MODELS OF EXPERT JUDGMENT

As we have seen, even the simplest models lead to more reliable decisions than human intuition alone. But models bolstered by expert judgment can work even better. In the hypothetical MBA applicant example above, we assigned the weights to each factor intuitively, based on our best judgment. But you can more reliably choose the weights for your model by collecting the best judgments of experts and then using that model to *outperform* the expert on new cases.

This process is called "bootstrapping" because you're pulling yourself to a higher level of performance by your own bootstraps. It works because of one simple idea. When a person makes a prediction, you get wisdom mixed in with "random noise": serious inconsistencies due to fatigue, boredom, and all the other factors that make us human. The ideal decision process would eliminate the inconsistencies but retain the real insights that underlie the prediction. This is precisely what bootstrapping does: *It eliminates the noise, and retains the core wisdom of the human expert.* When you put in the same facts a week later, you always get the same judgment.

### Bootstrapping Logic

In bootstrapping, instead of directly assigning weights, as we did in the MBA admissions case, you allow experts to make careful intuitive judgments on a series of cases, then you use a statistical technique (called "regression analysis") to *infer* what weights they were implicitly applying. The regression analysis calculates how much weight, on average, the experts put on each of the underlying criteria or factors to arrive at their rating. (Anyone who has studied statistics can conduct a regression analysis. Standard computer software packages exist for this.)

Bootstrapping is especially useful when experts are good at making judgments but can't articulate why they make them. It also helps when people don't feel comfortable stating their importance weights outright. Perhaps they don't trust themselves to be accurate, don't wish to expose their own "importance policy" to the scrutiny of others, or consider it demeaning or meaningless to capture their expertise in a set of simple numeric weights.[19]

For instance, a gifted claims handler with an excellent nose for sniffing out fraudulent cases was about to retire from her insurance company. She had the uncommon ability to make good intuitive decisions—decisions based on "automated expertise"—because she'd accumulated (and learned from) so much experience over the years. Unfortunately, she couldn't spell out how she did it. All she could say was that she looked at such factors as lack of adequate support data, valuable property that did not fit the insured's income level, evasiveness in the police report, financial difficulty such as loss of a job, personal problems like divorce, and frequent or suspicious past claims. By asking the adjuster to rate a wide cross-section of applications for fraud potential, the company could statistically infer what weights she used and thereby capture her valuable expertise before she left the company.

Dozens of studies show that this odd system actually produces superior judgments. Many researchers have compared intuitive judgments to those based on linear bootstrapped models—in fields ranging from the judgments of physicians to Wall Street analysts.[20] In nearly all the cases, the model produced by bootstrapping performed at least as well as the experts themselves—and usually better.[21] Many decision-makers use bootstrapping implicitly when they average the predictions of multiple experts. What they do, in essence, is cancel out much of the random error contained in any one expert's views. This is why "consensus forecasts" often beat most of the experts on which they are based.

Lesson: Models produced by bootstrapping—using the best judgments of experts to create a systematic model—nearly always outperform the experts themselves.

| Type of Tasks Experts Judged | Intuitive Prediction | Subjective Model | (Bootstrapping Effect) |
|---|---|---|---|
| Graduate Student Admission | .19 | .25 | (.06) |
| Cancer Patients Life Expectancy | −.01 | .13 | (.14) |
| Personality Test Scores | .28 | .31 | (.03) |
| Teaching Effectiveness | .35 | .56 | (.21) |
| Insurance Agent Performance | .13 | .14 | (.01) |
| IQ Test Scores | .47 | .51 | (.04) |
| Changes in Security Prices | .23 | .28 | (.05) |
| Means (over 15 studies) | .33 | .39 | (.06) |

*Figure 6-3* **Typical Bootstrapping Results**

## CREATING AN OBJECTIVE ASSESSMENT

Although decisions based on a subjective model (that is, one based on expert judgment) can come out far better than intuitive decisions, they're still wrong some of the time. Can you do still better? The answer is often no. But if the same decision is made repeatedly, the outcomes of past decisions are available, and you have good reason to expect that the future will resemble the past, then you can build an objective model of the choice.

You construct an objective model in exactly the same way as a subjective model. But instead of statistically inferring the decision weights from the subjective predictions of an expert, you infer them from actual past results. That's where the superior matching score of over .80 came from in the Colorado highway study. The past accident rates, which were known, were the basis for building an objective model. In dozens of areas, objective linear models prove excellent decision-making tools, far outperforming simple screening rules. Financial institutions use them extensively in evaluating credit applications. So does the IRS in choosing whom to audit. Insurance companies use them to estimate risk levels on the basis of actuarial data.[22]

They are also ideal for creating all kinds of estimates and forecasts. Indeed, both objective and subjective linear models can be valuable tools for preparing the estimates you'll need in the intelligence-gathering phase. A regression analysis will even give you the range and level of confidence we recommended in chapter 5 for all estimates and forecasts. Statistical analysis (of either an objective model or a bootstrapped subjective model) can also demonstrate that some of the information you have been collecting doesn't help in making predictions. If so, you can often avoid the cost of continuing to collect it.

Be cautious, however, in assuming that you can create objective models to predict the future, especially when trying to predict complex economic phenomena such as prices or market shares. There is considerable evidence that an objective model based on the past may be a poor or dangerous predictor in a changing environment.

## MIXING MODELS AND HUMANS

Models, especially objective ones, are almost always superior to human intuition. In a changing environment, however—where human expertise is used to *update* and *extend* the model—research has shown that a combined approach can add great value. In times of change, human intuition can not only predict but also understand why and when a predictor will be more or less valid. It can sense when changes in the environment mean that the past (on which the objective model is based) may not reflect the future, or which specific predictors will carry over to the future and which will not. In such cases, studies have shown that averaging the judgments of human experts and a decision model produce the most accurate results. The blend of model and human intuition hedges the bet that would otherwise place complete trust in one or the other.[23]

We'd be remiss to end this section without noting that decision weighting models can be misused. The epidemic of ranking surveys—from best cities to best employers to best universities—is an increasingly controversial use of this systematic tool in a seemingly scientific way. Most of these rankings are conducted by magazine publishers, who have found them to be extremely lucrative. However, if you are going to sell a rankings story year after year, you need surprises. No one is going to pay much attention if the same three cities (or companies or schools) top the list every year. Where does the volatility come from? Probably not from major changes in relative quality. Cities, companies, and schools rarely change that dramatically in a single year. Rather, the volatility comes from the survey methodology itself. Editors use a weighted average of factors (such as employee turnover and benefits for companies or class size, acceptance rate, and GPA for universities) to reach their final decision. And how are the weights assigned? Not only subjectively, but with deliberate variation from year to year.[24]

If "variance" sells, by all means use intuitive methods or rig the weights strategically. But if you want consistency, use a linear model. On average, it will yield greater accuracy.

## LEVEL 4: INCORPORATING VALUES INTO YOUR MODEL

When a decision is truly important and complex, it may pay to conduct a more comprehensive value assessment. Value analysis refines importance weighting techniques by considering how different factors affect broader goals and how increases in the rating of a factor add value. The technical details can be quite complicated, and you will need to channel much of the detail work to experts in decision analysis, but the concepts are not difficult. Once you know that this option exists, you will be able to gather the necessary resources when it's time to make that big, important decision.

First, value analysis goes beyond the lists of factors or criteria to uncover the true *values* of the decision-maker. It does this by linking the factors to key objectives. For instance, in the admissions case, you would start by determining the broad characteristics you were looking for in your applicants, such as intellectual ability, professional commitment, and leadership potential. Then you would use scientific methods to determine how well GMAT scores, undergraduate major, and so forth actually predict those three overarching criteria.

Second, value analysis addresses the fact that an increase in a given factor does not necessarily add value at a constant rate. In the case of admissions to an MBA program, for example, twenty years of work experience is not necessarily twice as valuable as ten years of work experience. At some point, work experience contributes to overall performance in smaller and smaller amounts. Similarly, you may believe that an increase in GPA from 3.6 to 3.8 is much more impressive than an increase from 3.0 to 3.2. Decision weighting models can't account for uneven changes in value. Value analysis can.

The technique that combines these refinements is called multi-attribute utility (MAU) analysis. This is where a trained decision analyst comes in. The process is costly in terms of time and effort, requiring one or more days with the analyst. Does all this refinement yield better decisions? Many analysts think so. MAU analysis has been applied effectively to such decisions as locating airports and power plants, prioritizing fire departments' services, and setting corporate objectives.[25] One company used it to decide which of three prototype testers for very large-scale integrated circuits to bring to market.[26]

A large oil and gas multinational used value analysis to help decide where to build a $500 million pilot plant to test a process that could convert natural gas into middle distillate fuels. More than ten countries were considered (from Germany to Malaysia to New Zealand), and they had dozens of advantages and disadvantages. In some countries the investment climate was very attractive; in others labor costs were low or the supply of natural gas abundant.

To make the decision, the executives identified four overriding objectives: financial attractiveness, the degree of uncertainty and risk, strategic fit, and organizational desirability. They connected the features of specific countries with these objectives in a "goal hierarchy." Senior executives then determined the weights for the higher-level objectives, and technical experts estimated and weighted the lower-level ones. Because the analysis was complete, careful, and generally honest, the company reached agreement on the overall ranking among the ten possible countries and built the plant in the country that came out on top.

General Motors also regularly uses value analysis to facilitate major corporate decisions. GM's decision support center sends two people—an econometric modeler and a facilitator of their "dialogue decision process"—to assist managers throughout the company.[27] Interestingly, creating the right frame turns out to be the most important component of this process. When redesigning a car, for example, representatives from manufacturing, design, marketing, finance, and engineering are all sent to the decision support center with their division's proposed plans. Of course, none of the department-sponsored designs are acceptable from the company-wide perspective. The five managers are sequestered in a room with the two decision support staff members, and nothing else happens until they have created a common frame. This process has taken as long as several weeks; but however long it requires, it must be done as the foundation for all that follows.

Whether or not to apply this kind of highly sophisticated technique to your decision boils down to a subjective trade-off between cost/effort and decision quality. Is one more day of analysis (and the associated cost) worth an increase in the quality or defensibility of your next decision? If big bucks are at stake, the answer is probably, *yes.*

## DIFFERENT METHODS; DIFFERENT RESULTS

Which decision-making method you choose matters. Different methods weigh criteria differently—and will likely lead you to choose different options. To illustrate this, we ran an experiment, applying three of the four methods to the decision many MBA students must make: where to relocate upon graduation. First, we asked our students to make a list of their top ten U.S. cities for relocation, assuming no differences in job attractiveness and equal salaries (adjusted for cost-of-living). They made intuitive decisions based on information from the *Places Rated Almanac*, which profiles ninety-seven U.S. cities in terms of climate, housing cost, health care, environment, crime, transportation, education, recreation, the arts, and economics.[28]

We also gave each student a personal computer software package that was programmed with procedures for threshold rules, dictionary rules, and value analysis.[29] The students chose their own thresholds and tightened or loosened them until the program came up with ten cities. For the dictionary rule, students ranked the attributes in order of importance and indicated for each how small a difference would constitute a tie. Whenever a tie occurred, the program would go to the next most important attribute as specified by the student.

The value analysis procedure required students to assign each attribute a weight and determine how increases in a factor's rating added value. For example, an increase in the average summer temperature might be greatly valued up to, say, 80 degrees F, and then flatten or decline in attractiveness. The computer program then performed the calculations and identified the top ten cities. Figure 6-4 shows the four rankings for one of our students.

| Intuitive Judgment | Threshold Rule | Dictionary Rule | Value Analysis |
|---|---|---|---|
| San Francisco | Boston | Seattle | Seattle |
| Honolulu | Buffalo | San Francisco | San Diego |
| Boston | Cincinnati | Cleveland | San Francisco |
| Chicago | Cleveland | Chicago | Cleveland |
| Nassau | Columbus | Milwaukee | Chicago |
| Sacramento | Pittsburgh | San Diego | Washington |
| Denver | Portland | Cincinnati | Portland |
| San Diego | San Diego | New York | Pittsburgh |
| New Brunswick | Seattle | Baltimore | Boston |
| New York | Washington | Dallas | Cincinnati |

*Figure 6–4* **City Selection via Four Different Methods**

Each student thus generated four lists of ten cities. On average, the value analysis method differed from each of the other methods about half the time. What accounts for these discrepancies? Simply the fact that the methods process and weight information differently. For instance, the student who placed Honolulu near the top of his list based on intuitive judgment may have had romantic ideas about living in Hawaii. However, because those ideas have little to do with his actual trade-offs among climate, cost of living, travel distance, and so forth, the city doesn't appear on the Top Ten lists generated by the other approaches. Similarly, Milwaukee appeared only on the list generated by the dictionary rule, apparently because that city scored high on a few important criteria (such as being near his family), but not on others.[30]

Interestingly, our study also demonstrated—once again—that people have an unreasonable faith in their intuitions. Although over 80 percent of our MBA students knew they had been beaten by their own decision-weighting models in a prior study, when it came to selecting cities to live in, these same students relied on the intuitive approach almost as much as the much more systematic value analysis. This held true even *after* they recognized that their intuitively generated list disagreed with the value analysis's top ten about half the time.

## CHOOSING A DECISION TOOL

It would be nice if there were a simple formula for determining which approach to use. Unfortunately there's not. Each of the four techniques we have described has its advantages and disadvantages. Once again, we suggest you choose the simplest method you can—without sacrificing reliability. To do so, you will need to consider the importance, complexity, and political or organizational ramifications of the decision at hand.

In terms of *importance* ask: how high are the stakes? What are the costs of a wrong decision? How frequently will the decision be made? Improving seemingly minor decisions that are made frequently, like loan or admissions decisions, may do as much good over time as making one big decision well, such as choosing the next CEO. You should also consider how much time and other resources you have to make the decision correctly.

Now consider *complexity*: is the information involved so complex that the decision-makers suffer from mental overload? Are the deeper values underlying a decision difficult to articulate? Time pressure, resource constraints, political ramifications, or issues related to justification may also influence your decision.[31]

Finally, consider the *organizational ramifications*: do you want others to know how much emphasis you gave to different factors? What if those characteristics are sensitive? Decision weighting and value analysis are transparent techniques. That is, the rules, priorities, and values on which you based the decision process are readily apparent to others. This is always good for decision-makers themselves who can now *privately* examine their process with full clarity. But can you tolerate the public, or even your boss, being able to examine the process in the same way? Will that transparency be beneficial or put you at risk? Much controversy has arisen in the U.S. over the practice of police profiling, which targets minorities for more frequent questioning. Similarly, banks making loan decisions or universities giving preference to the children of alumni or large donors might worry about the public scrutiny, or even legal liability, arising from a too-transparent decision policy. Thus, one of the attributes of higher levels of the pyramid—increased transparency of the process—is a double-edged sword.

That said, here are some general guidelines to help you make the tradeoffs between techniques:

**Intuition** is surprisingly unreliable for all but the most repetitive decisions, where expertise has become truly "automated." But because it takes so little effort, it may be appropriate for some small decisions with limited complexity. It may also be necessary in an emergency where there is no time for a comprehensive assessment or where a decision may be inherently intuitive, such as an artistic judgment. But don't be too quick to favor intuition even in these cases. What may seem like a purely intuitive judgment can often be broken down into components and analyzed. Orley Ashenfelter, a Princeton University economist, developed a simple model to predict the quality of new Bordeaux wines. Usually, wine experts carefully taste samples of a new year to predict its ultimate quality. To their surprise and dismay, a three-factor equation (measuring winter rainfall, average summer temperature, and harvest rainfall) does just as well.[32]

*Rules* take a little more effort, provide a bit more quality, are easy to explain and can often be used to defend a decision. But remember that they have built-in biases and dangers that must be carefully considered. And as times change, many golden rules no longer shine.

*Decision weighting* takes some effort the first time, but it can be used quickly thereafter. It yields high-quality decisions and very high clarity, but your importance weights are totally transparent. And the environment shouldn't change much if you're going to apply today's model to tomorrow's decisions.

*Value analysis,* while providing the highest-quality decisions, requires a maximum level of effort and may be very difficult to explain and use. Nonetheless, the final decision will be highly explicit in terms of the data employed, assumptions made, and values and weights assigned. If done right, it should withstand a fierce public or private inquiry. Once again, however, we caution you about the total transparency, all the more so because of the use of consultants.

---

Lesson: Choose the simplest technique you can—without sacrificing reliability. Remember, however, that the different methods process and weight information differently—and will often lead to different conclusions.

---

## IMPROVING ORGANIZATIONAL DECISIONS

Those who wish to spread these techniques through their organization have two tasks ahead: making the technical tools available and encouraging people to use them.

You may have to overcome a few technical hurdles, but just about anyone who knows a spreadsheet program can set up a table to calculate the simple form of decision weighting. A statistics expert will be needed to create the

## The Pros and Cons of Different Decision Approaches

| Method Used | Quality | Effort | Transparency* |
|---|---|---|---|
| 1. Intuition | Low | Low | Very Low |
| 2. Rules | Moderate | Little | Moderate |
| 3. Weighting | High | High/Low** | Very High |
| 4. Value Analysis | Very High | Very High | Often Low |

*Transparency refers to how easy it is to verbalize the rule, use it as a basis for learning, and self-audit, as well as to persuade or legitimate the decision to others.
**To construct an importance weighting model takes considerable effort the first time; however, thereafter it can be swiftly used again by plugging in new numbers.

more complicated regression model that determines implicit weights. In large organizations, enough in-house expertise may exist to examine all four approaches. Statisticians, operations researchers, or market researchers should be able to devise tests to measure the accuracy and distortion in intuitive judgments. They can also perform the regressions and perhaps would be able to apply value analysis. For smaller firms, outside consultants may be required, either from quantitatively oriented management consulting firms or academia. Few consultants, however, will be familiar with both the behavioral and quantitative literatures referred to in this chapter.

The more difficult problems, however, will be organizational rather than technical. You may encounter considerable reluctance and skepticism on the part of decision-makers. The benefits of intuitive or rule-based techniques are easy to recognize, whereas the costs are often invisible or delayed. Further, many people will have trouble understanding how the most sophisticated methods can help with decisions. (Only highly mathematical types will understand the theory and calculations of multi-attribute utility analysis, but a good analyst should be able to translate any technical aspect into lay terms.) Try to persuade them by emphasizing the dangers of purely intuitive or rule-based judgments. Then present the model as no more than an encapsulation of their considerable expertise. Don't give the model too much of a separate identity, lest it be viewed as a competitor. Emphasize that the model cannot run without their inputs and may be overridden by them if circumstances warrant. Finally, keep track of the model's performance, improve it, and slowly persuade your team that everyone is better off combining intuition and analysis rather than relying on one approach alone.[33]

At Harris Investment Management, a unit of the Harris Trust and Savings

Bank in Chicago, senior executives were concerned that although the analysts and portfolio managers often had good ideas about investment strategies, they were at times distracted by recent market information or the current strategy's poor performance. So they decided to create a model that would combine experts' insights (e.g., about the yield curve, national economy, specific industry sectors) to guide its overall investment strategy. Use of the models ultimately improved the company's bottom-line results, but it was not easy.

First, analysts and portfolio experts had to be persuaded that their intuitive judgments might not be totally free of bias (a delicate matter). Second, the experts needed to accept the model that incorporated their insights as their friend, not their rival. Third, the experts wanted the power to override the model in case its use would be clearly inappropriate (as during the 1987 stock market crash). Several intuitive experts left the bank because they perceived their role as having been "diminished" by the new process.

Each organization must find its own optimal balance for layering intuitive and analytic approaches. Sometimes a fifty-fifty combination of a bootstrap model and your top experts is best.[34] Harris used a combination to select bonds. Their bootstrap model took into account factors such as industry sectors, maturation profile, and interest rates, whereas analysts and portfolio managers considered trading liquidity, special bond features, ethical investment constraints, and new market information.

Here are some practical suggestions for disseminating better techniques for reaching conclusions within your organization:

 **Experiment with all four approaches.**
Make people aware that they use methods at different levels of the pyramid and that each level has its place. During your next retreat, when tough choices come up, split the group into three teams. Ask one team to tackle the issue intuitively, another team to use an explicit set of rules, and a third team to build an importance weighting model. Then see if they come back with different rankings, and if so, ask them why.

 **Create a "test-retest" study to demonstrate the limits of intuition.**
Identify where important decisions in your organization are currently being made on purely intuitive grounds. Check the track record of these intuitive experts and see if you can perform a test-retest study concerning their consistency. Are some of your experts perhaps as

unreliable as the radiologists or our MBA students? If so, consider bootstrapping.

 **Perform a "rule audit."**

What rules are commonly used in your organization and with what results? Do the people who use them appreciate the rules' distortions? Ask for cases where the rule would be greatly off the mark. Work with these decision-makers to fine-tune rules or update and adjust them to changes in the decision environment.

 **Encourage people to try analytical models.**

Explore opportunities for modeling in such areas as personnel, new product design, compensation, sales prediction, budget estimation, selecting R&D projects, and so on. Encourage your experts to create models based on their own criteria and then challenge them to outperform their own model.

 **Talk with colleagues.**

Discuss explicitly with your staff the trade-offs you are willing to make among consistency, distortion, speed, and clarity. Perfection has its price, and value analysis should be reserved only for the most complex and important decisions, especially those that are now-or-never and can't be reversed or substantially revised later. Help decision-makers consider those trade-offs and lead them to appropriate method selections. Challenge yourself and your colleagues to articulate the reasoning underlying every decision.

---

## Deciding Under Fire

You thought you had a week to analyze the data you have so carefully collected and reach a final decision; you've just learned that you have only twenty-four hours. Don't panic. And more important, don't abandon a good decision-making process. You still have twenty-four hours, not twenty-four minutes. Don't ask: is the option I'm leaning toward at this moment good enough? Instead, remember that you still must systematically evaluate all your decision options. If time is really short and systematic weighing (even on the back of an envelope) not really an option, try to rank your top alternatives by screening them against the most important decision criteria in your frame.

Fortunately, even formal decision weighting models can be built quickly. How? By using intuition to assign the importance weights. When you must resort to intuition as a decision tool, improve on it by using multiple people's intuition, if possible. Ask several colleagues to assign importance weights and then average the responses, thus eliminating extreme views. Better yet, preserve uncertainty by running the model with the *range* of intuitively-assigned importance weights. Looking at the extremes in each range allows you to apply the robustness test. If the outcomes don't differ much, you know you are selecting a robust alternative. If the outcomes differ greatly (and choosing the wrong alternative will be costly), you may need to find ways to hedge your bets, build in flexible options, or extend your decision-making deadline.

Finally, find someone whose perspective tends to be different from yours and ask for a half hour of their time to check through your reasoning process. Do they see anything you might have overlooked?

---

## APPLYING DISCIPLINE TO DECISION-MAKING

How far up the pyramid decision-makers should climb will have to be judged case-by-case. However, in our experience, decision-makers rely too much on the bottom-level approaches. There are notable exceptions. In some fields, such as credit rating, magazine-subscription solicitation, and stock analysis, where companies have a great deal of money at stake, people regularly use formal models to make decisions. But in many other domains they turn to formal models far less. In fact, in situations truly central to people's lives, like medical, legal, and personal financial decisions, people have been far less quick to recognize the increased quality of decision-making they could achieve by using more formal decision rules and systematic models.

We don't want to minimize the importance of highly trained experts. But professionals should rethink their roles. Their honed intuitive skills are crucial for framing questions, collecting evidence, and identifying the pertinent factors in a decision. But once the proper frame has been chosen and the right intelligence has been collected, the final choice calls principally for discipline in following the right rules. If organizations want to build greater quality into their decisions (as well as their products and services), decision-makers will need to focus more on the techniques toward the top of our pyramid. Shooting from the hip when many data points are involved is simply unprofessional. As the sixteenth-century British philosopher and statesman Francis Bacon observed, even in his far simpler world: "Neither hand nor mind, left to themselves, amounts to much; instruments and aids are the means to perfection."[35]

CHAPTER 7

# Managing Group Decisions

None of us is as smart as all of us.  —*Satchel Paige*

"**H**OW COULD WE have been so stupid?" demanded John F. Kennedy after his administration's invasion of Cuba had been soundly defeated at the Bay of Pigs. The invasion was one of the most ill-conceived in American history. Yet the planners of this operation included some of the smartest people in America. They didn't fail because they were stupid. They failed because Kennedy and his advisors stumbled over the most common traps lurking in group decision-making terrain. They agreed prematurely on the wrong solution. Inadvertently, they gave each other biased feedback that made the group as a whole feel certain that it was making the right choice. They discouraged each other from looking at the flaws in their assumptions. And they ignored dissenters who tried to speak up.

The trouble began with framing. Kennedy unquestioningly accepted the CIA's frame of the problem: "How can we help the Cuban exiles overthrow Castro?" and the CIA's only two alternatives: invade or do nothing. Once he was framed by others, the decision-making process only got further and further off track.

Intelligence was gathered poorly. Kennedy, his advisors, and the CIA planners ignored disconfirming evidence provided by the U.S. State Department, British intelligence experts, and others that would have challenged key assumptions. The plan rested on the belief that Castro's army and air force were weak (although evidence indicated otherwise), that the Cuban exiles had high morale and were willing to invade Cuba without U.S. troops (although CIA agents working with these exiles in Guatemala had recently put down a mutiny), and that the planned invasion was "secret" and would be a surprise (although the U.S. press had reported details of the training). Other disconfirming evidence was on file—but the right parties (e.g., those at the State Department's Cuban desk) were never asked for it.

And when it came to making the final decision, those who questioned the emerging majority view either censored themselves or were pressured to get on board. In a memorandum prior to the Bay of Pigs invasion, Arthur Schlesinger, Jr., wrote that he considered the proposed invasion of Cuba immoral. After learning of this, Robert Kennedy, then attorney general, took Schlesinger aside and told him: "You may be right or you may be wrong, but the President has made his mind up. Don't push it any further. . . . This is a time to be behind your President." Schlesinger remained silent when he attended meetings of the Kennedy team.

Here was a group of smart people who understood the grave international ramifications of their decision, but the result of their decision-making was an utter failure.[1] Unfortunately, the Kennedy policymakers have plenty of company in their errors.[2] Similar mistakes were committed in the group decisions that led the U.S. to mismanage the Vietnam War, General Motors to create the poorly conceived Corvair,[3] and NASA to launch the ill-fated space shuttle *Challenger*.[4] And thousands of equally disastrous but less well known examples reside within organizational archives and individual memories.[5] You undoubtedly have your own stories.

---

Lesson: Teams, on average, make better decisions than individuals. But some of the absolute worst decisions are also made by groups.

---

## GROUPS NEED A GOOD DECISION PROCESS

Teams increasingly pervade our organizational lives, and there's no reason to expect that will change anytime soon. Nor should it. Whether you love teams or hate them, groups are excellent decision-makers in many ways. They offer greater thinking capacity, multiple viewpoints (or, in our language, frames), a broader information base, and links to activities taking place in various parts of the organization. Discussion and the need for consensus moderate extreme views. Participation in the decision-making process can generate widespread buy-in when it comes time for action.

It might seem safe to assume that with so many good minds working together, an excellent decision must surely emerge. Right? Wrong! As anyone who has taken part in a group decision knows, high quality decisions do not automatically arise from a group of smart people with shared goals.

No matter how brilliant their members may be, groups aren't superhuman. Decision-making groups have their characteristic strengths, but they also have predictable weaknesses. And while research indicates that, on average, teams make better decisions than individuals, some of the absolute worst decisions are also made by groups.

And so we return again to what is perhaps the single most important point in our book: good decision *processes* are the best hope for good decision *outcomes*.

But as anyone who has ever led a group knows, good group processes do not emerge naturally; they must be managed—and they must be managed well. Kennedy's failure as a group leader in the Bay of Pigs decision was not that he managed destructively (e.g., he was not autocratically trying to generate support for a predetermined choice), but that he did not manage well. In this chapter we will turn to the principles and tools that can help decision-makers manage groups well.

Two caveats. The first: the subject of managing groups deserves an entire volume of its own, and indeed excellent ones have been written. In this chapter we will focus on *decision-making* in and by groups—and in particular, on *managing conflict* in groups, for it is in how well conflict is managed (or not) that most determines how well decision-making groups succeed. We will explore why people tend to avoid conflict, and why it should be embraced. We will also look at how well-managed conflict can improve decision-making. We will *not* cover, except in passing, issues of team building (nor will we distinguish between groups and teams), how groups should be composed, the motivation of groups, power and influence, and organizational culture and politics. These are important subjects, and readers interested in them would do well to consult some of the books we list in the endnotes.[6]

The second caveat: we will paint a somewhat simplified picture of group decision-making. For the purposes of our discussion, we will assume that the group has both the power and the desire to succeed. In reality, jealousy, animosity, and posturing can destroy group productivity. Dominant individuals can subvert the process. Personal agendas can derail attempts to move ahead. Or it can be a mission in futility: groups may be asked to generate decisions that have, in fact, already been made by those at the top.

Of course in every group, members bring private agendas and individual frames. However, we are going to talk about those cases where the private agendas are not so overwhelming that they preclude the possibility of good group process and where the individual frames are not so rigid that they can't be modified for the greater organizational good.

But even without the pitfalls of misaligned motivations, other potential enemies of good group decision processes abound. Ask people what they

## (a) Groupthink

Problem 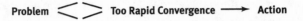 Too Rapid Convergence ⟶ Action

## (b) Ideal Group Process

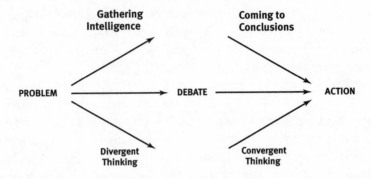

## (c) Debating Society

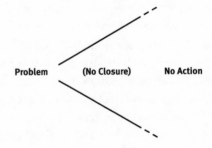

*Figure 7-1*

dread about group decision-making and they are likely to complain most about discussions that drone on and on without resolution, or deep, divisive conflicts that lead to a hostile impasse. These groups follow what we call the "debating society" model, depicted at the bottom of figure 7-1. In such groups the decision-making process forever expands. There's no closure, and no action.

However a second, less-well-recognized enemy to a good group decision process also lurks: too much conformity (see the top of the accompanying figure). In these cases you've barely had time to pass the donuts and the group is ready to adjourn. It seems ideal: no arguments, no meeting. Isn't that a decision-maker's dream? In this case, however, the dangers lurk below the surface, like hidden icebergs waiting to sink the ship. In fact, converging too rapidly on the chosen conclusion is as great a barrier (if not greater) to good decision-making as no closure at all.[7] For this reason, we explore it first.

---

Lesson: Too *little* conflict is as dangerous to a decision-making group as too much conflict.

---

## THE LURE OF PREMATURE HARMONY

Harmony (and the cohesiveness it implies) seems an appropriate goal for a productive group. After all, conflict is usually unpleasant. It slows down the decision-making process in long debates and requires a seemingly endless series of meetings. It can corrode previously collegial relationships. At worst, it torpedoes many groups, blowing a seemingly benign decision process out of the water and creating animosities that may linger long after the decision fades.

In contrast, it seems reasonable to expect that a cohesive group will perform well.[8] Consider Benjamin Franklin's comment upon signing the Declaration of Independence: "We must all hang together, or assuredly we shall all hang separately." To generate cohesion, many decision-makers ask, shouldn't harmony be a goal? Ultimately, yes. But in chapter 4, we saw how *undue* optimism and *false* efficiency can derail a good decision process. So, too, *premature* harmony can send a smart decision-making group into a brick wall.

The (mis)conception that "conflict is bad" and "harmony is good" leads people to believe that eliminating—or at least reducing—conflict will hasten decision-making. But it may be a false efficiency. Of course, a quick consensus is not always bad. If the group really does not have time for extended discussion, the problem is relatively simple, and the leader is fairly certain of the correct solution, agreement to preserve harmony can unite the team behind a decision. In a brief discussion, members can simply add ideas that may help them implement the chosen alternative. But for the vast majority of decisions, especially those of any import, the best process is at first *expansive*, with sufficient time for different opinions, converging on a final decision only *after* the group has considered the problem from diverse perspectives.

When a group strives for *premature* harmony, too few alternatives are examined and too few objectives taken into account. The decision frame or policy alternative first put on the table may be adopted, whether good or bad. Intelligence-gathering becomes one-sided, especially concerning the risks inherent in the preferred option. Confirming evidence is sought; disconfirming evidence (and disconfirming speakers) shunned.

The most successful leaders are acutely aware of this, as was Alfred P. Sloan, Jr., when as chairman of General Motors' board of directors, he said: "Gentlemen, I take it we are all in complete agreement on the decision here. . . . Then I propose we postpone further discussion of this matter until our next meeting to give ourselves time to develop disagreement and perhaps gain some understanding of what the decision is all about."

---

Lesson: How well conflict is managed determines whether decision-making groups fail or succeed.

---

## THE CASE FOR CONFLICT

Conflict has its place in fostering creativity and learning. Consider the words of the philosopher and educator John Dewey:

> Conflict is the gadfly of thought. It stirs us to observation and memory. It instigates to invention. It shocks us out of sheeplike passivity, and sets us at noting and contriving. . . . Conflict is a *sine qua non* of reflection and ingenuity.

The American poet Walt Whitman also called for embracing conflict, asking:

> Have you learned lessons only of those who admired you, and were tender with you, and stood aside for you? Have you not learned great lessons of

those who rejected you, and braced themselves against you? . . . and disputed the passage with you?[9]

At Nissan, car designers with diametrically opposed work styles, priorities, and worldviews are hired in "divergent pairs" specifically to generate creative conflict. Jerry Hirshberg, founder and retired president of the award-winning Nissan Design International (NDI) in La Jolla, California, developed this quirky employment plan. NDI's output, however, is far from quirky. The studio has won countless awards, and more than four million of their cars (including the Pathfinder sport utility vehicle, the Infiniti series, and the Mercury Villager minivan) have won consumers' votes as well. "I believe in creative abrasion," says Hirschberg. "And I mean abrasion. . . . That friction can produce wonderful creative sparks." Further, he insists, NDI's designers, modelers, and engineers "get a kick out of the pairings because they feel valued for their own quirks. They see that the boss doesn't just tolerate divergence—he courts it. So they feel free to be themselves."[10]

Rather than eschew conflict entirely, decision-makers would do well to learn what Hirshberg knows: the right kind of conflict can drive innovation. The key, however, is to distinguish between productive and destructive conflict. **Relationship conflict** (i.e., conflict between individuals in which perceived differences in style, background, or values are under attack) will distract any group from its productive work. It is always to be avoided, or at least resolved outside the group. However, moderate amounts of **task conflict** (i.e., differences of opinion about the task at hand and how it should be completed) are necessary and valuable if a group decision-making process is going to accomplish more than simple groupthink.

In fact, numerous carefully conducted research studies corroborate that low levels of task conflict are associated with poor decision-making, while higher (albeit not very high) conflict levels are related to superior performance. Higher conflict teams have more thorough and creative discussion of decisions, gain a richer understanding of the issues, and develop a more cognitively complex perspective. They use more information and they use it better. In contrast, low conflict teams, like Kennedy's group, tend to overlook key issues or simply avoid analyzing the downside risk of the consensus option. Their understanding of the issues is often superficial or one-sided. They make poor choices.[11]

When it takes place in an atmosphere of trust and mutual respect, moderate task conflict can push members to create a more robust frame, gather better intelligence, explore more options, and examine issues in more depth. In fact, groups are likely to outperform individuals in decision-making prowess only to the extent that *moderate task conflict arises among their members and such conflicts get resolved through balanced debate and careful intelligence-gathering*. When that happens, a group is likely to understand the issues better than an individual and is more likely to choose wisely. Without it, groups lose their effectiveness.[12]

---

Lesson: *Moderate task conflict* and *low relationship conflict* is the decision-making ideal. Only then are groups likely to outperform individuals.

---

## THE PULL TOWARD CONFORMITY

Unfortunately, research also finds that productive conflict within management teams is less widespread than might be expected from its rewards. Autocratic leaders in command-and-control regimes will minimize and even eradicate conflict. Consider this description of Iraqi president Saddam Hussein: "They say he states a position and then asks questions that he then proceeds to answer himself. He runs meetings with his commanders like a tribal leader or an arrogant corporate chairman, and those who murmur in private about his decisions, or who are perceived to have failed in their duty, are either retired or executed."[13] Most of us rarely face situations quite so extreme, yet the phenomenon is not unfamiliar. In any organization where the boss clearly favors those who share the same frame of reference, dissent is effectively precluded.

Even in the absence of authoritarian leadership, however, group members themselves can suppress conflict and generate the illusion of harmony. Why? In theory, two heads are better than one. But in practice, those two heads can find themselves operating as one, without even meaning to. Within groups, members often conform to the majority opinion rather than speak their minds. They often influence each other in ways that prevent the full benefit of their independent ideas from being realized.

A classic experiment, first conducted by Solomon Asch, demonstrates how remarkably powerful the desire to conform can be. Asch showed people four lines like those below. At left is the "test line"; the other lines are labeled A, B, and C.

Each participant in the experiment was asked whether the test line was equal in length to line A, B, or C. When people are asked this question individually, over 99 percent get it right. Most can clearly see that line B is the same length as the test line, and lines A and C are not.

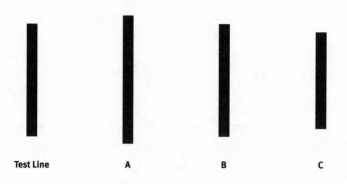

Test Line              A                B                C

Which line equals the test line?

*Figure 7-2* **Asch's Conformity Experiment**

But then Asch changed the procedure. He began asking people the question in groups, rather than individually. He also planted his research assistants as stooges, instructing them to give the wrong answer on purpose. What do you imagine happened to those who answered after the stooge before them said "line A"? Their error rate rose from under 1 percent to 3 percent. If they followed two stooges saying "line A," their error rate jumped—13 percent of them also said "A." When three or more stooges preceded them saying "A," then 33 percent of those being tested also said "A." Finally, when the group was told that a monetary reward for the group as a whole depended on how many members got it right, 47 percent of the people (excluding the stooges) gave the wrong answer.[14]

If the desire to conform can change these simple judgments, it's not surprising that others' opinions influence what people will say in a group, particularly when discussing a truly complex issue. When the implicit assumption is that everyone else agrees, individuals will tend to go along as well.[15]

The so-called Abilene paradox shows how this phenomenon plays out in group decision-making. In this apparently true story, a Texas family is sitting on its front porch on a hot, August afternoon. One person suggests a trip to Abilene, many miles away. Although no one really wants to go, everyone thinks that the others do and so each agrees. The subsequent trip to Abilene is hot, dusty, and unpleasant. Only afterwards do the family members realize that the initial suggestion, and everyone else's acquiescence, had been made just to please the others. No one really wanted to go to Abilene.[16]

## OVERCOMING GROUPTHINK

At its extreme, this pull toward conformity has come to be called "group-think." Kennedy's Bay of Pigs fiasco represents a prototypical example. Irving Janis, the researcher and author who first coined the phrase, defines groupthink as follows: "members of any small cohesive group tend to maintain esprit de corps by unconsciously developing a number of shared illusions and related norms that interfere with critical thinking and reality testing."[17] Groupthink most often occurs when there is a strong team spirit, high cohesiveness, limited contact with outsiders and outside ideas, high stress, and directive leadership. When groupthink takes over, camaraderie becomes valued over critical thinking, to the detriment of the decision at hand.[18]

Fortunately, groupthink and the pull toward conformity can be overcome. Fourteen months after the Bay of Pigs fiasco, John F. Kennedy and his advisors faced another decision-making crisis: the Soviet Union sent twenty thousand troops equipped with tactical atomic weapons and one-third of their atomic warheads to Cuba. However, U.S. policymakers had learned from experience; they approached this decision very differently from the start.

To begin, framing was broad. Robert Kennedy later recalled his brother's thinking: "Surely there was some choice between doing nothing and sending in bombers," JFK had said. Frank discussion with genuine dissension and vigorous debate became the norm. Several leaderless sessions with John Kennedy absent were held. Two subgroups met independently to generate recommendations. They actively searched for alternatives; many outsiders were consulted and treated seriously. Skepticism was widely encouraged; two key advisors were designated as critics. Reversals of judgment were welcomed. Ted Sorenson, special counsel to Kennedy, later noted: "Each of us changed his mind more than once that week on the best course of action to take." The illusion of invulnerability was gone.

After nearly two weeks of discussion, Kennedy ordered the island blockaded. Six days later Soviet prime minister Khrushchev agreed to remove the missiles, with a similar retreat by the U.S. of its missiles in Turkey.[19]

## Some Symptoms of Groupthink

❑ **Self-censorship** and the **illusion of unanimity**—Group members avoid speaking up against the majority for fear of being ridiculed or because they "do not want to waste the group's time." No one wants to be the first to speak against the dominant position. Because no one hears any dissent, each doubter assumes that he or she is the only one.

☐ **Pressure on dissenters**—Those who insist on dissenting are branded as a nuisance or "naysayers"; their loyalty is questioned. Exhortations to "pull our oars in the same direction," "line up our arrows," or "all work together on this" can deter those with minority views from raising their concerns.

☐ **Illusion of invulnerability**—A successful track record or the qualifications of group members lead people to assume that luck is "on our side" or "we can't lose."

☐ **Stereotypes**—Outsiders, such as competitors, are cast as less ethical, intelligent, farsighted, or committed to the public good. In contrast, the intelligence, commitment, and vision of team members are highlighted.

## HOW TO ENCOURAGE DIVERGENT VIEWS

To counter the pull toward conformity, group leaders must signal that conflict is appropriate and even expected. Here are some general principles for creating an atmosphere that welcomes divergence.

✧ **Invite dissenters.** The group leader's attitude toward disagreements will determine whether they lead to creative solutions or hard feelings. For example, if leaders see people with different ideas (especially subordinates) as "problem employees" or "troublemakers," group members are less likely to propose or accept alternative solutions. If the leader sees those employees as "idea people" or "innovators," constructive conflict is more likely to become the norm.[20] Groups are exceptionally perceptive about their leaders' views. There are all sorts of ways to punish dissenters—from overt comments such as "Most of us see it this way, why don't you?"—to more subtle but easily read body language that communicates displeasure or "politely" ignores an unwanted contribution. To encourage varied views, communicate from the start that task conflict is not only welcome, but desired. (Insist, however, that group members refrain from relationship conflict.)

✧ **Don't take sides too soon.** The pull to conform to a leader's views can be great, especially if the group leader holds a position of authority or respect in the organization. Once the leader's preferences become known, disagreeing is perceived as politically costly. Many group members' ideas—including some good ones—will not be heard. To avoid this, leaders should almost always avoid stating the final choice they would prefer. Announce at the start that you don't want to signal your views until there has been a thorough and candid discussion; then offer your opinion last. Japanese companies have an interesting custom that may be worthy of emulation. As a rule, they let the lowest-ranking member of a group speak first, then the next lowest, and so on. That way, no one is held back by fear of differing with an opinion a more senior person has already expressed.

◇ **Reduce the pressure to conform.** The less fear that a person has of becoming isolated, the more likely he is to speak his mind. In fact, the chances of a minority being able to shift the majority rise dramatically when more than one person presents the unpopular view. Many of the tools below will make it safer for those with minority viewpoints to speak up and be heard.

◇ **Establish norms supporting conflict and creativity.** Make it clear up front that task conflict is for thinking, not to win arguments, and that disagreement will not result in expulsion. People can battle other group members and still maintain mutual respect if the leader insists that members be critical of ideas, not of people. To keep the conflict focused on the task rather than on the relationship requires tact—and thus, suggestions must be couched accordingly. Clarify that the objective is to enhance, modify, challenge, and extend the ideas of the group, without any one person taking ownership of any one particular view. Especially when challenging a viewpoint strongly associated with certain people, care must be taken to disassociate the comments from the person. Instead of saying, "I disagree with Joe because . . ." try to rephrase it as "Let me qualify the useful ideas just offered by noting that. . . ."

The following true, if unusual, story demonstrates the lengths to which one manager went to persuade a reluctant group of employees to share their real views with him. This man, a middle manager at a major Chicago bank, decided that he wanted to run his own business. He left his job and bought a small, one-office bank on the south side of Chicago. His first morning at the new bank, this new CEO assembled his staff for the regular weekly meeting. "I'm not going to pretend to know our customers, our competitors, our neighborhood, or our operation," he told them. "But you do. I need your help. Tell me what we need to do to make this a better bank."

The response: dead silence. The bank's previous owner had been an autocratic, "command and control" manager. He exemplified the joke told about Samuel Goldwyn, the Hollywood mogul who was alleged to have said "I don't want 'yes men.' I want people who say 'no' even if it costs them their jobs." The bank's staff wasn't certain the new CEO meant what he said. If he didn't, the cost of speaking out could be high. No one wanted to be the first to test the waters.

The following Monday the CEO convened his staff again. The second meeting was a repeat of the first. The new CEO welcomed suggestions and was met with similar silence.

The third week the CEO began the meeting by introducing a banking industry consultant whom he had invited to offer advice. Fifteen minutes into the meeting the consultant raised his hand. "I think that what you just said is idiotic," he pronounced when the CEO called on him. The staff was stunned. (The original word was much stronger than "idiotic"—but also unprintable.)

"I appreciate your candor," said the CEO. "Thank you. We'll take a hard look at it."

Fifteen minutes later the consultant again raised his hand. "Once again, I've got to tell you that what you're talking here is idiotic." Again, the CEO thanked him and noted the advice would be considered seriously.

Twice more, every fifteen minutes for an hour, the consultant raised his hand and said the same thing. Each time the CEO thanked him for his candid, respected opinion. As the meeting adjourned, the staff lingered to see what would happen. The CEO immediately walked over to the consultant, shook his hand, and thanked him for speaking out.

There are two endings to this story. The first you can probably imagine. The following Monday, when the CEO asked his staff what should be done to make the bank better, the dam burst. His staff, of course, knew well what problems the bank was facing, and the information the CEO needed came forth in a torrent.

The second ending has to do with the consultant. He served his purpose—freeing the staff members to speak their minds. But why pay a consultant to come in and say "What you're doing is idiotic" four times?

In fact, the CEO didn't. The consultant wasn't a consultant at all, but rather his neighbor. The CEO had told him "Dress like you're going to a funeral, stand up and say idiotic every fifteen minutes, and I'll buy you dinner."

---

Lesson: For divergent views to emerge in a group, leaders must signal that conflict is truly welcome.

---

## CREATING CONSTRUCTIVE CONFLICT

Because most people associate disagreeing with being disagreeable, constructive dialogue is often easier in theory than in practice. For it to occur, conflict must be managed—and it must be managed well. Here are some tools that can help.

 **Create heterogeneous groups.**

To maximize the diversity in a group, choose people who strike you as approaching decisions in different ways. If members think about problems in many different ways, they're more likely to produce conflicting ideas. Thus they're more likely to teach each other something, and conflict among their views will lead to new insights.

You can bring together people with different thinking styles intuitively or by using tools such as the Myers-Briggs personality inventory.[21] People with different backgrounds also tend to think differently. Even if a decision seems to call exclusively for computer experts, for instance, try to include some marketing or accounting people on the team. Interestingly, some research has shown that age differences are particularly powerful in helping generate different views of a problem.

In addition to bringing together people with varying worldviews, the presence of diversity within a group also cues an *expectation* of conflict. When people engage with others who are clearly different from themselves, they are less likely to assume agreement and more likely to expect to hear contrasting viewpoints.[22]

 **Give two subgroups the same task.**

Subgroups can encourage healthy conflict. Remember the framing exercise ("Seeing Into the Shadows") where two separate groups were asked to develop criteria to select a new manager? It's common for leaders to break intelligence-gathering teams into subgroups to focus on *different* tasks. But it may be especially revealing to create two different subgroups for the *same* task. They're sure to come up with different perspectives on the issues at hand. Nissan Design International's practice of "hiring in divergent pairs" is a variation on this theme.

**Require anonymous "precommitment."**

Prior to any meeting, ask group members to write down anonymously their ideas about the best decision option, the background issues, or even the agenda itself. This can be done by e-mail and sent to the group leader (or to an independent facilitator) who removes individual names, collates the comments, then distributes the combined list to the entire group prior to the meeting. This technique not only overcomes the pull toward conformity, it also prevents the most vocal (e.g., the most overconfident but not necessarily the most astute) members from dominating the group's decision. In the Asch "line-length" study, for example, when people were asked to first write their answer on paper privately, the error rate dropped from 33 percent back down to 8 percent. Precommitment increased their resistance to conform even though the private notes would not be made public in any way.

Skiwear manufacturer Sport Obermeyer found that the more vocal members of their buying committee skewed the consensus forecast on trends for the winter clothing market, frequently causing forecasts to be significantly off target. So the company's executives, in collaboration with several researchers, conducted an experiment. Previously, the buying committee had provided a single consensus forecast for each style and color, arrived at after extensive discussion. In the experiment, they asked each member of the forecasting committee to forecast independently, rather than through a group process. The result? The average of the independent forecasts was usually *more accurate* than the forecasts generated through a consensus process. As a result, the company now uses the average of individual forecasts (modified by some basic statistical techniques), rather than the buyers' consensus forecast, to predict demand.[23]

 **Appoint a devil's advocate.**

A devil's advocate can serve to provide "permission" for dissent. Many more people are willing to be the second one to go against the tide than to be the first. In the Asch experiment described above, when just one participant out of seven gave the right answer, the error rate for the others dropped from 33 percent to just 6 percent. In other words, as long as *one* person diverged from the "consensus," others felt free to say what they really thought.

Research has shown that groups using a devil's advocate develop and consider more alternative solutions to a problem and select a higher quality recommendation.[24] Try assigning someone to be devil's advocate at each group meeting, and reward a job well done. Even a weak dissenter will help. One warning: don't designate the same person as the devil's advocate all the time (and try to discourage any one individual from volunteering for that role repeatedly). The group will just learn to ignore their input. You might also appoint two such advocates, as Kennedy did during the Cuban missile crisis, to avoid isolating a single dissenter.

 **Solicit more than one option from each member.**
Ask each individual to bring at least two alternative views on each major issue. Better yet, encourage three, four, or five options. (See Interlude A, "Improving Your Options," for a reminder of tools to help get ideas on the table.) Not only will the group have more alternatives to consider, but requesting multiple options from each individual helps prevent anyone from being too closely identified with (or taking too much pride in) a single view.

 **Use minority reports to gain a balanced perspective.**
Minority viewpoints stimulate divergent thinking and sometimes lead to new understandings and creative solutions. Even when a minority opinion does not alter the final decision, it forces the group to think about alternatives, better justify their chosen action, or find creative ways to alter the decision to meet a broader set of criteria.[25] Research shows that even when the minority viewpoint is wrong, it still improves the decision outcome by opening the group to alternate ways of thinking and increasing the chance of finding a creative, appropriate solution.[26]

 **Hold "second-chance" meetings.**
Don't let the urgency to "be done with it" prevent divergent views from emerging. To send a dramatic message, do as Alfred P. Sloan, Jr. did when he sent people away to think of possible issues that should be raised.

## THE FAILURE TO "COME TOGETHER"

Since we believe that not enough—rather than too much—conflict is the greatest danger to good decision-making, we have examined that situation first. But there are times when divergent opinions run rampant. Unbridled conflict can stalemate even a well-intentioned group, forestalling attempts to agree on a common solution. Such conflict may arise because important goals, values, or preferences are not shared. Deep conflicts can polarize a group, leading people to join emotionally rooted, opposing camps. Groups can also fail to reach a decision when its norms favor continued expansion over coming to a conclusion. This problem is more common in the public and not-for-profit sectors than in the corporate world (where someone is more likely to eventually step in and make an executive decision), but it can appear in any organization. It may occur on volunteer boards, when the group can't afford to alienate an influential donor, or in groups whose norm is to ensure that "everyone is on board" before any step is taken. At many university faculty meetings, norms favoring "academic freedom" and "intellectual creativity" mean that in any discussion of eight people there are nine opinions—and always room for one more refinement or unnecessary elaboration.

Whether because of polarized conflicts about values or goals, or norms that favor continued expansion, when a group continues to diverge—and diverge and diverge, the hopes for ever making a decision seem dim. Group members become frustrated and alienated; they stop coming back.[27] When the push for consensus goes on for too long, it may become a battle of attrition. Unfortunately, in such cases a committed vocal minority often has more energy than the majority—and their desired outcome reigns. Whatever the reason for the divergence, the goal is same: the group needs to come together and reach a conclusion.[28]

## REDUCE POLARIZATION TO HELP A GROUP COME TOGETHER

When a group fails to converge, the question becomes: how do you make the best of it? You can't always ensure that everyone will be happy with the eventual outcome. But you can ensure mutual respect and a belief in a good *process*.

Too often, coming to conclusions is understood through Western culture's adversarial frame: One side advances its arguments and the other side does likewise. A third party tries to reconcile or find the truth in the conflicting viewpoints. (This adversarial approach is especially used in the judicial process.) Some leaders mistakenly pit one strong-willed subordinate against another to battle out opposing points of view on an issue, believing that whoever can sell their opinion more effectively is necessarily right. Unfortunately, this method (like the battle frame it mimics) can be costly. It may further polarize the two sides. And as we have seen repeatedly in the overconfidence experiments, the person who is most certain does not necessarily have the "best" or the most correct information.

Better approaches exist. But before we present some of those tools, consider this example, taken from Denver, Colorado.[29] Police officers and members of minority communities held opposing views on a highly contentious topic: a proposal that police be equipped with more powerful bullets.

The police faced a life-threatening situation: After they shot fleeing armed suspects, the suspects were often able to get up and shoot back, wounding—and in at least one case killing—an officer. The department wanted to switch from traditional lightweight bullets to what was then a new, hollow-tipped bullet that would more reliably disable suspects.

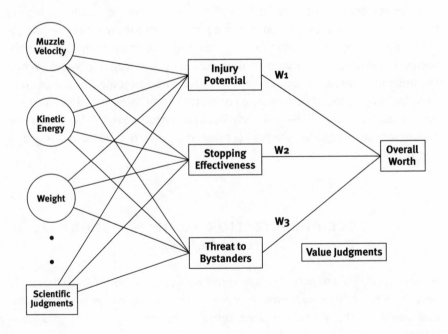

*Figure 7-3*

Members of minority communities and the American Civil Liberties Union were outraged. They declared that the new bullet would kill or maim innocent suspects and bystanders. The issue was brought to the Denver city council. Each side employed its own ballistics experts to testify in favor of its view. Unfortunately, that generated more vituperation. The one-sided experts were adding little to the city council's understanding.

The council turned to Professor Kenneth Hammond at the University of Colorado, a respected behavioral decision expert. Hammond set out to separate the factual opinions of people involved in the issue from their value judgments. He used a framework of the type shown in figure 7-3. At the far left are the objective characteristics of the various bullets: muzzle velocity, mass, kinetic energy, contours, and so on.

Unfortunately, those scientifically measurable characteristics meant little to politicians, community members, or even police officers. Community members might sense that heavier bullets were more dangerous than lighter ones, but their real concern was about potential injury, threat to bystanders, and stopping effectiveness (the variables in the middle column). Only experts in ballistics and medicine could determine how muzzle velocity, mass, kinetic energy, and so on (the objective characteristics) actually led to injury potential, threat to bystanders, and stopping effectiveness.

Hammond convinced the city council that experts respected by both sides should make the scientific judgments about how each bullet would score on these dimensions. However, value judgments must also be made about how much weight to put on each of the factors in the second column. That is, should stopping effectiveness weigh more or less in the final judgment than the potential for injury? Hammond emphasized that once the scientific judgments had been made, the experts possessed no additional qualifications for the value judgments that would ultimately determine which bullet the city should select. The city council, as representatives of the public, should make the value judgments about how much relative importance to assign each factor. The final choice would be based on both the scientific judgments about each bullet and the set of importance weights (shown in the diagrams as $W_1$, $W_2$, etc.).

It turned out that the ballistics and medical experts selected by each side differed little in their scientific judgments. They had previously favored different bullets only because they differed in their personal value judgments. Once outside of an adversarial atmosphere, the experts were able to add a great deal to the discussion. They told the city council that bullets with the greatest injury potential might not have the greatest stopping effectiveness. Some bullets, for example, that produced small, shallow cavities (less injury) nonetheless had considerable ability to render a suspect shot in the torso

incapable of returning fire. Hammond's group asked the experts to make scientific judgments on eighty different types of bullets.

Not surprisingly, city council members disagreed on the issue of how to
weight these judgments. The potential impasse was avoided by an agreement
to count the three main factors (stopping effectiveness, injury potential, and
threat to bystanders) as equally important. The researchers then applied
these equal weights to the scientific findings for the eighty types of bullets
being considered.[30]

The conclusion: the bullet that had the highest overall score was neither
the old bullet the police department had been using nor the new bullet they
proposed. It was a type of bullet not previously considered. This new bullet
was nearly equal in stopping effectiveness to the police department's proposed option. However, it presented no greater potential for injuring suspects or bystanders than the bullet the department had been using. The
result: a good decision process had succeeded in meeting both sides' key
goals.[31]

It may seem serendipitous that they were able to find a third, previously
unconsidered alternative. Some people may be thinking, "Yes, but what if
they hadn't found that new option. Would they have been able to come to a
good resolution?" It's a fair question. This kind of process will not resolve
every controversy. However, in our experience, a good decision process that
eliminates adversarial positioning—such as this one that helps separate facts
from values—often leads groups to an excellent, previously unconsidered, alternative that better can meet both sides' key goals.

 **Separate facts from values.**
**In choosing between the advantages and disadvantages of competing
options, decision-makers must often make value trade-offs.[32] Conflicts can usually be far better managed when participants are clear
about which components are factual and which reside in values or
policy judgments. Although both types of disagreements probably exist in most complex, emotionally charged debates, in some cases the
value conflict is the crux of the disagreement. In others, the factual issues are paramount. Of course, it is not always easy to untangle facts
from values, but as the Denver police bullet case demonstrated, the
rewards for such efforts can be great.[33]**

**To disentangle whether you are dealing with a factual or value dis-
agreement, ask what data would convince that person to change their
mind. Someone opposed to drug testing in the workplace, for example, might be asked what data would be convincing enough that the**

benefits would outweigh the costs. **If the person would under no circumstances favor workplace drug testing, then you know the issue is exclusively a question of values to this individual. If on the other hand the person would favor testing if there were sufficient statistical evidence that it, say, reduces accidents and corporate liability, then the debate can shift from values alone to the empirical evidence.**

We used this separating-facts-from-values technique to help an executive decide among three conflicting medical recommendations. His two-year-old daughter had been born with a hip defect, and he was frustrated and confused after three different specialists advised three different treatments. One urged a major operation, another a rigid brace, and a third advised waiting six months. We suggested that he ask the doctors to separate their scientific opinions from their personal values. While doctors' scientific opinions represent their medical expertise, and merit deep respect, their personal values are no better than anyone else's. Did the two doctors opposing the operation really expect a different result from the doctor who favored it? "No," they said. However, they did fear that the long period of recuperation would disrupt the social development of a two-year-old. Now the father could weigh the alternatives rationally. He knew that his wife and five other children could travel to the city where the operation and rehabilitation would be performed. They could provide plenty of social support for his daughter. He okayed the operation. It worked beautifully.

The Harris Trust and Savings Bank in Chicago used a similar approach to reach a decision about a new information system. Much money and time had been invested in a custom-designed information system, but opinions were strongly divided on whether to continue. The system was down too often, not always user-friendly, and rather costly. To prevent emotions from dominating this complex decision, they hired a consulting firm to coordinate the evaluation of the in-house system and compare it with five integrated systems available from outside vendors. Four criteria were used: (1) cost, (2) timeliness, (3) operating features, and (4) risk.

A surprising consensus emerged on how each of the six systems scored on each of the policy criteria. Next, a senior management group was asked to prioritize the four policy criteria (by distributing 100 points among them— the decision weighting technique discussed in chapter 6). These weights were then applied to the six systems. The in-house system was outscored by at least two of the external vendors' systems. The gap was big enough that fairly strong agreement could be reached on discontinuing development of the existing in-house system.

Separating facts from values is particularly useful when dealing with complex, emotionally charged issues such as those related to affirmative action, drug-testing in the workplace, trade vs. human rights, and so on. Of course, it cannot guarantee success because the values themselves may be irreconcilable.[34] But at least the discussion toward agreement is focused on the limited topic of values and not on the facts as well.

 **Listening to find common ground.**

In the midst of a heated controversy, people often forget that those on the other side might have legitimate concerns. They can become so invested in defending their own positions that they fail to listen well to what others are saying. As a result, polarized groups often miss the common ground they share and the opportunity to find not only a shared but a truly robust solution. The following process can help.

1. Ask people to listen, without interruption or planning a rebuttal, to the arguments advanced by an advocate of one view. If you doubt the sincerity of the listeners, give them the task of reciting the speaker's key points.
2. Have group members, especially those who disagree, ask the speaker for additional information about why that conclusion was reached. (Note: these questions should not be disguised challenges, but sincere attempts to elicit more information to clarify understanding.)
3. Record (e.g., on a white board or poster paper) the concerns and reasons given, without editing them, checking with the speaker to make sure that positions stated are being accurately reflected.
4. Designate a speaker for another point of view, and repeat the first three steps. If more than two camps exists, steps one through three can be repeated for each.
5. Review these and other people's concerns, pointing out the areas of agreement. Then ask the group to reframe the question, taking as many concerns from each side into account as possible.
6. Determine whether a robust solution can be found that addresses the issues and concerns raised on both sides.[35]

 **Try consensus mapping.**

Consensus mapping can help a team that is having difficulty agreeing on the problem they are facing. Have the group members write key aspects of the problem as they see it on individual Post-It notes. Members then cluster and recluster the notes according to theme or topic until there is some agreement as to how to represent the problem at hand in its full complexity.

 **Experiment with the "nominal group technique."**

This classic technique is designed to enhance creativity in generating ideas, provide a mechanism for resolving differences in ranking those ideas, balance participation among members, and enable them to present ideas anonymously. Steps 1–3 can be accomplished electronically before the meeting. For groups with access to the appropriate technology, steps 4–7 can also be accomplished electronically, facilitating anonymity and private (rather than public) voting. This anonymity can be particularly helpful in groups that are highly politicized or always divided along the same lines.

1. Ask individuals to write ideas anonymously
2. Collect and record those ideas in terse phrases
3. Add ideas and build on the ideas of others
4. Discuss each idea for clarification and pros/cons
5. Vote privately
6. Discuss the vote and revise alternatives.
7. Generate a final ranking[36]

 **Use outside process (not content) experts.**

An outside team leader or facilitator can help manage conflict within the group, present alternative perspectives for consideration, and keep the process on track. Good facilitators are skilled at preventing discussions from becoming personal and will allow all relevant issues to be raised. They are independent of the outcomes and issues, with no "personal agenda." Their loyalty is to a good process, not to a personally preferred option.

## WHEN TO STOP STRIVING FOR CONSENSUS

Striving for a consensus decision can be extremely powerful. It allows all team members to feel that the decision-making process has been fair, enables a group to be more confident that they have found the right decision, and ensures that everyone is "on board" when it comes time to implement. Sometimes, however, achieving unanimity is impossible—or at least will take more time than the group has. In such cases, the push for consensus can go on for so long that it becomes a test of endurance.

In fact, research has shown that allowing a group to debate for too long eventually backfires, with the leader bearing the brunt of the group's frustration. When fundamental disagreements drone on and on, with one or two people forcing a stalemate, members blame the group's leader for not intervening to stop the discussion.[37] The best solution in such a situation may be for the leader to step in and make a decision, or for the group to let the majority rule.[38] In doing so:

1. Make sure everyone feels that their point of view has been heard or understood.
2. Acknowledge the validity of each speaker's contribution.
3. Use the tools we offer in this chapter to help move the group on toward conclusion. Sometimes it is enough to get everyone to accept a deadline and the absolute need for a unified stance.
4. It should be understood from the beginning that in the face of utter stalemate, the decision will be made either by majority rule or by the leader (possibly informed by a majority vote).
5. Encourage conflict before the decision, but insist on 100 percent team spirit once implementation is underway.

## GROUP FRAMING AND INTELLIGENCE-GATHERING CHALLENGES

We have waited until now to devote an entire chapter to decision-making in groups since it is in the "coming to conclusions" phase that many group-related problems surface most visibly. However, groups can get tripped up by poorly managed conflict in any of the decision-making stages. Here's how such conflict may hinder good framing and intelligence-gathering. The principles and tools in this chapter apply to helping groups successfully navigate those stages as well.

## Framing

**The dangers of premature harmony:** The selected frame is inadequate, resulting in too few evaluation criteria. The frame's shadows are not well-understood. The best alternatives are bounded out of consideration.

**The failure to come together:** Frame conflict is not understood for what it is. Members remain unaware of each other's frames. They defend their frames or see others' frames in opposition. Much time is wasted in groups because of confusion about frames.

**The advantages of a well-managed group:** Groups can explore and integrate different perspectives, develop a shared (even robust) working frame, and better understand the chosen frame's highlights and shadows.

**Tips:** Know your own frames and those of others. Recognize and deal with frame conflict as soon as possible. Don't minimize the time spent on framing to avoid frame conflicts; it will resurface later. Reframe conflict as positive. Help the group see disagreements as conflicts between frames rather than between individuals. Guide the group toward true frame *alignment* (e.g., a shared working frame) rather than surface *agreement.*

## Intelligence Gathering

**The dangers of premature harmony:** The information search is restricted and focused on confirming evidence. The group fails to reappraise its options, examine the risks of the preferred action, or work out contingency plans. Disconfirming evidence is shunned.

**The advantages of a well-managed group:** Divergent thinking is central to excellent group intelligence-gathering. Groups can pool individual knowledge, expertise, and information. They can pool the ability to gather more intelligence. Creativity is enhanced, enabling the group to generate more options.

**Tips:** Encourage people to think as widely as possible and come up with as many unusual ideas as they can imagine. When the intelligence-gathering phase for a major decision is complete, the evidence on the table should be rich enough that no one feels ignored.

## Guidelines for a Good Group Process

The heart of good group management is encouraging the right kind of conflict within the group and resolving it fully and fairly through further debate and intelligence-gathering. Here are some general principles that can help you—and your group members—to ensure that this happens.

- ❑ **Manage the *process*.** It's not who makes the decision, but how. Have a process for the meeting and a clear agreement on who is responsible for managing it.

- ☐ Remember: **consensus is a goal, not a process.**
- ☐ **Listen.** Too often the opposite of speaking is not listening, but *waiting* to speak.
- ☐ **Separate "task conflict" from "relationship conflict."** Challenge ideas, not people. Once an idea is contributed to the discussion, it belongs to the group, not the person who suggested it.
- ☐ **Nurture issue-oriented conflict.** Ensure that conflict is centered on alternative courses of action and interpretation of facts, not on interpersonal animosity.
- ☐ **Distinguish facts from attacks.** Permit people to share facts, clarifications, and suggested actions. Encourage people to explain *why* they hold highly subjective judgments/opinions, feelings, and disagreements regarding certain ideas. Prohibit attacks on (or defenses of) people.
- ☐ **Ensure that the group listens to and respects minority views.** Even if an idea is rejected, a fellow group member should not be.
- ☐ **If you are the leader, refrain initially from stating your own opinions,** because many group members will fear to offer their own (possibly good) ideas if they contradict yours.
- ☐ **Encourage diverse views** (new ideas, criticisms) in the early stages of any group process. Then as more facts and insights are gained, guide the group toward convergence on a final choice.
- ☐ **Test your management of conflict.** How few dissenters are needed to reveal a fatal flaw? Ideally, just one. With sufficient conflict, does the group become *more* cohesive? It should, if the conflict is a productive competition among ideas.

## SURVIVING IN A MISMANAGED GROUP

Unfortunately, we all must deal with decision-making groups that are not really well managed—and in which we don't occupy the leadership role. How can you help such a group be more productive?

First, assess whether the leadership challenges stem from the leader's disposition (e.g., a leader who is autocratic, indifferent, indecisive, or inflexible by nature) or are being influenced by the situation at hand (e.g., an inexperienced leader or one whose attention is absorbed by other priorities). In the former case there may not be much you can do, unless the majority of group members agrees with you and can join together to work around the leader's shortcomings.

If, however, the challenges arise from the situation itself, you may be able to diplomatically suggest ways to help move the task along. Some good guidelines are:

- Try speaking with the leader privately about the decision process. Your career won't benefit from publicly undermining the boss (or even a colleague).
- Analyze the leader's frame, so you can try to speak in its terms. Ask what the leader thinks the challenges are.
- Be tactful and positive. The goal is to highlight the reservoir of insight that lies dormant in the group, not necessarily to "convert" your boss or fellow group members. Try offering support to the leader rather than challenging the leader's job performance.

Ask yourself what the group needs to do to make an effective decision. Is the key problem framing? Too few options? Biases or lack of direction in intelligence-gathering? Group management skills? The absence of a systematic approach to coming to conclusions? Which principles or tools are most likely to remedy the situation?

Focus on the decision process and, if necessary, supply articles or other authoritative sources on group management (see the end notes). Offer concrete suggestions about a particular tool or technique that may help. You may not be able to convert a bumbling leader into a stellar one, but you may be able to improve the decision process and help the leader get more from the team.

Before undertaking this kind of intervention, however, honestly assess your own vulnerability. If the task is intrinsically interesting or important to you and the team leader does not directly control your rewards, the risks are lower. So, too, if it is a multidisciplinary group or if you have a "professional" orientation with your peers residing outside of the group or organization. You are more vulnerable in challenging a group's direction to the extent that the group is highly cohesive and/or interdependent, the goals are ambiguous, and the team leader has special training in the subject or is your boss.[39]

---

## Groups Under Fire

Group decision-making can seem an insurmountable barrier when time is tight. However, the greatest strength of group brainpower (the notion that "all of us are smarter than any one of us") can still be brought to bear. Many of the tools in chapter 7 can be used on an accelerated timetable; we offer some examples below. The most important point to remember: premature harmony remains a danger, even if a decision is required in twenty-four hours. Don't be mesmerized by the goal of agreement and think that any step that makes agreement come sooner is correct. While you may have to give up on reaching consensus if you need to converge on a decision quickly, you don't want to bury divergent views. After all, the time spent listening to one of those divergent views now may save you from costly and time-consuming fixes later. Create subgroups, with each team assigned one option to advance. Ask each group to argue for the merits of its option and to list the potential flaws. Better yet, require precommitment: ask people for a private vote (by e-mail) before you put the teams together. Have them tell you which option they would choose and why. This will enable you to discern how much disagreement actually exists. Consider mixing the assigned subgroups so that some people must argue for an option they didn't choose.

## AS SMART AS ALL OF US

The principles for managing group decision-making are few to learn, but challenging to master. Learn to walk the narrow footpath between the abysses of premature harmony and never-ending conflict. Create a context in which people feel safe expressing divergent views. Help polarized groups separate facts from values and learn to listen to each other respectfully. And when necessary, abandon attempts to reach consensus, tap an alternative decision-making plan, and move on. These tasks are simpler to state than to execute. However, when decision-making groups are well managed, when both their characteristic strengths and common weaknesses are understood, then Satchel Paige is right: None of us is as smart as all of us.

# Implementing Your Chosen Option

No plan survives contact with the enemy.

—*Prussian field marshal Helmuth von Moltke, 1800–91*

I T ' S  T I M E  T O  A C T . Until this point, decision-making has been largely an intellectual exercise, an attempt to anticipate where and how things might be changed for the better. But now, for better or worse, the judgments you made during the framing, intelligence-gathering, and coming-to-conclusions stages are about to be put to the test.

While implementation per se is not really within the scope of this book, we want to recognize its importance. Most professionals spend the bulk of their time executing and managing decisions, not just making them. And while the merit of a particular decision should be based on the decision *process*, and not just the outcome (as we emphasized repeatedly in chapter 1), implementation is an important part of what produces great decision results.

Even more important, your decision-making process does not end when you decide which alternative to pursue. "Learning from experience"—an integral part of any good decision-making process—is yet to come. And after committing to a course of action, and before stepping back to assess the decision-making process, astute decision-makers will have the chance to alter and improve the decision they just made. This activity fits neatly into neither "coming to conclusions" nor "learning from experience," and yet it relates to both. Hence, we again insert an "interlude."

In it, we examine how to use experience to refine your conclusion in the *midst* of implementing it. This is particularly vital when operating in environments where uncertainty is high. In such situations you usually are forced to come to a decision based as much on fragile assumptions as on firm knowledge. And because assumptions about the unknown often turn out to be wrong, you will likely experience deviations—often huge ones—from your original plan. You may be able to adjust your course accordingly—if you have planned wisely and are watching well. This interlude suggests ways to do that. We will look first at how to systematically capture feedback as it emerges and while there is still time to make midcourse corrections. Then we will examine how to exercise the flexible options you may have been able to build into your decision plan.[1]

## MONITORING ACTION AND REACTION

Most complex decisions will require an elaborate, coordinated implementation process. A series of tightly sequenced, interrelated activities will be called for. Many people—both internal and external to your organization—may play a role. Time pressure and/or limited resources must be handled to get the job done on schedule. New or unfamiliar activities may be required to achieve the desired result. Ambiguous authority relationships, miscommunication, and/or poorly aligned incentives or attitudes within the implementation team may get in the way. Dumb, uncontrollable luck—good or bad—will inevitably intervene. And unless the decision is routine, it is unlikely that you will predict or anticipate all the possible futures. Midcourse corrections will be required. Fortunately, from the moment you begin to put your chosen alternative into action, feedback will emerge. The question is: are you prepared to use it?

In 1992, the Walt Disney Company launched its first European theme park near Paris. EuroDisney (now called Disneyland Paris) has become one of Europe's most popular paid tourist destinations. However, just two years after opening it had accumulated losses of more than $1 billion. Disney is known as an astute manager of theme parks; Disneyland in California, Disney World in Florida, and Tokyo Disney were each a profitable success. Why was the debut of EuroDisney such a financial disaster?

Part of the answer: erroneous assumptions. In the information-gathering stage, Disney executives made a large number of estimates about average food and beverage consumption, how long Europeans would tolerate waiting in line for a ride, price sensitivity to admission fees, and so on. The company expected half of the revenue to come from admissions, the other half from hotels, food, and merchandise. Many of these assumptions were based on Disney's prior successes in the U.S. and Japan. But no one questioned the appropriateness of applying that existing frame to Europe.

In fact, Europeans turned out to be far less willing than Americans and Japanese to shell out for this kind of entertainment. Disney was forced to drop adult ticket prices drastically. The average spending per visit was also far below plan. The park opened with fewer rides than in the U.S. and Japanese parks; with less to do, the average stay in the park's hotels was only two days rather than the four days projected. Nor did Europeans take to the U.S. and Japanese pattern of all-day "grazing" for their meals; when everyone sought to dine at noon, EuroDisney's restaurants were unable to seat them all.

But flawed assumptions, alone, needn't have saddled Disney with such tremendous losses. To understand that, we need the second part of the answer: poor monitoring. As empirical data emerged, Disney didn't have a systematic way to aggregate and channel this valuable information to the people who could do something about it. Instead, EuroDisney continued to operate on flawed assumptions—even when the data proved otherwise. Indeed, a basic framing blind spot, namely that an alcohol-free theme park would work just as well in Europe as elsewhere in the world, was corrected much too late. Had a good mechanism been in place to allow midcourse corrections, Disney could have at least cut its losses.[2]

In contrast to Disney's uncomfortable encounter with reality, consider Royal Dutch/Shell, an early practitioner of learning and adjustment in real time. Arie de Geus, head of Shell's strategic planning group during most of the 1980s, moved that group from traditional forecasting and scenario planning toward tools to stimulate organizational learning. Shell's approach anticipated a broader shift in companies from "command and control"–style planning to a "sense and respond" mode of managing in which improvisation is accorded higher priority. The challenge for organizations, de Geus notes, "is to recognize and react to environmental change before the pain of a crisis. . . . The issue is not whether a company will learn . . . but whether it will learn fast and early."[3]

The emerging field of project management offers one way for organizations to learn "fast and early" by providing an excellent framework for monitoring actions and collecting vital information about whether you are headed toward success. While the traditional command-and-control organization viewed implementation as secondary to planning and analysis, the newer frame places more weight on learning and adjustment in real time. As Disney so painfully learned, however, for feedback to be registered, interpreted, and acted upon, a project implementation plan with clear milestones and review points is crucial.[4]

---

Lesson: For emerging signs of success or failure to be used to refine a decision, a project monitoring plan with clear milestones and review points is crucial.

The literature on project implementation is vast and deserving of several chapters for a full review. In this interlude we restrict ourselves to highlighting some of the key principles from the perspective of good decision-making.

- **Every plan is a basis for change.** Respect uncertainty. Frame your plan as a flexible means to an end. Don't rigidly follow a predetermined route; notice alternative paths to your desired decision goals.
- **Navigate an appropriate course between rigid adherence to the plan and shooting from the hip.** Carefully gauge the balance between planning and adjusting as you go. The new frame doesn't jettison planning and analysis; it stretches the traditional frame to incorporate flexible, real-time responses.
- **Monitor in real time.** Don't wait for comprehensive quarterly reports when faster (but possibly incomplete data) can be obtained from the field. Remember Disney's problems in Europe: they stemmed primarily from poor tracking and slow response. Be sure to keep an eye on the mental biases that distort how you interpret the information available.
- **Prepare your organization for tactical and strategic adjustments.** Most organizations are hobbled by inertia and must be primed for change. Use contingency planning and organizational dress rehearsals for key turning points. The power of flexible thinking can only be fully realized if the organization knows when and how to adjust its course as time unfolds. Don't limit your effectiveness, however, by focusing too much on inertia.

Managers responsible for implementation often complain about employees' resistance to change, and they identify this as a major obstacle to successful implementation. One Swiss chemical company in the midst of a major change effort challenged this core assumption at its deepest level. They adopted the opposite view and argued that most people welcome change. After all, human beings are deeply curious and seek variety in the form of vacations, career change, new friends, sports, and so on. The CEO of this company does not view the problem to be the employees, but the managers themselves who fail as leaders to tap into people's natural desire for change and growth. In essence, this CEO reframed the implementation problem as mostly one of leadership rather than one of organizational inertia. When managers in that company refer to "resistance to change," they are politely reminded that they have misdiagnosed the problem and are wrongly blaming the victims (i.e., the workers).

**Develop a project implementation plan.**

The best intentions for correction or intervention will remain worthless if they are not activated when needed. Ask yourself, what information is required to properly judge progress? How frequently must it be updated? Who should be responsible for updating and reviewing that information? Be sure your plan includes both milestones and review points.

 **Track Real-Time Information.**

Watch both your operations and the competitive environment. As noted before, monitor the alignment between the resources you are investing and the benefits you expect. Ask yourself whether you are learning anything through continued intelligence-gathering that changes the balance. Is the value you expected to get the same value you expect today? Has the big picture shifted in any important ways? Is a frame shift required?

## EXERCISING OPTIONS

We talked in Interlude A about the value of adopting an options perspective. Real options are not static. Changing markets, competitor actions, unexpected research outcomes, shifting strategic priorities, and a host of other external and internal developments may affect decisions and the value of embedded options over time. While most discussions focus on the nature and value of real options *at a given point in time*, the real value of real options can only be realized through effective implementation *over time*. Without such attention, any potential value you developed in creating such options will inevitably erode.

Of course, as events unfold, some options won't be worth pursuing. Others, however, may be gold mines. To tell the difference, and to exercise the winning options in a timely and appropriate manner, you will need to have the structures and processes in place to continuously evaluate and reevaluate your options. Our Wharton colleague William Hamilton, who has written extensively about creating, valuing, and implementing real options, suggests the following steps.

1. **Monitor progress.** You need regularly updated information on project progress to decide when to exercise or defer options. Be sure you have identified the major uncertainties that should be monitored over time.

2. **Test and update assumptions.** Identify key assumptions and decision points at the outset. Test these against current conditions, either at regular intervals or when key project milestones or "event triggers" (e.g., a competitor action or an unexpected outcome) signal the need to reevaluate your assumptions. Each reevaluation iteration may require a new or revised decision tree to reflect the changes. The greater the uncertainty, the shorter the periods should be between project reviews.

3. **Exercise your options.** An option exercised too late may have little or no value. But organizational inertia and other sources of resistance to changing plans can make the implementation of real options difficult in practice. Continuous updating and review provide the basis for decisions to exercise, defer, or abandon identified real options. As projects and market conditions evolve, prior assumptions and expectations may need to be revised in response to updated information, and these decisions will change. Furthermore, because options often have limited windows of opportunity due to competitive actions or other shifts in the environment, timing is critical.[5] You have to know when to pull the trigger, or the plug.

## WHEN TO PULL THE PLUG

The question of whether and when to pull the plug on a project is particularly vexing for decision-makers. You may have decided correctly to proceed with a project based on what was known and knowable at the time, but often new information arises that puts the entire project in doubt. When that happens, decision-makers must strongly guard against a pernicious tendency to proceed (a phenomenon known as the status quo bias).[6]

Once major projects gain organizational momentum they may be nearly impossible to stop. At its extreme this bias results in such celebrated fiascos as the Sergeant York air-defense gun, in which the Pentagon kept sinking money into an ill-fated advanced model that failed to perform key tasks in field tests. Yet, the project wasn't terminated until well over a billion dollars had been spent, against the better judgment of many observers who noted the gun's fatal flaws early in its design.

Even when there may be broad agreement—made in the early planning phases, with a cool eye and detached view—to halt a project if a certain revenue level is not reached by a certain date, it's not so simple to pull the plug.

In the heat of battle, with egos and reputations now on the line, the decision to cut bait may be less obvious. Hope springs eternal, and new information may be gleaned that calls the original commitment into question. Decision-makers face a tough balancing act between the disciplines of precommitment strategies and continuous review, recognizing that the latter is subject to political and emotional distortion.

The best antidote against failing to cut losing projects is to place the burden of review in the hands of a neutral party. Even our analytically astute MBA students are more likely to pull the plug in a case study where they are presumed to be the new management team than in that same case setting when they play the role of the managers responsible for getting the project started in the first place. Just imagine what kind of biases real (rather than hypothetical) involvement can create for those who championed the decision. Such people are the least well positioned to review the project with a cool eye and to pull the plug when needed.

## IMPLEMENTATION AS LEARNING

In a brief interlude, we can only touch upon the managerial and organizational complexities of using experience to refine your decision in the midst of implementing it. We recommend the excellent resources cited in the endnotes for those who want to pursue this subject further.[7] But let us close with one final thought: decision-makers would do well to frame implementation as an opportunity for learning. Apart from the necessary tactical adjustments in any one project, implementation presents a chance to interact with reality in the context of a specific hypothesis. Although we all interact with reality much of the time, we mostly do so in a casual or undisciplined way (such as when we discuss business over lunch with a friend). Implementing a decision, in contrast, involves a highly focused interaction in which we track and follow the consequences of our actions in light of explicit predictions or assumptions underlying the plan. This augurs well for decision-makers, but only if they recognize that true learning—in the real world amid noise and distraction—requires discipline and analysis. With that, we turn to the final stage in our decision-making process: learning from experience.

# Learning from Experience

## CHAPTER 8

# The Personal Challenges of Learning

People sometimes stumble over the truth, but usually they pick themselves up and hurry about their business.

—*Winston Churchill*

A SUCCESSFUL ENTREPRENEUR, who had a reputation for being a man of few words, was once interviewed about his many accomplishments. The interchange went as follows:

*Reporter:* Sir, what was the key to your success?
*Entrepreneur:* Good decisions.
*Reporter:* And what was the key to those good decisions?
*Entrepreneur:* Experience.
*Reporter:* And where, sir, did that experience come from?
*Entrepreneur:* Bad decisions.

Most professionals can empathize with the entrepreneur's learning process. We all have made our way toward expertise on the stepping-stones of more bad decisions than we care to remember. And we'd like to say we learned from them. After all, studies have documented what most people intuitively know: that the ability to learn from experience is the main factor separating successful executives and professionals from those who achieve only middling results. Those who are not able to learn from experience continue to repeat poor decisions and work patterns that produce at best mediocrity, and at worst, failure. Research by the Center for Creative Leadership, for example, found that successful executives were better at:

- Routinely gathering feedback on personal and organizational performance
- Interpreting the information they received in constructive ways

- Using this information to adjust personal behavior and improve operational results
- Helping others recognize and use the lessons of experience to improve personal and organizational performance.

In a rapidly changing environment, you not only need to get better at doing what you do, you need to get better at getting better. Sadly, this is easier said than done. For what the reticent entrepreneur failed to note is that experience alone does not lead to better decisions. Experience, after all, offers only the raw ingredients for learning; it provides information about outcomes, telling us *what* happened. It does not guarantee learning, which requires understanding of what caused the outcomes or *why* they happened. That requires a systematic, conscious focus on learning itself.

---

Lesson: Experience is knowing *what* happened. Learning is knowing *why* it happened.

---

## EXPERIENCE IS INEVITABLE; LEARNING IS NOT

People—including intelligent, highly motivated people—do not learn as easily from experience as one might expect. Somewhere along the way, many if not most professionals stop learning and simply depend on accumulated wisdom and expertise to see them through—often while thinking they are continuing to learn. In a now classic experiment, researchers asked experienced psychologists and their secretaries to diagnose whether patients were suffering from brain damage using a standard test, called the Bender Visual-Motor Gestalt test. In this test, patients are shown figures (such as partly overlapping circles and triangles) and asked to draw them by hand. Research has shown that if certain features are present in the hand drawings (for example, disproportionate overlaps or missing intersections), the patient is likely to be suffering from brain damage. But the relevant symptoms can be hard to recognize. The test cannot easily be scored by computer; a trained professional has to judge whether truly significant distortions are present in the patients' drawings.

Both the psychologists and their secretaries were presented with a series of drawings that patients had produced. Since all the patients had gone through further diagnostic tests, the researchers knew which of the drawings were really produced by brain-damaged individuals. The psychologists and secretaries, of course, did not.

Surprisingly, the results showed that the experienced psychologists had learned little about interpreting patients' drawings from years of administering the test. They could correctly determine whether the patients had brain damage only about two-thirds of the time. The secretaries, who had heard the terminology and picked up snippets of knowledge over the years, were also right about two-thirds of the time.

What happened? The psychologists hadn't, on average, turned their experience into improved knowledge. Meanwhile their secretaries, who typed the test reports, had picked up enough knowledge to diagnose correctly the same (simpler) cases that the psychologists could. But the psychologists had not continued to learn and reach the expertise needed to diagnose more than two-thirds correctly.

In contrast to most of the group, one expert who specialized in this test was right 84 percent of the time, more often than anyone else studied. He had found ways to systematically analyze feedback from patient after patient to improve his skill.[1] His performance shows that it is possible to learn to use this test well. The average clinician, on the other hand, failed to learn continually from experience.

Lesson: Learning is not automatic. It requires a systematic examination of our experience.

## WHY PEOPLE FAIL TO LEARN

If learning from experience is so obviously useful, why do so many people fail to learn?

To a large extent, the world seems to conspire against learning, at least outside the classroom. The sheer number of demands on our time and attention—and the pace at which we must operate to do our jobs—can make learning difficult. Often there doesn't seem to be enough time to recognize and make sense of the information available to us. We may jump to conclusions or ignore data at our fingertips. The perspective we need may be right there in front of us, but as Winston Churchill so aptly observed, we hurry past, trying to complete the urgent task at hand.

At other times experience provides feedback that is far from clear. We may get no feedback at all on the outcomes of our decisions, or the information we need may be hard to decipher. Real-world events are often by nature ambiguous, making it hard to progress from knowing what happened to knowing why. Attempts to learn can also be hindered by organizational barriers, like the ways in which people create environments that reinforce existing knowledge rather than promote opportunities for change.

Finally, mental biases (of the kind we have been discussing throughout this book) make learning from experience a more difficult task than most people realize. Our personal defense systems—the needs to feel competent, consistent, in control, and comfortable—set a boundary around our capacity and willingness to learn and change.[2] We fool ourselves about feedback, failing to interpret the evidence from past outcomes for what it really says. When events come out well, self-aggrandizement leads us to see the success as the result of our own genius. If results turn out badly, we face an equally pernicious bias toward rationalization, creating an explanation that preserves our positive self-image. And even if we carefully prevent ourselves from rationalizing, we are often unable to reconstruct how we thought about an issue before we learned its outcome, and thus we may fail to draw the right lesson.[3]

From this perspective it might seem a wonder that anyone can learn anything at all. But here's the good news: many of the obstacles to learning are under your control. We will begin by discussing these *personal* barriers to learning in this chapter. These barriers arise from the way people think. Mere awareness coupled with a sincere desire to learn will do much to dismantle them. The adoption of one or more simple but systematic techniques will do the rest. We will turn to the *organizational* and *environmental* barriers to learning in chapter 9.

**Which of the following prevent you from learning from experience?**
- Limited or ambiguous information about decision results
- Not enough time to make sense of the information available
- No opportunity to test conclusions in new decisions
- Anxiety about appearing a poor performer
- Inability to see how observed outcomes might be interpreted differently
- A tendency to jump to conclusions
- Ignored or distorted feedback
- Difficulty separating skill from luck

## Reframe Yourself as a Learner

It may sound trivial, but the first step in increasing your ability to effectively translate knowing *what* happened into an understanding of *why* it happened requires adopting a learning mind-set. Too often, overconfidence and defensive routines hinder learning. If you think you already have most of the knowledge you need, there is not much room for learning. As John Wooden, former UCLA basketball coach, wryly observed: "It's what you learn after you know it all that counts."

But the ability to see ourselves as learners goes beyond protecting sore egos. It requires that we reframe the essence of our role as workers (i.e., as performers who deliver results). And it requires understanding a profound change in the managerial paradigm. The traditional command-and-control organization was oriented nearly exclusively toward performance. Those at the top were to do the thinking; those lower down the organizational hierarchy were to implement their bosses' thinking. And they were judged solely on how well they did so, that is, on how well they performed. As a "performer," evaluated primarily on outcomes, if your initiative fails, you fail.

In the new managerial paradigm, all employees need to use their brains as well as their hands. The emerging imperative that *every* individual in the organization learn follows directly from this paradigm shift. In today's organization, everyone—no matter what their position in the organization—must be both a performer (delivering successful results) and a learner (continually developing the capacity to deliver better results in the future). And as the half-life of knowledge plummets, learning now means not only adding to what you know, but dropping what you used to know that's no longer true.

---

Lesson: To succeed, whatever your organizational position, reframe yourself as both a "performer" and a "learner."

---

 **Adopt a learning mind-set.**

As a learner, you must focus not only on the decision outcome, but on the process you used. Ask yourself: "Did I use a good decision process?" If you didn't, did you learn from it? "Learners" fail not because they make a mistake (everyone does sooner or later), but because they repeat those mistakes. To become a learner, we must overcome our ego-driven tendencies to hide mistakes. We must take every opportunity to learn from our mistakes. (We will talk about mistakes further at the end of chapter 9).

 **Let go of obsolete concepts.**

Outdated beliefs inhibit new learning. In fact, a substantial portion of the time devoted to learning should be devoted to "unlearning." But old ideas tend to be comfortable. It is hard to let go of them, even after they have lost their utility. Dee W. Hock, founder and CEO emeritus of Visa International, offers the following approach to this difficult task: "We clutter our mind with so much old stuff that there is no room for anything new. We can't discard mental 'stuff.' But we can create a mental attic and put a sign on the door that says 'things I know that are no longer so.' Call all those old, best-loved ideas into question . . . and lug it into the attic if it's no longer useful."[4]

## YOU CAN'T FIX IT IF YOU CAN'T FIND IT

At a large healthcare products manufacturer, almost half the grievances reviewed by the benefits department involved parents who had neglected to enroll their newborns in the company's medical plans within the required thirty days of birth. In each case, the company's administrative review committee (comprised of benefit personnel and lawyers) always asked: did the parents *admit* that they forgot to enroll? Usually the answer was "yes"—technically absolving the company of responsibility. Unfortunately, the committee, dominated by a legal frame that emphasized potential liability, never asked *why* this problem continued to occur and what they might do differently to prevent it. An existing database of research, compiled after talking to the couples, was ignored during the committee meetings and underutilized later. It showed, for example, that a simple reminder to new couples would reduce the "forgot to enroll" problem. Had the committee adopted a learning frame, the time spent reviewing appeals could have been cut in half—or more. More important, they might have decreased employee frustration and increased productivity by enabling new parents to focus on their work rather than worrying about medical coverage for their newborns.

With a bit of thought, most readers will find that they can relate similar experiences within their own organizations. Most people—through fear, laziness, or the wrong frame—overlook or even destroy a good deal of information that does exist, and that could otherwise help them understand whether their decisions have been wise and how they might be made better in the future. This embarrassing if common oversight can lay claim to far more missed learning opportunities than it ought to.

The disastrous flight of the *Challenger* space shuttle on January 28, 1986, provides another, this time catastrophic, example of ignored feedback. Technicians had studied the problematic O-rings in the shuttle boosters after each of thirty earlier space shuttle flights. On seven of those flights they had discovered serious wear, called "scoring." Engineers were concerned that this O-ring damage was correlated with cold weather. When they learned that

NASA intended to launch the *Challenger* despite near freezing temperatures, they objected.

But the positive feedback from twenty-three damage-free launches had made top NASA officials overconfident. The worried engineers were asked to produce evidence that the launch-time temperatures might cause damage. The discussion focused on the data shown in the first of the accompanying plots. NASA officials remained unconvinced of the cold weather link. According to the charts in front of them, several problems had occurred in flights launched when temperatures were 70 degrees or higher. Top managers at NASA and Morton Thiokol (the rocket booster's builder) agreed that the evidence on whether cold temperatures caused O-ring problems was "not conclusive." They okayed the launch. The O-rings failed and the rocket exploded, killing everyone aboard.

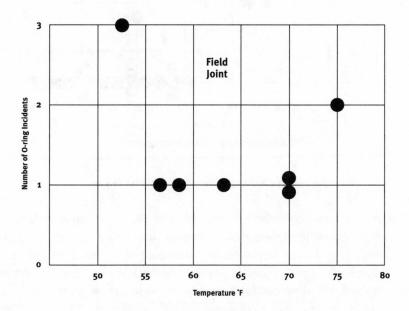

*Figure 8-1* **Challenger Data Reviewed Prior to Launch**

In reviewing the decision to launch, a new chart was produced. Note what is different. Data showing the temperature at launch-time for all flights in which *no* wear on the O-rings was discovered has now been added. Every one of the flights on which the O-rings escaped damage took place at a temperature of 66 degrees or above. Proper feedback would have shown that while the O-rings did indeed fail at a variety of temperatures, cold weather *enor-mously increased* the chance of O-ring failure.[5]

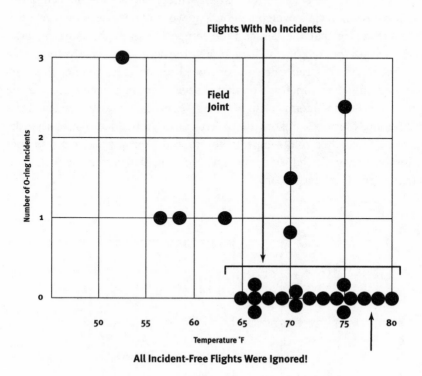

Figure 8-2 *Challenger* **Data from All Past Flights**

NASA's mistake—considering some, but not all, of the relevant data during intelligence-gathering—is more common than you might think. Sometimes people don't even recognize the relevance of the data they have. In particular, people often ignore important feedback about their failures because feedback about successful decisions seems somehow more relevant. A product manager at a major consumer goods company noted: "Of the new products we decide to field test, only the successes are evaluated. We don't try to determine why the other product ideas failed." Similarly, a consultant hired by a nonprofit social service agency to help it obtain grants began by trying to understand what characterized a successful grant application. He went to the agency's files only to find that all the unsuccessful applications— about 90 percent of the grant proposals written—had been destroyed.

Like NASA ignoring the O-rings that weren't scored, the converse can happen as well. One large bank we know decided to study why so many of its loans to medium and small businesses had gone sour in the early 1990s. Unfortunately, they restricted their analysis to the bad loans and failed to learn as much as possible by not contrasting them with the good loans. Success or failure, learning should be based on *all* the information available.

---

Lesson: Don't ignore information on outcomes you already possess—both good *and* bad.

---

Here's one more story, this time based on a study conducted at *Time* magazine by a team of decision researchers from Duke University. Accurate forecasts of advertising pages are vital to magazines since they are used both to make editorial commitments and predict the company's earnings for the year. Such forecasts are typically prepared by the publisher, advertising director, and business manager, who make their own independent predictions and then meet to arrive at a consensus forecast. The Duke researchers found that the managers performed well, not surprising given their extensive experience. Their estimates were off by an average of only about 10 percent (295 pages) annually. But the Duke researchers also found that a simple objective model (of the type we described in chapter 6) built from the data on actual ad sales—information easily available in the magazine's business records—made the managers' predictions look downright shoddy. When the model was used, the average forecast error was reduced 70 percent, dropping from 295 pages annually to just 89 pages. Further, the results were obtained in just a fraction of the eight to ten weeks per year that the managers spent at this task.[6]

Every opportunity should be used to find information that can improve decision-making, particularly repetitive decision-making. Yet this valuable feedback lay dormant, ignored at *Time* for years. We believe such lost opportunities abound at many organizations. For no good reason beyond ignorance or lack of discipline, much valuable feedback remains blissfully unanalyzed, seldom mined for all that it is worth.

 **Investigate fully the data available.**
There's no excuse for ignoring readily available feedback. Ask yourself: Am I making appropriate use of the information the organization has been retaining? What do we currently measure and record? Does anyone already track the information I need? Is the information in someone's head, a phone call away? Are there project files I could review? Is information being destroyed (e.g., the rejected grant applications) that could aid my learning now or later? Would modeling

techniques (e.g., *Time* magazine and those described in chapter 6) extract insights that I might otherwise miss?

 **Look from the outside/in.**

Use an "outsider's" perspective to learn something about your own experience. Ask yourself what your competitors could learn about you, your decisions, or your organization (from financial data, stock analysts' reports, former employees, and so on) if they set out to study it systematically. Are you neglecting information that would be freely available to them?

 **Stick to the facts.**

To learn well we must separate facts from inferences. When someone says "sales are down again because our competitor cut prices," one inference is made and three facts are claimed. First verify the facts. Are sales indeed down? Second, has this really happened before? And third, has your rival actually lowered prices? With the true facts in hand, try to generate *multiple* reasons why your sales may have dropped. (Remember the lessons in chapter 4 on seeking disconfirming evidence and testing multiple hypotheses.) The competitor's action is one possible explanation. Random fluctuation is another. And advertising effects or sales bonuses are yet another hypothesis.

## AMBIGUOUS FEEDBACK: DISTORTED AND CONFUSED

The real world is messy. So even when you take care to pay attention to all the information available, experience may provide feedback that is far from clear. If you open a new hamburger restaurant, for example, how much of your success stems from your excellent choice of location and how much from that lucky review by a celebrity who happened to be in the area? By the same token, if your restaurant fails, how much responsibility rests on poor decision-making and how much on government reports about "mad cow disease" that discouraged people from eating hamburger, a factor most certainly outside your control?

It's not always possible to determine how much of a given outcome really stems from skill and how much from luck. If you make the same kind of decision many times—e.g., hiring salespeople—the random factors tend to average out and it is usually safe to assume that your long-term success rate reflects skill rather than luck. But many of our most important decisions (such as what career to pursue, whether to accept a promotion or switch companies, and so on) are made only once or at most a few times in our lives.

No matter how wise you may be, this random "noise" greatly complicates learning from single or isolated experiences.[7] And in fact, at times you may be able to do no better than find incomplete or uncertain causal connections. Was it the location, or that lucky review? Can you claim decision-making skill or only good luck? And therein lies the next danger to learning from experience: a series of mental biases that stand ready to pounce on the fertile ground of that uncertainty, making it all the more difficult to apply the self-discipline needed to fight through the noise to figure out not only what happened, but why. We turn to these biases in the sections that follow.

## THE ILLUSION OF CONTROL

Victory has a thousand fathers; defeat is an orphan.

—the Duke of Wellington

The Spanish National Lottery is one of the oldest and largest lotteries in the world. Its Christmas-week drawing—affectionately called El Gordo ("the fat one")—is by far the largest; the event is televised and winners become celebrities overnight. One grand prize winner—asked by the Spanish media, "How did you know which ticket to buy?"—replied that he had searched until he found a ticket ending with the number forty-eight. "Why forty-eight?" the reporter queried. "For seven nights in a row," the enthusiastic winner said, "I dreamed of the number seven, and seven times seven is forty-eight . . ."[8]

Faulty math aside, the winner's equally flawed logic presents a much greater danger to learning and future decision-making. While it may be only human to claim credit when things turn out well and rationalize that we had no responsibility when they turn out badly, this mental bias is lethal to learning, destroying our chance to obtain objective feedback. Every outcome arises from a combination of skill (in both decision-making and implementation) and random chance—and it can be difficult to pinpoint exactly how much each factor contributed to the whole. But when this illusion of control distorts our perception of reality, it causes us to overestimate the odds of success and lay the wrong bets, as the Indiana Pacers painfully found out.[9]

A while back, the National Basketball Association held its annual player draft to assign teams the right to negotiate with each player about to graduate college. The prize that year was seven-foot-four Ralph Sampson of the University of Virginia. The two teams with the worst records in each of the NBA's two divisions—that year, the Indiana Pacers and the Houston Rockets—would decide who would have first choice (i.e., the right to pick Sampson) on the basis of a coin flip. Shortly before the coin toss the Pacers' manager confidently asserted: "We're going to win it. Somehow, some way, we're going to do it. We seem to be on a roll right now."

There is good reason to believe that the Pacers' management believed what they were saying. The Rockets had made an attractive offer to the Pacers for their half of the coin toss. (The offer was the number three pick in the 1983 draft, Houston's first pick in the 1984 draft, and the Pacer's choice of one of two established players on the Rockets' current team.) A Pacers representative said: "We turned it down . . . we're perfectly content to go into the coin toss, stare them right in the eye, and flip." On May 19 the coin was flipped. Houston won. Based on the above, it appears to us that the Pacers had walked away from an attractive offer because of an illusion.[10]

While we can laugh at those who claim control over obviously random events (such as a lottery or a coin toss), the illusion of control is pervasive, even among those who claim to know better. Once there is even a slight component of skill in a victory (as there is in almost all professional settings), it becomes extremely hard to acknowledge that a success may be due primarily to chance rather than ability.

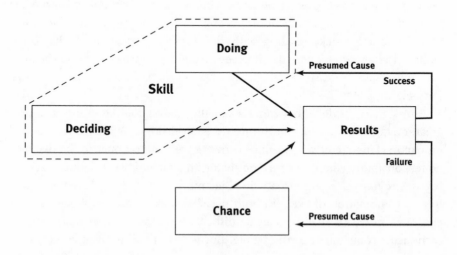

*Figure 8-3*

Like confidence, some sense of control over our environment is essential to our performance. Feeling powerless is debilitating. In one study, two experimental groups of workers were made to endure the same distracting background noise. Members of one group, however, were informed that they could turn off the noise at any time. Although they never touched the control switch, the group with control performed better than the group that had no control.[11] Similarly, dental patients who were told they have the power to flick a switch and turn off the drill, remained more relaxed than similar patients to whom no such control was granted—even if the people with the switch never exercised their power.

But *illusions* of control frequently cause people to repeat actions that in the past were followed by success, even if there's no reason to believe the actions did anything to cause the success. Only by realistically assessing the role of chance in successes can you learn which of your actions you should carefully repeat and which could be improved.

## SELF-SERVING RATIONALIZATIONS

Ninety-nine percent of failures come from people who have the habit of making excuses.  *—George Washington Carver*

If the tendency to claim credit for good outcomes causes us to overestimate our degree of control, most of us also possess a genius for underestimating our responsibility when things turn out badly. To avoid the pain of admitting mistakes we may distort our memory of what we actually did or said, unrealistically blame the failure on others or on supposedly unforeseeable circumstance, say our original prediction was misunderstood or misinterpreted, or change our current preferences so the failure seems less important, deciding that a desired outcome wasn't all that important to us after all.[12]

Self-serving explanations often seem entirely plausible. But since you can learn from mistakes only if you acknowledge them, rationalizations exact a heavy price. One Rand Corporation report, for example, documented cost underestimates on new energy plants. The average overrun on ten projects was 153 percent. The managers responsible blamed factors entirely outside their control, from bad weather to labor strikes to changes in construction specifications. Yet the Rand analysis showed that 74 percent of the cost-estimating errors could be traced to foreseeable, preventable causes; only 26 percent were due to factors outside management's control.[13]

Of course, the managers' rationalizations may have been partly aimed at improving their chances of obtaining future jobs. But they surely learned less from the experience of underestimating costs than they could have. (If you really must give your boss a misleading rationalization of why a project has failed, at least note privately what you would do differently the next time.) Rationalization, however, is usually driven by our internal desire to protect our egos rather than any real need to impress others.

To control the bias toward claiming undue credit for successes and rationalizing away failures requires intellectual honesty—the willingness to be as objective as possible. Acknowledge that some mistakes are inevitable; view them as learning opportunities. In fact, the person who never makes mistakes is unlikely to accomplish much. (We will talk more about seeing mistakes as learning opportunities in the next chapter.) For now, try the following approaches to accurately separate your real mistakes from chance events.

**Unambiguously define success beforehand; then measure it.**
Set clear criteria or milestones that unambiguously define success or failure. Determine what methods will be used to measure results, and make the separation between success and failure explicit. Specify to what extent you believe your own choices can influence the outcome of your effort. Then stick to those original criteria; don't move the goalposts after you've started the game. One human resource manager has created a spreadsheet where she logs (on a percentage basis) how good she thinks new hires will be and why. She then periodically reviews the sheet to compare her initial expectations with how well those employees actually do. Alternately, you might perform a "goal analysis"—explicitly listing the outcomes you want or dread— to flag those outcomes you will be least able to judge objectively in hindsight.

**Accept accountability; recognize limitations.**
Rather than exaggerate the role of bad luck when you fail, identify what you might have done to create a different outcome. Ask yourself: What should I have done differently? What problems did I mishandle? What did I avoid that should have been addressed? What more could I have done to get the result I wanted?

By the same token, when you succeed, honestly consider which actions contributed to success and which probably did not. Ask yourself: How much influence did I really have? How lucky was I? What role did others play? Did I know what I was doing or was I just guessing? (If you can't ask these questions in public, at least do so in private.)

 **Ask others for feedback.**

Ask people who had nothing to do with the project to review what happened. They are less likely to have preconceived ideas or vested interests in the outcome of an appraisal. Ask them what they think were the key factors in producing the final outcome and how your actions contributed to success or failure. Also ask: what more could I have done? What did I do well? What should I do differently next time?

---

Lesson: Beware of the tendency to inflate the contributions made by your skill when things turn out well and to overattribute failures to chance when they don't.

---

## THE "WE KNEW IT ALL ALONG" PHENOMENON

We've all experienced the 20/20 clarity of hindsight. Events often seem inevitable after the fact, even though they might have been very hard to predict beforehand. And novel analyses frequently sound obvious once we have heard the conclusions. To some small extent, we may actually understand a situation better when we think about it in hindsight. But in general, the clarity of hindsight is an illusion that hampers learning from experience. The more time elapses, the more we think that we predicted, or could have predicted, the eventual outcome all along.

The following study demonstrates the strength of this bias. Prior to President Richard Nixon's trips to China and Russia in 1972, two researchers asked students to consider fifteen possible outcomes, such as: the U.S. will establish a permanent diplomatic mission in Peking, but not grant diplomatic recognition; Nixon will meet Mao Tse-tung at least once; Nixon will see Soviet demonstrators; and so on.

The students were asked to assign a probability to each possible outcome. After the trip the students were asked in hindsight to assess the likelihood of these various outcomes and also asked to remember or reconstruct their original probabilities. When the pre- and post-trip tests were given two weeks apart, 67 percent of the students thought their original estimates were closer to the truth than they really were. When four to eight months elapsed between the tests, 84 percent thought they had predicted the truth.[14]

Why do such hindsight effects exist? We want to make sense of the world. Part of the hindsight bias may simply result from our need to feel that we knew what was likely to happen. But probably a larger part is a result of the way our minds process information. Our minds are not filing cabinets that store information the way it came in. Instead, we edit the information heavily, cut it up into pieces, and file the edited extracts in multiple parts of our minds, depending on what they are associated with. We synthesize and integrate new information into old knowledge. Like a glass of red wine poured into a bowl of clear water, the new blends with the old, and it becomes impossible to reverse the process. We truly cannot think the way we did before we knew that Nixon met with Mao during his trip to China. Similarly, adults cannot draw pictures as they did when they were four years old. (Even if adults draw stick figures, they use elements of perspective and proportion that children acquire only later.) We can't easily undo what we have learned.

Note the depth of the problem this creates for learning from feedback. Do the results of the China trip call for a reevaluation of the students' prior view of China or of communists? Do they suggest reevaluating China as a business partner? To judge accurately, the students should compare what they've learned with the assumptions that underlay their previous opinions. But they can't do that if they can't recall or reconstruct their earlier views.

Anyone who has worked as an advisor or consultant—or even presented business projections—knows this phenomenon well. Here's one example. A manager responsible for computer simulations of marketing strategies regularly received one of two responses to his simulation reports. The first: "This is so implausible that your model must be wrong; go back and check your assumptions." The second: "We already knew that." No matter how hard he worked, he couldn't win. By the time his boss had finished reading his reports, his most useful insights appeared obvious. The simulation manager finally moved to another position in frustration and disgust.

The best solution to this "nothing-really-new" dilemma is to ask people to predict or guess what you found *before they read your report*. Then you can demonstrate just how your analysis differs from their initial assumptions. In a presentation, ask the audience to write down their predictions prior to your revealing new findings. That way, you will most impress them with the value of what you have learned. Without such precommitment, people will probably say (and believe) that they knew your discoveries all along due to hindsight.

Similarly, when training new employees, don't present the outcome with the case. Make the trainees decide what they would have done in the same situation. This will convey the difficulty of the original decision and the uncertainty of the outcome. If the trainees get the outcome along with the case, the real flavor of the decision will get lost in a "knew it all along" feeling produced by hindsight.

The hindsight phenomenon is one reason you should record important agreements of all kinds in writing. Without a written record to turn to, people naturally come to believe different versions of the same fuzzy agreement once new information arises. Worse yet, they may have strategic reasons to misremember.

Unfortunately, the dangers of hindsight can't be entirely avoided by mere willingness to record predictions ahead of time. They are not solely rooted in our wishes, but also in the mechanisms of our mind—which are largely beyond our rational control. They demand that we take steps to prevent the problem when we first make our decisions. Scientists, athletes, and others who engage in endeavors of human achievement improve through the application of measurement, data collection, and systematic analysis. Try the following to help you do the same.

 **Use a "decision diary" to examine your predictions.**

To minimize hindsight effects, record your current predictions and opinions. Ask those who report to you to do the same. You needn't create an elaborate document. But write down not just the decision itself, but the rationale behind it. Compare the actual experience to the record of your initial expectations. Recording *predictions* for the success of a new branch office, the performance of a newly hired employee, the progress of a negotiation, and so on, will prevent self-serving interpretations where people claim that they knew right from the start that the chosen course of action would fail. Only by keeping some kind of record—and referring back to it from time to time—can you ensure that you will realize when you have something to learn. Ask yourself: What did you anticipate? How confident were you in the forecast? How much control did you think you might have on the outcome? Did trends play out as you expected?

 **Regularly record what you have learned.**

Even obvious insights can soon be forgotten. Most golf pros take notes when they play a course prior to a tournament and consult these notes during or after the game. One manager we know writes a "lesson learned" into her day planner daily. At the end of each month she reviews and compiles the entries, highlighting the most important. At the end of each year she reviews the list once again.

## ENSURING SYSTEMATIC LEARNING

Remember the clinical psychologists at the beginning of this chapter? Learning does not inevitably arise from experience—even from many years of experience. It takes time and disciplined effort, scarce commodities in a fast-paced world. Too often the demands of the next project drown out the lessons of the one just completed. For this reason, systematic learning analyses, in which you ask: "What have I learned, and what should I be learning, from recent experiences?" are integral to fully benefiting from that high-cost teacher: experience. They may take valuable time, but the potential payoff long-term—in higher quality, more reliable decisions—is well worth the investment. The structure and frequency of the learning analysis should depend on the particular situation, but everyone needs some form of learning analysis at regular intervals. Such an exercise forces you to draw reasonable conclusions, imprints the lessons of your experience in your mind, and enables you to plan strategically for learning in the future. The conclusion of a project may be a natural time to conduct a learning analysis. If you make decisions continually (for example, if you are a loan officer or a personnel manager), the analysis can be conducted once or twice a year—perhaps at the same time as standard performance reviews.

 **Conduct annual learning audits.**
Although sometimes intimidating in theory, the following procedure is almost always a surprisingly positive experience in practice. Once a year, request fifteen minutes with your boss. Spend an hour or two preparing a list of your "lessons learned" for the year. Notice not only what you have added to what you know, but what you have dropped because it is no longer true. (For example, consider not only what your key competitors do now that they didn't do a year ago, but also what they did then and no longer do.) Most people who conduct learning audits discover that they have learned more than they realize. Only when you sit down and reflect on it all at one time does that become apparent.

 **Analyze the decision process.**
Sometimes you can't get direct feedback on the outcome of a decision, or if you can it won't arrive in time to do you any good. Or perhaps the outcome in a particular case is determined as much by chance as by the quality of your decision. In these cases you have to focus not only on learning from *outcomes*, but on learning through analysis of

the decision *process* itself. A careful review of the decision processes is a vitally important part of obtaining feedback on your decisions.

*Examine the decision phases.* Ask yourself: What have I learned about my own frames? About the frames of others? What have I learned about the way we gather intelligence for our decisions? What have I learned about the process we use to reach final conclusions? In general, what do we value and not value about our decision processes?

*Examine how time was spent.* Was adequate time allocated to each decision phase? Was each stage completed successfully? Where did you spend too much time? Too little? How might you reallocate the time in your next decision?

 **Apply new learning.**

Carefully analyze how new information from the outcome of a recent project might cause you to revise a scenario you have already prepared for a future project. Consider changes to improve the quality and reliability of future decisions. What stage of the process could you perform better? Which strategies should you use more frequently? How could you avoid the traps you often encounter? What skills could you develop for making better decisions?

## Learning Under Fire

*People rarely have to figure out how to learn "under fire," as this stage can usually be postponed until the time pressure is off. However, it's important to remember that learning from experience needn't be a long, drawn-out process. A "lessons learned" analysis or audit of the decision process can be completed in an hour or less. Ask team members to e-mail you their view of the two most important lessons learned. (Warn them about the human tendency to claim credit for successes and rationalize failures. Let them know that you welcome their candor, and ask them not to discuss their answers with the others first). If you have a five-person team, you're likely to collect a list of seven to ten lessons. You can be almost certain that where there is overlap in the responses, there's importance.*

*A similar approach can be applied to learning from the decision process itself. Ask team members: Was the crux of the issue what we thought it would be? Did we allocate our time properly among the four stages? Was each stage completed successfully? How might we better allocate the time in our next decision? What have we learned about the process we use to reach final conclusions?*

*Finish by sharing the final list of lessons with your entire team; let them learn, too.*

## OVERCOMING INTERNAL BARRIERS TO LEARNING

In a rapidly changing environment, slow learning can ruin you and your organization. Fortunately, awareness alone can go a long way toward helping you learn. You can minimize the biases we've discussed if you remember the dangers and work to overcome them:

- *Reframe yourself* as a learner. Focus not only on the decision outcome, but on the process you used. Learn from your failures as well as your successes. And regularly ask what outdated beliefs it is time to discard.

- Don't fall into the trap of *claiming credit* for successes that have occurred by chance. When you succeed at something, honestly consider which of your actions seem to have contributed to your success and which probably didn't. Ask trusted colleagues to help you be objective in your evaluation.

- Avoid *rationalization* when you fail. If you exaggerate the importance of bad luck in your failures, you miss one of the biggest opportunities in all of professional life: the chance to learn from mistakes. You've paid the price, you may as well extract the lesson. When you receive negative feedback from previous decisions, at least take an honest look at it privately. If possible, discuss its importance with those you trust. Review scenarios you've created for the future and decide whether they should be changed.

- Minimize the effects of *hindsight bias* by keeping records of what you expected when you made your major decisions. Then compare the actual results to your expectations, and consider what lessons you should learn.

- Use *systematic learning analyses*. For long-term improvement in decision-making ability, discipline yourself to take time regularly to ask what you have learned.

We will turn to the organizational obstacles to learning in the next chapter. But you can do much to promote your own learning—regardless of your environment—with just these simple steps. As William Shakespeare's character Benedict exclaims in *Much Ado About Nothing*: "Happy are they that can hear their detractions and put them to mending."[15] Create an aptitude, even an enthusiasm for learning, and you will find that there is no limit on the extent to which you can get better at getting better.

CHAPTER 9

# Learning in Organizations

In times of change, learners inherit the earth, while the learned find
themselves beautifully equipped to deal with a world that no longer
exists.[1]  —*Eric Hoffer*

ROYAL DUTCH/SHELL'S Arie de Geus tells the following story. In the early 1900s, milkmen in England would deliver bottles of milk to the door of each country home. At that time the bottles had no cap, and two different species of British garden songbirds—the titmouse and the red robin—learned to siphon the sweet, rich cream from the top. Then, between the two world wars, dairy distributors began placing aluminum seals on the bottles. Cut off from the rich, abundant food source, individual birds—both robins and titmice—occasionally figured out how to pierce the seals. By the early 1950s the entire titmouse population in the United Kingdom—almost a million birds—had learned how to pierce the seals. However, although individual robins had been as innovative in breaking the seals as individual titmice, the red robins as a group never regained access to the cream. The knowledge never passed from the individual innovators who had learned to pierce the milk bottle seals to the rest of the species.

Scientists were curious about why. This difference in learning behavior could not be attributed to the birds' ability to communicate. As songbirds, both the titmice and the red robins had the same wide range of communication. Their social organizations, however, differed greatly. Red robins are territorial birds. A male robin will not allow another male to enter its territory. When threatened, the robin sends a warning as if to say, "Keep the hell out of here." They communicate in an antagonistic manner, with fixed boundaries they do not cross.

Titmice, by contrast, are a social species. They live in couples in the spring, until they have reared their young. By early summer, when the young titmice are flying and feeding on their own, the birds move from garden to garden in flocks of eight to ten. These flocks seem to remain intact, moving together around the countryside. The conclusion of the scientists who studied this case: birds that flock seem to learn faster. They increase their chances to survive and evolve more quickly.

"Any organization with several hundred people is bound to have at least a couple of innovators," says de Geus. "There are always people curious enough to poke their way into new discoveries, like the titmice finding their cream. However, keeping a few innovators on hand is not enough, in itself, for institutional learning. . . . Even if you develop a high-caliber system of innovation, you will *still* not have institutional learning until you develop the ability to 'flock.' "[2]

While the organizational support you receive for becoming a better decision-maker matters in all stages of our decision-making process, nowhere does it matter more—and nowhere do we address it more—than in learning from experience. As de Geus's story so aptly conveys, learning can only proceed so far as a solitary activity. In the last chapter we provided tools and strategies that you can employ largely on your own to enhance learning. In this chapter the picture is more complicated. Some of the barriers that block the route from "knowing what" to "knowing why" are built into the organization or the environment. They have to do with how and where information is stored and shared (or not), the way the real world distorts feedback on outcomes that are influenced by a complex mix of decision and action, and the organizational norms that determine whether learning behaviors are rewarded or punished. These barriers are not completely under your control (unlike the ones in chapter 8); you will need the cooperation of others to change them. Doing so will require more than the awareness we advocated in the last chapter; it will require systematically building opportunities for learning into the organizational environment. It requires learners to "flock."

Fortunately, the concept of institutional learning and the "learning organization" has experienced tremendous growth in the last decade. One of the first published references to the idea, "Post-Project Appraisals Pay," appeared in the *Harvard Business Review* only in the late 1980s.[3] A plethora of wonderful books, such as Peter Senge's *Fifth Discipline*, has been published since then—and nearly every organization now talks, in some way, about learning. The most successful have implemented widespread changes—including creating special units devoted to fostering learning—to ensure that it takes place. (Not surprisingly—in hindsight—this emphasis on learning occurred in a period of profound external change involving deregulation, globalization, new technologies, and generation shifts.)[4]

Since our focus in this book is not on organizations, but on people, we will be talking in this chapter primarily about how *individuals* learn—or not—*within organizations*. We will point out ways to be more like the social titmouse rather than the solitary robin. We will talk a bit about building a "learning organization" later in the chapter, but again we will focus primarily on the ways that individuals can impact learning—among their colleagues or within their group or unit. For readers who wish to explore this subject in more depth than we can provide here, we refer you to the numerous references in the endnotes.

## MISSING IN ACTION

You can't hope to capture the elusive "why" that signals learning from experience if you don't first know *what* happened. But far too often, organizational and environmental barriers prevent decision-makers from learning the results of their decisions. Sometimes considerable time may pass between when a decision is made and when the results are known. For example, if you approve the research department's request for a budget increase, it may take years before the results of your actions are known. By then you may be elsewhere in the organization and never learn whether the department did anything useful with the money. At many major multinational companies, senior managers are promoted every three to five years to different functions and countries, while their biggest decisions may take five to ten years to play out.

Other times, the barriers are far more arbitrary than the passage of time. The information you need may exist in the present, but be tracked or stored elsewhere in the organization. A marketing manager may have changed the products' price or advertising venue, for example, but the sales department is likely to have the best data on that decision's effect. Often local supervisors know best how policies developed in the personnel department really work—and the human resources director never learns what they know.[5]

Finally, people rarely learn what might have happened from the results of actions not taken. For example, you can learn about the success or failure of the job candidate you hire, but you usually learn nothing about those you reject. Perhaps candidate X, who wasn't selected for the position, would have been even more successful than the person offered the job. Even though they could, many investment professionals (and the rest of us amateurs, as well) don't track the stocks or funds we *don't* buy, and so rarely know whether they would have outperformed those we did select. Manufacturers miss feedback from the potential new products they choose *not* to pursue. Without this kind of missing feedback, we never learn whether our decision rules for predicting success are worth all that much.[6]

Getting better information on these missing outcomes needn't be time-consuming or complex. It must, however, be approached consciously and systematically, and may require some leadership and creativity. Below we cite several examples of organizations that recognized inadequate feedback and found ways to augment it. The result: much improved information on the quality of their decisions—and learning that led to better (and more profitable) decisions.

---

Lesson: When we don't capture information on the results of our actions—those options we passed over as well as those we chose—we never learn whether our decision rules are worth all that much.

---

 **Give decision-makers timely feedback on outcomes.**

Sometimes the solution to the problem of missing information is quite simple: give people access to it. When decision-makers miss learning the outcome of their decisions because of structural barriers in how information is tracked and stored, they should demand or build new feedback loops. Consider this story from Harrah's Casino in Atlantic City, New Jersey. Casinos typically provide credit to their customers to enable them to continue to play the games even when their cash is gone. The casino industry's standard for making loan decisions is reflected in the phrase taught to all new loan officers: "When in doubt, give it out." But casinos suffer millions of dollars in bad debt losses each year.

Frank Quigley, vice president of operations at Harrah's Atlantic City, decided to see whether he could improve his loan officers' decision-making abilities. Noting that loan officers were never told the results of their credit decisions, he instituted a simple change: the accounting office was required to tell loan officers whether or not each loan was repaid. As a result, his loan officers were able to refine their decision criteria; losses due to bad debt at Harrah's Atlantic City fell 25 percent in the first year alone and continued to fall thereafter.

 **Track the path not traveled.**

In many cases, it can be difficult or impossible to directly track the path not traveled. But sometimes it can be done—and it is always worth considering. Follow-up phone calls to attractive job candidates who choose to go elsewhere can provide a wealth of information with only a minimal investment of effort. One industry, money management, is becoming increasingly interested in tracking—via shadow portfolios—the normally missing information about the options not chosen. Once analysts have made their stock recommendations, policy committees typically decide how much money to invest in each. However, the most sophisticated of these firms also analyze how well the recommendations they *rejected* would have done. Because feedback (in the form of market prices) is available for both the accepted and rejected stocks, management can compare the quality of different analysts' recommendations without having to buy the stocks themselves. Indeed, in some firms, analysts' annual compensation is based on the performance of their complete "shadow portfolios"—all the stocks that they recommended, not just the ones they convinced the policy committee to invest in.

## BEWARE THE SELF-FULFILLING PROPHECY

In many complex decisions, deciding and doing are entwined in a way that is difficult—if not impossible—to separate. Did you select great sales representatives through a good hiring rule, or are their stellar end-of-quarter sales reports the result of enrolling average individuals in an outstanding training program? It may be a bit of both, but to learn about your hiring (i.e., decision-making) process requires that you know how much of the outcome came from a good decision versus how much from good training (i.e., implementation).

When you can't untangle whether (or how much) outcomes arise from decisions vs. implementation, you've laid the groundwork for a dangerous learning trap: the self-fulfilling prophecy. In these cases, we influence the outcomes of our decisions in ways that make the quality of the decisions themselves hard to judge. When senior managers choose people to mentor, they do much more than bet on their protégé's success. They also tell their protégés that they believe in them and provide advice, opportunities, and assistance to increase their success. Thus, it becomes even more difficult to learn whether the decision process for selecting that protégé was a good one. Is the protégé's success due to an excellent selection process, or the help given along the way? Similarly, a venture capital firm invests in the start-ups with the highest expected payoff and takes a seat on the board of directors.

On average, the start-ups do well. Did the VC firm choose wisely, or was its guidance the primary cause of success? Although in each case such actions make good sense, they confound later attempts to analyze the outcomes and learn from them.[7]

Self-fulfilling prophecies are perhaps most common in job interviews. Interviewers form impressions from reading job applications, then look for confirming evidence when they conduct the interviews. In one study, interviewers were told (randomly) that personality tests revealed the person they were about to interview was either warm or cold. Sure enough, after the interview, they described the interviewees exactly as they had been led to expect.[8] Sometimes, of course, prophecies can be self-destroying. The doomsday scenarios about Y2K problems are partly responsible for the absence of major malfunctions at the start of the new millennium.

Lesson: In many cases, we influence the outcomes of our decisions through subsequent actions. This makes the quality of the decisions themselves hard to judge.

## EXPERIMENTATION: DESIGNED FEEDBACK

Given this real-world complexity, how then do you learn from experience when you can't directly track the path not traveled or separate the impact of the decision from its implementation? One answer: you can conduct experiments.

Advertising executive David Ogilvy exemplified the experimenting spirit. To stay a step ahead of his competition, Ogilvy pursued a strategy of trying a few offbeat ads, ones that typically would be rejected under standard decision guidelines and that "conventional wisdom" predicted would fail. Indeed, most of these ads did flop; however, the few that succeeded against all expectation pointed the way to novel approaches, innovations that proved extremely profitable to Ogilvy's clients. What's more, the flops were not that costly. Ogilvy watched his "experiments" closely and quickly pulled the losers.[9]

Often the idea of experimenting seems counterintuitive to those not trained as scientists. We spend our professional lives trying to create successes. Why set up an experimental situation in which, in at least some cases, we are destined to fail? (For Ogilvy it was nearly all cases.) The answer has to do with the trade-off between short- and long-term goals. Experiments may be costly in the short-term. But long-term, they can show you how good your decision rule really is and how to build a better one, enabling you to make decisions more effectively in the future. Running an experiment may turn out to be undoable, but it shouldn't be unthinkable.

The old Bell system (before the 1984 breakup) used experimentation—on a large scale. As regulated monopolies, Bell system operating companies could not refuse service to new customers—even those they believed to be poor credit risks. However, the companies generally were allowed to cover these risks by requiring a deposit from a predefined percentage of customers. Thus, the companies wanted to identify those new customers who were most likely to default on their telephone payments, and then require deposits from exactly those people. The importance of an optimal decision policy for security deposits was magnified by the size of the Bell companies, with twelve million new customers per year when the experiment was conceived. The total bad debt at that time was over $450 million per year, $300 million alone from new accounts.

Bell executives turned for advice to researchers at Bell Laboratories, who suggested a counterintuitive experiment. Nearly one hundred thousand randomly selected new customers should be given telephone service without a security deposit. This bold action was certain to cost a lot of money in defaulted payments, but it would probably help build smarter selection rules.

But how much smarter? Would the future savings, if any, be worth the cost? After nine months the results of the study were in. New decision rules were built, one for each state. Bell Laboratories estimated that these more intelligent decision rules would save it $137 million per year, every year, for at least a decade. The experiment itself cost about one-tenth of that.[10]

Note that the revenue increase was not obtained by requiring more deposits. The reduction in bad debt was achieved solely by more intelligently identifying the high-risk new customers, based on more complete feedback. The phone companies required deposits not from *more* customers, but from *different* customers.

## STATISTICAL "EXPERIMENTS"

Sometimes you can't (or don't want to) conduct an experiment that involves deliberately violating your existing decision rules. Perhaps it will be too costly—in sheer dollars or in public perception. In those cases, you might want to conduct a statistical "experiment"—an analysis that tests whether your assumptions are realistic.

For example, suppose you want to test whether your hiring decision rules for sales representatives are well founded. You could run an actual one-year experiment in which you fill half (or maybe just a tenth) of the available slots with people who otherwise would have been rejected. The results would help you select new sales reps more effectively in succeeding years. But you don't want to really hire anyone you deem inferior—and you probably couldn't sell this experiment to the rest of your organization anyway.

Instead, you can perform a statistical study. Let's say your current decision rule takes account of your applicants' sales experience, their education, the impression made during an interview, and other factors. Are these really predictors of sales success in your company? If they are, then not only should the people you hire perform better than those you do not hire, but those who score *best* in the applicant pool should perform better than those who score just barely high enough to be hired. Do they? Look at their records and find out.

You won't get as full or complete an account of what factors predict success in sales through this kind of statistical analysis as you would by hiring a random sample of all applicants. And you could fall into the trap that tripped up NASA when looking at the problem Challenger flights, since the risk factor posed by temperature only became visible when examining all cases. But if you are rigorously honest, you may well demonstrate that some factors you considered important don't predict success at all.[11]

---

Lesson: Experiments can help us learn from experience when we can't directly track the path not traveled or separate the impact of the decision from its implementation. Experiments can create the needed experience.

---

## VIRTUAL "EXPERIMENTS": ACCELERATED FEEDBACK

Computer-based simulations let people test their decision-making abilities— and see the results immediately, without real-world consequences. Such simulations range from off-the-shelf software that can be run on your desktop computer and played in an hour to custom-designed games that require millions of dollars to create and days or weeks to play. Some of the latest simulations even incorporate virtual reality. Many simulations allow for generic learning, enabling players to experiment with a variety of strategies to achieve a desired result. Custom games enable decision-makers to test outcomes for a well-defined, real question. In both cases, decision-makers can take risks that might be cautiously avoided in real-world settings; in a virtual environment, "failure" costs nothing and feedback is immediate.[12]

Simulations can also allow decision-makers to test multiple options. One company, trying to choose between several strategic options, received computer-generated "quarterly performance data." Running the existing strategy led to falling profits, quarter after quarter. The team reluctantly changed its strategy, profits started to go up, and to their relief, by the end of "five years" the profits were significant. But fortunately, they didn't immediately return to the office and implement the new strategy. Remember missing information on the paths not taken? The consultant running the simulation suggested that they play again, this time sticking with their original strategy over the long haul just to see what would have happened. The unexpected result: over the long-term, profits from the original strategy were double that of their revised approach.[13]

The value of testing competitive strategies through simulation prior to launch was brought home powerfully to Shell Oil a few years ago when it considered building many unstaffed service stations requiring self-service by customers in order to greatly expand the company's presence in the retail market. The key question was how rivals would react. By building a competitive computer simulation, Shell Oil was able to test its new expansion strategy in ten different market segments, reflecting varying demographics, competitors, and consumer needs. The conclusion: Shell Oil would benefit in the short term, but would lose in the long run; don't proceed with the new unstaffed service stations. The reason: adding new stations would likely spark a "pump war" to protect market share in a zero-sum game. The company originally estimated $315 million in *additional* profits (above the expected $211) in one geographic market over five years by implementing the expansion strategy. But the computer simulation showed that it would eventually lose $133 million due to the probable pump war unleashed by its action.[14]

Compared to experiencing the $133 million loss for real, the simulation was a cheap and effective alternative, although it remains just that—a simulation. To be credible, key managers need to endorse the simulation and participate in its development. Often, a simulation model can be back-tested to see if it would have predicted market developments or competitive actions from the past. Further, a simulation model could be used to examine the robustness of a strategy across a variety of future scenarios. For example, how would Shell's marketing strategy have fared in the case of a severe recession, an aggressive new entrant, or a strong environmental group opposed to some or all of the gasoline companies?

The real value of a good simulation model is that it forces managers to surface their implicit assumptions and even mental models, while thinking through the consequences of their strategic actions, all in a spirit of joint learning rather than playing for real. Learning and play are often entwined, and most managers have too few opportunities to be playful when it comes to their business.

 **Consider experimenting.**

Ask yourself whether you can create a real, statistical, or simulated experiment to help pinpoint the true causes of the outcomes observed. The tools offered in chapter 4 can help ensure that you obtain undistorted information. Beware, in particular, of the tendency to use experimental results simply to confirm preexisting notions. Even rigorously trained scientists fall prey to this bias, as NASA's moon rocks story shows. Hoping to help settle competing theories of how the moon came into existence, NASA distributed its collection of moon rocks to numerous laboratories. Once all the labs had thoroughly investigated the samples, NASA hoped a scientific consensus would emerge. To their dismay the opposite happened. After studying the rocks, each research group was more convinced than ever that its own theory was correct. Somehow the identical evidence presented by the moon rocks was selectively analyzed and interpreted to protect existing theories and established positions.[15]

## THE LEARNING ORGANIZATION

We began this chapter by asserting that learning fully from experience requires organizational cooperation. While we hope you work in an environment that supports learning, many decision-makers must operate in organizations still struggling to integrate learning into their collective frame. For readers in this situation, your challenge is to assess and change as much of the organization as you care to, or can.[16]

How do you know to what extent your organization has stretched its traditional performance frame to incorporate learning? Try describing your organization's culture and norms. A learning culture is at the heart of a learning organization. Much of learning involves challenging old ideas and assumptions. Is such behavior allowed as a norm? Are decisions audited? Are lessons-learned reports prepared? Is helping the organization to learn (spreading knowledge) rewarded at the individual level? Is such cooperation captured in performance reviews? Are people evaluated for process as well as outcome? Are reviews designed to assess performance only or also to enhance learning?

How does your organization distribute responsibility for learning at the corporate or division level? Who is charged with aggregating knowledge and making it widely available? Are people evaluated, rewarded, and promoted for sharing knowledge? When do these activities appear on people's performance evaluations? This is the whole point of knowledge management. The rise in the number of CLOs (chief learning officers) and CKOs (chief knowledge officers)—jobs that didn't exist a decade ago—is testament to the recognition that unless someone is in charge of disseminating information across an organization, it is unlikely to occur.

The accompanying chart can help you decide to what extent you are part of a learning organization. Which column more accurately describes your organization? Then consider the principles and tools that follow. Perhaps you can apply them only within your own group, but from there they may spread throughout your organization.

## Learning Organizations

Do you have a learning organization? Review the accompanying table.[17] The left-hand column lists characteristics that lead to a learning organization; the one on the right, characteristics that detract from learning. Which better describes your organization or group?

| Positive Indicators | Negative Indicators |
| --- | --- |
| **Operating Characteristics** | |
| Anticipatory | Reactive |
| Long-term focus | Short-term/operating focus |
| Change=Opportunity | Change=Threat |
| Adapts/adjusts to change | Static organization/sterile culture |
| **Culture** | |
| Simple structure | Complex and bureaucratic |
| Participative management style | Autocratic or directive management style |
| Strong networking | Lack of sharing/disconnected functions |
| Open flow of information | Information used as power base |
| External scanning encouraged | Insular/lacking external contacts |

| Culture | |
|---|---|
| Encourages questioning and review | Closed mind-set/tunnel vision |
| Innovation/experimentation encouraged | Non-risk-taking |
| Failures used as learning opportunities | Failure punished |

| Development | |
|---|---|
| Individual development encouraged | Development aimed at conformity |
| Systems in place to support sharing, | Slow processing of information |
| review of experience, and provide | Lack of cross-functional |
| organizational memory | communication |

| Whole | |
|---|---|
| Greater than total individual | Fails to make full use of individuals |
| contributions | |

## DEVELOP A LEARNING CULTURE

Warning: The truth shall set you free, but first it may infuriate you. Here's a true story we find amusing, but telling: "An executive director of a trade association heard a speech by two psychologists about the uses of upward feedback. Inspired, he went back to his office, designed a confidential form [asking for feedback on his performance as a boss], and circulated it to his staff. Under the protection of anonymity, his employees no longer felt that they had to obey [his prior signals to tell him what he wanted to hear], and they told him what they really thought—which was not what he wanted to hear. Convinced by his expectations and preferences that somehow the evaluations he had received were neither fair nor credible, he reprinted the forms and sent them out again, but with the following note attached: 'I'd like you to fill out these forms again—and this time rate me accurately.' "[18]

It's hard to accept feedback when we find its content disturbing. Unfortunately, behaving like territorial robins, with their threatening chirps to "stay away," does little to promote real learning. Few decision-makers are as transparent as the ego-driven director just described. The same problem, however, occurs in most organizations—albeit in more subtle ways. And it doesn't just bias the feedback people provide their supervisors. It also leads people to temper the feedback they provide their subordinates.[19]

In the U.S. Marines, on the other hand, officers learn to master the art of announcing provisional plans, inviting everybody to shoot holes in them, and then plugging the holes before it really counts. Subordinates know to salute once the plan is finalized. Until then, they know to resist and challenge all ideas that may not work, even when it entails going over the head of an immediate commander. Marines with the skill and courage to follow this process are drawing together two of our earlier lessons. First, they are distinguishing deciding from doing. Second, they welcome conflict among ideas in the coming to conclusions stage, but not in the implementation of that action.[20]

 **Replace "defending and debating" with "listening and learning."**

Create a culture where people feel free to tell it like it is. Jerry Hirshberg, retired president of Nissan Design International, notes: "Many of the best ideas are communicated through whispers—in the hallway meetings that happen after the official meeting. That's because people worry about how the boss will react if they speak the truth. What's remarkable, of course, is that these whispered ideas are what companies are most hungry for. So the next time you feel yourself defending and debating, stop—and start listening and learning instead."[21]

## LEARN FROM OTHERS

Sometimes the most powerful insights already exist—in someone else's head. That someone else may be in another part of your organization, or in another organization or even industry. One CEO, in his desire to create a learning organization, encouraged his staff to learn as much as possible about other parts of the organization. They were to ask for whatever information they wanted, without any explanation or justification. He recognized that learning happens at the interstices, intersections, even fringes. The new mandate was a culture shock to his organization, where in the past information was "for your eyes only."

 **Seek out and share internal "best practices."**

Most people only use a fraction of the knowledge available in their organization. Xerox, on the other hand, is well-known for its zealous pursuit of benchmarking and sharing best practices. In 1993 its partially owned European subsidiary Rank Xerox created Team C, several dozen employees charged with helping divisions learn from one another. In a remarkably simple and successful effort, they collected sales data from every division and found eight cases in which one country dramatically outperformed the others. After brief site visits to determine what the leading office did, team members put together a book for sales and service managers that showed what each benchmark was, how their territory compared with it, and how the top performer's systems worked. (To avoid some of the usual challenges to such efforts, they selected cases so that no country was the benchmark more than once, allowed managers to decide which three or four best practices to implement, and set ambitious goals so that immediate action was required. No dithering or "further study" was allowed.) The results: an extra $65 million in sales (1.4 percent of total revenues) the first year that could be credited directly to the best practices initiatives, and a combined incremental sales growth of $200 million (3.64 percent of revenues) from two years' activity.[22]

   **Learn from other organizations.**

Benchmark yourself against top-performing organizations. These need not be in your own industry or profession. Stanford University researcher Kathleen Eisenhardt, who studies top-performing Silicon Valley firms, has found that they tracked real-time information on operations and the competitive environment; built multiple, simultaneous alternatives; consistently sought advice from those outside their firm; used consensus to reach decisions when possible, but moved ahead without it when it couldn't be found; and applied portfolio thinking, integrating every decision with other decisions.[23] No matter what industry you're in, more and more successful companies will find themselves looking like these agile high-tech organizations. To what extent is your organization already using these best practices?

Strategic alliances and partnerships are also excellent ways to learn from others. Although not necessarily formed primarily for this purpose, they usually present an easy opportunity to inject new perspectives or techniques into your own organization. Ask yourself "What do they do differently, does it work, and why?"

## TRANSFER KNOWLEDGE

Knowledge is precious—and even more so when it is shared broadly. But too often, key knowledge resides only in people's heads. To make matters worse, staff turnover—due to downsizing, shorter tenures for employees, and other organizational changes—has shortened the collective organizational memory. To enable new employees to draw on past experiences, develop formal procedures to capture information.[24]

 **Preserve organizational learning.**
Here's another story about the U.S. Marines, an organization that has honed the ability to learn quickly. "Every Marine is at heart a teacher and mentor, obliged to pass on his knowledge and the benefit of his experience to his subordinates," notes former Marine Commandant Charles C. Krulak. Seasoned Marines transfer wisdom to fresh recruits through repeatedly shared "sea stories," or accounts of their prior experiences. As a result, young soldiers acquire a repertoire of previous "cases" from which they can develop guidelines for future action.[25]

Other companies have turned to their intranets to create a virtual storehouse of knowledge. French computing-services giant Gemini Sogeti, for example, dubbed its intranet "Knowledge Galaxy." The system places accumulated knowledge, resources, and expertise within every employee's reach, enabling them to build upon past experience rather than repeat it. One project manager sent an electronic SOS for a software-development tool that would help it blend off-the-shelf software packages with a customer's business applications. Building the tool from scratch would take at least eighteen months. Two days later the company's British unit responded with a tool that could be tailored to meet the customer's needs. Within three weeks Gemini presented the solution and clinched the development contract.[26]

## LEARN FROM PAST EXPERIENCE

The philosopher George Santayana said it best, in his well-known phrase: "Those who cannot remember the past are condemned to repeat it."[27] Unfortunately, organizations too often tend to repeat their *mistakes,* while allowing *smart decisions* to be single occurrences.

 **Develop "learning histories."**

"In corporate life, even when experience is a good teacher, it's still only a private tutor. People in organizations act collectively, but they learn individually," say MIT researcher George Roth and consultant Art Kleiner. Together with their colleagues at MIT's Center for Organizational Learning, Kleiner and Roth have turned to the ancient practice of storytelling to develop a tool they call the **learning history** to help people collectively understand the meaning of an event. These written narratives—or case studies—offer two perspectives of a particular event, presented side-by-side. In the right-hand column, events are described by the people who took part, were affected by, or observed them. The left-hand column contains analysis and commentary by "learning historians"—trained outsiders and knowledgeable insiders—who identify recurrent themes, pose questions, and raise "undiscussable" issues. The document forms the basis for group discussions, both for those involved in the event and for others who also might learn from it. Kleiner and Roth's research indicates that this "jointly told tale" can help organizations make sense of major, often controversial incidents in a way that builds trust, stimulates collective reflection and learning, raises issues that people may not have had the courage to discuss openly, builds a body of generalized knowledge about what works and what doesn't, and successfully transfers knowledge from one part of the organization to another.[28]

 **Map the minefield.**

Identify and list important factors that often contribute to decision problems in your organization. Which decision traps are most common? Where does decision-making typically break down? Which groups have the most difficult time reaching agreement or finding good solutions? Why?

 **Conduct group learning audits.**

In the previous chapter we advocated systematic learning audits as the most powerful tool we know to ensure learning comprehensively from past experience. Like individuals, organizations wanting to promote **widespread** learning should institutionalize regular learning analyses. Use the questions at the end of chapter 8 to guide you.

British Petroleum was one of the first companies to do this systematically, with a decision-auditing system that has saved BP tens of millions of dollars. The Post-project Appraisal Unit, based at corporate headquarters, does nothing but analyze major recent decisions for lessons applicable to the company as a whole. By creating a separate unit, BP has encouraged objective decision auditing. The Post-project Appraisal Unit has great latitude in choosing what decisions to review (though it typically focuses on the biggest decisions, where much is at stake). A manager and several assistants report directly to British Petroleum's board of directors. Unit members interview in pairs. One asks questions while the other watches the interviewee for signs of doubt or less than complete candor. They conduct only six project appraisals per year because the corporation "can absorb only so much information at a time," said Frank R. Gulliver, one of the unit's founders. The unit not only chooses its own audit subjects, but is also charged with communicating its discoveries throughout the organization.[29]

Group learning audits can also be simple: John Seely Brown, chief scientist at Xerox Corporation, and his senior team have a two-hour lunch every Friday where they reflect on what they did well, what they did wrong, and what they can learn from it all.[30]

## "MISTAKES" VS. "INVESTMENTS IN LEARNING"

The following story is told about Thomas Watson, Sr., founder of IBM. An executive dejectedly approached Watson after making an error that had cost the company $10 million. "Go ahead," said the executive. "Fire me. I deserve it." "Fire you?" Watson responded. "I just spent ten million dollars educating you."[31]

We'd be remiss to conclude a chapter on learning without talking about mistakes. In fact, the fear of making mistakes—and their consequences—may be one of the most intransigent barriers to learning. It's not surprising. Contrast Watson with the division president we mentioned in chapter 1, who rhetorically asked us whether he should promote the person with a track record of 50 percent mistakes, or the one who had made no mistakes. Until recently, attempting to bury (or at least rationalize) mistakes was the norm in corporate culture. For example, researchers examined CEOs' letters to shareholders in annual reports of eighteen large corporations over a period of eighteen years starting in the mid-1960s—three hundred and twenty-four letters in all. They found that management claimed credit for 83 percent of the positive events while accepting blame for only 19 percent of the negative events.[32] We found similar results when we looked at private divisional reports in a large corporation.

This norm, however, appears to be changing—perhaps as a result of the growing value being placed on learning from experience. Annual reports in the 1990s were more likely than their predecessors to quote corporate leaders reporting bad news and taking clear responsibility.[33] Euphemisms and evasiveness were out; candor was in. While this may have been in part a public relations response to changing public expectations, it highlights the changing frame dominating successful organizational behavior today.

John Chambers, president and CEO of Cisco Systems, has said: "Anyone who takes risks and does not make mistakes is kidding themselves—you're not taking a risk. And companies who say, 'We're risk takers' and then you ask their key employees, what happens if you miss and they say, 'I get shot,' they aren't risk takers either."[34] At Procter & Gamble the motto is: "Fail cheap, fast, and frequently." And therefore: Learn cheap, fast, and frequently.

Not many organizations frame risk-taking like Cisco, or P&G, and we can't always make them. But we can use whatever power and freedom we have within our own organizations to nudge them in the right direction.

To create a learning organization, leaders must create an environment in which people are not punished for making honest mistakes, but rather only for failing to learn from their mistakes. The U.S. Department of Veterans Affairs (formerly the Veterans Administration; VA) deserves credit for enthusiastically embracing the notion of learning from mistakes in a profession that has traditionally shunned public admissions of failure. While doctors have always conducted "postmortems," cultural and legal norms created many barriers to collective learning from experience. Infallibility was valued; mistakes represented a failure in character; and opportunities for malpractice lawsuits were minimized. Although individual physicians might learn from their mistakes and change their behavior accordingly, such learning often took place in a vacuum, without the learning being transferred to the doctor's organization—or the profession as a whole.

In 1999 the VA asked James Bagian, a physician, engineer, and astronaut, to use his scientific experience to examine the *process* behind medical errors. And in May 2000 the VA announced that it had hired NASA to replicate for the 172 VA hospitals the program that has been so successful in improving aviation safety: establishing a system where errors could be reported without fear of penalty and the information analyzed to create safeguards against future mistakes.

The VA's three-year, $8.2 million experiment is no small matter. The prestigious Institute of Medicine reported in 1999 that medical mistakes kill 44,000 to 98,000 hospitalized Americans a year. In the new VA/NASA initiative, any health worker can report mistakes they make or witness. After the worker is interviewed for more details, identifying information is stripped from the database. NASA-hired medical experts will then analyze how an error happened and seek design procedures to prevent it from happening again.

When an airplane crashes, says Bagian, "Aircraft-investigation people don't come in and say, 'Whose fault is it?' They say, 'What happened?' " And then they try to fix it so that it doesn't happen again. The new system is set to launch in January 2001. But some quick process improvements have already been seen from Bagian's initial work, such as using bar-coding of medications to combat drug mix-ups due to sloppy handwriting and similar drug names.[35]

Perhaps no industry has embraced framing mistakes as "investments in learning" as fully as fast-moving technology organizations. Albert Yu, senior vice president, Intel's Microprocessor Products Group asserts that "failure is just part of the culture of innovation. Accept it and become stronger. The infamous Pentium flaw in 1994 was devastating. . . . It was incredibly painful to the company, and to me, personally. But we managed to become better as a result. It marked a real transition. I'm a different person today. I've beefed up the way we validate our technology before it gets out the door. We went from having a product-engineered orientation to a consumer orientation. We broke down barriers inside the company because we were all involved in an emergency. . . . Now we know that we can respond to any crisis ten times faster than before."[36]

---

Lesson: To create a learning organization, leaders must create an environment in which people are not punished for making honest mistakes, but rather only for failing to learn from their mistakes.

---

 **Don't bury your failures; learn from them.**
The old adage says "surgeons bury their mistakes." That may be true (although the VA initiative calls that saying into question), but you shouldn't do the same. Periodically list your failures; if the list is

short, be suspicious. Ask others (who are not too dependent on you) to augment the list. Systematically consider what you can learn from them.

Explore others' failures as well. Marketing consultant Robert McMath, for example, has collected more than seventy-five thousand consumer products—thousands of the one-time-hopefuls that flopped. They are on display in his New Products Showcase and Learning Center in central New York. Major consumer goods manufacturers visit not only to view the collection but to listen to him talk about what's been tried, what's failed, and why.

## DON'T WAIT FOR THOSE AT THE TOP

We recognize that our call to enhance the way individuals can learn within your organization is not a simple charge—especially if you don't hold the position at the top of the organizational chart. Even if you do hold a senior management title, the route toward a learning organization is not without its potholes. Sometimes "shock treatment" is needed to jump-start deep change. When one organization first began asking for "retrospective assessments," managers complained about the extra paperwork. Within a few weeks, however, senior executives there had 100 percent compliance. How? They held up paychecks until people complied. It sent an enormously powerful signal that the assessments mattered and would be used.

The U.S. Army has long been one of the most systematic users of simulation and lessons-learned analyses to efficiently correct mistakes, sustain successes, and engage in a process of continuous learning and improvement. The lessons are analyzed and disseminated by military intelligence schools, the Center for Army Lessons Learned, and the Training and Doctrine Command. The Army's learning system is showcased in a recent case study by the Harvard Business School. Yet when retired general (and former executive director of the Center for Creative Leadership) Walter Ulmer encouraged Army leaders to apply their finely honed learning process not just to battles and war games but to managers at the Pentagon, his suggestion was soundly rejected.[37]

However, lest we sound too pessimistic about individuals' abilities to change their organizations, let us close with some more encouraging examples. You may not be able to change incentives and rewards across the entire organization, but if you manage a division, or even a single group—you *can* create an effective learning environment within your own sphere and set an example of success for the organization as a whole.

Chris Turner, formerly at Xerox Business Services, notes: "Many organizations harbor an underlying assumption: Change is the province of some 'official change group' that surely must exist in an obscure department somewhere in the company. In other words, it's someone else's task to create the 'learning organization.' But real learning and change require you to become a participant-observer in your own environment—that you stop what you're doing, step back, look, and then challenge every thought and practice that perpetuate outdated mind-sets, from training programs to Power-Point presentations. . . . Thinking creates the structures that create an organization's behavior. Learn how to rethink, and you start to change."[38]

Terry Chandler, former national sales director for Eli Lilly's Neural Science Division and one of the best developers of people that we know, believes that modeling how to learn is a powerful tool. "If you can instill an environment where people can express their views, regardless of their title or position, you reach better final decisions," he says. "People want to bring their issues out, but framing it so as to give them permission to do so can be challenging." For that, Chandler turns to metaphors, and in particular, to a story he loves to tell new staff members about the "dead moose on the table." He begins: "I had a colleague five or six years ago who liked to hunt moose in the Northwest. He came home from one of those trips and brought me a set of moose antlers.

"Anyone who knows anything about moose knows that it is a large, cumbersome animal with a foul odor. In our discussions about his hunting trips, the phrase was coined. Now, anyone in our group who has an important issue that needs to be raised says 'let's put the moose on the table' or 'I have a moose on this subject.' That phrase raises people's antennas and focuses their attention. And it has been one of my slogans that I've used since that time to help get differences of opinion out into the open."

Chandler also shares stories with his staff about things he has tried that didn't work as expected, as well as what he learned from those experiences. Managers, he advocates, must themselves model that it's okay to "fail fast" so long as you "fix it fast." Better yet, find others in your group with a high level of confidence willing to take that public challenge with you.

Finally, Chandler suggests, take learning from experience one step further. "We're quick to quit and we're slow to stroke," he says. "Whether the task is ultimately successful or not, do you take time to analyze learning and do you celebrate short-term victories? . . . Make sure you find ways to celebrate even the small victories. In a business environment where so much pressure is put on performance, you have to put time on people and what they do to get the task done. Corporate America can be like a classroom with learning. But you have to ensure you have a good instructor at the front."[39]

---

Lesson: Real learning requires you to become a participant-observer in your own environment. Even if you don't control rewards across the entire organization, you can create an effective learning environment within your own sphere.

---

Author Minna Antrim has said, "Experience is a good teacher, but she sends in terrific bills."[40] Given the high costs of experience, how much better if we could learn from it fully. The challenges are many—even more so because many barriers to learning are outside our individual control. But the effort to overcome them—to create an environment that supports individuals to learn within organizations—is well worth the cost. And as you try, it would be wise to keep in mind the British songbirds, and aim to be more like the social titmice than the solitary robins.

CHAPTER 10

# Bringing It All Home: The Decisions of RealHome.com

**June 22, 2000**

Richard J. Roll, CEO and founder of RealHome.com, knows the importance of making fast, accurate decisions. "With home ownership clearly ranking among life's most stressful challenges, any mistakes can cost dearly," he says. That's why he's built an online company offering homeowners and first-time home buyers access to the information, advice, and services they need to help them make more informed decisions about one of their most significant investments.

But Roll might as aptly have made that statement about his own undertaking, and he doesn't forget it for a moment. Building an Internet business clearly ranks among life's most stressful challenges, and any mistakes can cost dearly.

A typical day, if there is such a thing for an e-entrepreneur, buzzes with decisions, many of which can make—or break—the company. Some of those competing for his attention this morning: Should he target strategic investors or pure venture capitalists as he searches for next-stage financing? Which of the three investment banking firms that have been recommended should he hire? Are personnel changes required to reflect RealHome's increased emphasis on business-to-business rather than business-to-consumer marketing? How much should the company spend to acquire new members given that the market no longer places a high value on that metric? How quickly should they develop wireless applications, and in what ways? Does he want to try to acquire a hot strategic partner that would offer interesting synergies? And should he explore selling the company to a larger, better capitalized firm? But now Roll has another decision to add to the list.

Last week, less than three months after RealHome.com opened its virtual doors, chief operating officer (COO) Lars Halstead (not his real name) resigned to become CEO at a much larger, publicly traded direct marketing company. Roll, who couldn't possibly match that offer, wished him well and they parted amicably. But now he had to decide what to do. Did he want a new COO, or could key tasks and responsibilities be reshuffled? Halstead, who had been with RealHome for eight months, was an experienced general manager with an extensive background in database and consumer direct marketing. Did he want to find someone with a similar background and skills or look for a different set of qualifications? Would the company be better served by a president or executive vice president, with greater responsibilities, as they prepared for the next phase of growth and an upcoming IPO? What did he, and the company, most need?

Although RealHome.com is a young company, Roll's roots in the consumer finance and home ownership industries run deep; so does his experience as an entrepreneur. After receiving his MBA from Harvard Business School in 1977, Roll worked initially for Citicorp's consumer marketing department, where he launched the bank's first IRA and Keogh accounts. He left when the bank decentralized and wanted him to run a branch in Queens, outside New York City. "That just wasn't on my career chart," Roll says with a laugh.

Instead, he launched his own business—Best Years Marketing, Inc., publishers of the "Best Years Guide to Better Retirement Living," a national Sunday magazine supplement—and coauthored two books: *The Best Years Book: How to Plan for Fulfillment, Security, and Happiness in the Retirement Years* and *Getting Yours: Financial Success Strategies for Young Professionals in a Tough Era.* The recession of the early eighties sapped Best Years' principal advertisers, and the venture folded. But other businesses soon followed: the Financial Marketing Corporation of America, a direct marketing consulting company which assisted financial institutions to upgrade the returns from their low-yielding mortgages, which Roll sold in 1987; Mortgage Monitor, a technically sophisticated mortgage audit service that assisted thousands of U.S. homeowners to recover millions of dollars in mortgage overcharges; and the American Homeowners Association (AHA), a national membership–based organization providing services and advocacy related to buying, selling, and maintaining a home.

Roll's shift from advising the banking industry to advocating for consumers occurred gradually, but the change had marked significance. In 1993 at the invitation of the New York State attorney general, he testified before the U.S. House Banking Committee about the then-common practice of overcharges in the mortgage servicing industry. That testimony helped bring about major reforms in mortgage banking and resulted in refunding some $5 billion of mortgage escrow overpadding to homeowners. By the time AHA was founded in 1994, Roll had heard the cries of thousands of homeowning consumers, and he had committed to leveling the playing field between knowledgeable service providers and their less-well-informed customers. "Innovations linking consumers with information must run in my blood," Roll chuckles; his father was the creator of the toll-free "800" number.

This vision formed the philosophical underpinnings of AHA, which by 1999 had grown to nearly $6 million in revenues. But what was an appealing, membership-based, affinity group mass marketing model in the mid-1990s had started to fall out of favor with investors by the end of the decade. The well-publicized accounting scandals associated with Cendant, Inc., a high-profile membership direct-marketing powerhouse, cast a shadow of doubt over the entire industry. The rise of the Internet was also taking its toll on direct marketing ventures. Like many other entrepreneurs and investors, Roll knew that growth resided online. So in early 1999, after a careful analysis of the risks and opportunities, Roll took his homeowners' club to cyberspace; RealHome.com was born. With this new venture, Roll hoped to tap even more deeply into the $425 billion home ownership services market.

Just three weeks after RealHome.com's April 2000 launch, PC Data Online ranked it as the third fastest growing site on the Internet. Gomez Advisors cited it among the top five home-buying sites. Proud of that recognition, Roll projected the number of registered RealHome members to grow to as many as four million by year's end. He knew that the question of how to structure and staff his senior management team would be vital to that hoped-for success.

## RealHome.com—at a Glance

**What:** *A one-stop web-based shopping and information environment as well as a vibrant virtual community for homeowners and first-time home buyers. Providing free access to competitively-priced transactions, products, and services related to every stage of buying, selling, financing, maintaining, and improving the home; online minicourses; objective information and advice; home listings; contractor directories including member ratings of products and services; member ratings of home products and services; virtual "back fence" homeowner community.*

**Goal:** *To bring market power, sizable savings, and superior service to consumers and to become a dominant player in the $425 billion home ownership services market.*

**Employees:** *Thirty-two employees (as of June 2001). Top management team: president & CEO, COO, chief technology officer, vice president of new business development, vice president of finance.*

**Revenue sources:** *Referral-fee partnerships with service providers, discounted real estate sales commissions, and a premium, fee-based membership subscription. Mass advertising space will not be sold on the site (except for premium displays in proprietary online directories); permission-only marketing to members.*

## THE INITIAL ASSESSMENT

*Our contact with RealHome.com began with one of us (Paul) joining the RealHome.com board of directors.* When we offered Roll decision coaching in return for recounting his decision process in this book, he had already begun to ask himself the kinds of "meta" questions required in a good decision-making process. Before plunging into the decision to hire a new COO, Roll stopped to ask whether he actually needed a COO at all or wanted instead to take this opportunity to restructure his senior management team. And although he must complete most decisions at Internet speed, he had decided that he could take up to three months on this one, satisfied to have an offer extended by Labor Day. Operating plans were in place and on track, and the delay could help conserve cash. In the meantime, a job description had been posted and an executive search firm engaged. Several intriguing resumes were already in hand.

In addition to the questions Roll had already asked himself, we posed some others to help him focus on how he thought this kind of decision ought to be made:

- *What's the crux of this issue? Which of the four stages—framing, intelligence-gathering, coming to conclusions, and learning from experience—will be the most challenging in this case?* Without a doubt, Roll agrees, hiring decisions turn on the quality of intelligence-gathering: you must get the right people to apply, evaluate their resumes and references, and conduct useful, unbiased interviews. Gathering that intelligence is messy. You must assess people based on brief, artificial encounters and predict how they will perform in the future. That will be the most challenging stage. However, framing the decision correctly is also essential. He must decide what kind of person he needs and what criteria will frame his decision. In the unpredictable, fast-changing Internet environment, creating a stable decision frame is no small task. Thus, he can expect to move back and forth between the first two decision stages, refining the framing as he gathers more information.

- *What are the special challenges affecting this kind of decision?* Roll identifies his biggest challenge as generating good options in the first place (a topic that bridges the framing and intelligence-gathering stages, as discussed in Interlude A. "The best people are not readily visible," he says. "It's not that they're not available, because they might be under the right circumstances. It's just that their resumes have not been submitted." He notes that he will need to invest time in making sure he casts a wide enough net. Other key challenges relate to intelligence-gathering and coming to conclusions. Privacy laws restrict what questions may be asked of job applicants; some important information is off-limits. Interviewing (as well as other intelligence-gathering activities) is fraught with mental biases that must be studiously avoided in order to make a rational decision.

  Further, Roll says, it is hard to rank people against each other. "You need to filter and screen to create a short list, but I don't really know yet exactly what I want. When you make a hiring decision, you have to do successive rankings based on incomplete information."

  And finally he notes, "You can't wait until you have explored all your options to reach a decision, because the best applicants will disappear. At some point, you have to stop the search process and make a decision based on the information and options you have." Decision researchers call this type of dilemma the "parking space" problem: if you drive past an empty parking space looking for a more attractive spot closer to your destination, you may find no other spot available while losing the first spot to another driver.

- *Where do his own strengths and weaknesses lie in making decisions of this type? How good is he at sizing up people and assessing their compatibility with him and others in the company? How experienced is he in finding key talent, and in what ways might his past experience be biased or unrepresentative?* Like many people, Roll has a hard time fully answering these self-evaluative questions. But he says, "I've gotten better at both selecting and developing good employees. This is the first time in my career as an entrepreneur that I've been able to afford the quality of people we now have, and I've gotten lots of positive feedback about the quality of our team." In what way might his past experience be biased or unrepresentative? He's not sure. But as an experienced entrepreneur, he feels confident about sizing people up.

- *Where might he get help, if needed, in resolving this issue, especially now that he is twice as busy without Halstead's daily support?* In addition to using both online and offline recruitment ads and his own informal network to recruit applicants, Roll has engaged an executive search firm. But that solution introduces its own challenges that he must keep an eye on: the biases of his headhunters. "It's human nature to want to do the least work for the greatest fee," Roll says. "Agents are likely to go for the low-hanging fruit—the people who are raising their hands, the organizations they are familiar with—rather than do the research necessary to find the ideal candidate. You need to recognize that and counter it. I try to make their biases explicit in my own mind so I can factor them into the decision process."
- *Whose decision is this? Who else should be involved?* Legally, the decision rests with the CEO, but the board of directors and the rest of the management team will likely be consulted as well. Roll also intends to talk with a former board member who provided sage advice during the hiring of the previous COO.

Roll is a thoughtful, successful, experienced executive. He has developed a metadecision that appears to make sense. But only as he immerses himself in the decision process itself will he—and we—find out if he is right.

## REALHOME.COM—A FOCUS ON FRAMING

**June 30, 2000**

Ask Richard Roll to talk about what RealHome.com is best at, and it won't be long before the subject of consumer empowerment arises. "We provide marketplaces in which vendors compete for the business of our members, but we are vendor-neutral," he says. "We preselect quality vendors, provide an interface, and make it possible for consumers to make an effective decision among competitive bids. To me, that is the model of consumer advocacy in the twenty-first century. We don't have sweetheart deals. You can't buy banner advertising. We try to provide content that's objective and thorough. We don't try to steer you one way or another. We don't pull any punches."

This consumer advocacy frame is vital to Roll. That's not surprising given that RealHome.com builds on AHA's legacy of providing consumers with enough information and collective clout to become power-wielding "Davids" as they take on the "Goliaths" in the marketplace. So the bright, easily navigated RealHome site features "RealHome University" with 120 interactive homeowner minicourses, a first-time buyers course, financial calculators and tools, competitive marketplaces featuring 100 lenders and 20 major insurance carriers, a half-million home listings, links to help buyers research schools and communities, as well as directories of contractors and professionals (including member ratings of service providers). A "virtual back fence" operates through online message boards where members can share information and advice with their "Real Neighbors" or consult "Real Experts."

The new COO clearly will have to share a commitment to this frame, "not in the bleeding heart sense," says Roll, "because we're tough businesspeople. But this person will have to be passionate about providing superior value to the consumer. A fast-buck artist won't work out here."

To help Roll further clarify his frames, we ask him to pick a metaphor for his business and how it operates. He mentions several, but his enthusiasm for one quickly surfaces. "Basketball is an important metaphor for our business, and perhaps for Internet businesses in general," he says. "Everyone is playing on the same fixed court. The ball isn't changing. The baskets are fixed. But what's happening on the court is changing constantly: the interplay among players, the formation of positions to set up plays. The ball is always somewhere else. You're driven perceptually within the dimensions of the court and the clock. You can't forget the clock.

"In basketball," he continues, "players aren't running around in their own world. There's a high level of interactivity—with those on your own team and with the other team. You need to be agile, aware, and have the physical ability to put it all together. At the end of the day, what matters is how many baskets you made and whether you won. It's all execution."

In fact, Roll applies this metaphor to his own employees, noting, "I let go of an administrative assistant because I felt she was in her own world. In our company, you need that level of heightened awareness for what's happening around you."

And Roll's role on that basketball team? He has several answers to our question. The first: "I try to be like Michael Jordan. I'm good at a lot of these things, but I can't do it myself. I can only do it with my teammates." Immediately, however, he realizes that while this comparison captures some of how he sees himself, it shadows other equally important aspects of what he does. After all, every metaphor has its limitations. "I'm more like a player-coach," he modifies. "Part of my job is to motivate, to manage. I'm a very active player, but I'm also the manager."

The qualities he values and how he sees himself within his organization are further refined when we ask him for additional metaphors.

"I've often felt like the conductor of an orchestra." What kind of orchestra? "Classical. In my job, I'm rotating to different parts of the orchestra, focusing my attention, prompting them. But they're playing the music, I'm not."

Roll also likes the sailing metaphor. Like a basketball game, he notes, sailing requires a high degree of attention. "You must remain constantly aware of the weather, other boats, your passengers, their comforts and needs"—all variables which can change quickly and without warning.

How does he recognize when someone has those characteristics? "You look for signals that they are not paying attention," he says, citing a recent unsolicited candidate for a sales and marketing job who left Roll a voicemail message in a "cocktail lounge voice" and mispronounced the name of the person who had referred him to RealHome. It's obvious, Roll says, when that awareness is lacking. But how do you know when it's there? "You can just see how they move around the room, how they watch the ball, how they conduct themselves."

## THE COO FRAME, ADAPTED

With this awareness of some of Roll's thinking frames, especially his passion for consumer advocacy (David versus Goliath) and the basketball metaphor for running an Internet business, we turn to the decision at hand. His first framing issue:

- *What job to fill?*

Does he want to adopt the traditional COO frame (operational, internally-focused, responsible for day-to-day management)? Does he want to frame it in terms of replacing Halstead and his particular set of skills and contributions? Does he want to take this opportunity to recast the position to that of president or executive vice president, with greater responsibilities? Or does he need to fill the job at all? Would he be better to frame it in terms of function rather than position, distributing the COO's responsibilities to a wider executive team?

Roll's framing response is clear. "I'm going to hire a COO," he says. "We can't yet afford a president of the necessary stature." That's the first framing boundary he sets. Compensation limits have bounded a president or executive vice president out of consideration. The second boundary is a time metric: Roll is hiring a COO to meet his needs six months to a year from now; three-year concerns are out of the picture. Finally, while he is clearly proud of his employees, his existing staff is not yet seasoned enough to create an expanded executive team, distributing the COO's responsibilities among them. That option, too, has been bounded out of consideration. Thus, Roll must now frame a second question, and this time the task is more challenging:

- *What kind of person does he need?*

What skills and experience are essential? To what extent is he looking for someone who could step in for him when necessary, dealing with the lawyers, investment bankers, media, and so on? To what extent is knowledge of emerging technologies, such as wireless, important? To what extent should the new COO be responsible for driving revenue and the bottom line?

In addition to the traditional COO frame's highlights (e.g., internally focused, someone who can keep the show running), Roll adds several of his own: he'd like someone whose strengths complement his own and who has the ability to bring "something extra" to the table immediately.

Lars Halstead's style, he notes, was "diametrically opposed" to his own. The former COO was more linear and methodical, good at focusing on the operational details. While Roll kept his eye on the forest, Halstead focused on the trees (as indeed a COO should). But while Halstead was largely responsible for day-to-day implementation, he also helped develop strategy and revenue forecasts. And while Roll had been the only senior executive at the company when Halstead came on board, he now likes the idea of having another truly seasoned executive to share the rapidly growing responsibilities.

"The growth of the company requires having multiple shoulders," he says. "I want an additional senior manager who is seasoned, confident, mature, and trustworthy, and who in my absence is capable of holding the fort. The COO must be able to help departments plan their objectives, drive measurable results, and interface with outside sources." Other criteria: he wants a highly quantitative person who can grapple with income streams, has specific dotcom and direct marketing experience, and is regarded by others as a serious businessperson. Finally, there's what Roll calls "window dressing"— someone whose experience and fit will make sense to potential investors.

But while he can articulate this initial frame, Roll is loath to elaborate much further. "I'll have a hard time telling you exactly what kind of person I'm looking for until I've interviewed a few," he says. In large measure, that's due to the nature of Internet businesses. In a traditional company it's possible to articulate exactly the characteristics you want your COO to have. In the Internet world, very few people have the exact portfolio of skills needed. One strong applicant is the former commander of a nuclear submarine. "When I look at his resume, I'm reminded of other attributes I want: discipline, loyalty, running a tight ship, and so on," Roll says.

To complicate matters, new attributes emerge in the Internet world daily.

Wireless is currently the hot issue for web-based businesses. "Is it more important now than six months ago that our COO is familiar with technology?" Roll asks, not yet certain how he will answer this question. After all, the number of people who possess that level of technology knowledge is limited.

Further, the Internet world itself seems to morph overnight. "One year ago, Internet businesses were regarded as their own world, with their own culture and rules," Roll says. "Today they are just another business, with the same rules of good business as any other. So a year ago we would have needed a COO with online experience. Now, we need someone who can help grow the business in a more traditional way. The key question is how have they taken a business from one level to another. It doesn't have to be an Internet business at all." (Readers may recall that the Internet bubble started to deflate in April of 2000, only a few months prior to Roll's comments.)

For the new COO, therefore, flexibility—the capability to grow, learn, and adapt—will be another key attribute. "The playing field changes radically every month," Roll continues. "It's like the other team brought on a new roster of players. This month the market is no longer valuing the acquisition of registered users for business-to-consumer marketing. It's valuing our ability to leverage the content we've created with other business partners. We've had to shift the revenue streams we were focusing on. We think our model is still strong and on target. We set out to create a world-class Internet site for homeowners and home buyers, and by all measures we succeeded in doing that. I tell my staff, the good news is we won this game. The bad news is we have to win a new game."

In such an unpredictable environment it's hard to create a stable decision frame ahead of time. But our four-stage process was never intended to be as linear as it appears in a book; there will always be a reassessment of earlier stages from the more experienced perspective of later ones. And decision-makers, no matter how many of our tools they apply, will move from one stage to the next with incomplete information and less-than-ideal clarity. Thus, Roll is prepared to embark on the search with his initial COO frame, expecting to refine it further as his intelligence-gathering gets under way.

## Roll's Initial COO Hiring Frame

*Decision Criteria*

1. Seasoned, confident, mature, trustworthy; can "hold the fort" in my absence
2. Serious businessperson; can drive results, help plan objectives, interface with outside sources

3. Highly quantitative (can grapple with assumptions and variables that drive income streams)
4. Dotcom and direct marketing experience
5. Has taken a business from one level to another
6. Flexibility, IQ, capability to grow, learn, adapt
7. Discipline, running a tight ship

## REALHOME.COM—FINDING THE RIGHT PERSON FOR THE JOB

**July 10, 2000**

Of the four hundred resumes he's received to date, Richard Roll has created two piles. In one pile are applicants from the three states (New York, New Jersey, and Connecticut) that make up the greater New York City metropolitan area, where RealHome.com is based. In the other pile, everyone else. To control interviewing costs he's looking primarily at the first pile for now.

A few people catch his eye. There's the former nuclear submarine commander Steven Fisher (all of the job candidates have been given pseudonyms), who's currently leading an international team negotiating protocols for a $4.6 billion nuclear reactor project in Asia. Fisher goes onto the list of those Roll will interview. So does George Lang, a general manager with extensive experience in consumer products and services as well as brand marketing. Lang has held primary responsibility for a $125 million product line and most recently has grown a start-up brand to $50 million in less than eight months.

Frank Havens, currently senior vice president for operations and CFO for a large manufacturer/distributor of medical equipment and scientific instruments, also gets Roll's attention. Haven's resume claims that he grew the company internally as well as through acquisitions, turning a $400,000 loss into a $7 million profit and adding $100 million in revenues. In addition, as a CPA he has extensive experience in financial services, and Roll wants to talk with him further. Susan Stevenson, one of the few women in the applicant pool, also makes the cut for an initial screening interview. She's a senior marketing executive with experience both in multinational corporations and small high-tech start-ups. Several years ago she helped launch one of the first U.S. broadband wireless access businesses.

In spite of Roll's stated preference for tri-state candidates, he's not applying his screening threshold rigidly. There's one West Coast candidate, Jim Rossini, whom, Roll says with a laugh, he has been "trying to knock off the list, but he keeps coming back strong." Rossini has fifteen years' experience as president and CEO of several financial service businesses, with a track record for successful turnarounds and leadership in e-business development.

## GENERATING GOOD OPTIONS

Roll anticipated in his initial analysis that discovering good "options"—that is, candidates qualified for a senior management position in an Internet company—would be one of his biggest challenges. To cast a wide net, he has tapped into a variety of networks: online recruitment; ads in newspapers, including the *New York Times*; word of mouth; and an executive search firm. Several of the resumes he has seen intrigue him. Still, the candidate pool is less than ideal. "I talked with our executive search firm this morning, and they said that thus far, the people who have raised their hands as being interested in dotcom companies aren't the caliber in which we're interested," he noted. Although there are now people with enough relevant experience to consider seriously, no one candidate has the breadth of expertise he would like. That challenge could trap a less experienced decision-maker.

"Because we don't have all the criteria set in our minds in advance, it's easy to be seduced by someone who is strong in one criterion," Roll observes. "For example, we're all in love with the nuclear submarine commander. But when you drill down into the skill set needed to oversee businesspeople and develop business plans . . . that is, the entire range of executive and financial skills needed to generate good business options, he hasn't had those experiences. In spite of his obvious strengths, he hasn't grown a business. When it comes to generating business solutions, an experienced businessperson knows what the options are. An inexperienced person may not."

To his credit, Roll has not only been looking for ways to increase his options, he has also begun to think about creating flexible options. "Maybe the way to reduce the risk is to engage the top individual in a three-month trial period, as a consultant," he muses. "That way, I could assess the fit, the chemistry with our company, the person's skill set. It would give us a chance to assess both the pleasant and unpleasant surprises that come after an initial hire of this nature."

Harking back to his basketball metaphor, he also takes a portfolio perspective. "I haven't found anyone yet who is so compelling that I'm saying 'we've got to have that person.' I'm not even sure that ideal person exists. They may have to be created." He's toying with the possibility that he will have to reconfigure the job, taking on certain aspects of the position himself.

Stevenson, for example, has great depth in marketing, but may not yet be ready to handle all the financial responsibilities. "No player is necessarily perfect," Roll says. "But if you can meld those strengths with others already on the team and can change some plays, you can have an effective team. The trick is to anticipate management gaps, to figure out which can be adequately managed and which can't. You don't want to find that out only after you're in the game."

## GATHERING INTELLIGENCE

**July 24, 2000**

On the surface, gathering intelligence about a new hire is straightforward. Resumes, interviews, and references are the standard tools. But the dangers of overconfidence and mental biases run deeper than most people realize. To begin, most people are far too sure of the diagnostic value of interviews. In fact, studies have shown that the ability to generalize from a typical interview setting to normal business operation is limited.[1] Neither the interviewer or the interviewee acts "normal" in an interview. Job candidates put their best face forward in interviews, but decision-makers tend to assume that the data received are far more representative than they are. To further complicate matters, certain relevant questions (e.g., about a candidate's family situation, lifestyle, and future plans) are off-limits in the U.S.

Finally, interviewers must overcome the inevitable mental biases: accepting the most available information, anchoring on the current candidate pool (rather than the ideal for the job), selectively perceiving or remembering the information presented, giving too much weight to either the first or the most recent candidates interviewed, and the pull toward seeking confirming (rather than disconfirming) evidence. And all of this must take place, of course, within the context of trying to sell your company while also testing and evaluating the candidate.

"One of the pitfalls," Roll acknowledges, "is being too concerned about approval or being nice. You're recruiting, and you don't want to turn people off. But you need to ask 'What is the person made of? Is that anything like what you're looking for?' " To help that process, Roll has made clear to candidates that the initial screening interview will be structured primarily to consider their accomplishments, not to discuss the job or the company.

"I like to start with the resume," he says about his own intelligence-gathering style. "It's a road map of the person's experience. But after the initial sort, the interview is the essential intelligence-gathering tool. In the interview, I want to find out how this person thinks. I drill down into what they really did and try to understand the pattern: what help they had or didn't have. Sometimes people take credit for things they didn't do, weren't responsible for, and couldn't replicate. I also throw out to them actual situations we've faced. It gives me a benchmark, hearing that person react, how much ability this person has to grapple with that."

Roll correctly tests multiple hypotheses—an important tool to avoid the confirmation pull—in his interviews. To date, he's screened twelve candidates. "With Havens," he says for example, "he ran twelve product lines. I asked myself whether he was just an operations guy or whether he actually grew the business as he claims credit for. Does he really understand distribution and dealing with the customer? I ask myself—and them: who else was involved in running the show?"

He also seeks disconfirming evidence. "When I hired Lars," he says, "I wanted to know why he left his previous position if he had done such a great job. I still wound up hiring him. But I wanted to know, what broke down? Was it possible to avoid this situation, and how? I wanted to understand his weaknesses in advance so I could steer around them. That's possible, assuming you're not trying to make a silk purse out of a sow's ear." At the suggestion of one of his former board members, he tracked down the CEO of Halstead's former company, putting the question to him as well.

In addition to the questions Roll is already asking, we suggest several other disconfirming questions he might want to include. First, he might ask candidates to what extent random luck was involved in their accomplishments, with a question like: "How much of your indicated accomplishments was due to your skill and how much to luck? Did the market go your way? Were there other factors outside your control that contributed to the great results?"

Second, besides thinking about whether this person will "fit the job and my company, and why," he would do well to use pro/con reasoning, asking: "Why *won't* this person fit? In what ways is the candidate's experience *not* analogous to the requirements of this job? Why might this person fail?"

Finally, we ask Roll about his biggest hiring mistakes. He shares several stories, all about lower-level hires. Certainly there are differences between assessing lower-level employees and senior managers, but we ask him to think about what lessons might be applicable. Several themes emerge: a desperate need to fill the position, candidates who overstated their worth and abilities, people who presented themselves as poised and competent in an interview setting but couldn't function in the fast-paced work environment, and coached references. In one case, he notes, "The candidate came from a company we respected. That blindsided us." The overall lesson he can bring to this decision: the need for an immediate solution led him to make up his mind too early, based on first impressions, and then he didn't seek disconfirming evidence.

Since we last spoke with him, Roll has refined his decision frame, developing a list of fourteen evaluation criteria on which each candidate will be rated from 1 (low) to 5 (high). He has also built a simple intelligence-gathering tool from it: a scoring sheet on which each candidate will be rated immediately following the interview. Such a document will help him avoid some of the "availability" biases when it comes to evaluating the information he has gathered, such as being unduly influenced by the most recent, memorable, or lengthy interviews. It will also enable him to compare candidates more objectively. He plans to use it for the "short-list" of four to five candidates who make it past the first screening interview. And after those second interviews he will turn to reference checks, many of which he will do himself and some of which he may delegate.

---

## RealHome.Com, Inc.
## Initial COO Candidate—Evaluation Criteria
### Rating Comments (1–5; 5 = Good)

Applicant: _____ Date: _____

Chemistry _____

Style _____

Growing of Revenue & Profit _____

Services/Financial Service

Comparable Experience _____

People Management _____

Leadership _____

Business Acumen _____

Direct Marketing Experience _____

Negotiation _____

Quantitative Skill _____

Learning Curve _____

Technology _____

Marketing/PR _____

Intelligence/Analytical Skill _____

Additional Comments _____

_____

**July 27, 2000**

We didn't have time to finish our intelligence-gathering discussion with Roll. It took place as he was en route by car from Connecticut to a meeting in New York City, and eventually the need to continually change network carriers on his cellphone became too much. So we reconvene three days later.

We begin by pointing out that although developing an evaluation sheet was a wise move, fourteen items will be difficult to compare when it comes time to weigh the candidates against each other. We suggest to Roll that he group his criteria into a few broad categories. He can then relate those categories to his frame to make sure that all relevant aspects are covered. Doing so also will ensure that each category receives due attention and help him judge whether overlapping attributes are unwittingly used. Finally, if he decides to pursue a systematic weighted ranking process to aid in his final selection, it will be simpler to do so using broad categories rather than fourteen independent attributes. Roll likes our grouping idea and revises his rating sheet accordingly.

---

## RealHome.Com, Inc.
## Revised COO Candidate—Evaluation Criteria
### *Rating Comments (1–5; 5 = Good)*

Applicant: _____ Date: _____

### *Company Fit*

Chemistry _____

Style _____

Learning Curve _____

### *Business Skills*

Growing of Revenue & Profit _____

Services/Financial Service _____

Comparable Experience _____

Business Acumen _____

Direct Marketing Experience _____

Marketing/PR Experience _____

Quantitative Skill _____

Negotiation Skill _____

## Management Skills

People Management _____
Leadership _____
Intelligence/Analytical Skill _____

## Technology Expertise

Technology _____
Additional Comments _____
_____
_____

---

Roll also has good news about the candidate pool. This morning the executive search firm sent him the resume of another candidate, Eric Stein. Although Roll won't interview him until tomorrow afternoon, he's excited. Stein appears to be the strongest candidate yet. An executive vice president at a $350 million direct marketing company with more than twenty-two years' direct marketing experience, he's also worked in insurance marketing and association-type financial services. He most recently led his division's e-commerce initiatives, boasts a solid track record of increasing sales and profits, oversaw a staff of fifty, and comes with a strong recommendation from the search firm that has already placed several good employees with RealHome.

It's clear that Roll is well on his way to gathering solid intelligence, and has a good grasp on the potential challenges and traps along with some of the ways to overcome them. But we take a moment to think about what other tools we can offer. Fault trees make sense for repetitive decisions in stable cases where things are highly structured. But they don't work as well in cases like these where there are many possible (and difficult to predict) causes for failure. Further, as Roll is unlikely to hire many COOs, it's not worth taking the time that building a fault tree requires. Likewise with full-fledged scenario planning. If Roll were looking out beyond a year, we'd recommend thinking about two to three scenarios for RealHome and its Internet environment. But he's hiring for the next six months.

Prospective hindsight, on the other hand, is likely to yield some enlightening insights. In this case, Roll would imagine life at RealHome.com eight months into the future. For each top candidate, he must assume that that person had been hired and didn't work out, and then ask himself "Why not?" We suggest he keep this tool in mind as he continues interviewing and prepares to move into the coming to conclusions stage.

## REALHOME.COM—CHOOSING A COO

**September 11, 2000**

It's just past Labor Day, Roll's original deadline for hiring a COO. But no candidate to date has scored sufficiently strongly on his decision criteria. (Remember the excitement over Eric Stein? His interview resulted in a clear "thumbs down." He was actually described as "too depressing.") Just two weeks ago Roll was close to exercising the flexible option he had developed: hiring his top two candidates as consultants. It would be a "stopgap" measure, enabling him to obtain some of the professional assistance he so desperately needs. And by using the additional information gathered through working with them more closely, Roll could continue to consider whether to offer one of them the COO position.

Last Friday, however, as the company was closing for the long Labor Day weekend, his assistant Charlotte informed him that John Hartounian (not his real name) was available to be interviewed. Hartounian, who has fifteen years' management experience with six years as a CFO and then COO for a non-U.S. wireless telecommunications company, had been on Roll's original "to interview" list. But with Hartounian working in Africa and Roll often on the road, they had been unable to schedule a face-to-face interview—until now.

We warned readers in the introduction that while every decision goes through four stages—framing, intelligence-gathering, concluding, and learning from experience—these stages are not always linear. Although he was well into the "concluding" process, Roll decided to return to intelligence-gathering. So on the Saturday of Labor Day weekend he interviewed Hartounian. The following week Hartounian spoke with five other RealHome.com managers, and Roll, Hartounian, and their wives had dinner.

This morning Roll is decidedly enthusiastic. Hartounian, he says, was immediately impressive. He has grown a business from a start-up to $150 million in revenue, is an accomplished and articulate fund-raiser, and understands key business concepts "with a mature insight." His extensive experience in the wireless industry, technological expertise that RealHome clearly needs, places him high on the technical learning curve. Although born in France, Hartounian received his MBA in the U.S. and is socialized to the U.S. business culture. Finally, he has been a COO, a fact that is particularly important to Roll.

"He has the business acumen and has been through the entrepreneurial growth experience," Roll tells us. "Most people don't have the experience of changing a company's culture as it grows from a start-up to $150 million in annual revenues. Hartounian does. He isn't an ingenue; he has been through the rough-and-tumble of business. Even more, there were no negatives in the interview, no showstoppers. He was better in person than on paper."

Roll also mentions Hartounian's business values—his commitment, drive, attention to building infrastructure, emphasis on teamwork and accountability as well as his articulate, thoughtful, even reflective approach. These are all part of what we would call Hartounian's entrepreneurial business frame. "He's practical, but innovative and ambitious," continues Roll. "I liked that. It comes down to how you deal with business issues. To be successful in this kind of company, you have to have a gas pedal and a brake pedal and know when to use which." Such frame alignment, at the level of values, is essential between senior executives who must work closely together; if it does not exist, future problems are likely in both substance and style. But Roll knows that he not only needs to assess Hartounian's fit with RealHome, but also to figure out the frames of Hartounian would bring to his side of the decision process: whether to accept a job if it were offered. As Richard listened during the interview, several highlights emerged: ownership potential, family-friendly, and the team culture. Hartounian didn't have an equity stake in his previous position, but clearly wanted (and felt he deserved) ownership. The father of two young children, he was seeking to travel less. And he was clearly drawn to what he saw as RealHome's solid team and accomplishments to date.

There was one drawback: Hartounian had scored close to zero on one of Roll's decision criteria—he had no direct response marketing experience. But Roll was prepared to offer him the position anyway.

What made you decide 'Yes, this is the one'?, we ask. Once you gathered all the information, what method did you use to reach a conclusion?

"I listened for (a) signs that my top criteria were being met and (b) fatal flaws," Roll responds. "I also got feedback from the other members of my company who spoke with him. Because we've had numerous discussions about what we were looking for, they knew what was involved. In this case they were uniformly positive. He seemed like a 'player.' I wasn't seeking a consensus from my staff, but that was another data point. It helped to inform my decision."

Roll also listened to what Hartounian's references had to say, not only verifying the data received, but seeking more information on the context of that data: who else was involved in the accomplishments Hartounian had claimed, what was his actual role, what might he have done better or differently?

On the surface it might appear that Roll has relied heavily upon intuition to reach his decision, a choice approach whose limitations we have gone out of our way to warn you about. But remember, early on in this decision process, Roll developed and refined a detailed decision frame with explicit criteria. While he didn't use any of the formal decision weighting models we suggested, he did use his frame as a decision aid to come as close as possible to those models without plugging in the actual numbers and calculating final values.

This brings us to a lesson that we cannot repeat often enough: our systematic decision-making process provides a guideline, not a recipe. Use the techniques we offer to avoid distortions and biases, but don't do more than you have to. In coming to conclusions, decision-makers need two elements— good alternatives, and a systematic way to evaluate them. In this case Roll didn't have many great alternatives. But he did have a well-developed decision frame for evaluation, a frame that he refined throughout the interview process, becoming increasingly clear on the relative value of each criterion. The last step, were he to use a formal decision weighting approach, would have been to plug in the numbers. But given his limited alternatives, Roll didn't need such a detailed analysis to separate his "best" alternative from the merely "second best." Doing the math would only have confirmed the obvious.

Finally, Roll has considered the possibilities that this might be the wrong decision. Acknowledging those possibilities, he says, "In hiring someone, there's always a risk. The question now becomes how to manage that decision into effectiveness. You need a plan to deal with and mitigate the risk. That involves coaching a new employee. When it comes to direct marketing, Hartounian has a steep learning curve confronting him. I think he will climb it quickly. But at the same time, I will continue to oversee those marketing tasks until he does." Roll has also structured the compensation package to further mitigate risks, noting that Hartounian's stock options in the company vest over time. Thus, says Roll, if it doesn't work out, it hasn't been a great financial risk.

Two weeks after interviewing him, Roll offered Hartounian the job. Hartounian accepted. He is to begin at RealHome on October 23.

## REALHOME.COM—LEARNING FROM EXPERIENCE

### January 15, 2001

Remember that when the decision process began, at the metadecision and framing stages, we counseled Roll to look back and consider what he had learned from past hiring experiences that might be applicable to this one. At this point, we suggest Roll cull lessons from this new experience—while it is still fresh in his mind—that he might be able to use in the future.

Hartounian has been on the job now for nearly three months. It is still too soon for Roll to make anything like a final evaluation of the *outcome* of his decision (that is, whether he made the best possible hire), but so far so good. It looks like he picked the right person. What he can, and we think should, do now is glean insights from two other kinds of learning activities: (a) monitoring and modifying his decision while implementing it and (b) evaluating his decision-making *process*.

"How's Hartounian working out?" we ask. "Great," Roll responds. "I just got back from a week's vacation and asked other people on my staff how it went. They all told me what a great job he was doing."

Of course, the implementation track has not been without its bumps, but Roll has not been surprised. As he told us in September, before he hired Hartounian, "You need to plan how to manage your decision into a success by coaching the new employee." Now, he says, he's doing just that.

"John initially felt like he was hit with a tidal wave," Roll reports. "There's a lot of product knowledge and technical content in our company, and it's really a ninety-day learning curve before it all starts to come together. I could see it happening. After all, he didn't have experience in affinity marketing. Three or four weeks into his tenure with the company, I could see that he needed to be more proactive; he was letting me do too much. Perhaps he didn't want to make a mistake. That's okay at the start, but after a certain point you can't hang back. I gave him a wake-up call and he responded very effectively. It was important for me to communicate with him about how we work, how we think, to make sure he was being brought into the company's culture rather than having to figure it out by himself.

"But," Roll quickly continues, "Hartounian had the intellectual capacity, temperament, commitment, drive, and entrepreneurial experience—those things that were apparent when I selected him. I wanted someone who would be taken seriously as a businessperson, who had the ability to learn—and I got that. We've worked well as a team. All in all, I have no doubt that it has been the right decision." Of course, Roll is continuing to monitor Hartounian's progress in adapting to the COO position and he plans a six-month evaluation.

And how about the decision-making process itself? We asked Roll to do a quick analysis of the decision process with us. Was the crux of the issue what he thought it would be? Would he change how he allocated time between the four stages? What has he learned that might be useful in such decisions in the future?

Roll immediately responds that what was most important in retrospect was "having clear criteria, sticking to them, casting a wide net, and going through enough candidates to get a sense of who was out there and what the trade-offs were." Back in June, when we began, Roll had anticipated that intelligence-gathering would be the critical stage—getting the right people to apply and evaluating them thoroughly and without bias or distortion. And he saw generating good options (i.e., candidates) as his biggest challenge. In retrospect, he was largely correct. There is an ebb and flow to recruiting for this type of job. But whether many (or few) good candidates are available depends on external circumstances such as layoffs, restructurings, and so on, factors outside the decision-maker's control. "There are no fish for a while, then you will have a whole school," he says.

At the same time as he determined that getting good candidates would be key, Roll had also pinpointed at his metadecision stage the importance of framing the decision correctly, deciding what kind of person he needed and what criteria he would use to build his frame. It is the importance of this framing challenge that strikes him even more forcefully now. "My criteria became refined and clarified," he says, "as I saw people who appeared to meet the criteria on paper but weren't a great cultural fit for my company. And vice versa, seeing people who were a good cultural fit (like the former submarine commander), but who didn't have the required business background or experience. Not compromising on those criteria—even when it looked like my options were limited—was essential."

He also notes that when you start to get resumes from different levels at the same company, you find that several people all take credit for the same accomplishment. "That was dramatically revealing," Roll says. "You really have to prove and check out what people actually did. Checking references—and asking them about who was really responsible for what—can be extremely informative."

We continue to probe for additional learning, but perhaps because this is the second COO Rolls has hired, he can't identify much more that he has learned from the process at this time. His previous COO hiring experience certainly explains why he was able to develop decision criteria that remained so stable throughout the process and, in his word, needed only "refining." But like many busy CEOs, Roll clearly remains more focused on performance (e.g., monitoring Hartounian's progress) than on devoting time to learning analyses. He is justifiably pleased with his decision outcome—and he has every right to be.

Yet to our minds, the issue is not only whether one has made the right decision, but also whether one can learn—even from one's successes. We make one final suggestion about what we would do if we were in his shoes, recommending that he e-mail his top managers with a single question: What are two or three lessons that you learned in this hiring process that might be of use to us in the future?

One of us (Jay) recently took part in this kind of lessons-learned analysis and was surprised and humbled by the experience. Five of the eight lessons in the final report had been obvious to him from the start, but the other three were significant observations that he had not even considered. Unfortunately, true learning cultures are still the exception in most organizations. Fortunately, learning something you didn't previously know may not take a great deal of time.

In the meantime, Roll has completed his decision in a manner that appears to bode well for him, his staff, and the continued success of his company.

*May 29, 2001.* As we go to press, we check in with Roll one last time to see if any new learnings have materialized. The good news is that Hartounian is still progressing well. But Roll remarks that "he is still taking responsibility for only a minority part of the business, and I have still been too involved on a day-to-day level. This is partly because of my greater background in the membership, real estate, financial services, and direct marketing arenas." Apparently, the learning curve is steeper than Roll had expected.

When we asked Roll whether in hindsight he wished that he had done anything different, he replied, "I would want to have more clearly understood exactly what Hartounian's experience was in the growth of the prior business he worked for, and at what stage it was when he joined it—I think I misunderstood something in there, in the interviewing process; but it has turned out not to be material. The coaching process I emphasized before was essential regardless."

Did he wish that he had waited longer, so that he could have taken more advantage of the talent flooding the market in the wake of the dotcom shakeout? Roll observed, "I think the so-called flood of talent is a flood of people, not necessarily talent. And even those with talent would need to be vetted in the same way I did it, and a lot of digging is required to get to the bottom of what kind of stuff the person is made of."

Finally, we asked whether any significant changes had occurred in the overall business since we last spoke with him (four months earlier). He observed that "we have had less success than planned in generating license and transaction fees through our Powered by RealHome strategy, partly because many of our dot-com partners have fallen by the wayside. And so, in order to reduce our monthly burn rate, I shifted the company's focus to growing our online AHA memberships profitably." His final comments reminded us how fluid decision-making can be in the real world, occurring amid continually changing circumstances. This makes it even more important that managers follow a sound process. We think Richard Roll did just that.

*Note:* Readers who would like additional information about RealHome.com can find it on the Web at www.realhome.com.

EPILOGUE

# Learning into Action

*The winds are always on the side of the ablest navigators.*

*—Edward Gibbon*

## IT'S TIME TO PLAY THE GAME

Here's where we must stop and you must take over. We've given you a proven process for good decision-making that can be usefully applied to problem-solving and critical thinking in general and can also improve major components of strategy formulation and negotiations. Along with the four-stage framework, we have provided the concepts, skills, and tools you need to make the process work for you.

Our advice has been general, as it must be for a wide audience of readers. But your challenges aren't general. They are quite particular. That's why to finish this book, you must take over. Like the coaches we promised we would be, we've taught you what we can in book form. Now it's time for you to go out and play the game. But before you do, let us leave you with some closing words.

✧ **Respect the process, but don't become a slave to it.** This decision-making process is not a recipe where you can stir two cups framing with three-quarters of a cup intelligence-gathering and deliver a savory dish to the waiting guests. It's a conceptual approach—rooted in cognitive science—that requires both discipline and creativity. We have offered you guidelines, not algorithms. Take shortcuts wherever possible; the process of decision-making shouldn't ever become arduous, painful, or rigid. But don't pretend the four stages don't exist. Either you will take charge of them, or they will control you.

✧ **Practice until these skills are second nature.** An excellent tennis player doesn't just have great strokes, but knows which stroke to use when. She knows when to rush the net, when to hit the ball with slice, and when with topspin. And in the midst of a championship game, she can do so almost without thinking, freeing her to focus on strategy. That's possible because she has practiced extensively. So, too, in becoming an excellent decision-maker, you will need to practice these principles and skills until they become second nature.

✧ **Conduct a personal assessment.** Experience has shown that even when readers know they're getting good advice, the knowledge they gain from books may change their behavior only slightly. They rarely benefit as much as those working under live coaches where students get highly specific advice tightly focused on their particular errors, and have someone watching to see that they put that advice into action. We want our advice to make a decisive difference. So we suggest that you conduct a decision audit. Begin by reviewing the exercise in chapter 1 that asked how you typically spend your decision-making time. How would you ideally allocate your time in the future? What barriers might hinder a proper allocation of time and how can they be removed? Then take a look at the self-assessment tools in Appendix A. Identify the areas where you most need to practice and, if you haven't done so already, select some tools to bring to your next decision. In addition to self-knowledge, it helps to know the court you will play on, as your environment will dictate the complexities and challenges you face.

✧ **Continue to adapt this decision-making process.** Finally, create a continual learning process. This book is written on paper, not cast in stone. Retain those tools that work. Discard others that may have become outdated. Keep your eyes open for new decision-making tools, and add the best ones to your repertoire. In other words, adapt this process to your needs and style. An Organizational Challenges survey appears in Appendix B.

✧ **Spread the word.** We invite you to consider becoming a public champion for critical and innovative thinking. First, there's no better way to understand something than to try to teach it to others. You may understand the concepts in this book, but trying to coach others will hone your understanding. Second, the benefits of enhanced decision-making will only be fully garnered if many people within your organization start to adopt more disciplined approaches in making decisions. Share our decision-making principles and tools with the people you supervise. Try to become a highly visible decision coach and champion. If you can, share these tools more widely in your organization, in your teams, or perhaps even with your boss.

In addition to applying new decision-making tools, try to create occasions for action learning. This might take the form of internal decision squads who tackle especially vexing and important issues, or weekly dialogues structured around the main topics of this book. Asking a few simple questions such as "In which ways do our frames limit us?" "How good are we at learning?" or, "How effective are our team decision-making meetings?" can enrich a few brown-bag luncheons. Some people take a half day every quarter to review how their group makes decisions, and how they could make them even better. Such an activity should not be used to punish, or even reward, individuals for particular decisions but as an exercise for learning.

One entrepreneur we know invited the people in her company to read one chapter each month of our earlier book, *Decision Traps*, and then share their reactions with the group via e-mail. She shares our view that nothing is as powerful as people recognizing and reflecting on these insights in the context of their own jobs and experience. If you're in a position to do so, consider making decision-making prowess part of your staff's performance evaluation. (Can they move beyond awareness to usage? Are they recognizing subtle concepts, such as overconfidence or reframing? Are they championing critical and innovative thinking?)

## WARNING: ILLUSIONS STILL AHEAD

One final caution: Being warned about an optical illusion doesn't make it disappear. Try one last experiment with us. Which of the lines on the next page is shortest? By now you can probably guess the correct answer (the two lines are the same length), but can you really see them as the same?

So, too, with the decision-making biases and illusions in this book. Just knowing the distortions are there won't make them go away. They must be guarded against vigilantly. But as with the figure below, consistently applying a frame around them (such as the framework we've presented in this book) will help.[1]

With that caveat, we've completed our pep talk. It's your turn now. We hope that every decision you make will be a winning one. You now have the tools to do it right the first time.

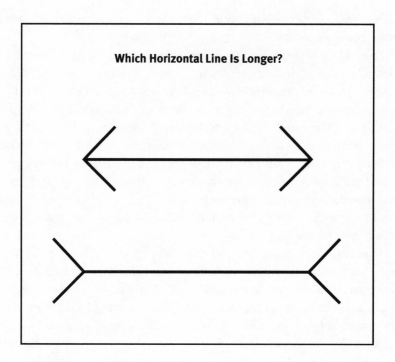

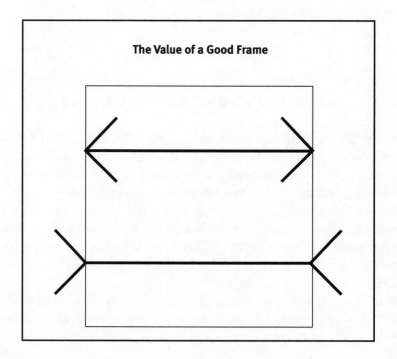

# Appendix A

**Decision Audits**

1. Start your decision audit by answering these questions:

   a. In the past, how has your time been divided among the decision-making phases?

   b. How will you divide your time in the future? This indicates how you may want to change your decision process.

   c. What barriers hinder a proper allocation of time? How can they be removed? For example, do you have enough time for intelligence-gathering? Are your records too poor to permit proper learning from feedback?

Now that you've read the book. . . .

# Appendix A

## Time Allocation Worksheet

| | What share of your time did you devote to each phase in the past?* | What share of your time do you intend to devote to each phase in the future?* |
|---|---|---|
| Framing | —% | —% |
| Gathering Intelligence | —% | —% |
| Coming to Conclusions | —% | —% |
| Learning from Experience | —% | —% |
| | 100% | 100% |

*Distribute 100 points within each column to reflect your actual and intended time allocations.

## Auditing Your Decisions

2. After you've evaluated your use of time, list several recent decisions, including a:
   - Decision in which you achieved good results because you followed a good decision process, and a
   - Decision in which you suffered bad results because of a poor decision process.

3. For several of the good decisions, evaluate why you think a sound process was followed in each. Make sure you address all phases of the decision process, and get the perspectives of knowledgeable others if available. Think about how these good processes can be codified and spread throughout your organization.

4. Next, select some decisions where a rather poor process was used, and evaluate their processes in the same way (across phases and with the perspective of relevant others). As before, focus on process issues, not just the outcome. What are the lessons to be learned? To what extent were the barriers to good decision-making personal, group-related, or institutional in origin?

5. *Team audits* can also be highly effective. Your work group can meet to complete both the Time Allocation Worksheet and the decision evaluations in steps 2–4 above. Such group exercises offer two big advantages. More people result in more perspectives and less rationalization.

And people are often more motivated in groups to do a thorough job—even in a group of just two.

6. Groups may also benefit from the Group Assessment form that follows. Note that this last evaluation tool covers the larger organization, within which your group must function.

## Decision-Making

*Group Assessment*

If your primary objective is to ensure high quality decision-making throughout the operation, here are some important questions to consider:

1. Assess the current quality of decision-making and problem-solving within the organization.

☐ Are the individuals at each level making sound decisions?
☐ Are groups making good decisions? How do you know?
☐ Are interdepartmental decisions managed well?
☐ Are cross-level decisions and implementation managed well?
☐ Which decisions are managed well and which are not? For example: We make good hiring decisions but are not good at determining why performance problems persist.

2. Identify the main obstacles currently hindering more effective decision-making within the division.

☐ What are the values, patterns, rewards, and constraints of decision-making within different operations?
☐ Where does decision-making break down: framing the issue(s), gathering intelligence, developing options, selecting or crafting the solution, planning, implementing the strategy, or learning from feedback and experience?
☐ Why does it falter: lack of skill, low reinforcement, inadequate feedback, organizational barriers?
☐ How does the behavior of senior managers positively or negatively affect decision-making practices throughout the operation?
☐ Which policies, procedures, or organizational systems hinder rather than help the decision process?

3. Determine actions or changes that are needed to support more consistent and effective decision-making throughout the organization.

❑ Which barriers are most significant?
❑ Which are the easiest to resolve?
❑ Which are the most important to resolve?
❑ What individual and organizational strengths can be used to counter or eliminate these barriers?

4. Gain agreement on how these actions or changes will be implemented.

❑ What organizational support will be required to ensure that the desired gains in problem-solving and decision-making are achieved?
❑ How do we achieve these changes with a minimum of disruption?
❑ How will we know when the desired improvements have been achieved?
❑ How can we ensure that the improved capability does not deteriorate over time?

# Appendix B

**Organizational Challenges in Decision-Making**

We have listed below some of the questions we pose in our longer surveys about organizational decision-making. Please review them and then add additional questions that are important for your group or organization. This kind of survey constitutes a preliminary diagnosis for identifying where improvements are most urgently needed. It should be complemented with decision audits and deeper analysis.

**Directions:** Ask a representative group of managers in your organization to rate how frequently they encounter the following challenges at work when making a decision alone or in a group.

**I. Deciding How to Manage the Decision**

| | Frequency Encountered | | | | |
|---|---|---|---|---|---|
| | *Never* | *Seldom* | *Sometimes* | *Often* | *Always* |
| 1. There is a lack of experience with similar problems or decisions. | 1 | 2 | 3 | 4 | 5 |
| 2. Too many things compete for my attention as a manager or professional. | 1 | 2 | 3 | 4 | 5 |
| 3. The deadlines for deciding are too tight. | 1 | 2 | 3 | 4 | 5 |
| 4. Stakeholders have competing priorities or values, are vying for control of the decision, or politicking for parochial solutions. | 1 | 2 | 3 | 4 | 5 |

| | Never | Seldom | Sometimes | Often | Always |
|---|---|---|---|---|---|
| 5. Resources (time, energy, budget, people) needed to understand or address issues are inadequate. | 1 | 2 | 3 | 4 | 5 |

**II. Framing the Issues**

| | Never | Seldom | Sometimes | Often | Always |
|---|---|---|---|---|---|
| 6. Decision objectives are unclear, hard to define, or conflicting. | 1 | 2 | 3 | 4 | 5 |
| 7. We filter or distort the information we receive. | 1 | 2 | 3 | 4 | 5 |
| 8. People have conflicting views about what is happening or what should be done. | 1 | 2 | 3 | 4 | 5 |
| 9. Some people don't even recognize that there is a problem or that it needs to be solved now. | 1 | 2 | 3 | 4 | 5 |
| 10. Diagnosis of the source of the problem is hard because cause and effect relationships are not clear. | 1 | 2 | 3 | 4 | 5 |

**III. Gathering Intelligence**

| | Never | Seldom | Sometimes | Often | Always |
|---|---|---|---|---|---|
| 11. The available information is inadequate to resolve the uncertainty inherent in the problem. | 1 | 2 | 3 | 4 | 5 |
| 12. Key information is simply "off limits." | 1 | 2 | 3 | 4 | 5 |
| 13. People interpret or evaluate the same information differently. | 1 | 2 | 3 | 4 | 5 |
| 14. The consequences of some options are hard to anticipate. | 1 | 2 | 3 | 4 | 5 |
| 15. There is not enough time, budget, or people to gather the intelligence needed. | 1 | 2 | 3 | 4 | 5 |

**IV. Coming to a Conclusion**

| | Never | Seldom | Sometimes | Often | Always |
|---|---|---|---|---|---|
| 16. Multiple objectives or competing interests must be satisfied. | 1 | 2 | 3 | 4 | 5 |

| | Never | Seldom | Sometimes | Often | Always |
|---|---|---|---|---|---|
| 17. The available information is too incomplete or unreliable to support a clear decision. | 1 | 2 | 3 | 4 | 5 |
| 18. Alternative evaluation strategies produce different choices. | 1 | 2 | 3 | 4 | 5 |
| 19. Fear of uncertainty, potential risks, or possible failure paralyze the decision process so no choice is made. | 1 | 2 | 3 | 4 | 5 |
| 20. People shoot from the hip and don't follow a systematic process. | 1 | 2 | 3 | 4 | 5 |

## V. Learning from Experience

| | Never | Seldom | Sometimes | Often | Always |
|---|---|---|---|---|---|
| 21. Decision flaws become apparent during implementation but no one evaluates and improves the decision. | 1 | 2 | 3 | 4 | 5 |
| 22. Priorities, resources, or values shift during implementation. | 1 | 2 | 3 | 4 | 5 |
| 23. People cover mistakes to avoid blame, ridicule, or sanctions. | 1 | 2 | 3 | 4 | 5 |
| 24. Poor decisions are rescued by skill during implementation. | 1 | 2 | 3 | 4 | 5 |
| 25. We don't apply lessons learned from our similar past decisions. | 1 | 2 | 3 | 4 | 5 |

# Notes

## Introduction

1. David Fairchild's anecdote about Herbert Hoover is found in his memoir, *Exploring for Plants*, New York: The MacMillan Company, 1930, p. 5.

2. Nortel Networks CEO John Roth was quoted in "Buying Into the New Economy," by Mark Heinzl, *Wall Street Journal*, July 25, 2000, p. B1.

3. The phrase "The Winner-Take-All Society" is the title of a book (*The Winner-Take-All Society: How More and More Americans Compete for Ever Fewer and Bigger Prizes, Encouraging Economic Waste, Income Inequality, and an Impoverished Cultural Life*, New York: Free Press, 1995) coauthored by our colleague, Robert H. Frank, professor of economics at Cornell's Johnson Graduate School of Management and also Goldwin Smith professor of economics, ethics, and public policy in Cornell's College of Arts and Sciences; and codirector of Cornell's Center for Behavioral Economics and Decision Research. The book's other author is Philip J. Cook of Duke University. The changing nature of management has been described in several well-known books, starting with Tom Peter's *Thriving on Chaos: Handbook for a Management Revolution*, New York: Alfred A. Knopf, 1987; Peter Drucker's *Post-Capitalist Society*, Harper Business, 1993; and Charles Handy's *The Age of Unreason*, Harvard Business School Press, 1989. Gary Hamel and C. K. Prahalad in *Competing for the Future*, Boston, MA: Harvard Business School Press, 1994, especially emphasize the need to look forward whereas David Hurst in *Crisis & Renewal: Meeting the Challenge of Organizational Change*, Boston, MA: Harvard Business School Press, 1995, emphasizes the importance of meeting the challenge of organizational change. Regarding the latter, see also Kathleen Eisenhardt and Shona L. Brown, *Competing at the Edge*, Boston, MA: Harvard Business School Press, 1998, and Stephen Haeckel and Adrian J. Slywotsky, *Adaptive Enterprise: Creating and Leading Sense and Respond Organizations*, Harvard Business School Press, 1999. The importance of managing evolutionary as well as

revolutionary change is further emphasized in Richard Leifer, Christopher M. McDermott, Gina Colarelli O'Connor, Lois S. Peters, Mark Rice, and Robert W. Veryzer, *Radical Innovation,* Harvard Business School Press, 2001, and in Gary Hamel, *Leading the Revolution,* Boston, MA: Harvard Business School Press, 2001. The challenges posed by uncertainty and complexity are perhaps nowhere more evident than when managing disruptive technologies, as highlighted in Clayton M. Christensen's *Innovator's Dilemma,* Harvard Business School Press, as well as in George S. Day and Paul J. H. Schoemaker (eds.), *Wharton on Managing Emerging Technologies,* Wiley, 2000. The latter book characterizes the challenge of managing discontinuity as being a profoundly "different game," a view also echoed in Charles Handy's *The Age of Paradox,* Boston, MA: Harvard Business School Press, 1994.

4. The continual breaking of athletic records is, of course, also partly due to improved equipment (e.g., vaulting poles or running shoes) as well as to increased numbers of people shooting for the record. The more people, over time, who attempt to break a record, the greater the sample becomes from which the record-breaker gets drawn. In many sports (e.g., gymnastics, speed skating, diving), however, the major factor in breaking records appears to be improved coaching and deeper insight into the physical and psychological aspects of the sport.

5. For this research, see Justin Kruger and David Dunning, "Unskilled and Unaware of It: How Difficulties in Recognizing One's Own Incompetence Lead to Inflated Self-Assessments," *Journal of Personality and Social Psychology* 77, no. 6 (1999): 1121–34.

6. To fully acknowledge and cite the contributions of Daniel Kahneman and Amos Tversky are beyond the scope of this writing. However, their most important papers and many related ones by students and colleagues are gathered in *Choices, Values, and Frames,* edited by Daniel Kahneman and Amos Tversky, Russell Sage Foundation, Cambridge University Press, 2000. This latter volume was completed by Kahneman after his friend and coauthor's untimely death in June 1996. Their earlier work, again with related papers by others, is collected in *Judgment under Uncertainty: Heuristics and Biases,* edited by Daniel Kahneman, Paul Slovic, and Amos Tversky, Cambridge University Press, 1982.

7. The work of the late Herbert Simon is even more widespread and difficult to acknowledge since it came earlier and influenced not only decision-making but much of cognitive science. However, a sense of his broad range of thinking on topics related to decision-making can be found in *The New Science of Management Decision,* Prentice Hall, rev. ed., 1977; *Administrative Behavior,* The Free Press, 4th ed., 1997; *Models of Bounded Rationality,* MIT Press, vol. 1, 1981, vol. 2, 1982, vol. 3, 1997; and in two books of invited lectures presented at MIT and Stanford, respectively, *The Sciences of the Artificial,* 3rd ed., MIT Press, 1996, and *Reason in Human Affairs,* Stanford University Press, 1983. As intriguing as any of the above is his remarkably frank autobiography, *Models of My Life,* New York: Basic Books, 1991.

8. For those who want to pursue behavioral decision research in more detail than our book allows, two excellent and highly readable books are available: *Judgment in Managerial Decision Making* by Max H. Bazerman, John Wiley & Sons, 4th ed., 1998, and *Rational Choice in an Uncertain World: The Psychology of Judgment and Decision Making* by Reid Hastie and Robyn M. Dawes, Harcourt Brace Jovanovich, 2001. The

most influential of the primary literature has been reprinted in several anthologies: *Judgment Under Uncertainty: Heuristics and Biases*, edited by Daniel Kahneman, Paul Slovic, and Amos Tversky, Cambridge University Press, 1982; *Judgment and Decision Making: An Interdisciplinary Reader*, edited by Terry Connolly, Hal R. Arkes, and Kenneth R. Hammond, Cambridge University Press, 2nd ed., 2000; *Research on Judgment and Decision Making: Currents, Connections, and Controversies*, edited by William M. Goldstein and Robin M. Hogarth, Cambridge University Press, 1997; and *Choices, Values, and Frames*, edited by Daniel Kahneman and Amos Tversky, Russell Sage Foundation, Cambridge University Press, 2000. See also *Smart Choices* by John S. Hammond, Ralph L. Keeney, and Howard Raiffa, Harvard Business School Press, 1998. A broader, integrative perspective is offered in *Decision Making: Descriptive, Normative and Prescriptive Interactions*, edited by David Bell, Howard Raiffa, and Amos Tversky, Cambridge University Press, 1988. We also highly recommend the seminal writings of James G. March as collected in *Decisions and Organizations*, Basil Blackwell, 1998. Finally, two entertaining popular treatments of the principles of decision-making applied to personal money management are Gary Belsky and Thomas Gilovich's *Why Smart People Make Big Money Mistakes*, New York: Simon & Schuster, 1999, and Max H. Bazerman's *Smart Money Decisions: Why You Do What You Do with Money (and How to Change for the Better)*, New York: Wiley, 1999.

9. Social, political, and emotional aspects of decision-making are important and have been covered in numerous books and articles. A classic is Irving L. Janis and Leon Mann, *Decision Making: A Psychological Analysis of Conflict, Choice and Commitment*, New York: Free Press, 1977. We also recommend Jeff Pfeffer's book, *Managing with Power: Politics and Influence in Organizations*, Harvard Business School Press, 1992; Daniel Goleman's bestseller, *Emotional Intelligence*, Bantam Books, 1995; and Lee G. Bolman and Terrence E. Deal's *Reframing Organizations*, San Francisco: Jossey-Bass Publishers, 1997. For academic studies of the role of affect (i.e., emotion and stress) in decision-making, see A. John Maule and Ola Svenson (eds.), *Time Pressure and Stress in Human Judgment and Decision Making*, New York: Plenum, 1993. Also, we recommend Mary Frances Luce, John W. Payne, and James R. Bettman, "The Emotional Nature of Decision Tradeoffs," chapter 2 in *Wharton on Making Decisions*, Stephen J. Hoch and Howard C. Kunreuther (eds.), New York: John Wiley & Sons, 2001, pp. 17–36.

10. Behavioral decision research enjoyed a flurry of inspired research in the late 1970s and 1980s, followed mostly by critiques, refinements, and extensions in the 1990s. Its basic tenets found rich application in areas such as negotiations, finance, and organizational behavior. Nonetheless, the field has remained largely laboratory-bound. It often studies heuristics and biases in stylized experiments where a normative answer can be readily adduced from a rational benchmark (because a "bias" can only be firmly established relative to an accepted standard of accuracy). Less well understood is how and when these biases operate in the real world, or particularly, if or when they counteract or exacerbate each other. Important questions also remain about how various biases and cognitive processes combine in groups or organizations and what their aggregate effects are in competitive markets with dynamic feedback. Various authors have argued that these biases may be less severe in the real world, notably G. Gigerenzer's "How to Make Cognitive Illusions

Disappear: Beyond 'Heuristics and Biases,' " *European Review of Social Psychology* 2 (1991): 83–115; G. Gigerenzer, U. Hoffrage, and H. Kleinbolting's "Probabilistic Mental Models: A Brunswikian Theory of Confidence," *Psychological Review* 98 (1991): 506–28; and G. Gigerenzer's "On Narrow Norms and Vague Heuristics: A Response to Kahneman and Tversky," *Psychological Review* 103 (1996): 592–96. Other authors have argued that we need better models of naturalistic decision-making, e.g., see *Naturalistic Decision Making*, edited by Caroline E. Zsambok and Gary Klein, Lawrence Erlbaum Associates, 1997, or for a European view, see Peter Juslin and Henry Montgomery (eds.), *Judgment and Decision Making: Neo-Brunswikian and Process-Tracing Approaches*, NJ: Lawrence Erlbaum Associates, Inc., 1999.

### Chapter 1

1. Robert Rubin's comments on decision processes were made in a commencement address at the University of Pennsylvania, May 17, 1999, and reprinted in that university's *Almanac Supplement*, May 18/25, 1999, pp. S-2–S-3. It is worth adding that the distinction between process and outcome is central to the field of ethics. Can noble ends ever justify questionable means, such as killing a man who is about to bomb a village? For classic essays on this subject, see J. J. C. Smart and Bernard Williams, *Utilitarianism: For & Against*, London, UK: Cambridge University Press, 1973, as well as chapter 21 in Jonathan Baron, *Thinking and Deciding*, Cambridge University Press, 2nd ed., 1994, pp. 422–49.

2. This well-known Lewis Carroll quote and its context can be found on p. 84 of *Alice's Adventures in Wonderland and Through the Looking Glass*, Stockholm: Zephyr Books, 1946.

3. Thinking of decision-making as a process consisting of phases has a long intellectual tradition. John Dewey in chapter 10 of his book *How We Think*, D. C. Heath & Company, 1910, characterized problem-solving as consisting of (1) defining the problem, (2) identifying the alternatives, and (3) choosing the best one. Herbert Simon similarly proposed a three-phase process consisting of intelligence, design, and choice (see his *New Science of Management Decision*, Prentice-Hall, 2nd ed., 1977). Our four-phase framework especially highlights framing and learning (relative to other approaches).

4. Our simplified diagram depicts the first two stages as characterized by divergence and the latter two as characterized by convergence. While this is true, overall, each of the four stages requires a balance of divergent and convergent thinking. Searching for other frames and developing new perspectives requires creative thinking, as does the generation of new options. However, the act of choosing a preferred frame requires convergence and closure. Intelligence-gathering is largely a diverging phase, in which additional information and interpretations of facts are sought. But convergence is required to distill the available intelligence into numeric estimates and ranges, possibly via quantitative models. The choice phase is primarily concerned with convergence, narrowing down the options to the most preferred. But in thinking about how much importance to ascribe to various criteria—such as whether safety is more or less important in buying a car than, say, mileage—some

divergent thinking is needed as well. Lastly, the learning phase also entails a balance. Making sense of the observable outcomes requires the development and eventual testing of multiple hypotheses (divergence). But summarizing the learning into a few pithy lessons or pointers entails convergence.

5. The statistics on where managers spend their decision-making time come from surveys of participants in our executive training programs over many years. These numbers reflect a wide variety of industries, multiple levels of managers, and different cultures.

6. There is little formal treatment of the concept of a metadecision in the research literature on decision-making. However, several authors have discussed the problem of deciding how to decide. A solid, relatively early treatment is Eric J. Johnson and John W. Payne's article "Effort and Accuracy in Choice," *Management Science* 30 (1985): 395–414. Their book with James Bettman offers more comprehensive coverage (Payne, Bettman, and Johnson, *The Adaptive Decision Maker,* 1993). Others have written wisely on the topic of decisions that might not get made (Ruth M. Corbin, "Decisions that Might Not Get Made," in *Cognitive Processes in Choice and Decision Behavior,* ed. Tom S. Wallsten, Lawrence Erlbaum, 1980). Part of this involves counterfactual reasoning, such as asking what would have happened if a decision had not been made or had been made differently. An extensive cognitive and social literature on counterfactual thinking exists. For example, see *What Might Have Been: The Social Psychology of Counterfactual Thinking,* N. J. Roese, and J. M. Olson (eds.), NJ: Lawrence Erlbaum, 1996. For a formal treatment of metadecisions, see Alan E. Singer's "Strategic Thinking without Boundaries: Transitions and Meta-Decisions," *Systems Practice* 9, no. 5 (1996), and Zhongtuo Wang's "Meta-Decision Making: Concepts and Paradigm," *Systems Practice* 13, no. 1 (2000).

7. The actual Dewey quote is, "It is a familiar and significant saying that a problem well put is half-solved." See John Dewey, *Logic: The Theory of Inquiry,* New York: Henry Holt, 1938, p. 108.

8. John Sculley's quotes are taken from his memoir, *Odyssey,* Harper & Row, 1987, pp. 20–22.

#### Chapter 2

1. For further details, see "Encyclopaedia Britannica," Harvard Business School Case N9-396-051, December 1995; for an update, see "Dusting Off the Britannica," *Business Week,* October 20, 1997, and "Bound for Glory?: The Venerable Encyclopaedia Britannica Struggles to Survive in an Electronic Age," *Chicago Tribune Magazine,* March 1998. By 1997, Britannica had begun to profoundly reframe itself. In the *Business Week* article cited above, newly arrived publisher Paul Hoffman noted: "We want to be recognized as a publishing company in the broadest sense." During this time, it fundamentally changed its business model. The CEO, Peter Norton, retired in 1995 in the face of declining market share, and formidable new competitors such as Microsoft, Times-Mirror, and Bertelsmann. The sales force was disbanded in 1996 after the company lost well over half its sales. Information would now be given away free; advertising would be allowed; multichannel access was to be

encouraged—from print to Internet to wireless. Britannica.com Inc. was formed as a new corporate entity to "fuse the remarkable legacy of *Encyclopaedia Britannica* with all the power and possibility of technology." The company's new vision is to become the most trusted source of information, knowledge, and learning in digital media (see www.Britannica.com).

2. The contrasting frames in this box may not all speak for themselves. For the win-win view of negotiations, see Roger Fisher and William Ury with Bruce Patton, editor, *Getting to Yes: Negotiating Agreement Without Giving In*, Penguin Books, 2nd ed., 1991. A more elaborate discussion of distributive bargaining is offered in Roy J. Lewicki, Joseph A. Litterer, David M. Saunders, and John W. Minton, *Negotiation: Readings, Exercises, and Cases*, Irwin, 2nd ed., 1993. The broader view of competitors was fully developed in Michael E. Porter's *Competitive Strategy: Techniques for Analyzing Industries and Competitors*, The Free Press, 1980. The view that an organization is a nexus of contracts is more formally explicated in Eugene F. Fama, "Agency Problems and the Theory of the Firm," *Journal of Political Economy* (1980): 88, 288–307, as well as Eugene F. Fama and Michael C. Jensen's "Agency Problems and Residual Claims," *Journal of Law and Economics* (1983): 327–49.

3. The sixteenth-century Hindu fable of the six blind men and the elephant was immortalized in the West by the nineteenth-century American poet John Godfrey Saxe, *Poetical Works*, Houghton Mifflin Co., 1884.

4. Functional blindness—i.e., the tendency to frame problems from one's own functional or occupational perspective—was demonstrated quite some time ago by DeWitt C. Dearborn and Herbert A. Simon in "Selective Perception: A Note on the Departmental Identification of Executives," *Sociometry* 21 (1958): 140–44.

5. This traditional frame difference is being subjected to some interesting forces of change. For one, Southern European managers are finding their "pyramid of people" or "village hierarchy" frame moving toward the greater, if less personal, efficiency of the functional frame. As pan-European organizations emerge and managers are rotated more frequently for breadth of development, electronic communication becomes a frequent necessity, and so on, the Southern social frame is looking more and more Northern. The embracing of Japanese management techniques in the 1980s further narrowed the difference. This Eastern tradition challenged both the Northern and Southern European frames. Although ultimately more compatible with the Northern frame's focus on functional efficiency (just-in-time delivery to cut inventory costs, rigorous attention to quality to reduce costly defects and re-work, etc.), the use of teams, worker participation (e.g., in "quality circles"), and the like has changed both frames.

6. The Kinko's story is told by Paul Roberts in "Kinko's—The Free-Agent Home Office," *Fast Company* 12 (December 1997): 164.

7. In the list of old versus new management or business frames, 24/7 refers to organizations working 24 hours 7 days a week (e.g., via a website, call center, or set of international trading desks). This markedly contrasts with the traditional workday starting at 9 A.M. and ending at 5 P.M. The balanced scorecard approach seeks to measure performance in four key areas: (1) financial, (2) internal operations, (3) customers and supplier satisfaction, and (4) innovation. This contrasts with a singular focus on rate of return on investment (ROI) or economic value added (EVA).

For further details, see Robert S. Kaplan and David P. Norton, "Using the Balanced Scorecard as a Strategic Management System," *Harvard Business Review* (January–February 1996): 75–87, or Robert S. Kaplan and David P. Norton, *Balanced Scorecard: Translating Strategy into Action,* Harvard Business School Press, 1996. Knowledge management refers to the systematic and comprehensive codification, storage, and retrieval of information across organizational boundaries, in real time with the very latest data. Such management systems are increasingly important for knowledge workers operating in an information economy. For details, see Thomas Davenport and Laurence Prusak, *Working Knowledge,* Cambridge, MA: Harvard Business School Press, 1998; John Browne and Steven E. Prokesch, "Unleashing the Power of Learning: An Interview with British Petroleum's John Browne," *Harvard Business Review on Point,* February 1, 2000; and David A. Garvin, *Learning in Action: A Guide to Putting the Learning Organization to Work,* Harvard Business School Press, 2000. Learning cultures are inquisitive and externally focused, experimental and innovative. They share information freely, reward risk-taking, and rely on cross-functional teams. In contrast, performance organizations tend to be internally oriented, focus on making the numbers, reward consistency, dislike ambiguity and deviations, and rely on rules and procedures. The key is to strike the right balance for any given company in a particular industry and time period, given the amount of external change and rate of competitive innovation. Regarding the latter, see Richard A. D'Aveni, *Hypercompetition: Managing the Dynamics of Strategic Maneuvering,* The Free Press, 1994. Coopetition refers to balancing cooperation (through partnership and alliances) with the traditional focus on competition (via price cutting, advertising campaigns, lawsuits, etc.). The classic reference here is Adam M. Brandenburger and Barry J. Nalebuff, *Co-opetition,* New York: Doubleday, 1996. Virtual organizations are an important new organizational form in which the boundaries and geographic location of the firm are less well defined. Workers may operate part-time, being neither traditional nine to five employees nor independent contractors. Important assets and capabilities of the firm (such as intellectual property or sales and marketing) may be jointly owned with strategic partners. And the work may be conducted in cyberspace. Such virtual network firms may not have a central office or indeed any office that is owned by the firm itself. For a comprehensive view of these and other organizational forms, see Jennifer Herber, Jitendra V. Singh, and Michael Useem, "The Design of New Organizational Forms," chapter 17 in *Wharton on Managing Emerging Technologies,* G. Day and P. Schoemaker (eds.), Wiley, 2000, pp. 376–92.

8. The pervasive influence of metaphors is discussed in George Lakoff and Mark Johnson's classic *Metaphors We Live By,* University of Chicago Press, 1980. A more in-depth treatment of metaphors and categories of the mind in general is offered in George Lakoff's innovative and controversial book *Women, Fire and Dangerous Things,* University of Chicago Press, 1987. For recent discussions, see Sabine Massen, *Metaphors and the Dynamics of Knowledge,* Routledge, January 2001; Robert Claiborne, *Loose Cannons, Red Herrings, and Other Lost Metaphors,* W. W. Norton & Company, July 2001; or Andrew Goatly, *Language of Metaphors,* Routledge, February 2001.

9. The new product development/stud poker quote example is taken from Thomas J. Peters and Robert H. Waterman, Jr., *In Search of Excellence,* New York: Warner Books, 1982, p. 143.

10. This is a decidedly simplistic overview of an extremely complex field. For more on mental models, see Rob Ranyard, *Decision Making: Cognitive Models and Explanations*, Routledge, 1997, or C. Marlene Fiol and Anne Sigismund Huff, "Maps for Managers: Where Are We? Where Do We Go From Here?," *Journal of Management Studies* 29, no. 3 (1992): 267–85. The classic references to mental models and their cognitive functions are: *Mental Models*, edited by Dedre Gentner and Albert L. Stevens, Lawrence Erlbaum Associates, 1983, and Philip N. Johnson-Laird, *Mental Models*, Harvard University Press, 2nd ed., 1983.

11. Our concept of thinking frame is much closer to the original notion of frame as it appeared in the field of artificial intelligence (AI) in the mid-1970s than to the decision frame concept in behavioral decision research. It was defined in AI as a method of organizing our knowledge about a concept to help focus attention and facilitate recall and inference. Thus, frames were defined as the mental structures or frameworks within which new information is interpreted through concepts acquired via previous experience. Our notion of thinking frames is also closely related to what are called schema and scripts in cognitive psychology. Like the AI idea of a frame, schemas organize into a coherent whole a multitude of different component concepts and events. In the area of decision-making, Kahneman and Tversky brought the concept of decision frames to great prominence by demonstrating that changes in the surface features of the decision frame can alter choices. Their specific definition is: "We use the term 'decision frame' to refer to the decision-maker's conceptions of the acts, outcomes, and contingencies associated with a particular choice. The frame that a decision-maker adopts is controlled partly by the formulation of the problem and partly by the norms, habits, and personal characteristics of the decision-maker" (Amos Tversky and Daniel Kahneman, "The Framing of Decisions and the Psychology of Choice," *Science* 211 [1981]: 453–58).

### Chapter 3

1. Debra E. Meyerson, and Joyce K. Fletcher, "A Modest Manifesto for Shattering the Glass Ceiling," *Harvard Business Review* (January–February 2000): 127–36.

2. The assumptions about how General Motors looked at its world in the late sixties are from Peter Senge, *The Fifth Discipline*, NY: Currency, Doubleday, 1990.

3. For references about Federal Express's foray into Europe, see Hoover, *Handbook of American Business*, 1995, Hoover, Inc., pp. 488–89.

4. Steven E. Prokesh, "Unleashing the Power of Learning: An Interview with British Petroleum's John Browne," *Harvard Business Review* (September–October 1997): 147–68.

5. Gary Hamel, "Bringing Silicon Valley Inside," *Harvard Business Review* (September–October 1999); see also his book, *Leading the Revolution*, Harvard Business School Press, 2000.

6. Desmond Mpilo Tutu, "Truth and Reconciliation: Toward a Just Society," given as the Henry E. and Nancy Horton Bartels World Affairs Fellowship Lecture at Cornell University, Ithaca, NY, April 10, 2000. See also: Desmond Mpilo Tutu, *No Future Without Forgiveness*, New York: Doubleday, 1999. For a comparison of the two

historical frames and a more detailed rationale for creating a new frame, see, in particular, chapter 2: "Nuremberg or National Amnesia? A Third Way." Alex Boraine, deputy chairman of the Truth and Reconciliation Commission, also tells this story in *Inside South Africa's Truth and Reconciliation Commission*, New York: Oxford University Press, 2001.

7. Elias H. Porter, "The Parable of the Kitchen Spindle," *Harvard Business Review* 40, no. 3 (May–June 1962): 58–66.

8. Howard Perlmutter at the Wharton School has developed an interesting framework to encourage deep dialogue among organizational stakeholders. He identifies various dialogue deficits that limit effective communication, such as lack of trust, cognitive misperceptions, false assumptions, etc. In addition he recommends seven types of processes that can improve and deepen dialogue within organizations, ranging from bridging to bonding to blending. This framework of deep dialogue encompasses both the cognitive aspects of communication, such as frames, and the affective and cultural elements as well (Howard Perlmutter: personal communication). See also H. V. Perlmutter, "On Deep Dialog," 1999, working paper, Emerging Global Civilization Project, the Wharton School. Other good references on dialogue are David Bohm, *On Dialogue*, Lee Nichol, ed., London and New York: Routledge, 1996; Daniel Yankelovich, *The Magic of Dialogue: Transforming Conflict into Cooperation*, Simon & Schuster, 1999; and William Isaacs, *Dialogue and the Art of Thinking Together*, NY: Currency, 1999.

9. Frank G. Rogers, *The IBM Way*, New York: Harper & Row, 1986, p. 125.

### Interlude A

1. Personal communication from Manuel Sole. The storage tank was built in a wrong location (but only by several crucial meters) at the Complejo Jose Antonio Anzoategui in Puerto La Cruz, Venezuela.

2. The quotes from Vinton Cerf, Robert Dennard, and Frederick Smith were taken from "Here's An Idea!" by Jill Rosenfeld, *Fast Company* 33 (April 2000): 97.

3. For a systematic approach to innovative thinking, see the seven principles discussed in Gerald Nadler and Shozo Hibino, *Breakthrough Thinking*, CA: Prima Publishing & Communications, 1990. A useful toolkit for managers is offered in Morgan D. Jones, *The Thinker's Toolkit: Fourteen Skills for Making Smarter Decisions in Business and in Life*, NY: Random House, 1995, with techniques ranging from conceptual to analytical. For examples of breakthrough thinking in various corporate settings, see P. Ranganath Nayak and John M. Ketteringham, *Breakthroughs!* San Diego: Pfeiffer, 1994. This book details the events surrounding the development of major commercial breakthroughs such as the VCR, Federal Express, the Sony Walkman, and the microwave oven among many others.

4. Xerox PARC's "Workscapes of the Future" project was described in Elizabeth Weil, "Brainstorming the Future," *Fast Company* 8 (April 1997): 100. The BrainStore's BrainNet is described in Anna Muoio, "Great Ideas in Aisle 9," *Fast Company* 33 (April 2000): 46.

5. Michael Gazzaniga, *The Mind's Past,* University of California Press, May 1998.

6. Alan G. Robinson and Sam Stern, *Corporate Creativity,* Berrett-Koehler Publishers, 1998, pp. 9–11.

7. Numerous excellent books on creativity can be consulted for more specific techniques. See in particular such classics as Paul Watzlawick, John H. Weakland, and Richard Fisch, *Change: Principles of Problem Formulation and Problem Resolution,* W. W. Norton & Company, 1974; James L. Adams, *Conceptual Blockbusting,* Reading, MA: Addison Wesley Longman, 1986; Edward de Bono, *Lateral Thinking: Creativity Step by Step,* New York: Harper & Row, 1973; and Roger van Oech, *A Whack on the Side of the Head: How You Can Be More Creative,* New York: Warner Books, rev. ed., 1998, which even comes with a Wack Pack of cards. For creativity in an organizational context, see Robert Lawrence Kuhn, ed., *Handbook for Creative and Innovative Managers,* New York: McGraw-Hill, 1987; Jane Henry (ed.), *Creative Management,* Sage Publications, 1991; and Alan G. Robinson and Sam Stern, *Corporate Creativity,* San Francisco: Berrett-Koehler Publishers, 1998, pp. 9–11. For a comparison of techniques, see Kenneth R. MacCrimmon and Christian Wagner, "Stimulating Ideas through Creativity Software," *Management Science* 40, no. 11 (November 1994): 1514–32.

8. Options thinking is also referred to as "real options" or "shadow options" analysis in contrast to financial options and the associated Black-Scholes pricing formula. Important parallels between financial and real options analysis exist which are more fully explored in Lenos Trigeorgis, *Real Options,* Cambridge, MA: MIT Press, 1996; Keith J. Leslie and Max P. Michaels, "The Real Power of Real Options," *McKinsey Quarterly* 3 (1997): 4–22; and Timothy A. Luehrman, "Investment Opportunities as Real Options: Getting Started on the Numbers," *Harvard Business Review* (July/August 1998): 51–67. For options analysis in applied settings such as Enron and Hewlett-Packard, see "Exploiting Uncertainty," *Business Week,* June 7, 1999, pp. 118–24. For a link to strategy, see Timothy A. Luehrman, "Strategy as a Portfolio of Real Options," *Harvard Business Review* (September–October 1998): 89–101.

9. The Enron and Hewlett Packard stories are reported in "Exploiting Uncertainty," *Business Week,* June 7, 1999, pp. 118–24.

10. In the context of this book, our discussion of the important subject of "real options" is necessarily limited. For a more comprehensive and highly readable discussion, see our colleague William F. Hamilton, "Managing Real Options," chapter 12, in George S. Day and Paul J. H. Schoemaker (eds.), *Wharton on Emerging Technologies,* New York: Wiley, 2000, pp. 271–88. While most discussions of real options have focused on *valuing* options, Hamilton emphasizes that "options don't just represent a new framework for valuing decisions. They represent a different *process* for structuring and managing these decisions. A different approach to valuation is important, but is only part of the picture." We thank him for allowing us to draw extensively from his work.

11. The valuation of real options can typically be accomplished by folding back a decision tree that captures all downstream choice points and uncertainties. For details, see John F. Magee, "How to Use Decision Trees in Capital Investment," *Harvard Business Review* (September–October 1964): 79–96; James E. Smith and Robert F. Nau, "Valuing Risky Projects: Option Pricing Theory and Decision Analy-

sis," *Management Science* 41 (May 1995): 795–816. Approximations using financial valuation tools—such as the Black-Scholes formula—are also possible at times for real options; see Stewart C. Myers, "Finance Theory and Financial Strategy," *Interfaces* 14, no. 1 (January/February 1984): 126–37; K. Avinash Dixit and Robert S. Pindyck, "The Options Approach to Capital Investment," *Harvard Business Review* (May/June 1995): 105–15; and Lenos Trigeorgis, ed., *Real Options in Capital Investments,* Westport, CT: Praeger, 1995.

12. Various studies have shown that people may reject gambles in isolation that they would gladly accept in combination (or vice versa), underscoring that how you package the options and express their consequences may greatly affect the choice you make. You may sometimes find that while neither of two options is attractive when examined in isolation, the combination is a risk you would be prepared to take. Consider this simple example: Option A involves a 50-50 chance of gaining $100 or losing $100. Option B offers a ⅓ chance at gaining $200 and a ⅔ chance of losing $100. When examined in isolation, neither of these two options may be attractive. However, when combined into Option C, the new gamble entails four possible payoffs, namely getting $300, $100, $0, or losing $200, with probabilities of ⅙, ⅙, 2/6, and 2/6 respectively. The combined option is clearly different from either of its components, offering just a ⅓ chance of loss compared to ½ for A and ⅔ for B. The combined gamble may be attractive to people whereas its components may not. And this example ignores that the outcomes from Option A and B may be correlated, which further changes the risk profile of Option C.

## Chapter 4

1. The overconfidence quotes are taken from *The Experts Speak* by Christopher Cerf and Victor Navasky, Pantheon Books, 1984. This excellent compendium contains an alarming number of authoritative misstatements from highly accomplished people in many walks of life.

2. The Adam Smith quote is the one commonly cited. In fact, the correct quote is, "The overweening conceit which the greater part of men have of their own abilities is an ancient evil remarked by the philosophers and moralists of all ages. Their absurd presumption in their own good fortune has been less taken notice of. It is, however, if possible, still more universal. There is no man living who, when in tolerable health and spirits, has not some share of it. The chance of gain is by every man more or less overvalued, and the chance of loss is by most men undervalued, and by scarce any man, who is in tolerable health and spirits, valued more than it is worth." From "An Inquiry into the Nature and Causes of the Wealth of Nations," book 1, chapter 10, *Of Wages and Profit in the Different Employments of Labour and Stock,* Washington, DC: Regnery Publishing, Inc., 1998, p. 126.

3. For more detail, see J. Edward Russo and Paul J. H. Schoemaker, "Managing Overconfidence," *Sloan Management Review* 33, no. 2 (winter 1992): 7–17.

4. The literature on overconfidence is extensive. An authoritative discussion can be found in "Overconfidence: It Depends on How, What, and Whom You Ask" by Joshua Klayman, Jack B. Soll, Claudia Gonzalez-Vallejo, and Sema Barlas in

*Organizational Behavior and Human Decision Processes* 79, no. 3 (September 1999): 216–47. The classic overview of early overconfidence studies is by Sarah Lichtenstein, Baruch Fischhoff, and Lawrence Phillips, "Calibration of Probabilities: The State of the Art to 1980," In *Judgment Under Uncertainty: Heuristics and Biases*, edited by Daniel Kahneman, Paul Slovic, and Amos Tversky, Cambridge University Press, 1982 pp. 306–334. This paper also addresses the effects of feedback and training. The data on physicians can be found on Jay J. Christensen-Szalanki and James B. Bushyhead, "Physician's Use of Probabilistic Information in a Real Clinical Setting," *Journal of Experimental Psychology: Human Perception and Performance* 7 (1981): 928–35. The data on physicists can be found in an unpublished paper by Max Henrion and Baruch Fischhoff, "Uncertainty Assessments in the Estimation of Physical Constants," Carnegie Mellon University, Department of Engineering and Public Policy (January 1984). The Asian cross-cultural studies can be found in George N. Wright and Lawrence D. Phillips, "Cultural Variations in Probabilistic Thinking: Alternative Ways of Dealing with Uncertainty," *International Journal of Psychology* 15 (1980): 239–57. Researchers have critically examined how robust the overconfidence bias or phenomenon is across modes of response (e.g., probabilities vs. ranges), types of tasks (general vs. specific topics; or easy vs. hard questions), and what role regression towards the mean might play in explaining the typical finding of regressive calibration curves. A special issue of the *Journal of Behavioral Decision Making* (vol. 10, no. 3, 1997) was devoted to these issues, and generally concluded that the overconfidence bias was real rather than being an artifact of the methodology employed. See especially Peter Ayton and Alastair G. R. McClelland, "How Real is Overconfidence?" in *Journal of Behavioral Decision Making* 10, no. 3 (1997): 279–86.

5. For readers interested in how entire nations can fall into overconfidence, we recommend Barbara Tuchman, *The March of Folly*, Alfred A. Knopf, 1984. This book explores why countries continue to wage war, with both sides thoroughly confident that they will win.

6. Ford's Edsel fiasco has been described many times. For a brief analysis, see Robert F. Harley, *Bullseyes and Blunders*, John Wiley & Sons, 1987.

7. In July 1982 the tiny Penn Square Bank of Oklahoma City touched off a national banking crisis that brought down the Continental Bank of Chicago and seriously hurt a bevy of other major financial institutions. The cause was bad loans in oil and gas, many of which Penn Square had sold to Continental Bank. Most of these loans went bad, resulting in the collapse of Penn Square while leaving the FDIC with a $4.5 billion bill to bail out Continental Bank. A major lawsuit was filed in the wake of this fiasco against the accounting firm Ernst & Whinney, which eventually defeated the claims. For further details, see Jeff Bailey's report in the *Wall Street Journal* of April 1, 1987, entitled "Continental Illinois Ex-Chief Aids the FDIC." A more comprehensive account is offered by Phillip L. Zweig in *Belly Up: The Collapse of the Penn Square Bank*, NY: Ballantine Books, 1986.

8. Much of the work on the consequences of investor overconfidence has been done by Terrance Odean and his colleagues. See his paper "Do Investors Trade Too Much?" in *American Economic Review* 89 (December 1999): 1279–98. A one-page overview of the problem was published in the *Wall Street Journal*: "In the field of in-

vesting, self-confidence can sometimes come back to haunt you," by Jonathan Clements, September 22, 1998, p. C1.

9. Will Durant, *The Story of Philosophy*, New York: Washington Square Press, 1961, p. 354.

10. James R. Emshoff and Ian I. Mitroff, "Improving the Effectiveness of Corporate Planning," *Business Horizons* 21 (1978): 49–60. A penetrating analysis of the bias toward confirming evidence has been presented by Joshua Klayman and Young-Won Ha, "Confirmation, Disconfirmation and Information in Hypothesis Testing," *Psychological Review* 94, no. 2 (1987): 211–28. Klayman and Ha argue that whether disconfirmation or confirmation is most suitable depends in complex ways on the kind of task one faces; see also Joshua Klayman, "Varieties of Confirmation Bias" in Jerome Busemeyer, Reid Hastie, & Douglas L. Medin (eds.), *Decision Making from a Cognitive Perspective*, New York: Academic Press [Psychology of Learning and Motivation, vol. 32], 1995, pp. 365–418.

11. Robert A. Olsen, "Desirability Bias among Professional Investment Managers: Some Evidence from Experts," *Journal of Behavioral Decision Making* 10 (1997): 65–72.

12. Kurt A. Carlson and J. Edward Russo, "Jurors' Distortion of Evidence in a Mock Legal Trial," *Journal of Experimental Psychology: Applied* 7 (June 2001). See also J. Edward Russo, Margaret G. Meloy, and T. Jeffrey Wilks, "Predecisional Distortion of Information by Auditors and Salespersons," *Management Science* 46, no. 1 (2000): 13–27. The distortion of information toward our preferred beliefs or positions is an old phenomenon. What is new, and only starting to be appreciated, is how big distortion can be without being recognized. The jurors, auditors, and salespeople who distorted very substantially were largely unaware they were doing so. This means that they were fully convinced of their final choice, even though it was based to a large degree on their own distortion of the information provided. They could not tell the distorted evidence from the real thing. Sometimes we can recognize our own distortion, with some embarrassment. When you root for a national athlete or your college team, you tend to score your side more positively or to see its rules infractions as less severe. But these distortions are guided by the deeper beliefs of nationality and alumni status, beliefs of which we are generally aware. What is so dangerous about the distortion of information during decisions is that it can occur without any prior preference for one option. It happens with alarming ease.

13. How much weight to give to evidence, pro or con, is a complex issue depending both on the strength of the evidence itself and the credibility of its source. Research suggests that people overweigh the strength of evidence (e.g., how well a candidate did in an interview) relative to the credibility of that type of evidence (the limited insight that can be gained from any single short interview). Whenever credibility is low, as is often the case in business decisions, but the strength of the evidence is highly suggestive, overconfidence is likely to occur.

14. The remark about Leonardo da Vinci is by Kenneth Clark, as quoted in Michael J. Gelb, *How to Think Like Leonardo da Vinci*, 1998, p. 50.

15. The counterargument question referred to in the text was stated as follows: "Our company's current liabilities (defined as notes payable, short-term loans, etc.)

were $1,971 million and $1,441 million as of December 31, 19xx, and March 31, 19xx, respectively. For October 31, 19xx, the company's current liabilities will be (circle one):

(a) greater than $1,900 million

(b) less than or equal to $1,900 million

Give your subjective probability that you will be correct: ____%."

16. The full study can be found in Jayashree Mahajan, "The Overconfidence Effect in Marketing Management Predictions," *Journal of Marketing Research* (August 1992): 329–42. In a similar vein, researchers have found that when listing pros and cons, the cons do the most good in countering overconfidence. See Stephen J. Hoch, "Availability and Inference in Predictive Judgment," *Journal of Experimental Psychology: Learning, Memory, and Cognition* 10 (1984): 649–62.

17. The Bertrand Russell quote is from *Collected Papers of Bertrand Russell*, vol. 11, London: Routledge, 1997, p. 142. The actual quote is: "The Greeks were fruitful in hypotheses, but deficient in observation. Aristotle, for example, thought that women had fewer teeth than men, which he could not have thought if he had had a proper respect for observation."

18. These and other relevant statistics on school-related deaths can be found in the 2000 *Annual Report on School Safety* (published by the U.S. Departments of Education and Justice), which draws data from such sources as the U.S. Center for Disease Control and the U.S. Department of Justice.

19. The youth violence trends and public responses are reported in Kim Brooks, Vincent Schiraldi, and Jason Ziedenberg, *School House Hype: Two Years Later,* by the Justice Policy Institute, a youth advocacy think tank based in Washington, DC, and the nonprofit Children's Law Center in Covington, Kentucky, April 2000. It is an update to their 1998 report, *School House Hype: School Shootings and the Real Risks Kids Face in America.* The report provides an overview of polling and crime data on youth violence and school shootings as well as a legislative, legal, and policy analysis of the debate over school safety. The data on youth homicide arrests comes from the FBI. The data on the decrease in school-associated violent deaths comes from the National School Safety Center. The "one in two million" risk of dying a violent death in an American school comes from calculating that data against the 52 million students in American schools. The phone poll assessing fears of a school shooting in the respondents' own community was conducted by the *Wall Street Journal* and NBC News; they spoke with 1,004 adults. The two polls comparing the increase in fears from the 1997–98 to the 1998–99 school years were conducted by Gallup for *USA Today*.

20. Similar results on availability bias come from a survey of 165 staff members at Consumers Union, the publisher of *Consumer Reports* (December 1996, p. 52). Staff members were given twenty-two selected causes of death and asked to rank them according to which was responsible for the most deaths in the U.S. in a given year. The reported rank is an average of the responses. The accompanying table shows results of the survey for six of those causes, along with the actual figures of annual deaths due to each cause. Invariably the majority of people surveyed ranked the second item in each pair as causing more deaths each year. In each case, however, the first item is the correct answer. (Note: the original survey simply listed the

causes. We've paired them here to help highlight the discrepancies. Notice that the higher ranked item in each pair gets more often reported in the press as a cause of death.)

| Cause of Death | People's Rank | Annual U.S. Total (in. 1,000s) |
| --- | --- | --- |
| Alcohol-related | 3 | 108 |
| Motor-vehicle accidents | 1 | 42 |
| Secondhand smoke | 5 | 40 |
| AIDS | 2 | 30 |
| Drowning | 6 | 4.8 |
| Fires in the home | 4 | 3.2 |

Figures of deaths/year are based on 1996 data in the USA.

21. Availability bias can also lead to undue optimism. Because we fail to envision important pathways in the complex net of future events, we become unduly optimistic about predictions based on the fewer pathways we actually do consider. The limited paths that are evident (e.g., the expected and the ideal scenarios) may exert more weight on likelihood judgments than they should. Bridge players provide a telling example of how availability can cause undue optimism. More experienced bridge players are better calibrated bidders because they take into account more unusual events or hands. Less experienced players believe they can make hands they often cannot, precisely because they fail to consider uncommon occurrences. Gideon Keren, "Facing Uncertainty in the Game of Bridge: A Calibration Study," *Organizational Behavior and Human Decision Processes* 39 (1987): 98–114.

22. On January 4, 1990, two and a half months after he killed his wife, Charles Stuart's body was found in the Mystic River beneath the Tobin Bridge, an apparent suicide. In testimony in the 1995 federal trial of the Boston Police Department's handling of the case, the first detective in charge said that he had initially suspected Stuart. However, he was removed from the case in favor of detectives who aggressively pursued Stuart's explanation of attack by an African-American (Ralph Ranalli, "Cop Who Eyed Stuart 'Shut Out,' " *Boston Herald*, June 27, 1995).

23. Gregory B. Northcraft and Margaret A. Neale, "Experts, Amateurs, and Real Estate: An Anchoring-and-Adjustment Perspective on Property Pricing Decisions," *Organizational Behavior and Human Decision Processes* 39 (1987): 84–97.

24. For completeness, we note that the actual instructions in the Attila the Hun example were to "add 400 to your home phone number." Thus, the range of anchors was A.D. 400 to 1399, not A.D. 0 to 999. We translated the data in the figure by subtracting 400 so that it would correspond to the simpler form of the anchoring question that we present in the text.

25. The Boeing 747 was eventually one of the most profitable aircraft in history.

However, "It wasn't until 1978 that sales reached the official breakeven point of four hundred established early in the program—meaningless when achieved because of the stupendous budget overrun" (p. 287 of Eugene Rodgers, *Flying High,* New York: Atlantic Monthly Press, 1996). The final cost of the 747's development may never be fully known. The company's admission of $750 million is considered low, but even that matches Boeing's net worth of $762 million in 1965, the year the project started (p. 279, ibid.).

26. The tendency to seek mostly incremental solutions was referred to as "local search" by Richard Cyert and James March, *A Behavioral Theory of the Firm,* Englewood Cliffs, NJ: Prentice-Hall, 1963. A more extensive discussion of incrementalism is offered in Charles E. Lindblom, "The Science of Muddling Through," *Public Administration Review* 19 (1959): 79–88, under the heading of "disjointed incrementalism." Others, however, have argued that incremental approaches are often the only way to proceed within complex bureaucracies; see James B. Quinn, *Strategies for Change: Logical Incrementalism,* Homewood, IL: Richard D. Irwin, 1980.

## Chapter 5

1. This diagram can be found in Hugh Courtney, Jane Kirkland, and Patrick Viguerie, "Strategy Under Uncertainty," *Harvard Business Review* (November–December 1997): 66–81. Note how the overall posture and approach to dealing with uncertainty migrates from confident analysis to portfolio and options approaches to evolutionary learning models. Note as well that the McKinsey typology concerns both the intelligence-gathering stage of our framework as well as the coming to conclusions stage, addressed in the next chapter. As we emphasized earlier, our four stages are not strictly sequential in real-world applications, but require a back-and-forth approach until the right path to solving the problem has been found. The McKinsey illustration underscores this point by highlighting that the type of information to be gathered (stage two in our framework) depends on how the problem will be resolved (stage three), a matter that ideally should have been anticipated in the metadecision. For more on the four-level framework in the figure, see Hugh Courtney, *20/20 Foresight: Crafting Strategy in an Uncertain World,* Boston: Harvard Business School Press, 2001.

2. For an early history of probability forecasts of weather, see Allan Murphy, "Some Extensions and Clarifications," *Weather and Forecasting* 13 (March 1998): 5–15. The excellent calibration of weather forecasters is documented in Allan Murphy and Robert Winkler, "Probability Forecasting in Meteorology," *Journal of the American Statistical Association* (September 1984). For accountants, see Lawrence Tomassini, Ira Solomon, Marshall B. Romney, Jack L. Krogstad, "Calibration of Auditors' Probabilistic Judgments: Some Empirical Evidence," in *Organizational Behavior and Human Performance* 30 (1982): 391–406.

3. Based on Schoemaker's discussions with Shell executives in Exploration & Production (EP).

4. We don't want to create the false impression that feedback and accountability, as useful as their combination can be, get at the root of the problem. Re-

searchers are only recently examining the cognitive processes underlying the generation of a confidence estimate. One promising view is that your level of confidence depends most on the internal conflict that you experience in coming up with your answer or best guess. That is, although confidence should measure your likelihood of being correct, it is really based on the amount and kind of conflict you experience in selecting your choice or estimated value. Elke Weber of Columbia University has made this argument and applied her ideas to physicians in her paper, "Confidence Judgments as Expressions of Experienced Decision Conflict."

5. The classic demonstration of the value of pro and con arguments (and especially the con ones!) is Asher Koriat, Baruch Fischhoff, and Sarah Lichtenstein, "Reasons for Confidence," *Journal of Experimental Psychology: Human Learning and Memory* 6 (1980): 107–18.

6. The idea of prospective hindsight is discussed and documented in Deborah J. Mitchell, J. Edward Russo, and Nancy Pennington, "Back to the Future: Temporal Perspective in the Explanation of Events," *Journal of Behavioral Decision Making* 2 (1989): 25–39.

7. Prospective hindsight works to increase the number and specificity of the reasons generated by increasing the perceived certainty of the event. What matters most is not the time perspective, looking back versus looking forward, but the certainty of the event. People work more effectively to generate reasons for an event when it is certain compared to when it is uncertain. This is true even if the event is in the past, but the person generating reasons for it is not certain which way it turned out.

8. Regarding the fault tree study, a third group of managers was given the shorter fault tree provided to Group 1, with one difference. Space was provided for each manager to list up to six more causes. Some managers who used this chart failed to list any additional causes. They estimated probabilities similar to those of the first, highly biased, group. However those managers who did write in six additional causes of their own choosing—which were often different from those we had listed for the second group—provided probabilities similar to those of Group 2. This study of restaurant managers can be found in Laurette Dube-Rioux and J. Edward Russo, "An Availability Bias in Professional Judgment," *Journal of Behavioral Decision Making* 1 (1988): 223–37. It extends the first such demonstration (involving car mechanics), by Baruch Fischhoff, Paul Slovic, and Sarah Lichtenstein, "Fault Trees: Sensitivity of Estimated Failure Probabilities to Problem Representation," *Journal of Experimental Psychology: Human Perception and Performance* 4 (1973): 330–44. A subsequent paper by J. Edward Russo and Karen J. Kolzow ("Where Is the Fault in Fault Trees?", *Journal of Experimental Psychology: Human Perception and Performance* 20 [1994]: 17–32) pinpointed availability bias as the primary cause of underestimating the size of the "all other" category.

9. Our treatment of this subject is necessarily brief. For a more extensive description of this tool, see Paul J. H. Schoemaker, "Scenario Planning: A Tool for Strategic Thinking," *Sloan Management Review* (winter 1995): 25–40. For a conceptual and behavioral perspective, see Paul J. H. Schoemaker, "Multiple Scenario Developing: Its Conceptual and Behavioral Basis," *Strategic Management Journal* 14 (1993): 193–213. For a methodology to link scenarios to competitor analysis, core

capabilities, and strategic vision building, see Paul J. H. Schoemaker, "How to Link Strategic Vision to Core Capabilities," *Sloan Management Review* (fall 1992): 67–81. For a forecasting perspective, see W. R. Huss, "A Move Toward Scenarios," *International Journal of Forecasting* 4 (1988): 377–88. For connecting scenario planning to project evaluation, using Monte Carlo simulation, see Paul J. H. Schoemaker, "When and How to Use Scenario Planning: A Heuristic Approach with Illustration," *Journal of Forecasting* 10 (1991): 549–64.

10. For a discussion of scenario planning at Royal Dutch/Shell, see Paul J. H. Schoemaker and Cees A. J. M. van der Heijden, "Integrating Scenarios into Strategic Planning at Royal Dutch/Shell," *Planning Review* 20 (1992): 41–46; Pierre Wack, "Scenarios: Uncharted Waters Ahead," *Harvard Business Review* (September–October 1985): 73–89; Pierre Wack, "Scenarios: Shooting the Rapids," *Harvard Business Review* (November–December 1985): 139–50; and Peter Schwartz, *The Art of the Long View*, New York: Doubleday, 1991. The Anglo-American Corporation example is discussed in C. Sunter, *The World and South Africa in the 1990s*, Cape Town: Human and Rousseau Tafelberg, 1987. In September of 1991, political leaders met near Stellenbosch to explore the so-called Mout Fleur scenarios, with special involvement from the ANC (African National Congress), a political party that had been outlawed during the era of apartheid. A video titled "The Flight of the Flamingoes" describes the four scenarios and the process used to create them. The video can be ordered via fax (021-959-3242) from the Institute for Social Development, University of the Western Cape. An account of how Shell helped create the Mout Fleur scenarios can be found in Robbie E. Davis-Floyd, "Storying Corporate Futures: The Shell Scenarios," *International Journal of Futures Studies* 1 (1996). This document can also be found as a chapter in *Corporate Futures*, George Marcus (ed.), Chicago: University of Chicago Press, 1997. For additional scenario applications in practice, see Cees van der Heijden, *Scenarios: The Art of Strategic Conversation*, NY: Wiley, 1996; Gill Ringland, Keith Todd, and Peter Schwartz, *Scenario Planning: Managing for the Future*, NY: Wiley, 1998: and Liam Fahey and Robert M. Randall (eds.), *Learning from the Future*, NY: Wiley, 1998.

11. Personal communication, Frank Quigley, vice president of operations, Harrah's Atlantic City, April 2000.

12. The two dimensions of the scenario matrix specifically include the following. The playing field question concerns the rules and regulations under which credit unions can operate (both state and federal), the role of nontraditional new entrants, the scrutiny given by Congress (which had considered a bill to tax credit unions) as well as the game plans of the various players (from focusing on profit to market share to competing on innovation). The technology dimension covers such issues as the role of internet banking and e-commerce (websites, portals, etc.), check imaging and processing (electronic vs. paper), new user verification methods such as iris scans, smart cards, the importance of data mining, new back-end systems to streamline operations, etc. Each cell of this initial matrix was then developed in greater detail—by adding other trends and appropriate outcomes from all other uncertainties—resulting in four full-fledged scenarios. Readers can find complete descriptions of these four scenarios at www.cues.org.

13. The Dutch Central Planning Bureau's wide-ranging global scenarios are dis-

cussed in A. de Jong and G. Zalm, *Scanning the Future,* The Hague: Central Planning Bureau, Sdu Publishers, 1992.

14. The scenario planning tips (along with many others) and the observations from Keith Kendrick about scenario planning at AT&T are found in a conference report, *Managing Uncertainty through Scenario Thinking,* issued by the Emerging Technologies Management Research Program at the Wharton School, University of Pennsylvania. This report (#96-1) is based on the proceedings of a senior management workshop presented on November 1, 1996, organized by Paul J. H. Schoemaker.

15. The data for the horse-race handicappers are from a study by Paul Slovic and Bernard Corrigan, presented in their talk to the Institute for Quantitative Research in Finance, "Behavioral Problems of Adhering to a Decision Policy," May 1, 1973, and also briefly described on pages 166–67 of Slovic's chapter, "Toward Understanding and Improving Decisions," in W. C. Howell and E. A. Fleishman (eds.), *Human Performance and Productivity: Vol. 2, Information Processing and Decision Making,* Hillsdale, NJ: Erlbaum, 1982. The essentially flat curve for accuracy results from three of the eight handicappers decreasing in accuracy, two improving, and three staying about the same. In an unpublished paper prepared for a seminar entitled "Behavioral Problems of Adhering to a Decision Policy," Slovic attributes the flat curve to information overload. For example, when the handicappers were presented with the same races a second time (to test their consistency), they proved less consistent with forty pieces of information than with five or ten. We gratefully acknowledge Paul Slovic for providing us with the necessary background information on this telling study.

16. The reasons why experienced decision-makers processing large amounts of information do not extract the maximum benefit are not well understood. We believe that they are often distracted by unusual values, such as extreme cases. Also, there is a tendency to be unduly influenced by the first and last data items seen and to give less weight to those in the middle. Although experts are often good at "chunking" large amounts of data into easily remembered portions or subtotals, they still fall victim to information overload. A remarkable series of articles by Lynne Reder of Carnegie Mellon University contrasted a 1,000-word summary with the original 5,000-word introductory chapter in a college textbook (on African geography). She and her coauthors found that the students, when given equal time (twenty to thirty minutes), learned more from the summary. Based on quizzes using objective questions, the summary proved superior to the full text in (1) helping students remember explicitly stated information, (2) inferring information implied but not explicitly stated over periods as long as twelve months, and (3) learning new information (e.g., additional insight into African geography).

### Interlude B

1. The headquote is from Romano Guardini, *Letters from Lake Como: Explorations in Technology and the Human Race*, William B. Eerdmans Publishing Company, 1994, p. 102.

2. We thank Professor Razvan Andonie of the Transylvania University of Brasov, Romania, for his helpful comments on this interlude.

3. An updated recommendation of the best product out of billions of available configurations gives consumers the feedback they want and enables sellers to keep them involved in the Internet-mediated dialogue. However, the cost of this interim feedback is a heavy computation burden. Unlike most product recommendation systems, the calculation of the best product in WiseUncle's Advisor doesn't happen only once, at the end, but each time a question has been answered. This requires that the AI-based computation of the best personal computer be very fast. If consumers are to get the feedback they want and sellers are to keep them involved and motivated, it must happen after every question.

4. For more on rule-based (or expert) systems, see Joseph C. Giarratano, *Expert Systems: Principles and Programming*, PWS Publishing Company, 3rd ed., 1998.

5. We can think of such fuzzy logic systems as employing probabilistic weights in assigning truth or falsehood to statements such as a loan being nonperforming. But fuzzy logic rules extend beyond the rules of probability. They have proved rather successful in designing systems to improve autofocus features in cameras, self-diagnosis and correction of washing machines, or how to route an elevator most quickly to a particular floor in a complex office building with multiple elevator shafts. For more on fuzzy systems, see Earl Cox, *The Fuzzy Systems Handbook: A Practitioner's Guide to Building, Using, and Maintaining Fuzzy Systems*, Morgan Kaufmann Publishers, 2nd Book&CD ed., 1998.

6. For more on network structures, see Marilyn McCord Nelson and W. T. Illingworth, *Practical Guide to Neural Nets*, Addison-Wesley Publishing Company, 1994, and Lance Chambers (ed.), *The Practical Handbook of Genetic Algorithms: Applications*, 2nd ed., CRC Press, 2000.

7. Consider, for example, buying a computer online via Dell, which derives an increasing percentage of its revenues from this channel. When you visit their website (Dell.com), several user-friendly screens appear that guide you to appropriate usage and product categories (home, small office, or big business; PCs, printers, software, accessories, etc.). But then, you are pretty much on your own. When one of us (Paul) decided to buy the Dimension brand from Dell (on the vague assumption that it was faster and more sophisticated than the alternatives), a complex barrage of choices awaited him. Should the Pentium 4 processors be 1.4 or 1.5 gigaHertz? Is the "enhanced quiet keyboard" really superior to the regular one? Is the 32MB NVIDIA GeForce 2 MX 4X AGP graphics card really better than some other equally obscure alternative? In fairness to Dell, there are some explanatory paragraphs associated with each product feature, but they still require considerable knowledge of computers. Even though Dell is as successful as any of the online PC

sellers, we think the consumer needs and deserves more help. Not only will the new decision-aiding technologies provide such help, they go a step further by adapting the computer to the consumer, rather than vice versa.

8. Note that in the purchase of a personal computer, as challenging as picking the best out of a billion options may be, there is little uncertainty to contend with. That is, you know what product you'll get when you order it. This is not true for many managerial decisions about new products to be launched, job candidates to be hired, or the demand in different retail locations.

## Chapter 6

1. The headquote is from *Samuel Butler's Notebook*, selections edited by Geoffrey Keynes and Brian Hill, London: Jonathan Cape, 1951, p. 222.

2. This chapter builds on Paul J. H. Schoemaker and J. Edward Russo, "A Pyramid of Decision Approaches," *California Management Review* 36, no. 1 (fall 1993): 9–31.

3. The letter by Ben Franklin to Joseph Priestley, dated September 19, 1772, has been reprinted in *The Benjamin Franklin Sampler* (Fawcett, 1956) as well as in several books on multiattribute decision-making (e.g., Milan Zeleny's *Multiple Criteria Decision Making: Past Decade and Future Trends*, vol. 1, McGraw-Hill Book Company, 1984).

4. There exist many different meanings and views on the role of intuition. For some, intuitive decision-making denotes the height of human intellectual achievement, whereas others view it as a self-serving cover for ignorance. Excellent overviews of the complex subject of intuition can be found in a book by Robin Hogarth, *Educating Intuition*, University of Chicago Press, 2001, and in an article in the *Harvard Business Review* by Alden M. Hayashi, "When to Trust Your Gut," vol. 79 (February 2001): 59. For applications of intuition in time-pressured decisions, see Gary Klein, *Sources of Power: How People Make Decisions*, Cambridge: MIT Press, 1998. Of related interest is Gary Klein and Karl E. Weick, "Decisions: Making the Right Ones, Learning From the Wrong Ones," *Across the Board* (June 2000). Finally, the view of intuition as tacit knowledge is well stated by Herbert A. Simon in an article written with Michael J. Prietula, "The Experts in Your Midst," *Harvard Business Review* (January–February 1989): 120–24. For a wide range of managerial views on intuition, see Weston H. Agor (ed.), *Intuition in Organizations*, NY: Sage Publications, 1989. An empirical comparison of intuitive versus more analytic judgments is offered by Kenneth R. Hammond, Robert M. Hamm, Janet Grassia, and Tamra Pearson, "Direct Comparison of the Efficacy of Intuitive and Analytical Cognition in Expert Judgment," *IEEE Transactions on Systems, Man, and Cybernetics* SMC-17, no. 5 (September–October 1987). An illustration of the dangers of intuition in the emotional area of medical decision-making can be found in Donald A. Redelmeier, Paul Rozin, and Daniel Kahneman, "Understanding Patients' Decisions: Cognitive and Emotional Perspectives," *Journal of the American Medical Association* 270, no. 1 (July 1993): 72–76. See also the Letters section of the *Journal of the American Medical As-*

*sociation* 270, no. 20, November 24, 1993, p. 2432, for "Patient Decision Making—Reply," by the same authors.

5. The radiologist example was taken from Paul J. Hoffman, Paul Slovic, and Leonard G. Rorer, "An Analysis-of-Variance Model for Assessment of Configural Cue Utilization in Clinical Judgment," *Psychological Bulletin* 69 (1968): 338–49. Note that these were highly trained professionals making judgments central to their work. In addition, they knew that their medical judgments were being examined by researchers, so they probably tried as hard as they could. Still, their carefully considered judgments were remarkably inconsistent.

6. To arrive at 23 percent, we took the reported mean intra-expert correlation of .76 and calculated the chance of getting a reverse opinion between two cases from one time to the next. In general, a (Pearson product-moment) correlation of $r$ translates in a $[.5 + \arcsin (r)/\pi]$ probability of a rank reversal of two cases the second time, assuming bivariate normal distributions. See Maurice Kendall, *Rank Correlation Methods*, London: Charles Griffen & Co., 1948.

7. These kinds of "test-retest" studies are rarely conducted in business. While they are simple to understand, they are harder to perform. To make the test valid, people must completely forget their initial judgments before they make their second one. Such total forgetting is difficult to achieve.

8. The importance weighting techniques to be discussed shortly have the disadvantage of simplemindedness but the advantage of perfect consistency. If the intuitive judgments predict GPA better, then the level of inconsistency may not have been that great. However, if the models' predictions are closer to the actual GPAs, then the advantage of removing inconsistency must be pretty sizable—big enough to overcome any disadvantage of "simplemindedness." We examined this with our GPA experiment. Since we knew the true GPAs for each of the fifty test cases, we could perform the key comparison. The correlation of the intuitive judgments with the actual GPAs was only .34. The importance weight models' estimates correlated .39 with the true GPAs. Of the 128 subjects tested, 81 percent were unable to outperform their own simplistic linear (regression) models. The inconsistency in their intuitive judgments must have been greater than any advantages stemming from deep insight, subtlety, or human complexity. Put differently, the unrecognized inconsistency in our intuition is so great as to turn any advantages of human judgment over a simple model into a net loss. In essence, the students (or rather their simple models) surpassed themselves.

9. The dangers of intuition are well-demonstrated empirically (via test-retest reliability studies), but the underlying mechanisms producing the inconsistencies are less well understood and may be numerous in cause. Attention shifts such as momentary distractions, contrast effects with earlier cases, or alternative ways of looking at the case may all cause a different response when examining the same case the second time around. Other factors besides the response mode and problem presentation may influence intuitive choices. For example, most of us suffer from a serious status quo bias in that we favor the option we have over the option we don't have (William Samuelson and Richard Zeckhauser, "Status-quo Bias in Decision Making," *Journal of Risk and Uncertainty* 1 [1988]: 7–59). Studies have demonstrated this effect by randomly giving people one of two gifts, say a baseball cap versus a

coffee mug. Then people are offered the opportunity—without cost or pressure either way—to exchange whatever they received for the other item. One would expect about half the group to exchange items (since the chance is 50-50 that you in fact received the item you more preferred at the start). In fact, only a fraction of people wish to exchange their hat or mug for the other item (Daniel Kahneman, Jack L. Knetsch, and Richard H. Thaler, "Experimental Tests of the Endowment Effect and the Coase Theorem," *Journal of Political Economy* 98 [1990]: 1325–48). Once they possess whatever item they were given, they value it more than before. One explanation for this is that giving up an item once it has been received (in return for the other item) entails a feeling of loss. And most people register losses more vividly than comparable gains (which is why few of us would want to flip a fair coin for, say, one hundred dollars (Daniel Kahneman and Amos Tversky, "Prospect Theory: An Analysis of Decisions Under Risk," *Econometrica* 47 [1979]: 263–91). For alternative explanations, see Gretchen B. Chapman, "Similarity and Reluctance to Trade," *Journal of Behavioral Decision Making* 11, no. 1 (March 1998): 47–58. Also, exchanging the gift is a more willful act than merely choosing one of two items, and thus more prone to regret or criticism. In general, acts of omission (not choosing or acting) are safer than acts of commission (see Jonathan Baron and Ilana Ritov, "Reference Points and Omission Bias," *Organizational Behavior and Human Decision Processes* 59, no. 3 [September 1994]: 475–98). For this reason, Ford Motor Company now requires that all options be put on an equal footing when making choices, including the option of doing nothing. Thus the burden of proof is shifted from beating "doing nothing" to picking the alternative that is truly best for the organization.

10. In the behavioral decision-making literature, these rules of thumb and other mental shortcuts are called "heuristics." The term comes from the Greek word for "discover."

11. For more on industry- and occupation-specific rules, see Seth Godin and C. Conley, *Business Rules of Thumb*, Warner Books, 1987. Many of the examples cited in this box were taken from this book. For a rather positive view on the use of rules in business, see Kathleen M. Eisenhardt and Donald N. Sull, "Strategy as Simple Rules," *Harvard Business Review* (January 2001): 107–16. The authors contend that in complex, evolving environments, the best we can do is use simple rules. These can be how-to rules, boundary conditions, priority rules, timing rules, and exit rules. Examples are cited from Yahoo!, eBay, and Enron.

12. The story of the food products company and its scientific rule is quite troubling. The junior manager who heard us lecture on the topic recognized the problem and explained it to his superiors. They were either unable to understand the trap they had fallen into or unwilling to hear the message. In fairness to his superiors, the circularity trap that the company fell into is quite subtle. When we present this trap to managers, many of them think it is awkward, even embarrassing, but not necessarily dangerous. Yet it is exactly this trap that the cookie company fell into: they kept picking B over A, and then C over B, D over C, and so on, until they had significantly undermined their market share and eroded profits. They could have easily seen this if only they had compared D with A, as consumers implicitly did when comparing D with unchanged competitor brands. For a highly technical

# Notes

review of the circularity trap inherent in the dictionary rule, see Peter C. Fishburn, "Lexicographic Orders, Utilities, and Decision Rules: A Survey," *Management Science* (July 1974): 1442–71, as well as Amos Tverky's original analysis, "Intransitivity of Preferences," *Psychological Review* 76 (1969): 31–48.

13. Of course, the accuracy of different rules of thumb varies considerably, depending on the specific criteria and cutoffs, as well as the option set itself. One study found that that the dictionary and threshold rules yield about 80 percent and 30 percent, respectively, of the accuracy attained by optimal rules. For more on this subject, see John W. Payne, James R. Bettman, and Eric J. Johnson, *The Adaptive Decision Maker*, Cambridge University Press, 1993.

14. This kind of choice system is known in academic jargon as a *linear model*. "Linear" is simply a mathematical term for combining the separate pieces of evidence by adding the weighted "pro" factors and subtracting the weighted "cons." See R. M. Dawes and B. Corrigan, "Linear Models in Decision Making," *Psychological Bulletin* 81 (1974): 97–106.

15. S. Rose, "Improving Credit Evaluation," *American Banker*, Tuesday, March 13, 1990. For an application to the repayment of medical students' loans, see R. Cooter and J. B. Erdmann, "A Model for Predicting HEAL Repayment Patterns and Its Implications for Medical Student Finance," *International Journal of Human-Computer Studies* (1998). For an article of historical interest, see H. A. Wallace, "What is in the Corn Judge's Mind?" *Journal of American Society for Agronomy* 15 (1923). For more detail on how to build linear models—both objective and subjective—see Alison Hubbard Ashton, Robert H. Ashton, and Mary N. Davis, "White-Collar Robotics: Levering Managerial Decision Making," *California Management Review* 37, no. 1 (fall 1994): 83–109. Especially useful is their discussion of possible objections to using linear models in applied settings, using their example of predicting advertising space for *Time* magazine (see pp. 95–101).

16. Kenneth R. Hammond, Robert M. Hamm, Janet Grassia, and Tamra Pearson, "Direct Comparison of the Efficacy of Intuitive and Analytical Cognition in Expert Judgment," *IEEE Transactions on Systems, Man, and Cybernetics* SMC-17, no. 5 (September–October 1987).

17. The linear model has a history of well over fifty years. A seminal work was Paul Meehl's *Clinical Versus Statistical Prediction*, University of Minnesota Press, 1954. A primary contributor to the subsequent work is Robyn Dawees of Carnegie Mellon University. Two of his papers are particularly accessible to nonprofessional readers: "Clinical versus Actuarial Judgment," written jointly with David Faust and Paul Meehl, *Science* 243 (1989): 1668–73, and "The Robust Beauty of Improper Linear Models in Decision Making," *American Psychologist* 34 (1979): 571–82. The 1979 Dawes paper is also reprinted in the anthology *Judgment Under Uncertainty: Heuristics and Biases*, edited by Daniel Kahneman, Paul Slovic, and Amos Tversky, Cambridge University Press, 1982.

18. Of course, the use of intuition to assign weights may be inaccurate. A person may assign different weights from one time to the next. One way to guard against such random error is to compare pairs of factors. For instance, how much more important is the quantitative GMAT than the verbal GMAT? Work experience is how many times more important than the personal essay? After judging every

possible pair of factors, you will need to use a statistical technique to average out the inconsistencies. (See Thomas L. Saaty, *The Analytic Hierarchy Process*, New York: McGraw-Hill, 1980.) Alternative methods for obtaining weights in subjective linear models are discussed and empirically compared in Paul J. H. Schoemaker and Carter C. Waid, "An Experimental Comparison of Different Approaches to Determining Weights in Additive Utility Models," *Management Science* 2 (1982): 182–96. For a more detailed description and comparison, see Appendix A in Paul Kleindorfer, Howard Kunreuther, and Paul J. H. Schoemaker, *Decision Sciences: An Integrative Perspective*, Cambridge University Press, 1995. However, we offer the caveat that such refined techniques may not be worth the extra effort in many cases. Indeed, some authors have argued that the weights don't matter much in many cases and that equal weighing is good enough. See, for example, Hillel J. Einhorn and Robin M. Hogarth, "Unit Weighting Schemas for Decision Making," *Organizational Behavior and Human Performance* 13 (1975): 171–92, and Howard Wainer, "Estimating Coefficients in Linear Models: It Don't Make No Nevermind," *Psychological Bulletin* 83 (1976): 213–17. Nonetheless, cases exist where the choice is sensitive to the exact weights.

19. Sometimes being overly explicit about one's weighting scheme can be detrimental, as Ford Motor Company discovered in its celebrated Pinto lawsuit. Ford's managers had carefully calculated that the cost of adding a reinforced gas tank would not be justified by the expected number of lives saved from rear-end collision fires. An internal memo rejected a safety improvement that in the early 1970s cost $11 per car, figuring that the savings of $49.5 million in fewer deaths and injuries was not worth the $137 million it would cost to add this safety feature to 11 million cars and 1.5 million light trucks. In making this trade-off, Ford valued saving a human life at $200,000 and avoiding the typical injury at $67,000 in 1970s dollars. Such explicit weighting of pros and cons, especially putting a price tag on human life, hurt Ford with the jury. However, such judgments are unavoidable: either they are made intuitively or explicitly. And in some cases it may help you in court to say that your personnel or credit decisions use formulae that explicitly exclude criteria deemed illegal (such as gender, race, or redlining). The Ford Pinto story was reported in J. Dowdy, "Pinto Madness," *Mother Jones* 18 (September–October 1977).

20. A readable and provocative prospectus for this structured numerical approach to making medical decisions can be found in "Better Decisions Through Science," by John A. Swets, Robyn M. Dawes, and John Monahan, *Scientific American* (October 2000): 82–87.

21. For a general review of bootstrapping studies, see Colin Camerer, "General Conditions for the Success of Bootstrapping Models," *Organizational Behavior and Human Performance* 27 (1981): 411–22. It builds on and refines Kenneth R. Hammond, C. J. Hursch, and F. J. Todd, "Analyzing the Components of Clinical Inference," *Psychological Review* 71 (1964): 438–56.

22. As we discussed in Interlude B, the growing field of artificial intelligence provides a number of additional techniques to build objective linear models for highly complex technical decisions. These new technologies include neural nets, rule-based systems, Bayesian networks, fuzzy logic, and genetic algorithms. A particularly intriguing application of these newer methods (and some old ones as well)

is automating some decisions. For an illustration in marketing decisions, see Randolph E. Bucklin, Donald R. Lehmann, and John D. C. Little, "From Decision Support to Decision Automation: A 2020 Vision," *Marketing Letters* 9, no. 3: 235–46.

23. Sales of fashion apparel through direct mail catalogs were estimated intuitively by eight buyers. See Stephen H. Hoch, "Experts and Models in Combination," in Robert Blattberg, Rashi Glazer, and John D. C. Little (eds.), *The Marketing Information Revolution*, Harvard Business School Press, 1994. A model to predict sales of the same items was created, based on the previous year's sales data and catalogs. The predictive success, where again 1.00 is perfect, was .76 for the buyers and .77 for the model. But a 50-50 average of both judgments reached a .80 success level. This may not seem like a big improvement, but let's reframe it (by switching reference points) from success to failure rate. The 50-50 mixture fails 20% of the time, the buyers 24%. In terms of merchandise, that's 20% more, (24-20)/20, left on the shelves to be discounted or discarded. For a discussion of *how* and *when* combining decision models and human intuition is likely to result in improved accuracy, see Stacey M. Whitecotton, D. Elaine Sanders, and Kathleen B. Norris, "Improving Predictive Accuracy with a Combination of Human Intuition and Mechanical Decision Aids," *Organizational Behavior and Human Decision Processes* 17, no. 3 (1998): 325–48. Also see Stephen H. Hoch, "Combining Models with Intuition to Improve Decision," and chapter 5 in Stephen H. Hoch and Howard Kunreuther (eds.), *Wharton on Making Decisions*, New York: Wiley, 2001, pp. 81–102.

24. Almost as much ink has been generated on critiquing major ranking efforts as on the rankings themselves. One article that prominently highlights the distortion of the decision weights is former *Slate* writer, Bruce Gottleib's "Cooking the Books: How *U.S. News* Cheats in Picking its Best American Colleges," August 31, 1999 at http://slate.msn.com/crapshoot/99-08-31/crapshoot.csp.

25. For more on the application of decision analysis and the multiattribute utility model, see Ralph L. Keeney and Howard Raiffa, *Decisions with Multiple Objectives*, New York: Wiley, 1976, and Ralph L. Keeney, *Value Focused Thinking*, Boston: Harvard University Press, 1992. The formal or quantitative approach to decision-making is well explained in Robert Clemen, *Making Hard Decisions: An Introduction to Decision Analysis*, Boston, MA: PWS-Kent Publishing Co., 2nd ed., 1996. See also Howard Raiffa's classic book *Decision Analysis: Introductory Lectures on Choices Under Uncertainty*, Addison-Wesley, 1968, and, at a more advanced level, Ralph Keeney and Howard Raiffa, *Decisions with Multiple Objectives: Preferences and Value Tradeoffs*, John Wiley & Sons, 1976. For behaviorally oriented perspectives, see Detlof von Winterfeldt and Ward Edwards, *Decision Analysis and Behavorial Research*, Cambridge University Press, 1986, or Paul J. H. Schoemaker, "The Expected Utility Model: Its Variants, Purposes, Evidence, and Limitations," *Journal of Economic Literature* 20 (June 1982): 529–63.

26. The integrated circuits case is described in Ralph L. Keeney and Gary L. Lilien, "New Industrial Product Design and Evaluation Using Multiattribute Value Analysis," *Journal of Product Innovation Management* 4 (1987): 185–98. After a careful analysis of how much the customer valued improvements within each attribute, it became clear that one of the three testers was unacceptable and that the remaining

two were very close to each other, scoring 13 and 15 respectively on a 0–100 scale. Since these were prototypes, much room for improvement remained. Also, it could now be determined how much this customer would be willing to pay for improvement in a given design parameter. For instance, the difference between the top two testers translates into about $300,000, which is useful information for pricing as well as product development decisions. Furthermore, this type of value analysis can help the marketing group determine which product features to emphasize most for a particular customer, and even how many products to introduce and where to position them in the market's value space.

27. GM's dialogue decision process is described by Michael W. Kusnik and Daniel Owens in "The Unifying Vision Process," *Interfaces* 22 (November–December 1992): 150–66.

28. David Savageau and Richard Boyer, *Places Rated Almanac*, New York: Prentice-Hall, 1993.

29. The software program we used was developed by Jack Hersey, Howard Kunreuther, and S. Schocken at the Wharton School, University of Pennsylvania. It is described in "Integrating Prescriptive and Descriptive Analyses Using A Computer-Based Decision Support System," Working Paper, Department of Decision Sciences, The Wharton School, University of Pennsylvania, April 1984.

30. Of course, we don't know for sure that the value analysis identified the best options for each student. This would require many hours with each person to model his or her true preference in fine detail. However, the method used in this experiment comes closest to such a full-blown value analysis. And our main point holds: different methods generate different conclusions.

31. Taking less time and effort to make a decision is an important consideration that decision research increasingly appreciates. Making the best decision means not only choosing the best alternative (referred to as "maximizing the utility of the chosen alternative"), but also minimizing time, effort, and other decision-making costs. This perspective is discussed in J. Edward Russo and Barbara A. Dosher, "Strategies for Multiattribute Binary Choice," *Journal of Experimental Psychology: Learning, Memory and Cognition* 9 (1983): 676–96, and in the book *The Adaptive Decision Maker* by John W. Payne, James R. Bettman, and Eric J. Johnson, Cambridge University Press, 1993. See also Kathleen M. Eisenhardt, "Speed and Strategic Choice," *California Management Review* 32, no. 3 (1990): 1–16.

32. P. Passell, "Wine Equation Puts Some Noses Out of Joint," *New York Times*, March 4, 1990, p. 1; Orly Ashenfelter, D. Ashmore, and Robert Lalonde, "Bordeaux Wine Vintage Quality and the Weather: Bordeaux," *Chance Magazine* 8, no. 4 (fall 1995): 7–14.

33. For a thorough discussion of possible objections to using a linear model and their rebuttals, see Alison Hubbard Ashton, Robert H. Ashton, and Mary N. Davis, "White-Collar Robotics," *California Management Review* 37, no. 1 (fall 1994): 95–101.

34. Robert Blattberg and Stephen H. Hoch, "Database Models and Managerial Intuition: 50% Model + 50% Manager," *Management Science* 36, no. 8 (1990): 887–99.

35. The Francis Bacon quote can be found in Robin Hogarth, "Judgment, Drug Monitoring and Decision Aids," in W. H. W. Inman (ed.), *Monitoring for Drug Safety*, Lancaster, England: MTP Press, 1980.

### Chapter 7

1. This chapter has benefited from the substantial input of our Cornell colleague, Randall S. Peterson. We are grateful for his assistance.

2. Further analysis of the Bay of Pigs fiasco, and the Kennedy quote, are provided in Irving Janis, *Groupthink: Psychological Studies of Policy Decisions and Fiascos*, Houghton Mifflin, 2nd ed., 1982. For a critical review of groupthink as a psychological model, see Won-Woo Park, "A Review of Research on Groupthink," *Journal of Behavioral Decision Making* 3, no. 4 (October–December 1990): 229–46. An alternative view—focusing on the role of reference points in the explosion of the space shuttle Challenger in 1986—is presented in James K. Esser and Joanne S. Lindoerfer, "Group-Think and the Space Shuttle Challenger Accident: Toward a Quantitative Case Analysis," *Journal of Behavioral Decision Making* 2, no. 3 (1989): 167–78. Yet another test of the role of reference points in risky group decision-making is offered in Glen Whyte and Ariel S. Levi, "The Origins and Function of the Reference Point in Risky Group Decision Making: The Case of the Cuban Missile Crisis," *Journal of Behavioral Decision Making* 7 (1994): 243–60. This excellent decision involved many of the same policymakers as in the Bay of Pigs.

3. General Motors' Corvair problems are discussed in J. Patrick Wright, *On a Clear Day You Can See General Motors*, Wright Enterprises, 1979, and Ed Cray, *Chrome Colossus: General Motors and Its Times*, McGraw-Hill, 1980. While GM's Corvair boasted an innovative rear-engine design and sporty styling, employees objected to safety concerns from the start. It was only after the automobile's engine failures were exposed by consumer advocate Ralph Nader (*Unsafe at Any Speed*, 1965) that the company responded. As Wright noted: "There wasn't a man in top GM management who had anything to do with the Corvair who would purposely build a car that he knew would hurt or kill people. But, as part of a management team pushing for increased sales and profits, each gave his individual approval in a group to decisions which produced the car in the face of the serious doubts that were raised about its safety, and then later sought to squelch information which might prove the car's deficiencies" (pp. 67–68).

4. The space shuttle disaster is examined in "Report of the Presidential Commission on the Space Shuttle Challenger Accident," I and II (June 6, 1986). Also see the SCRHAAC Report, *Post-Challenger Evaluation of Space Shuttle Risk Assessment and Management*, National Academic Press, 1988. The Challenger story has been recounted in several books. Noteworthy among these is the organizational perspective of Diane Vaughan, *The Challenger Launch Decision: Risky Technology, Culture and Deviance at NASA*, Chicago: University of Chicago Press, 1996. A briefer presentation of this book is available in Diane Vaughan, "The Trickle-Down Effect: Policy Decisions, Risky Work, and the *Challenger* Tragedy," *California Management Review* 39, no. 2 (1997): 80–102. The book itself was reviewed separately by three scholars in

the June 1997 issue of *Administrative Science Quarterly*. For a link to groupthink, see James K. Esser and Joanne S. Lindoerfer, "Group-Think and the Space Shuttle Challenger Accident: Toward a Quantitative Case Analysis," *Journal of Behavioral Decision Making* 2, no. 3 (1989): 167–78.

5. The best-documented examples of group blunders are found in the public sector, not necessarily because they occur there with greater frequency, but because public officials must leave more information available to researchers than corporate executives. In particular, postmortems of public blunders are part of the public record; corporate reflections, if they occur, are usually not.

6. For realistic insights about leadership, ranging from mountain climbing to drug discovery and fire fighting, see Michael Useem, *The Leadership Moment: Nine True Stories of Triumph and Disaster and Their Lessons for Us All*, Times Books, 1999. The role of power and influence in organizational decision-making is well covered in Jeffrey Pfeffer, *Managing With Power: Politics and Influence in Organizations*, Harvard Business School Press, 1992. The dynamics and social significance of groups are addressed in Rupert Brown (ed.), *Group Processes: Dynamics Within and Between Groups*, Blackwell Publishers, 2000, whereas David Nadler and Janel L. Spence (eds.), *Executive Teams*, Jossey-Bass, 1997, explores the special challenge of senior management teams; see also Jon R. Katzenbach and Douglas K. Smith, *The Wisdom Teams: Creating the High-Performance Organization*, HarperBusiness, 1994. Each of these latter books draws heavily on real-world case studies.

7. These three profiles of group decisions were suggested to us by John Carroll of MIT during some of our joint seminars. We gratefully acknowledge his contribution.

8. Group cohesiveness has often been used as a possible predictor of group performance. Although the association between cohesiveness and performance may be reasonable and consistent with anecdotal evidence, it is not at all empirically clear that the effect actually exists or under what conditions it appears. In fact, some research suggests that the most direct effect might be from performance to cohesiveness rather than the other way around. For an analysis of the cohesiveness-performance relationship, see Brian Mullen and Carolyn Copper, "The Relation Between Group Cohesiveness and Performance: An Integration," *Psychological Bulletin* 115, no. 2 (1994): 210–27.

9. The Walt Whitman passage is slightly abridged from the original in *Leaves of Grass, Comprehensive Edition*, edited by Blodgett and Bradley, New York: NYU Press, 1965, pp. 605–6.

10. The story of Nissan Design International's "divergent pairs" hiring and the quotes from Jerry Hirschberg are from "Opposites Attract," by Katharine Mieszkowski, *Fast Company* (December–January 1998): 42–43. Hirschberg describes his approach to creativity in his book, *The Creative Priority: Driving Innovation in the Real World*, HarperBusiness, 1998.

11. Karen A. Jehn, "A Multimethod Examination of the Benefits and Detriments of Intragroup Conflict," *Administrative Science Quarterly* (June 1995) suggests that *moderate* task conflict and *low* relationship conflict is the ideal. Excessive task conflict leads to problems with commitment in the "coming to conclusions" stage. For an excellent comparison of management conflict and performance, see Kathleen M.

Eisenhardt, Jean L. Kahwajy, and L. J. Bourgeois III, "Conflict and Strategic Choice: How Top Management Teams Disagree," *California Management Review* 39, no. 2 (winter 1997). The researchers studied twelve top management teams in technology-based "Silicon Valley" firms; a third of these had *very high* conflict, another third *very low* conflict. They found the highest conflict top management teams led the highest performing firms. Firms with lower conflict executive teams did less well. For other studies on the subject of conflict, decision-making, and performance, see A. Amson, "Distinguishing the Effects of Functional and Dysfunctional Conflict on Strategic Decision Making: Resolving a Paradox for Top Management Teams," *Academy of Management Journal* (1996); D. Schweiger et al., "Group Approaches for Improving Strategic Decision Making: A Comparative Analysis of Dialectical Inquiry, Devil's Advocacy, and Consensus," *Academy of Management Journal* (1986); R. Priem, "Top Management Team Group Factors, Consensus, and Firm Performance," *Strategic Management Journal* (1990); D. Tjosvold, *The Positive Conflict Organization*, Addison-Wesley, 1991; Karen A. Jehn, "A Multimethod Examination of the Benefits and Detriments of Intragroup Conflict," *Administrative Science Quarterly* (1995); Lisa H. Pelled, "Demographic Diversity, Conflict, and Work Group Outcomes: An Intervening Process Theory," *Organization Science* 7 (1996).

12. Work by Randall Peterson and Tony Simons suggests that both trust and consensus decision-making play a pivotal role in enabling groups to separate task and relationship conflict. High trust groups can separate the two. In low trust groups, task conflict leads to relationship conflict. Tony Simons and Randall S. Peterson, "Task Conflict and Relationship Conflict in Top Management Teams: The Pivotal Role of Intragroup Trust," *Journal of Applied Psychology* 85 (2000): 102–11. For a discussion of how consensus decision-making moderates group conflict, see Randall S. Peterson and Tony Simons, "(Mis)Trust, Decision Acceptance, and Implementation: The Moderating Impact of Consensus Decision Rules in Top Management Teams," unpublished working paper, Cornell University, 2001.

13. *New York Times*, international edition, Sunday, January 27, 1991, p. 16. Appeared just prior to the Allied invasion of Kuwait.

14. Two British researchers analyzed 133 conformity studies using an Asch-type line judgment task, drawn from seventeen countries, to see whether the level of conformity has changed over time and whether it is related cross-culturally to individualism-collectivism. An analysis of the U.S. studies found that conformity *has* declined since the 1950s. In addition, collectivist countries tended to show higher levels of conformity than individualist countries. See Rod Bond and Peter B. Smith, "Culture and Conformity: A Meta-Analysis of Studies Using Asch's (1952b, 1956) Line Judgment Task," *Psychological Bulletin* 199, no. 1 (1996): 111–37. Asch's classic conformity experiment was first published in Solomon E. Asch, "Studies of Independence and Submission to Group Pressure," *Psychological Monograms* 70 (1956). Subsequent extensions are reviewed in Serge Moscovici, "Social Influence and Conformity," in *The Handbook of Social Psychology*, edited by Bardner Lindzey and Elliot Aronson, 3rd ed., Random House, 1985.

15. Groups in which a majority leaning exists may suffer from polarization via two subtle mechanisms. The first concerns the amount of airtime and attention the majority and minority views receive. Once the minority realizes that its view is not

going to prevail in the argument, it may simply give up or present its case without vigor and conviction. In addition, a more subtle effect may operate whereby group members change their own view on the matter in order to retain their aspired position relative to the group. For instance, when evaluating a job candidate, most managers feel that they are pretty discriminating and critical in detecting weaknesses or flaws in any single applicant. Suppose, in fact, that your view of the candidate is mildly negative and now you meet with your colleagues to discuss the case. Whereas you thought that you were more critical than most of your colleagues, you now discover that they share your concerns, and that some are even more critical than you are. This may prompt you to speak up even more vigorously against the candidate, to signal to yourself and others how critically-minded you are and what high standards you adhere to. Although this shift of opinion may help you feel better about yourself, it will not help the candidate, especially since other group members may similarly shift their positions to the more critical side. The upshot is that a mildly critical assessment made by people alone may snowball into a harshly critical group assessment, a phenomenon known as group polarization (or extremity shift). So, groups will often end up being more extreme in their judgment than the prior opinions of the group members would lead one to expect, provided there is a majority leaning to begin with. When two roughly equal factions exist, the group may actually moderate extreme views and end up in a less extreme position. The polarization effect was originally referred to as the "risky shift" phenomenon; see J. A. F. Stoner, "Risky and Cautious Shifts in Group Decisions: The Influence of Widely Held Values," *Journal of Experimental Social Psychology* 4 (1968): 442–59.

16. The Abilene paradox is cited in Kathleen M. Eisenhardt, Jean L. Kahwajy, and L. J. Bourgeois III, "Conflict and Strategic Choice: How Top Management Teams Disagree," *California Management Review* 39, no. 2 (winter 1997). It appears (apparently for the first time) in *The Abilene Paradox and Other Meditations on Management*, by Jerry B. Harvey, Lexington, MA: Lexington Book, D. C. Heath and Company, 1988. Harvey tells the story in the first person.

17. The Janis quote can be found in Irving L. Janis, *Victims of Groupthink*, Boston, MA: Houghton Mifflin, 1972. See pp. 35–36 of the chapter "A Perfect Failure: The Bay of Pigs."

18. Groupthink has derailed many intelligent decision-making groups. But a caveat is needed. While the groupthink framework offers a useful perspective on team dynamics, it has, however, been critiqued in research circles for failing to offer clear predictions. This shortcoming derives in part from the generality of the concepts and the high degree of plasticity with which they can be applied in hindsight. Whereas we accept the process and mechanisms by which groupthink can be produced, readers must be careful not to label all group failings as necessarily being due to groupthink. This caveat applies not just to groupthink, but to overconfidence bias or the confirmation trap as well. Especially in complex real-world cases, multiple factors may be at play. For example, the tragedy of the 1986 *Challenger* launch in which the shuttle exploded shortly after takeoff has been interpreted and attributed to groupthink. Yet, the investigation by a presidential commission identified poor internal reporting systems as the main culprit, and a separate congressional inquiry blamed specific individuals in terms of their competency for the

positions they held within NASA. Yet other studies interpret the *Challenger* case as
due to excessive risk-taking in the domain of losses, based on the core principles of
prospect theory (see James K. Esser and Joanne S. Lindoerfer, "Group-Think and the
Space Shuttle Challenger Accident: Toward a Quantitative Case Analysis," *Journal of
Behavioral Decision Making* 2, no. 3 [1989]: 167–78). Finally, a careful field study by
Diana Vaughn (*The Challenger Launch Decision*, University of Chicago Press, 1996) focuses on the gradual decline of individual responsibility and the normalization of
danger as the prime reasons, thus emphasizing cultural factors relating to the ba-
nality and anonymity of bureaucratic decision procedures.

19. An interesting conference held twenty-five years after the Cuban Missile Crisis brought together several U.S. and Soviet policymakers involved in this historic
episode of October 1962 as chronicled by James G. Blight and David A. Welch, *On
the Brink: Americans and Soviets Reexamine the Cuban Missile Crisis*, NY: Noonday Press,
1989. This retrospective revealed significant misperceptions on both sides, including the Kremlin's serious consideration of a nuclear attack against the U.S. (see
Aleksandr Fursenko and Timothy J. Naftali, *One Hell of a Gamble: The Secret History of
the Cuban Missile Crisis*, W. W. Norton & Company, 1998). Recently released audio-
tapes further underscore how close the world really came to the brink, as documented by Ernest R. May and Philip D. Zelikow, *The Kennedy Tapes: Inside the White
House During the Cuban Missile Crisis*, Belknap Press, 1998. For a classic interpretation of this historic crisis through multiple conceptual lenses, see the new edition
of Graham T. Allison and Philip Zelikow, *Essence of Decision: Explaining the Cuban Missile Crisis*, New York: Longman, 2nd ed., 1999.

20. In studying the role of the leader in group problem-solving, Norman R. F.
Maier and L. Richard Hoffman found that the acceptance and support of solutions
by group members to be lower in groups in which the leader reported "problem employees" and greater in groups where the leader perceived "idea people." See, for
example, Maier and Hoffman, "Acceptance and Quality of Solutions as Related to
Leaders' Attitudes Toward Disagreement in Group Problem Solving," *Journal of Applied Behavioral Science* (1965): 373–86.

21. The Myers-Briggs test of cognitive style is discussed in Isabel Briggs Myers
and Mary H. McCaulley, *Manual: A Guide to the Development and Use of the Myers-Briggs
Type Indicator*, Consulting Psychologists Press, 1985. The test is based on Carl Jung's
book *Psychological Types*, Harcourt Brace, 1923. See also Isabel Briggs Myers, *Gifts
Differing*, Consulting Psychologists Press, 1988. For a direct link to decision-
making, see Alan J. Rowe and Richard O. Mason, *Managing with Style: A Guide to Understanding, Assessing, and Improving Decision Making*, San Francisco: Jossey-Bass Publishers, 1987.

22. The suggestion about age spreads is also from Eisenhardt's work with top
management teams cited above.

23. The story of Sport Obermeyer's experiment on individual vs. group forecasts
is recounted by Marshall Fisher, Alter Obermeyer, Janice Hammond, and Ananth
Raman, "Accurate Response: The Key to Profiting from QR," *Bobbin Magazine*, 1994.

24. A significant body of research demonstrates that the devil's advocate technique improves group performance over nonconflictual, expert-based approaches.
For a report on a laboratory experiment on the effects of devil's advocacy, see Jo-

seph S. Valacich and Charles Schwenk, "Devil's Advocacy and Dialectical Inquiry Effects on Face-to-Face and Computer-Mediated Group Decision Making," *Organizational Behavior and Human Decision Processes* 63, no. 2 (August 1995): 158–73.

25. See, for example, C. J. Nemeth, "Differential Contributions of Majority and Minority Influence," *Psychological Review* 93 (1986): 23–32.

26. C. J. Nemeth, O. Mayseless, J. Sherman, and Y. Brown, "Exposure to Dissent and Recall of Information," *Journal of Personality and Social Psychology* 58 (1990): 429–37. See also C. J. Nemeth and J. Wachtler, "Creative Problem Solving as a Result of Majority and Minority Influence," *European Journal of Social Psychology* 13 (1983): 45–55.

27. For a discussion of how consensus decision-making moderates group conflict, see Randall S. Peterson and Tony Simons, "All for One, One for All? The Effects of Consensus Decision Making in Moderating Top Management Team Conflict," unpublished working paper, 2000. See also C. J. Nemeth, "Interactions Between Jurors as a Function of Majority vs. Unanimity Decision Rules," *Journal of Applied Social Psychology* 7 (1977): 38–56.

28. C. E. Miller, "The Social Psychological Effect of Group Decision Rules," in P. B. Paulus, *Psychology of Group Influence*, Hillsdale, NJ: Lawrence Erlbaum, 3rd ed., 1989. See also Randall Peterson, "Can You Have Too Much of a Good Thing? The Limits of Voice for Improving Satisfaction with Leaders," *Personality and Social Psychology* (February 1999).

29. The Denver Police Department controversy and its resolution are explained in Kenneth R. Hammond and Leonard Adelman, "Science, Values, and Human Judgment," *Science* (1976): 389–96. Also see Kenneth R. Hammond, et al., "Linking Environmental Models with Models of Human Judgment: A Symmetrical Decision Aid," *Transactions on Systems, Man and Cybernetics* SMC-7 (1977).

30. Hammond and his colleagues achieved the equal weight agreement in part through the use of the subjective model we talked about in the last chapter. He asked each decision-maker to give hypothetical judgments for dozens of bullets which were described only by their stopping effectiveness, injury potential, threat to bystanders, etc. Indeed, some of these judged bullets were purely hypothetical. They didn't exist. Then he used the technique of the subjective model to infer the importance weights on the factors that each decision-maker was implicitly using to make judgments about the bullets. Thus, every participant from Denver's mayor on down was able to see their own importance weights reflected mirrorlike in their subjective model. Instead of sharpening the differences between the two sides, it focused their disagreement where it belonged, on the people's different values, (as reflected in their importance weights), not on the facts, and most especially not on the bullets themselves, which were a blend of both. This focus on values narrowed the debate and helped lead to the successful compromise of equal weighting.

31. The focus on process rather than outcomes per se is also often the key to win-win negotiations. As explained in Roger Fisher, William Ury, and Bruce Patton, *Getting to Yes: Negotiating Agreement Without Giving In*, Penguin Books, 2nd ed., 1991, less experienced negotiators often get stuck in rigid positions instead of focusing on principles first. Positional bargaining is focused on outcome, whereas "principled" negotiation addresses first the process by which the issues are to be resolved, and

then applies the facts accordingly. The key: focus on interests and process, not positions.

32. An excellent discussion on separating fact and value decisions in public policy debates can be found in "Psychologists as Policy Advocates: The Roots of Controversy," by Peter Suedfeld and Philip E. Tetlock, in Suedfeld and Tetlock (eds.), *Psychology and Social Policy*, New York: Hemisphere Publishing Corporation, 1992. These authors deal with the related challenges of making scientific reasoning value-free (a worthy if not perfectly achievable goal) and controversies where the sides, though needing to reach an agreement, are thoroughly opposed in values. Fortunately, in most situations that decision-makers face, there is at least some commitment to the organization's overall goals that can provide a common basis for bridging a gap in values. For more on this topic, level four of our pyramid, see Peter C. Gardiner and Ward Edwards, "Public Values: Multiattribute Utility Measurement for Social Decision Making," in *Human Judgment and Decision Processes*, edited by Martin F. Kaplan and Steven Schwartz, Academic Press, 1975.

33. As Suedfeld and Tetlock (cited in the previous note) point out, much research suggests that the relationship between one's interpretation of the facts and one's own value preferences is substantial. They note: While it can be hard to separate whether factual assessments shape value judgments from the reverse, decision-makers often align their factual assessments and value preferences in consistent and predictable ways. Because disentangling the factual and value components of policy disagreements is so difficult, some researchers have concluded that the effort should be abandoned. (See, for example, Knud S. Larsen, ed., *Dialectics and Ideology in Psychology*, Norwood, NJ: Ablex, 1986.) Yet there is also an impressive social science literature on assessing the risks of technological innovation that offers guidelines for balancing factual and value components. See, for example, Baruch Fischhoff, Sarah Lichtenstein, Paul Slovic, Stephen L. Derby, and Ralph L. Keeney, *Acceptable Risk*, New York: Cambridge University Press, 1981.

34. John Forester, "Dealing with Deep Value Differences," Susskind, McKearnan & Larmer-Thomas (eds.), *The Consensus Building Handbook: A Comprehensive Guide to Reaching Agreement*, Thousand Oaks, CA: Sage, 1999.

35. The "listening to find common ground" tool is adapted from Cherie R. Brown and George J. Mazza, *Healing into Action: A Leadership Guide for Creating Diverse Communities*, Washington, DC: National Coalition Building Institute, 1997.

36. Consensus mapping and the "nominal group technique" are described in Deborah Ancona, Thomas Kochan, John Van Maanen, Maureen Scully, D. Eleanor Westney, *Managing for the Future: Organizational Behavior and Processes* (Module 5: Team Processes), South-Western College Publishing, 1996. Also see Vince Barabba, *Meeting of the Minds: Creating the Market-Based Enterprise*, Boston: Harvard Business School Press, 1995.

37. Randall Peterson, "Can You Have Too Much of a Good Thing?: The Limits of Voice for Improving Satisfaction with Leaders," *Personality and Social Psychology* 25, no. 3, (March 1999).

38. In a study of top management teams in the fast-paced minicomputer market, Kathleen M. Eisenhardt found that while teams strive for consensus, they also have fallback plans. If consensus is not easily forthcoming, they let the leader de-

cide or they vote. See "Speed and Strategic Choice: How Managers Accelerate Decision Making," *California Management Review* 32, no. 3 (1990): 1–16.

39. Steven Kerr, formerly at the University of Southern California and now with General Electric, presents thirteen characteristics that he calls "substitutes for leadership," that is, factors that will allow individuals to succeed regardless of a group's leadership. (These traits are: (1) ability, experience, training, and knowledge; (2) professional orientation; (3) indifference toward organizational rewards; (4) unambiguous, routine, and methodologically invariant tasks; (5) task-provided feedback concerning accomplishment; (6) intrinsically satisfying tasks; (7) organizational formalization; (8) organizational inflexibility; (9) advisory and staff functions; (10) closely-knit, cohesive, interdependent work groups; (11) organizational rewards not within the leader's control; (12) spatial distance between superior and subordinates; and (13) subordinate need for independence.) The advice in this section is based on his work. For further discussion, see S. Kerr and J. M. Jerrnier, "Substitutes for Leadership: Their Meaning and Measurement," *Organizational Behavior and Human Performance* 22 (1978): 375–403, and S. Kerr and J. W. Slocum, "Controlling the Performance of People in Organization," in P. C. Nystrom and W. H. Starbuck, *Handbook of Organizational Design*, vol. 2, New York: Oxford University Press, 1981, pp. 116–34.

### Interlude C

1. The subject of implementation has received much attention in the strategy literature since many large change efforts in organizations fail outright or encounter major obstacles. It is not clear to what extent this problem traces to poor strategies versus poor implementation. Indeed, these two causes may not be distinguishable since a good strategy (or decision) should be implementable, almost by definition. Several lessons from the strategy field seem to apply to decision implementation in general: (1) Successful implementation requires and hinges on leadership, which in turn involves explaining the vision clearly, instilling passion, and operationalizing it. (2) Many organizational change efforts are messy and experience setbacks, but with the right attitude of continuous learning and perseverance they may succeed. (3) Incentives and rewards must be well aligned with the implementation effort, as must the norms and values that define the organization's culture. (4) Decision rights (i.e., who is allowed to decide what) must fit the problem, and people must have the requisite skill and information to act appropriately.

2. A good overview of the EuroDisney fiasco can be found in Rita Gunther McGrath and Ian C. MacMillan, "Discovery-Driven Planning," *Harvard Business Review* (July–August 1995).

3. Arie de Geus, "Planning as Learning," *Harvard Business Review* (March–April 1988): 70–74. See also Arie de Geus, *The Living Company*, Boston: Harvard Business School Press, 1997.

4. Much attention has been given at senior levels to the importance of measuring and monitoring organizational performance. Perhaps it all started, or restarted, with the total quality movement of the 1970s, which emphasized the importance

of managing with facts and data, and inculcated a more statistical approach to understanding organizational processes. This movement was followed by a renewed financial emphasis, reflecting deregulation, globalization, and the increasing pressures of Wall Street, in the form of measuring economic value added (EVA). This approach painstakingly measures the return on all the various uses of capital within a firm, and has much improved the return on assets in many industries. Before EVA, many managers were blissfully unaware of where and how much capital they were using. More recently, the balanced scorecard has come into vogue, starting from the premise that people do what gets measured and rewarded. In addition to better measures for financial performance, the balanced scorecard approach has highlighted the importance of metrics in four areas, namely (1) finance, (2) customer satisfaction and market performance, (3) internal operations and morale, and (4) renewal and innovation. Different strategies will require somewhat different metrics within each of these four quadrants of the balanced scorecard. This philosophy can apply to grand change initiatives involving shifts in strategy as well as to smaller operational projects. Ideally, each important decision has its own miniscorecard, so deviations can be quickly spotted and corrected as part of the implementation effort. One challenge is that the most accurate measures of performance often have a lag built in (like quarterly accounting reports). A truly balanced scorecard contains lagging indicators, concurrent metrics, and even leading indicators that anticipate potential problems. These latter ones will likely be more subjective, but also more timely and actionable.

5. William F. Hamilton, "Managing Real Options," in George S. Day and Paul J. H. Schoemaker (eds.), *Wharton on Emerging Technologies*, New York: Wiley, 2000, pp. 271–88.

6. Whenever significant investments of money, time, or emotion have been made, the status quo bias is often driven by the sunk-cost fallacy, an improper drawing of mental boundaries. When costs are truly sunk (i.e., incurred in the past), they should not exert an influence on the current decision. Although it is a natural tendency to look back, this often interferes with sound decision-making. Many investors or traders, for instance, would be better off if they did not know the historical cost of their positions. As one investment pro (George Soros of Quantum Fund) put it, "I don't believe in making money back. Once you have lost it, you have lost it. You lose it or make it, but you don't make it back" (*Fortune*, February 29, 1988, p. 113). For both academic and managerial analyses of sunk-cost fallacies, see Richard Thaler, "Toward a Positive Theory of Consumer Choice," *Journal of Economic Behavior* 1 (1980): 50; Hal Arkes and Catherine Blumer, "The Psychology of Sunk Costs," *Organizational Behavior and Human Decision Processes* 35, no. 1 (1985): 124–40; and Barry M. Staw and Jerry Ross, "Knowing When to Pull the Plug," *Harvard Business Review* (March–April 1987). Thaler's article also discusses opportunity costs. A formal application in economics can be found in Val Eugene Lambson and Farrell E. Jensen's "Sunk Costs and Firm Value Variability: Theory and Evidence," *American Economic Review* 88, no. 1 (March 1998): 307–13.

7. Whether implementation is an afterthought or the heart of real-world decision-making depends on how rational you think organizations are or can be. And this in turn depends on the nature of the decision, the type of organization you

work in, and indeed the culture and stage of industry evolution. In Paul J. H. Schoe-maker, "Strategic Decisions in Organizations: Rational *and* Behavioral Views," *Journal of Management Studies* 30, no. 1 (1993): 107–29, four views are offered of how things get done in organizations ranging from rational to organizational, political to contextual. Each of these perspectives would approach the challenge of implementation differently.

## Chapter 8

1. The results of the Bender Gestalt experiments are published in an article by Lewis R. Goldberg, "The Effectiveness of Clinicians' Judgments: The Diagnosis of Organic Brain Damage from the Bender Gestalt Test," *Journal of Consulting Psychology* 23 (1959): 25–33. The secretaries actually got 67 percent correct while their clinical psychologist bosses got only 65 percent. A third group, third-year doctoral students in clinical psychology, achieved 70 percent correct. None of these three percentages were reliably different from the others in statistical terms.

2. For a fuller discussion of the political and emotional aspects of learning from experience, see Russ Vince, "Experiential Management Education as the Practice of Change," in Robert French and Christopher Grey (eds.), *ReThinking Management Education*, London: Sage Publications, 1996. Although the article focuses on developing the practice of experiential management education, his observations and conclusions on learning and change as well as on how we learn to limit learning apply to our broader discussion here. He notes: "The struggle to learn and to change can be both complex and uncomfortable, involving strong feelings and prolonged uncertainty. Defenses to change contribute to keeping things manageable, but also restrict change."

3. In science, a variety of safeguards exists to maximize learning. Blind peer review, testing multiple hypotheses, control studies, and careful training in logic and data analysis try to instill values and attitudes of critical thinking and skepticism about received wisdom. And yet, even successful scientists succumb to the biases discussed in this chapter. All humans must continually balance wishful thinking, ego protection, and selective perception with the search for truth. And often great intellects can fool themselves even more than ordinary souls. As Thomas Kuhn observed when studying how new ideas take hold in science, it requires the passing of an entire generation of scientists trained in the "old school" of thought. Once entrenched in the paradigms that made them successful, very few scientists can accept the new radical ideas of their "immature" graduate students (such as natural selection or quantum mechanics). See Kuhn's classic book, *The Structure of Scientific Revolutions*, University of Chicago Press, 3rd ed., 1996.

4. Dee W. Hock's quote was taken from an interview in *Fast Company* 26 (July–August 1999), "The Art of Smart."

5. The space shuttle example was taken from Siddhartha R. Dalal, Edward B. Fowlkes, and Bruce Hoadley, "Risk Analysis of the Space Shuttle: Pre-*Challenger*Prediction of Failure," *Journal of the American Statistical Association*, 84, no. 408 (December 1989): 945–57. For an excellent analysis of how better visual displays of data

might have helped in this case, see Edward R. Tufte, chapter 2, in *Visual and Statistical Thinking: Displays of Evidence for Making Decisions*, Cheshire, CT: Graphics Press, 1997.

6. Alison Hubbard Ashton, Robert H. Ashton, and Mary N. Davis, "White-Collar Robotics: Levering Managerial Decision Making," *California Management Review* 37, no. 1 (fall 1994).

7. Our inability to detect relationships between variables when masked by noise is discussed further in Dennis L. Jennings, Teresa M. Amabile, and Lee Ross, "Informal Covariation Assessment: Data-Based Versus Theory-Based Judgments," in *Judgment Under Uncertainty: Heuristics and Biases*, edited by Daniel Kahneman, Paul Slovic, and Amos Tversky, Cambridge University Press, 1982.

8. El Gordo at Christmas 2000 was the most recent to this book's publication date. It distributed a first prize of $255 million (out of $1.14 billion in total). Roughly half of Spain's citizens participated through the purchase of a lottery ticket, and the televised drawing is a national event. Although its tradition dates back to the mid-eighteenth century, the lottery now has a website, www.elgordo.com, so its activities are available to the Spanish-speaking population globally. The story of the winner cited here was retold in a *Los Angeles Times* article (December 30, 1977, pt. 1, p. 13).

9. A fuller discussion of self-serving attribution biases can be found in Richard Nisbett and Lee Ross, *Human Inference: Strategies and Shortcomings of Social Judgments*, Prentice-Hall, 1980. An interesting discussion of the ways marketers' self-serving biases relate to decision outcomes can be found in Mary T. Curren, Valerie S. Folkes, and Joel H. Steckel, "Explanations for Successful and Unsuccessful Marketing Decision: The Decision Maker's Perspective," *Journal of Marketing* 56 (April 1992): 18–31. The careful reader might note that the prizewinner of the Spanish lottery is not explicitly claiming skills. Yet he's clearly claiming credit for something more than luck and as such is falling prey to an illusion of control.

10. The illusion of control exhibited by the management of the Indiana Pacers concerning the 1983 National Basketball Association player draft is described in the May 19, 1983, edition of the *Palatine* (Illinois) *Daily Herald*, sec. 4, p. 2.

11. The need to feel in control is discussed more fully in Ellen Langer, "The Illusion of Control," *Journal of Personality and Social Psychology* 32 (1975): 322–28. The examples involving dental patients and workers in noisy circumstances are discussed in Lawrence C. Perlmuter and Richard A. Monty, "The Importance of Perceived Control: Fact or Fantasy?" *American Scientist* 65 (November–December 1977): 759–65. Shelley E. Taylor and Jonathon D. Brown offer an interesting perspective on the positive value of illusions in "Illusion and Well-Being: A Social Psychological Perspective on Mental Health," *Psychological Bulletin* 103, no. 2 (1988): 193–210. The relationships among the illusion of control, wishful thinking, and optimism are subtle, as examined in David V. Budescu and Meira Bruderman, "The Relationship Between the Illusion of Control and the Desirability Bias," *Journal of Behavioral Decision Making* 8 (1995): 109–25. The value of optimism—as a learnable cognitive skill for children—is more fully explored in Martin E. P. Seligman, Karen Reivich, Lisa Jaycox, and Jane Gillham, *The Optimistic Child*, Harperperennial Library, 1996. A wider ranging set of essays on optimism and hope is offered in Jane E. Gill-

ham, *The Science of Optimism and Hope: Research Essays in Honor of Martin E. P. Seligman* (*Laws of Life Symposia Series, Vol. 2*), Templeton Foundation Press, 2000.

12. A pointed discussion of the subtle ways in which we rationalize is offered by Elliot Aronson's excellent article "The Rationalizing Animal," *Psychology Today*, 1973, which in turn is based on Leon Festinger's classic, *Theory of Cognitive Dissonance*, Stanford University Press, 1957. A more up-to-date and lighthearted version of how we fool ourselves daily is offered by Henry Beard, Andy Borowitz, John Boswell, and Roz Chast, *Rationalizations to Live By*, Workman Publishing Company, 2000.

13. The Rand report data were taken from "Understanding Cost Growth and Performance Shortfalls in Pioneer Process Plants," by Edward W. Merrow, Kenneth E. Phillips, and Christopher W. Myers, September 1981, Rand Corporation Report R-2569-DOE, prepared for the U.S. Department of Energy, and "A Review of Cost Estimation in New Technologies: Implications for Energy Process Plants," by Edward W. Merrow, Stephen W. Chapel, and Christopher Worthy, July 1979, Rand Corporation Report R-2481-DOE, also prepared for the Department of Energy.

14. The study of hindsight bias as it related to Nixon's trips to China can be found in an article by Baruch Fischhoff and Ruth Beyth entitled " 'I Knew It Would Happen'—Remembered Probabilities of Once-Future Things," *Organizational Behavior and Human Performance* 13 (1975): 1–16. Hindsight bias is especially problematic in legal trials, where witnesses' memories get distorted. The accuracy and confidence of eyewitness testimony are discussed in *Eyewitness Testimony: Psychological Perspectives*, edited by Gary L. Wells and Elizabeth F. Loftus, Cambridge University Press, 1984. See also Eugene Winograd's review "What You Should Know About Eyewitness Testimony" in *Contemporary Psychology* 31, no. 5 (1986): 332–34. For causes of hindsight bias, see Terry Connolly and Edward W. Bukszar, "Hindsight Bias: Self-Flattery or Cognitive Error?" in *Journal of Behavioral Decision Making* 3 (1990): 205–11.

15. *Much Ado About Nothing*, act II, scene II.

## Chapter 9

1. The headquote is Aphorism #32 in Hoffer's *Reflections on the Human Condition*, New York: Harper & Row, 1973, p. 22.

2. Arie de Geus, *The Living Company*, Boston: Harvard Business School Press, 1997, pp. 134–35. De Geus was head of strategic planning at Royal Dutch/Shell in the 1980s. His story about flocking is based on research by Jeff S. Wyles, Joseph G. Kimbel, and Allan C. Wilson, "Birds, Behavior and Anatomical Evolution," *Proceedings of the National Academy of Sciences* (July 1993).

3. Frank Gulliver, "Post-Project Appraisals Pay," *Harvard Business Review* (March–April 1987): 128–32. The article discusses the practice of decision audits at British Petroleum. An even earlier example of institutionalized learning in organizations is provided in David Dery, "Erring and Learning: An Organizational Analysis," *Accounting, Organizations and Society* 7, no. 3 (1982): 217–23.

4. The emphasis on creating learning cultures was pioneered by Peter Senge in

his well-known book, *The Fifth Discipline*, Currency/Doubleday, 1990. For a shorter version, see Peter M. Senge, "The Leader's New Work: Building Learning Organizations," *Sloan Management Review* 32, no. 1 (fall 1990): 7–23, and for elaborated essays, see Sarita Chawla and John Renesch (eds.), *Learning Organizations: Developing Cultures for Tomorrow's Workplace*, Productivity Press, 1995. The strategic significance of learning—especially about the future—was well underscored in Gary Hamel and C. K. Prahalad, *Competing for the Future*, Boston: Harvard Business School Press, 1994. Organizational obstacles to learning and change—especially concerning new technologies—are thoroughly addressed in Clayton Christensen, *The Innovator's Dilemma*, Boston: Harvard Business School Press, 1997.

5. Researchers at MIT have shown how difficult learning can be in complex environments with delayed or nonlinear feedback loops. Using computer simulations of the airline and consumer product industries, in which teams of managers make five to eight decisions per quarter for a stretch of, say, forty quarters, team learning happens slowly and incompletely. In one study, managers were unable to beat—on a fourth attempt—simple programmed decision rules that look at only one quarter (and have only a memory going back one quarter). In yet another study, human teams were unable to beat a random strategy. Furthermore, they failed to recognize that the other "team" was picking decision variables at random from pre-specified ranges. These studies underscore the importance of systematic approaches and the power of bootstrapping. For practical examples, in diverse industries, of dynamic modeling, see John D. W. Morecroft and John D. Sterman, *Modeling for Learning Organizations*, Productivity Press, 1994. An integrated treatment of dynamic systems modeling is offered in John D. Sterman, *Business Dynamics: Systems Thinking and Modeling for a Complex World*, Irwin Professional Publishers, 2000. For a detailed study of how poorly human teams learn in a dynamic feedback environment, see John D. Sterman, "Modeling Managerial Behavior: Misperceptions of Feedback in a Dynamic Decision Making Experiment," *Management Science* 35, no. 3 (1989): 321–39, as well as John D. Sterman, "Boom, Bust and Failures to Learn in Experimental Markets," *Management Science* 39, no. 12 (1993): 1439–58. The study about random teams can be found in Robin M. Hogarth and Spiros Makridakis, "The Value of Decision Making in a Complex Environment," *Management Science* 27, no. 1 (1981): 93–107.

6. A somewhat silly but all too common example of how missing feedback leads to erroneous conclusions is demonstrated by the following actual report, which appeared in *Management Focus* (November–December 1984) and is quoted in Robyn M. Dawes, *Rational Choice in an Uncertain World*, New York: Harcourt Brace Jovanovich, 1988: "Results of a recent survey of 74 chief executives indicate that there may be a link between childhood pet ownership and future career success. Fully 94 % of the CEOs, all of them employed within Fortune 500 companies, had possessed a dog, a cat, or both, as youngsters. . . . The respondents asserted that pet ownership had helped them develop many of the positive character traits that make them good managers today, including responsibility, empathy, respect for other living beings, generosity, and good communication skills." The missing feedback that might have led to a different conclusion? Had the survey included other, less successful, people, the researchers might have found that the vast majority of them also had child-

hood pets. What then would they have said about the link between pet ownership and future career success?

7. Researchers call these confounding factors "treatment effects." A "treatment" is anything done after a judgment that influences the outcome. The self-fulfilling prophecy is a common form of treatment effect: a prediction that comes true not so much because of the quality of the prediction but because of actions by someone who believed in it. Such outcomes are usually desirable. But the cost is distorted feedback. Here are two additional examples. An article in *Bartender* magazine offered a guide to predicting big tippers on the basis of the drinks they order. The best tippers are supposed to order scotch or vodka on the rocks, or bourbon or cognac straight. Those who order grasshoppers, sours, or brandy alexanders presumably are more parsimonious. But waiters who are trying to predict potential big tippers are likely to give expected big tippers exceptional service. Not surprisingly, these preferred customers tend to leave the bigger tips. But was it because the waiters accurately spotted good tippers, or was it simply because they gave some customers better service? The predictions from *Bartender* magazine are summarized in the July 12, 1982, issue of the *Chicago Tribune*, sec. 3, p. 2. The second example: a classic study of elementary school teachers illustrates how a prophecy can subtly fulfill itself. Teachers were told that some of their pupils were "late bloomers," i.e., that the results of a recently administered test showed them to have great potential for improvement. In fact, these students had performed neither better nor worse than the rest of the class on the test. The only thing special was their teachers' belief that they had untapped potential. Nonetheless, the "late bloomers" were soon outperforming the rest of the class on average. Somehow the teachers caused the unfounded prophecy to be fulfilled. (We know that when teachers believe students to be bright they are more likely to maintain eye contact, smile, nod their heads, and give other nonverbal indications of approval.) This study was conducted by Robert Rosenthal and Lenore Jacobson and published in their book *Pygmalion in the Classroom*, Holt Rinehart & Winston, 1968. A review of how exactly the self-fulfilling prophecy about students' performance takes place has been offered by Lee Jussim, "Self-Fulfilling Prophecies: A Theoretical and Integrative Review," *Psychological Review* 93, no. 4 (1986): 429–45. See also Robert K. Merton, "The Self-fulfilling Prophecy," in his book *Social Theory and Social Structure*, Macmillan Publishing Co., 1968. Recent summaries of numerous studies in education are offered by Robert T. Tauber, *Self-Fulfilling Prophecy*, Praeger Pub. Text, 1997, and in organizations by Nicole M. Kierein and Michael A. Gold, "Pygmalion in Work Organizations: A Meta-analysis," *Journal of Organizational Behavior* 21 (2000): 913–28.

8. For a discussion of the self-fulfilling prophecy in job interviews, see the work of Robert Dipboye, "Self-Fulfilling Prophecies in the Selection-Recruitment Interview," *Academy of Management Review* 7 (1982): 579–86. This classic study has been replicated and analyzed thoroughly. An analysis of the larger issues of the impact of expectancies on actual behavior was written by Edward E. Jones, "Interpreting Interpersonal Behavior: The Effects of Expectancies," *Science* 234, no. 3 (October 1986): 42–46. See also David H. Tucker and Patricia M. Rowe, "Relationship Between Expectancy, Causal Attributions, and Final Hiring Decisions in the Employment Interview," *Journal of Applied Psychology* 64 (1979): 27–34.

9. For more on David Ogilvy's approach to advertising, see his autobiography *Ogilvy on Advertising*, Vintage Books, 1985, or his earlier book *Confessions of an Advertising Man*, Ballantine Books, 1963.

10. The remarkable study by the Bell system is reported by J. L. Showers and L. M. Chakrin in their paper, "Reducing Uncollectible Revenues from Residential Telephone Customers," *Interfaces* 11 (1981): 21–31. Since then, one benefit of the TQM movement has been a greater appreciation in management of controlled variation and managing with facts and numbers. The upshot has been better learning and control of complex systems in manufacturing and operations.

11. One reason that this statistical experiment is not as informative as a real one is that a real one includes a wider range for each factor. You might like to know, for example, whether there aren't some very good sales reps who have not completed college (e.g., three years of college or even self-educated), but you can't find out from statistical experiments because there are no real sales reps without a college degree.

12. Simulations tailored to industries or topics are available from consultants, educational institutions, and through in-house development. Many readers will be familiar from their business school days with such classic simulation games as INTOP or MARKSTRAT. These games have since been enhanced using multimedia. For a thorough discussion of simulating competitive market responses, see David J. Reibstein and Mark J. Chussil, "Chapter 17: Putting the Lesson Before the Test: Using Simulation to Analyze and Develop Competitive Strategies," *Wharton on Dynamic Competitive Strategy*, John Wiley & Sons, Inc., 1997. Examples of how leading companies use simulation to improve innovation are offered in Michael Schrage, *Serious Play*, Harvard Business School Publishing, 1999.

13. The story of the Harris Chemical Group, as well as the unnamed company's use of computer-based simulation, is told in more detail in Peter Carbonara, "Game Over," *Fast Company* 6 (December 1996): 128. That issue of the magazine contains several other stories related to computer-based simulations.

14. For further details of this case and a fuller discussion of the benefits of simulation, see David J. Reibstein and Mark J. Chussil, "Putting the Lesson Before the Test: Using Simulation to Analyze and Develop Competitive Strategies," chapter 17 in George Day and David Reibstein (eds.), *Wharton on Dynamic Competitive Strategy*, New York: Wiley, 1997, pp. 395–423.

15. The article describing the moon rock study can be found in Ian I. Mitroff and Richard O. Mason, "On Evaluating the Scientific Contribution of the Apollo Moon Missions Via Information Theory," *Management Science* 20, no. 12 (August 1974), pp. 1501–13. A total of ten hypotheses were examined relating to the origin of the moon, its temperature history, etc. The authors found that more well-known scientists were less open-minded about new evidence, and that the data overall belie the image of the objective, rational scientist. They argue that the lunar science community, like all scientific communities, is "best described as a hierarchy rather than as a democracy" (p. 1511).

16. David A. Garvin, "Building a Learning Organization," *Harvard Business Review* 71, no. 4 (July–August 1993): 78–91. Garvin suggests that learning organizations are skilled at five main activities: systematic problem-solving, experimenta-

tion with new approaches, learning from their own experience and past history, learning from the experiences and best practices of others, and transferring knowledge quickly and efficiently throughout the organization. See also Garvin's book, *Learning in Action: A Guide to Putting the Learning Organization to Work*, Boston: Harvard Business School Press, 2000. For varied examples of how organizations have implemented learning approaches, see Peter M. Senge, Art Kleiner, Charlotte Roberts, Richard B. Ross, and Bryan J. Smith, *The Fifth Discipline Fieldbook: Strategies and Tools for Building a Learning Organization*, Currency/Doubleday, New York, 1994.

17. The chart of indicators for a learning organization was adapted from John W. Slocum and Clive J. Dilloway, "Discussion Group Report: The Learning Organization," *Executive Development for Global Competitiveness*, Albert A. Vicere and Virginia T. Freeman (eds.), Peterson, NJ: Peterson's Guides, Inc., 1992, 45–53.

18. Mardy Grothe and Peter Wylie, *Problem Bosses*, New York: Ballantine Books, 1987, p. 46. Quoted in Eileen C. Shapiro, *How Corporate Truths Become Competitive Traps*, New York: Wiley, 1991, p. 64.

19. Marie Waung and Scott Highhouse, "Fear of Conflict and Empathic Buffering: Two Explanations for the Inflation of Performance Feedback," *Organizational Behavior and Human Decision Processes* 71, no. 1 (July 1997): 37–54.

20. David H. Freedman offers an in-depth look at learning within the U.S. Marine Corps in *Corps Business: The 30 Management Principles of the U.S. Marines*, HarperBusiness, 2000. The book articulates the lessons that can be learned from this organization that has honed the ability to develop rapid, strategic responses to fast-changing environments. For a related article that also draws on Marine experience for management lessons, see Jon R. Katzenback and Jason A. Santamaria, "Firing Up the Front Line," *Harvard Business Review* (May–June 1999): 107–17.

21. William Rosenzweig's and Jerry Hirshberg's comments come from "Unit of One," *Fast Company* (April–May 1998): 102. Now at Venture Strategy Group, Rosenzweig was also cofounder, president, and "Minister of Progress" for the Republic of Tea. Hirshberg is the author of *The Creative Priority: Driving Innovative Business in the Real World*, HarperCollins, 1998.

22. The story of Rank Xerox's benchmarking and best practices initiatives is told in more detail in Thomas A. Stewart, "Beat the Budget and Astound Your CFO," *Fortune*, October 28, 1996, pp. 19–20.

23. For insights about how Silicon Valley companies succeed in fast-changing environments, see Homa Bahrami, "The Emerging Flexible Organization: Perspectives from Silicon Valley," *California Management Review* 34, no. 4 (summer 1992): 33–52, or Kathleen Eisenhardt and Shona Brown, *Competing on the Edge: Strategy as Structured Chaos*, Boston: Harvard Business School Press, 1998.

24. Developing and sustaining organizational memory is not unconditionally positive. See Christine Moorman and Anne S. Miner, "The Impact of Organizational Memory on New Product Performance and Creativity," *Journal of Marketing Research* 34 (February 1997): 91–106. Data from ninety-two new product development projects indicate that higher organizational memory levels enhance the short-term financial performance of new products, and greater memory dispersion increases both the performance and creativity of new products. The researchers find, however, that under some conditions of high environmental turbulence, high memory

dispersion actually detracts from creativity and has no effect on financial performance. To harvest the full value of organizational learning, organizations must
understand the subtle ways in which different features of organizational memory
influence product development.

25. The quote from former Marine commandant Charles C. Krulak can be found
in the foreword to David H. Freedman's *Corps Business: The 30 Management Principles
of the U.S. Marines*, HarperBusiness, 2000, cited earlier. It also appears in a review of
Freedman's book, "Leadership Book: Corps Business in a High-Speed Environment," *Wharton Leadership Digest* (May 2000).

26. Gail Edmondson, "One Electronic SOS Clinched the Deal," *Business Week*,
February 26, 1996, p. 83.

27. The quote from George Santayana can be found in *The Life of Reason*, vol. 1,
Amherst, NY: Prometheus Books, 1905.

28. Art Kleiner and George Roth, "How to Make Experience Your Company's
Best Teacher," *Harvard Business Review* (September–October 1997): 172. For more
information about learning histories, see MIT's Learning History Research Project
home page at <ccs.mit.edu/lh>.

29. For a summary of British Petroleum's decision auditing, see Frank R. Gulliver, "Post-project Appraisals Pay," *Harvard Business Review* (March–April 1987):
128–32. For additional examples of decision audits, see E. Frank Harrison, *The
Managerial Decision-Making Process*, Houghton Mifflin, 1981, concerning the Cuban
Missile Crisis and the TFX bomber plane (i.e., Robert McNamara's failed attempt
to have the U.S. Navy and Air Force *jointly* develop a sophisticated fighter plane,
circa 1962.) Brief audits of five bad decisions are offered in Paul C. Nutt's *Making
Tough Decisions*, Jossey-Bass Publishers, 1989, involving President Carter's failed Ira-
nian rescue mission, RCA's $175 million video disc fiasco, San Francisco's embar-
rassing Bay Area Rapid Transit (BART) system, record cost overruns in building a
stunning opera house in Sydney, Australia, and ITT's ill-fated construction of a pulp
paper plant that had to be closed within five years. Regarding the Cuban Missile Crisis, also see Graham Allison's classic, *The Essence of a Decision*, Prentice-Hall, 1967.
For direct contrasts between good and bad decisions involving the same industries,
see Robert Hartley's *Bullseyes and Blunders*, New York: John C. Wiley, 1987.

30. John Seely Brown's quote was taken from an interview in *Fast Company* 26
(July–August 1999), "The Art of Smart."

31. The Thomas Watson quote may be apocryphal. We have tried to trace it, but
without success. Certainly, it is something Watson *could* have said. In a 1931 speech,
he stated: "I do not believe in criticizing a man simply for making a mistake. If he
shows that he has given the proper amount of thought to a matter, he shows that
he has tried to do the right thing—and I am ready to forgive thoughtful mistakes."

32. The self-serving rationalizations in CEOs' letters to shareholders can be
found in work by Gerald Salancik and James Meindl, "Corporate Attributions as
Strategic Illusions of Management Control," *Administrative Science Quarterly* 29
(1984): 238–54.

33. For examples of the new "openness" in corporate annual reports, see Patrice
Duggan Samuels, "Annual Reports: Upfront and Unstarched," *New York Times*, Sun-

day, April 9, 1995, p. F5, and Richard Gibson, "Hardee's Sees the Enemy—And It Is Them," *Wall Street Journal*, December 18, 1995, p. B4.

34. The John Chambers quote is from James Daly, "John Chambers: The Art of the Deal," *Business 2.0* (www.Business2.com), posted October 1, 1999.

35. Three articles that document the medical profession's shift regarding learning and mistakes are Lucian L. Leape, "Error in Medicine," *Journal of the American Medical Association* 272, no. 23 (December 21, 1994): 1851; Joseph P. Shapiro, "Doctoring a Sickly System," *U.S. News & World Report*, December 13, 1999, from which the James Bagian quote is taken; and an Associated Press report by Lauran Neergaard, "Routine Tests on Newborns May Save Lives," May 30, 2000. Since this new initiative is just being launched, we cannot yet report on its success. It will undoubtedly entail much fine tuning, training, and culture change to systematically surface medical errors. And such challenging obstacles as self-serving distortions, internal blaming, and litigation risks will need to be addressed. But this is the price of the learning that will eventually lead to an improved health care system.

36. Pat Dillon, "Innovation: Albert Yu," *Fast Company* 20 (December 1998): 132. Yu describes this Pentium story in his book, *Creating the Digital Future: The Secrets of Consistent Innovation at Intel*, Free Press, 1998.

37. See Thomas E. Ricks, "Lessons Learned: Army Devises System to Decide What Does, and Does Not, Work," *Wall Street Journal*, May 23, 1997, p. A1, for a description of corporations' interest in the Army's learning approach. Ulmer's statement is based on personal communication, October 1997.

38. A consultant and writer, Chris Turner is the author of *All Hat & No Cattle*, Perseus Books, 1999, about the nature of institutions. This quote was taken from an interview in *Fast Company* 26 (July–August 1999), "The Art of Smart."

39. The quotes from Terry Chandler are based on our interviews with him.

40. The Minna Antrim quote is from *Naked Truth and Veiled Illusions*, 1902.

### Epilogue

1. The figures are taken from Amos Tversky and Daniel Kahneman, "Rational Choice and the Framing of Decisions," *Journal of Business* 59 no. 4, part 2 (October 1986): S251–S284.

# Index

*Page numbers in italics refer to illustrations.*